Coleridge
A Coleridge reader

DATE DUE
THIS BOOK MAY BE KEPT
SEVEN DAYS
**A FINE OF TWO CENTS WILL BE CHARGED FOR
EACH DAY THE BOOK IS KEPT OVER TIME.**
FORM 392B SCHOOL SPECIALTY SUPPLY, SALINA, KAS.

APR 2 4 1981			

Inquiring Spirit

A

COLERIDGE

READER

Coleridge, Samuel Taylor

Edited by

Kathleen Coburn

MINERVA PRESS

TO
MY MOTHER AND FATHER

CONTENTS

ACKNOWLEDGEMENTS

It is a pleasure to express my thanks to the various members of the Coleridge family who have given me the use of their manuscripts. They made possible the collecting of many things in this book.

I rejoice to think that those who have most profited by what he has taught them, do not and cannot form a school.

FREDERICK DENISON MAURICE, 1842

Coleridge nous apparaît continuellement en quête d'aperçus nouveaux, de conciliations plus riches.

GERMAIN D'HANGEST, 1943

INTRODUCTION

COLERIDGE has too long been the special property of 'the *literati* by profession', a class about which he always had some doubts. In his day he enjoyed the company of chemists and physicists, medical men, politicians of every stripe, farmers, tanners, lawyers, painters and musicians, publishers, newspaper editors and journalists, civil servants, clerks, housewives, innkeepers, teachers and children, parsons and professors, as well as poets and novelists and an assortment of the *literati*. There is no lack of testimony that these people enjoyed him and found their interests reciprocated by him. He ought to belong to them all again.

Contrary to a very general impression, Coleridge was not just the inspired talker, a financial burden and practical problem to friends who supported the man Coleridge for the sake of the poet. It is perfectly clear to any reader of the letters that he entered into the lives and concerns of his acquaintances with a zestful mind interested in all manner of things and able to forget itself in its own energy. For example, take his relation to Thomas Poole and Humphry Davy. When he talked to Poole, a tanner and agriculturalist, he asked him about the processes of tanning and the economics of agriculture. He stored up for him in his notebooks hints on how to plant trees and the sorts and uses of fertilizers. When Poole had a chemistry problem in his tanyard, it was Coleridge who asked questions of Davy, the solutions of which helped to further Davy's career. He also went to the Pneumatic Institution in Bristol and took part in some of the early experiments of Davy and Beddoes with nitrous oxide and other gases. Two or three years later when he was in Germany, in 1798–9, sugar was being experimentally produced from sugar beets, for the first time on any scale. Coleridge visited the laboratory, talked to the Director and took notes on the whole process; and he may even have brought back some of the seeds to Davy. (He made a notebook memorandum to get some.) Davy was an adviser to the Board of Agriculture and would be interested. Sugar beets were not grown in England, so far as I can find out, till several decades later, but Coleridge, in the sugar shortage during the Napoleonic Wars and the blockade of the West Indies, may have been the first Englishman to think that the sugar ration might be supplemented by a crop at home.

Or take his relation to Daniel Stuart the editor of the *Courier*. It has long been known that Daniel Stuart stood in the role of patron to Coleridge for some years, and helped him with loans of money and his practical knowledge during the production of Coleridge's periodical the *Friend*. What is less well known is the extent to which Stuart relied on Coleridge for advice on editorial policy in both domestic and foreign affairs. It puts a new complexion on things, puts his requests to Stuart in a truer context, to see, in the manuscript letters, Coleridge hard-pressed with all sorts of incredible obstacles in publishing the *Friend*, writing in a large desperate-looking hand about some new frustration, and yet, in the same letter, writing long paragraphs in detailed answer to some question of Stuart's as to the latest decision of the Cabinet or the recent appointment of the Commander-in-Chief of the Army. It is not altogether surprising, therefore, to anyone who knows this Coleridge, to find Sir Robert Peel, when his Factory Act of 1818 was in danger of being defeated, asking him to write a pamphlet for circulation among members of Parliament. Coleridge was ill in bed, but he responded with a trenchant brochure, here reprinted. It was credited at the time with helping to pass the Bill.

I am far from arguing that Coleridge was a practical person, but rather that the many-sidedness of his interests and his sheer mental energy and initiative have not been fully recognized. One of the purposes of this anthology is to try to suggest the richness of that manifold. Another purpose is to suggest what it is that gives his 'myriad-mindedness' (to borrow from him a phrase he applied to Shakespeare) its special focus and its particular vitality in our own time.

Coleridge said of the *Lyrical Ballads* that he and Wordsworth hoped by their choice and treatment of subjects, to excite in the first place an interest in familiar everyday things by showing anew their intrinsic wonder, and secondly, to make clear the inner truth and reality in the unfamiliar and 'supernatural'. This twofold tearing away of the veil, of commonplaceness from the matter-of-fact, and of remoteness from the wonderful, is characteristic of his purposes everywhere. The familiar is not so simple, nor are the common assumptions about it always to be taken for granted; and the strange and marvellous may be simpler and more common than we know. Of nothing are these truths so true as of the workings and products of the human mind.

Familiar things like words, for instance, are not dead counters or coins. They change, grow, split, carry overtones, defeat themselves. Grammar, it follows, is not the mechanics of language. Logic, if confined to Aristotelian propositions, is not commensurate with the requirements of thought. Science does not deal, though it may assume it does so, only with facts; it is based on hypotheses, and fictions. Education is not so simple as has been supposed; it is not a matter of pouring from big funnels into little ones under the overhanging rod; it is the training of a complex human personality and the inducements must be positive. In 1813 in a lecture on education he raised issues that are still being fought out to-day.

Obversely, the strange and unfamiliar may have laws and significance if we but look. Dreams are strange, if common, experiences, but are they merely what they commonly appear to be? Are they mere accidents? Do they not indicate something illuminating about the content and the degrees of consciousness, and about the associative processes of the waking as well as the sleeping state? And what of trances, oracles, mesmerism? Need these, from Pythagoras to the contemporary animal magnetists, be put down to trick and imposture? How does one mind work on another? What do we know about the imagination? In the tales of daemonology and witchcraft, are there not many cases that suggest pathological states? As he reads old John Webster's *Discovery of Supposed Witchcraft*, he concludes that the states of mind in witches and bewitched are not so far from 'normal' as is supposed, and that what was needed was not the strong arm of the law so much as a new kind of care—a 'neuro-pathology' (see 40). 'Medicine hitherto has been too much confined to *passive* works—as if fevers &c.— were the only human calamities. A Gymnastic Medicine is wanting, not a mere recommendation but a system of forcing the Will and *motive faculties* into action. There are a multitude of cases which should be treated as Madness—i.e. the genus madness should be extended and more classes and species made, in practice, tho' of course, not in name' (Notebook 14). This was written about 1808.

The more one reads Coleridge the more impressed one becomes with what can only be called a psychological approach to all human problems. Whether it be punctuation, or political sovereignty, a criticism of *Richard II*, the position of the mediaeval Church, or the baby talk of children, the state of Ireland or the work of the alchemists, he sees it as a piece of human experience, understandable in relation to the whole human organism, individual or social, so far as that organism can be comprehended as a whole. Politics are not a matter of events, facts, theories, and the isolated external circumstances only. No more is what passes for logic. Nor chemistry. Emotion comes in, motives, unknown ones as well as those that are acknowledged. Unknown especially to the participants.

This psychological approach has long been attributed to Coleridge as a literary critic but has not been so well recognized in other parts of his work. Everywhere it depends on his acute sense of the experiencing, integrating self, the complex human personality. In a comment on the margins of Thomas Taylor's *Proclus* he protests against neo-platonism: '. . . Amid all these fine flights concerning the Soul, the Intellect, and the One, what becomes of poor "I",—of the *Self* of each person? Whence comes, whither goes, the personality?' And in the margins of Tetens, 'What is a Thought but "I" thinking?' In personality, clearly or obscurely, everything is connected with everything else. The necessity of seeing every problem in its relations and perspective, in a perspective increasingly multiple the more one knows, accounts for that sense of defeat by the complexity of his materials that sometimes paralysed him before he had fairly set out. 'I seem to myself to distinguish Power from Strength and to have only the former,' he writes Davy in 1804. Power without Strength. To a more naïve mind the tasks he set himself would have been simpler, or rather, a more naïve mind would not have seen them at all. For was he not groping towards a *Gestalt* psychology before the gestaltists? And in his reflections on consciousness, on the importance of the study of consciousness, on the sub-conscious (he used the phrase 'below consciousness') and on the unconscious, had he not a glimmering of Freudianism before Freud? And would he not have recognized in Jung's doctrine of the collective unconscious, ideas that had in his own mind a sometimes dim and confused, but something more than merely primordial existence? His anticipations he could not at that time either formulate or develop with any scientific precision. He had not the medical knowledge, the case histories, the vocabulary or the hundred years of science between him and them. But he would have greeted some things in the work of all of them with a shout of recognition. This we know from his insight in a diversity of contexts. His interest in children as a source for the study of mental processes, in primitive people and their reactions and attitudes, in the personal literature of memoirs and biography, in dreams and other less conscious experiences, these he shared with many of his contemporaries; but in his insight into them he is closer to later psychologists. I venture to suggest, too, from the nature of his comments on them, that his defence of less rationalistic minds, for instance, mystics like Bruno and Jacob Boehme (Böhme), was aroused more by sympathetic psychological understanding than by any agreement in mystical opinions. Coleridge has been much maligned in regard to his interest in these and other aspects of the irrational.

It becomes clear to a reader of the many passages of self-searching and confession, especially in the notebooks, that his awareness of the existence of almost unrecognized psychological factors in all human activity, comes from his awareness of himself. It has been said by Professor Elton that no man observes the imaginative process so closely in the very act of creation, as he. And the self-observation goes on, not only during the creation of poems, but continually, whatever he is engaged in. Why is it, he notes in a notebook entry in 1803— was he afraid of being laughed down if he had put the question anywhere else?—that a certain pair of black woollen bloomers he wears, creates an intolerably irritating skin condition? Doctors might well attend more to 'cutaneous diseases' he thinks, about which they know little or nothing. The entry goes on amusingly, about the possibility of beauty being really only skin deep, and becomes very involved, but the main thing is that such questions depend on accurate observation in defiance of expectation and conventions of thought. (The concept of allergies was not really developed until about 1915.) His conclusions are tentative in such fields, and not always correct. Emotions, particularly fears, distort the view. This he knows.

(See 18, 37.) But the correctness of the observation, remarkable as it is, is less important than that the observations should be made at all.

What is farthest-reaching and most creative in other fields, in his literary criticism, philosophy, social criticism, theology, is rooted multifariously in and rises out of his own experience. It surely does not invalidate his critical or systematic views at all to suggest that in this sense their great strength and piercing insight depends largely on the subjective element in them. Perhaps 'personal' would be a less dangerous if less accurate word.

At his best, both in criticism and creation, he was able to take the materials of inner experience and to objectify them into works or fragments of truth or art—even in such a poem as 'Kubla Khan' which seems to have appeared out of the air. In a paper entitled 'The "Dream" of Kubla Khan', Miss Elisabeth Schneider interprets the poem as referring to the *Dejection* theme, the loss of joy, of song, of the vision of Paradise, of the creative power which once he had, and which, could he revive it, would enable him to build the pleasure dome of poetry. The whole article with its discussion of opium, and dreams, and its analysis of the origin and meaning of 'Kubla Khan,' is interesting, but what is pertinent here is that 'the purest piece of black magic in the English language' (Lowes) is the product of an imagination that is able to create a beauty of form and order out of deeply realized personal agony. Similarly 'The Ancient Mariner' clearly contains a large element of personal allegory— of fear, and guilt, and loneliness.[1] Again the inner materials have taken shape in art; and it would be possible to show, if this were the place for it, that of Coleridge's many unsuccessful poems, a number fail because, as in 'The Three Graves', the external materials are not sufficiently deeply realized to be subjectively endorsed; and conversely, as in the 'Destiny of Nations', because the subjective feelings are not sufficiently

[1] This is also fully discussed in a recent paper, by Mr. George Whalley, in the *University of Toronto Quarterly* for July 1947.

externalized either in the images of the natural world or in the medium of simple descriptive language.

The criticism of all kinds sometimes stands or falls for the same reason. Plato, for instance, as described in the fifth of the *Philosophical Lectures* has a good deal of Coleridge about him. He 'began in meditation, thought deeply within himself of the goings-on of his own mind and of the powers that were in that mind, conceived to himself how this could be, and if it were, what must be the necessary results and agencies of it, and then looked abroad to ask if this were a dream or whether it were indeed a revelation from within, and a waking reality. He employed his observation as the interpreter of his meditation, equally free from the fanatic who abandons himself to the wild workings of the magic cauldron of his own brain, mistaking every form of delirium for reality, and from the cold sensualist who looks at death as the alone real life of the world, by not considering that the very object was seen to him only by the seeing powers, and what a little further consideration would have led him to deduce, that that which could make him see it must be an agent, and a power like his own, whilst that which was merely seen, which was purely passive, could have no other existence than what arose out of an active power that had produced it.'

The adequacy of the description will be judged by philosophers according to their bent. There is no doubt about its source. Not that Coleridge's most sympathetic interpretations are reserved for those with whom he agrees; but he knows best those with whose mental process he can identify himself in some degree or other. The Stoic ethics fail, and he dismisses them, because the Stoic distorted his own inner nature, denied it in his concern with the externals of behaviour. Democritus on the other hand, whose atomism is inadequate and in its later manifestations anathema to Coleridge, received much fuller attention and respect because, in making his atoms into forms and essences, he invented 'a notion borrowed altogether from

18

what he found within himself, namely the sense of power'. A sense of power, though doubtless, for Democritus, with a sense of strength.

The same acute personal realization (in the true sense of the word) runs through the social criticism. When he wrote his strong plea—and one of his firmest pieces of prose—on behalf of Sir Robert Peel's bill to reduce the working hours of children in the cotton factories, he wrote from the conviction that the arguments of the opposition, based on the hue and cry of 'free labour', were deceptive, and that the labour of the children was not free at all, that they were in fact slaves of an expanding commercial enterprise. This he knew and felt from his personal knowledge of what freedom is and what slavery is. Slavery, he says, is a state of 'hopelessness' [1]; slavery to commerce, or slavery to opium are psychologically very much the same thing. Opium he described late in life, in 1832 to Green, as 'the curse of my existence, my shame and my negro-slave inward humiliation and debasement'. He knew what it felt like to be a negro slave, or a factory child. Slavery to anything prevents the fullest integration of the person and blocks creative activity. Hence the cotton-children must be made free. It is not a question of working hours but of life itself, of releasing them from the clutches of Death-in-Life.

So it is with slavery to opium and ill-health ; and slavery too, to childhood fears, to unhappiness in marriage, to hopeless love. They all prevent that energetic pushing through to an order of things that would have made his own life more useful. This he knows too, and makes it, in 'Dejection', the subject of the saddest and most devastating piece of self-criticism in English poetry.

That the fulcrum of Coleridge's thought is his awareness of the psychological factors in any kind of human experience, and that it derives its power from his own subtle and complex

[1] I have referred to this briefly in the Introduction to the *Philosophical Lectures of S. T. Coleridge*, p. 58.

personal realizations, is, at the very least, a part of the truth about Coleridge.

The relations of things to one another and to his experience are often more remote and strange than in the examples I have cited. His public and even his private audiences felt this frequently. He himself was often troubled by obscure and difficult connexions he could not always hold on to, let alone articulate. And so the sentences grow and grow, the parenthetical qualifications and explanations thicken between the start and the finish, the page fills with the convoluted sentences of his at times verbose, gangliated prose. But this sense of the links, of the complexity, of interdependent inter-relations, not merely among ideas, the products of thought, but in the very process of knowing, makes Coleridge a questioner rather than a systematizer, provocative rather than dogmatic, a noser of nettles rather than a hunter of the hare. (See 114.) His is the kind of not-rigidly-compartmentalized mind that asks questions that are more important than the answers. And those persons who would much rather have questions answered than asked do not generally like Coleridge. It is, however, this genius for questioning and for holding some judgements lightly and tentatively, that gives him that 'seminal quality' that John Stuart Mill detected and that helps to make him intellectually congenial to our time.

In days when we value crystallized systems less and inquiry more, when the area of the unprovable has encroached on the proved, when the relative finds a less frightened acceptance than it once did, when investigations of psychology and sociology begin to be to this century what physics and chemistry and biology were to the last, we are more receptive to Coleridge. We can be more receptive than his contemporaries and certainly much more than the generations that succeeded him. Aside from the change in mental emphasis and interest, we have some advantages over his contemporaries. We care less about his not completing the 'Opus Maximum', although ironically enough we know that much more of it was actually written than they believed. We do not receive his letters telling us that works written only in his mind, or in fragments on the margins of other peoples' books, are 'practically ready for the press'. Many of the sources of irritation and moral condemnation (though Sir Edmund Chambers's summary of his career rings with stern disapproval) have disappeared. On the hither side of the autopsy performed on him, and even without our knowledge of the long years of insidious, undiagnosed ill-health, we see in the list of his publications an impressive achievement. Not including the numerous editions of his poems, twelve volumes[1] of his work were published in his life-time; and fifteen[1] more have been published since his death. If all the manuscript remains were to be published they would easily run to as many as a dozen more. The charge of idleness levelled against Coleridge is understandable from his friends and acquaintances who had no total picture of the man's intellectual labours to go by, who were not in a position to appreciate the distance between him and most of them, and who judged by practical and tangible results. At this time of day, the charge of laziness and dilatoriness is a libel, and covers up a different sort of impatience with Coleridge.

Many persons dislike the tentative and exploratory. They want system and answers if only to refute them. But Coleridge must seek his audience among those who no longer expect to find in books, even by poets and philosophers, the whole truth arranged neatly and labelled as specifics for human ills. On the whole, however, are we not ready as never before to value those reachings out of the mind for what lies on the peripheries of knowledge and experience, to explore, as well as the interior of darkest Africa the still darker interior, at once familiar and unfamiliar, of the Town of Man-Soul? Coleridge should belong to us all again. At least he will meet half-way any reader who

[1] Counting major works only.

prefers being stimulated to being comforted. And to some he will bring his comfort too.

POSTSCRIPT ON THE TEXT

Possibly an anthologist need not defend himself for what is omitted. Yet the responsibility for not distorting an author is particularly great when one deals in unpublished materials. I have tried to be scrupulous, especially in quoting from manuscripts, to quote fully enough to be fair to Coleridge's intention. In the selection of subjects treated and works quoted from, I can only say what Lamb wrote to Coleridge (confessing that he had *not* sent him a present of a pig). 'Pardon me if I stop somewhere.' It required considerable self-denial and strength of purpose to omit from this anthology a selection of the lesser known poems that might easily have gone into the first section. But the poems are available in a good complete modern edition and in many smaller ones. The *Biographia Literaria*, the *Shakespearean Criticism*, and a volume of *Miscellaneous Criticism* are published in modern editions also, and I have not quoted from any of them. Four volumes of letters are published, two in 1895 by E. H. Coleridge and two more in 1932 by E. L. Griggs. But the *Friend*, the *Essays on His Own Times*, the *Aids to Reflection*, the *Statesman's Manual*, the *Confessions of an Enquiring Spirit*, even the *Table Talk*, where are they? I have selected from these, and from others of the less well-known works, because the latter are in any practical sense unavailable, either not reprinted since the early editions or hidden away in obscure publications.

About one third of the items have never been published, and in these cases I have retained Coleridge's eccentricities of spelling and punctuation with only slight modifications. I do so that the reader may haply remember to take them as Coleridge, in a notebook, (as usual thinking about how his own and other minds work) enjoined: as 'Hints and first Thoughts, often, too, *cogitabilia* rather than actual *cogitata a me*', that they 'may not be understood as my fixed opinions—but merely as suggestions of the disquisition; and acts of obedience to the apostolic command of "Try all things: hold fast that which is good" '.

This is not a golden book of Coleridge nor any book of *Gems*. Nor does it pretend to be a representative anthology of either themes or works. I must at the outset disclaim any attempt to set forth fairly or precisely, with due emphasis all round, what one needs to read in order to form a just estimate of the man or a full impression of his mind. Here is not Coleridge in his quiddity. Here is a basket of plucked plums and windfalls, collected while rummaging about in the more recondite materials. Working towards an edition of Coleridge's notebooks has made it necessary to go through everything, published and unpublished, and this anthology is an attempt to share with the common reader some of the fruits of research, fruits that gleam, sometimes obscured by the heavy but still green foliage on the Coleridge tree.

I have arranged the items in the order that seems to me on this twelfth day of March, 1949, illuminating, and I have sworn to stop juggling. "The kind reader" will observe that at least half the items might have been put in any other section than the one where now he finds them. I should like him, just as a point of interest, to try to decide where he would have put item 200 and item 227.

I

'GENUINE
SELF-RESEARCH'

Psychologically, Consciousness is the problem,
the solution of which cannot too variously be
re-worded, too manifoldly be illustrated. . . .
Almost all is yet to be achieved.

Notebook 51

PSYCHOLOGY

No detailed study of Coleridge as psychologist has ever been made, nor did he write anything systematic on what remained for him an all-pervading interest. The nearest approach to a definitely psychological study is to be found in an unpublished rough sketch of an essay 'On the Passions', from which some excerpts are given. See item 52. But Coleridge's psychological wisdom must be found sporadically, in statements on dreams, childhood, men and their motives, various mental states, daemonic energy and the occult generally, particularly witchcraft, and the creative process in poets and other artists. Some of these materials will be found in the *Biographia Literaria*, the *Miscellaneous Criticism* edited by T. M. Raysor, and in the *Philosophical Lectures*. For the rest and best, it is still to be published in the notebooks from which I have been able to give only a few specimens here.

It is well recognized that from earliest times poets have discovered intuitively many of the later observations of scientific psychology. Coleridge's insights have that kind of intuition as one of their sources; but they also derive from close observation and an effort to be precise in noticing the laws of cause and effect in the human as in the natural world. After a brief flirtation with mechanical Associationism, the Behaviourism of his day, he developed views along the lines of a *Gestalt* psychology, denying that man is the mere sum of his parts, and insisting on a totality, an organism,

> 'Dark fluxion, all unfixable by thought
> A phantom dim of past and future wrought.'

As well as asking the usual direct question of an experience, 'What does it mean to me?' he asked himself, 'What is the content of consciousness? What lies below consciousness, unknown to me?' Here he points forward to Freud. It is perhaps worth noticing that he would never have agreed with Freud's separation of the intellect and the imagination. For him the dividing-line between reality and illusion was not so sharp and clear, nor were science and art so mutually exclusive. He would not have called art play—or science all work, for that matter. The imagination for Coleridge contains both conscious and unconscious elements, and far from being an escape into illusion, is a means of ordering the chaos of reality, and one of the ways of access to truth. As I have pointed out in the Introduction, he appears to have come close to Jung and the idea of a collective unconscious in language and myth and in religion and art. On this last point, his Royal Society lecture on the *Prometheus of Aeschylus* is as startling now as it was baffling to his audience in 1825. The poems read the richer for an awareness of the psychological materials in them.

I

'GENUINE
SELF-RESEARCH'

I. KNOW THYSELF

How can a truth, new to us, be made our own without examination and self-questioning—any new truth, I mean, that relates to the properties of the mind, and its various faculties and affections? But whatever demands effort, requires time. Ignorance seldom *vaults* into knowledge, but passes into it through an intermediate state of obscurity, even as night into day through twilight. All speculative truths begin with a postulate, even the truths of geometry. They all suppose an act of the will; for in the moral being lies the source of the intellectual. The first step to knowledge, or rather the previous condition of all insight into truth, is to dare commune with our very and permanent self. It is Warburton's remark, not the Friend's, that 'of all literary exercitations, whether designed for the use or entertainment of the world, there are none of so much importance, or so immediately our concern as those which let us into the knowledge of our own nature. Others may exercise the understanding or amuse the imagination; but these only can improve the heart and form the human mind to wisdom.'

The recluse hermit oft'times more doth know
Of the world's inmost wheels, than worldlings can,
As Man is of the World, the Heart of Man
Is an Epitome of God's great Book
Of Creatures, and Men need no further look.
                                    Donne.
                                              Friend.

2. THOUGHTS AND MOTIVES

A manuscript note on the front flyleaf of Tetens' *Philo-sophische Versuche*, Bd. 2.

In the Chapters on Liberty and Necessity the old Delusion goes thro' all—the motives, nay the reflections and deliberations (*Bewegungsgründe, Ueberlegungen, Reflexionen*) are reasoned on as outward things—i.e. outward to the Soul, tho' inside of the Soul's imagined Residence-chamber. A. determines himself that and the other, therefore, A. does not determine himself! What are the motives but my impelling thoughts—and what is a Thought but another word for 'I thinking'?

                                              MS.

3. MIND DISTINGUISHED FROM CONSCIOUSNESS

I feel that there is a mystery in the sudden by-act-of-will-un-aided, nay, more than that, frustrated, recollection of a Name. I was trying to recollect the name of a Bristol Friend, who had attended me in my Illness at Mʳ Wade's. I began with the Letters of the Alphabet—A B C &c.—and I know not why, felt convinced that it began with H. I ran thro' all the vowels, a e i o u y, and with all the consonants to each—Hab, Heb, Hib, Hob, Hub and so on—in vain. I then began other Letters—all in vain. Three minutes afterwards, having completely given it up, the name, Daniel, at once stared up, perfectly insulated, without

any the dimmest antecedent connection, as far as my consciousness extended. There is no explanation, ὡς ἐμοίγε δοκεῖ, of this
fact, but by a full sharp distinction of Mind from Consciousness
—the Consciousness being the narrow *Neck* of the Bottle. The
name, Daniel, must have been a living *Atom*-thought in my
mind, whose uneasy motions were the craving to recollect it—
but the very craving led the mind to a reach [?] which each successive disappointment (=a tiny pain) tended to contract the
orifice or *outlet* into Consciousness. Well—it is given up—and
all is quiet—the Nerves are asleep, or off their guard—and then
the Name pops up, makes its way, and there it is!—not assisted
by any association, but the very contrary—by the suspension
and *sedation* of all associations.

MS.

4. OUR ONENESS

*In Illustration of what I have written in my Cottle-book
[Notebook 21] on Envy suspected where only resentment is
felt, and an uneasiness at a non-harmony, the wish not to see
any thing admirable where you find, especially in the moral
character, any thing low or contemptible, and the consequent
wish to avoid the struggle within—this anti-monadic feeling,
this (what shall I say?) *knowing*, *feeling*, a man to be *one*, yet not
understanding how to think of him but as two—in illustration
of this* I confess that it has cost and still costs my philosophy
some exertion not to be vexed that I must admire, aye, greatly,
very greatly, admire *Richardson*. His mind is so very vile a mind
—so oozy, hypocritical, praise-mad, canting, envious, concu-
piscent. But to understand and draw *him* would be to produce
[a character] almost equal to any of his own, but in order to
do this, '*down proud Heart down!*' as we teach little Children to
say to themselves—*bless them!*—(N.B. my fat boy, Derwent!)
—all hatred down! Charity, Calmness, an heart fixed on the
good parts, tho' the *Understanding* is surveying all. Richardson

31

felt truly the defect of Fielding, or rather what was not his excellence, and made that his *Defect*, a trick of Uncharitableness often played chiefly, tho' not exclusively by Contemporaries. Fielding's Talent was *Observation* not *Meditation*, but Richardson was not Philosopher enough to know the difference—say rather, to understand and develop it. *Strange! to bring two such names together, as Cottle's and Richardson's—yet amid and in spite of the vast difference there are points of resemblance and I must not be afraid to look steadily at them.

N.B. That deep intuition of our *oneness*—is it not at the bottom of many of our faults as well as Virtues—the dislike that a bad man should have any virtues, a good man any faults —and yet something noble and incentive is in this.*

MS.

5. SELF-ANALYSIS

As individual to individual, from my childhood, I do not remember feeling myself either superior or inferior to any human being; except by an act of my own will in cases of real or imagined moral or intellectual superiority. In regard to worldly rank, from eight years old to nineteen, I was habituated, nay, naturalized, to look up to men circumstanced as you are, as my superiors—a large number of our governors, and almost *all* of those whom we regarded as greater men still, and whom we saw most of, *viz.* our committee governors, were such—and as neither awake nor asleep have I any other feelings than what I had at Christ's Hospital, I distinctly remember that I felt a little flush of pride and consequence—just like what we used to feel at school when the boys came running to us—'Coleridge! here's your friends want you—they are quite *grand*', or 'It is quite a *lady*'—when I first heard who you were, and laughed at myself for it with that pleasurable sensation that, spite of my sufferings at that school, still accompanies any sudden reawakening of our school-boy feelings and notions. And O, from sixteen to

nineteen what hours of Paradise had Allen and I in escorting the
Miss Evanses home on a Saturday, who were then at a milliner's
whom we used to think, and who I believe really was, such a
nice lady;—and we used to carry thither, of a summer morning,
the pillage of the flower gardens within six miles of town, with
Sonnet or Love Rhyme wrapped round the nosegay. To be
feminine, kind, and genteelly (what I should now call neatly)
dressed, these were the only things to which my head, heart,
or imagination had any polarity, and what I was then, I
still am.

Allsop.

6. FEELING

I devote this brief scroll to Feeling: so no more of disquisition,
except it be to declare the entire coincidence of my experience
with yours as to the very rare occurrence of strong and deep
Feeling in conjunction with free power and vivacity in the
expression of it. The most eminent Tragedians, Garrick for instance, are known to have had their emotions as much at command, and almost as much on the surface, as the muscles of
their countenances; and the French, who are all Actors, are pro-
verbially heartless. Is it that it is a false and feverous state for the
Centre to live in the Circumference? The vital warmth seldom
rises to the surface in the form of sensible Heat, without becoming hectic and inimical to the Life within, the only source of
real sensibility. Eloquence itself—I speak of it as habitual and at
call—too often is, and is always like to engender, a species of
histrionism.

In one of my juvenile poems (on a Friend who died in a
Frenzy Fever), you will find that I was jealous of this in myself;
and that it is (as I trust it is), otherwise, I attribute mainly to the
following causes:—A naturally, at once searching and communicative disposition, the necessity of reconciling the restlessness of an ever-working Fancy with an intense craving after a

resting-place for my Thoughts in some *principle* that was derived from experience, but of which all other knowledge should be but so many repetitions under various limitations, even as circles, squares, triangles, etc., etc., are but so many positions of space. And, lastly, that my eloquence was most commonly excited by the desire of running away and hiding myself from my personal and inward feelings, *and not for the expression of them*, while doubtless this very effort of feeling gave a passion and glow to my thoughts

> Sloth-jaundiced all! and from my graspless hand
> Drop Friendship's precious pearls, like hour-glass sand.
> I weep, yet stoop not! the faint anguish flows,
> A dreamy pang in Morning's feverish dose.
> Is this piled earth our Being's passless mound?
> Tell me, cold grave! is Death with poppies crowned?
> Tired sentinel! 'mid fitful starts I nod,
> And fain would sleep, though pillowed on a clod.

and language on subjects of a general nature, that they otherwise would not have had. I fled in a Circle, still overtaken by the Feelings, from which I was ever more fleeing, with my back turned towards them; but above all, my growing deepening conviction of the *transcendency of the moral to the intellectual*, and the inexpressible comfort and inward strength which I experience myself to derive as often as I contemplate truth realized into Being by a human Will; so that, *as I cannot love without esteem, neither can I esteem without loving*. Hence I *love* but few, but those I love as my own Soul; for I feel that without them I should—not indeed cease to be kind and effluent, but by little and little become a soul-less fixed Star, receiving no rays nor influences into my Being, *a Solitude which I so tremble at, that I cannot attribute it even to the Divine Nature.*

Allsop.

7. DISTINCT CONSCIOUSNESS

Few are so obdurate, few have sufficient strength of character, to be able to draw forth an evil tendency or immoral practice into distinct *consciousness*, without bringing it in the same moment before an awaking *conscience*. But for this very reason it becomes a duty of conscience to form the mind to a habit of distinct consciousness. An unreflecting Christian walks in twilight among snares and pitfalls! He entreats the heavenly Father not to lead him into temptation, and yet places himself on the very edge of it, because he will not kindle the torch which his Father had given into his hands, as a means of prevention, and lest he should pray too late.

Aids to Reflection.

8. SELF-SLAVERY

Art thou under the tyranny of sin? a slave to vicious habits? at enmity with God, and a skulking fugitive from thy own conscience? O, how idle the dispute, whether the listening to the dictates of *prudence* from prudential and self-interested motives be virtue or merit, when the *not* listening is guilt, misery, madness, and despair! The best, the most *Christian-like* pity thou canst show, is to take pity on thy own soul. The best and most acceptable service thou canst render, is to do justice and show mercy to *thyself*.

Aids to Reflection.

9. 'TRUE NOTION OF SLAVERY—HOPELESSNESS'

What makes a slave a slave? If I mistake not it is oppressions—it is the being in a state out of which he cannot hope to rise; and he who is placed where there is no motive for action but where the miserable thing he is must ever remain, in the same sphere, is a slave, and a pitiable one.

Philosophical Lectures.

10. PSYCHIATRY

Medicine hitherto has been too much confined to *passive* works —as if fevers &c.—were the only human calamities. A Gymnastic Medicine is wanting, not a mere recommendation but a system of forcing the Will and *motive faculties* into action. There are a multitude of cases which should be treated as Madness— i.e. the genus madness should be extended and more classes and species made, in practice, tho' of course, not in name.[1]

MS.

11. MADNESS

Madness is not simply a bodily disease. It is the sleep of the spirit with certain conditions of wakefulness; that is to say, lucid intervals. During this sleep, or recession of the spirit, the lower or bestial states of life rise up into action and prominence. It is an awful thing to be eternally tempted by the perverted senses. The reason may resist—it does resist—for a long time; but too often at length, it yields for a moment, and the man is mad for ever. An act of the will is, in many instances, precedent to complete insanity. I think it was Bishop Butler, who said, that he was all his life struggling against the devilish suggestions of his senses, which would have maddened him, if he had relaxed the stern wakefulness of his reason for a single moment.

Table Talk.

[1] In a letter he suggests a 'new Charitable institution, under authority of a legislative act, namely, a *Maison de Santé* (what do the French call it?) for lunacy and idiocy of the *will*, in which, with the full consent of, or at the direct instance of the patient himself, and with the concurrence of his friends, such a person under the certificate of a physician might be placed under medical and moral coercion. I am convinced that London would furnish a hundred volunteers in as many days from the gin-shops, who would swallow their glass of poison in order to get courage to present themselves to the hospital in question. And a similar institution might exist for a higher class of will-maniacs or impotents. Had such a house of health been in existence, I know who would have entered himself as a patient some five and twenty years ago.' *Letters*, II. 767-8.

12. A CONTINUALLY DIVIDED BEING

[*page cut*] . . . all the realities about me lose their natural *healing* powers, at least, diminish the same, and become not worthy of a Thought. Who that thus lives with a continually divided Being can remain healthy! And who can long remain body-crazed, and not at times use unworthy means of making his Body the fit instrument of his mind? Pain is easily subdued compared with continual uncomfortableness—and the sense of stifled Power!—O this is that which made poor Henderson, Collins, Boyce, &c. &c. &c.—*Sots*—awful Thought—O it is horrid—Die, my Soul, die!—Suicide—rather than this, the worst state of Degradation! It is less a suicide! S.T.C.

I work hard, I do the duties of common Life from morn to night, but verily 'I raise my limbs, like lifeless *Tools*'. The organs of motion and outward action perform their functions at the stimulus of a galvanic fluid applied by the *Will*, not by the Spirit of Life that makes Soul and Body one. Thought and Reality two distinct corresponding Sounds, of which no man can say positively which is the Voice and which the Echo.

O the beautiful Fountain or natural Well at Upper Stowey! [*A line and a half of verse is here obliterated with heavy ink.*] The images of the weeds which hung down from its sides, appeared as plants growing up, straight and upright, among the water weeds that really grow from the Bottom, and so vivid was the Image, that for some moments and not till after I had disturbed the water, did I perceive that their roots were not neighbours, and they side-by-side companions. So—even then I said—so are the happy man's *Thoughts* and *Things*—in the language of the modern Philosophers, Ideas and Impressions.

MS.

13. AN OPIUM ALLEGORY

In Mr. Burchell's *Travels in South Africa* there is a very curious description of a singular Thorn-plant, which must have been quoted in some one of the Reviews or Philosoph[ical] Journals as I have never seen the Book itself. This I must refer to for— *Impatiens?* or *Noli me Tangere?*

The extract from Burchell, which was to have been inserted here, is as follows: I was preparing to cut some specimens of it [the Haakedoorn, or Hookthorn, or *Acacia detinens*]; which the Hottentots observing, warned me to be very careful in doing so, otherwise I should certainly be caught fast in its branches. In consequence of this advice, I proceeded with the utmost caution, but with all my care a small twig caught hold of one sleeve. While thinking to disengage it quietly with the other hand, both arms were seized by these rapacious thorns, and the more I tried to extricate myself, the more entangled I became; till at last it seized hold of the hat also; and convinced me that there was no possibility for me to free myself, but by main force, and at the expense of tearing all my clothes. I therefore called out for help, and two of my men came and released me by cutting off the branches by which I was held. In revenge for this ill-treatment, I determined to give to the tree a name which should serve to caution future travellers against allowing themselves to venture within its clutches.

Coleridge comments: Surely the wit of man could not present a livelier emblem of a Sinner entangled in the snares of a sinful Habit, without love to the Sin, nay with unutterable dread and condemnation of the same, tempted by no expectation, impelled by no desire, but goaded on by the inexorable *Want*, stung and chased onward by uncontrollable Restlessness, and cowed by the Pain that subsists in the bewildering Dread of Pain.

> Lured by no vain Belief
> Nor Hope that flatters Grief
> To lawless Spells they flee
> And borrow short Relief
> At frightful Usury——

MS.

14. MENTAL ANARCHY

Why need we talk of a fiery hell? If the will, which is the law of our nature, were withdrawn from our memory, fancy, understanding, and reason, no other hell could equal, for a spiritual being, what we should then feel, from the anarchy of our powers. It would be conscious madness—a horrid thought!

Table Talk.

15. A DEATH-WISH

Sunday, June 22nd 1806. Globe, Pisa. The concrete in nature nearest to the *abstract* of Death is Death by a Flash of Lightning. Repeatedly during this night's storm have I desired that I might be taken off, not knowing when or where. But a few moments past a vivid flash passed across me, my nerves thrilled, and I earnestly wished, so help me God! like a Love-longing, that it would pass through me!—Death without pain, without degrees, without the possibility of cowardly wishes, or recreant changes of resolve. Death without deformity, or assassin-like self-disorganization. Death, in which the mind by its own wish might seem to have caused its own purpose to be performed, as instantaneously and by an instrument almost as spiritual as the Wish itself!

> Come, come, thou bleak December Wind,
> And blow the dry Leaves from the Tree.
> Flash, like a Love-thought, thro' me, Death
> And take a Life, that wearies me.

MS.

16. JOHN WORDSWORTH'S DEATH

Sarah Hutchinson
S. T. Coleridge

39

Dorothy and Mary Wordsworth
William Wordsworth
Malta.

Shall I ever see them again? And will it not [be] better that I should not? Is my body, and the habits and state of mind induced by it, such as to promise that I shall be other than a new Sorrow? O dear John! would I had been thy Substitute!

MS.

17. NERVOUS WEAKNESS

A person, nervously weak, has a sensation of weakness which is as bad to him as muscular weakness. The only difference lies in the better chance of removal.

Table Talk.

18. POWER WITHOUT STRENGTH

9 August 1831. From my earliest recollection I have had a consciousness of Power without Strength—a perception, an experience, of more than ordinary power with an inward sense of Weakness. O more than ever, tho' I can and it would perhaps be instructive, to trace it thro' the different periods of my Life, in characteristic instances—more than ever do I feel it now, when I have to struggle day after day with life-loathing Sickness, as my first Good-Morning to you! with life-wearying uneasiness of the lower Bowels, the more depressive, the meaner, duller and more obscure the disquieting Sensation, which forces away my attention to itself—and last, the dread at night, lest my night should be turned into day by the withholding of my best outward Relief, the partial Oblivion of Sleep. More than ever do I feel this now, when all my fancies still in their integrity are, as it were, drawn *inward* and by their suppression and compression rendered a mock substitute for

Strength—the sprays, boughs and branches compressed into a branchless leafless Trunk. But O Almighty God! who in thy free Mercy convertest manifoldly our evils from the weakness of the flesh into thy own good, O sanctify this affliction, to a deeper and more effectual Seeking of thee, as the Alone Strength thro' the mediator of thy goodness, Christ Jesus!

MS.

19. OF HIMSELF

I never from a boy could under any circumstances feel the slightest dread of death as such. In all my illnesses I have ever had the most intense desire to be released from this life, unchecked by any but one wish, namely, to be able to finish my work on philosophy. Not that I have any author's vanity on the subject: God knows that I should be absolutely glad, if I could hear that the thing had already been done before me.

Illness never in the smallest degree affects my intellectual powers. I can *think* with all my ordinary vigour in the midst of pain; but I am beset with the most wretched and unmanning reluctance and shrinking from action. I could not upon such occasions take the pen in hand to write down my thoughts for all the wide world.

Table Talk.

20. A SELF-CASTIGATION

Mem. Alas! What use will *Mem.* be? The fullness, but much more the *undesigningness* of my mind, the habit and incapability of having any co-object with the point. I am arguing, *totus in illo, et mei et audientium immemor*, make it of no use. Nevertheless, *Mem.* not to allow myself to be [page cut].

MS.

21. SELF-KNOWLEDGE

The hypochondriac, or the intemperate man,—and his endless fruitless Memoranda, fruitless and perhaps pernicious as familiarising his mind to the Contemplation, the lazy Contemplation of his own Weakness.

MS.

22. 'FROM THE SOUL ITSELF MUST ISSUE FORTH'

I am never very forward in offering spiritual consolation to any one in distress or disease. I believe that such resources, to be of any service, must be self-evolved in the first instance. I am something of the Quaker's mind in this, and am inclined to wait for the spirit.

Table Talk.

23. LOVE AND FRIENDSHIP

Sympathy constitutes friendship; but in love there is a sort of antipathy, or opposing passion. Each strives to be the other, and both together make up one whole.

Table Talk.

24. GENIUS AND TALENT

To carry on the feelings of childhood into the powers of manhood, to combine the child's sense of wonder and novelty with the appearances which every day for perhaps forty years has rendered familiar,

> With sun and moon and stars throughout the year,
> And man and woman——

this is the character and privilege of genius, and one of the marks which distinguish genius from talent. And so to represent

familiar objects as to awaken the minds of others to a like freshness of sensation concerning them—that constant accompaniment of mental, no less than of bodily, convalescence—to the
same modest questioning of a self-discovered and intelligent
ignorance, which, like the deep and massy foundations of a
Roman bridge, forms half of the whole structure (*prudens inter-
rogatio dimidium Scientiae*, says Lord Bacon)—this is the prime
merit of genius, and its most unequivocal mode of manifestation. Who has not, a thousand times, seen it snow upon water?
Who has not seen it with a new feeling, since he has read
Burns's comparison of sensual pleasure,

> To snow that falls upon a river,
> A moment white—then gone for ever!

In philosophy equally, as in poetry, genius produces the
strongest impressions of novelty, while it rescues the stalest and
most admitted truths from the impotence caused by the very
circumstance of their universal admission. Extremes meet;—a
proverb, by the by, to collect and explain all the instances and
exemplifications of which, would constitute and exhaust all
philosophy. Truths, of all others the most awful and mysterious,
yet being at the same time of universal interest, are too often
considered as so true that they lose all the powers of truth, and
lie bed-ridden in the dormitory of the soul, side by side with
the most despised and exploded errors.

Friend.

25. TWO RACES OF MEN

'There are many men, especially at the outset of life, who, in
their too eager desire for the end, overlook the difficulties in
the way; there is another class, who see nothing else. The first
class *may* sometimes fail; the latter rarely succeed.'

Allsop.

26. GREAT MINDS ANDROGYNOUS

I have known *strong* minds with imposing, undoubting, Cobbett-like manners, but I have never met a *great* mind of this sort. And of the former, they are at least as often wrong as right. The truth is, a great mind must be androgynous. Great minds—Swedenborg's for instance—are never wrong but in consequence of being in the right, but imperfectly.

Table Talk.

27. SPURZHEIM AND CRANIOLOGY

Spurzheim is a good man, and I like him; but he is dense, and the most ignorant German I ever knew. If he had been content with stating certain remarkable coincidences between the moral qualities and the configuration of the skull, it would have been well; but when he began to map out the cranium dogmatically, he fell into infinite absurdities. You know, that every intellectual act, however you may distinguish it by name in respect of the originating faculties, is truly the act of the entire man; the notion of distinct material organs, therefore, in the brain itself, is plainly absurd. Pressed by this, Spurzheim has, at length, been guilty of some sheer quackery; and ventures to say that he has actually discovered a different material in the different parts or organs of the brain, so that he can tell a piece of benevolence from a bit of destructiveness, and so forth. Observe, also, that it is constantly found, that so far from there being a con-cavity in the interior surface of the cranium answering to the convexity apparent on the exterior—the interior is convex too. Dr. Baillie thought there was something in the system, because the notion of the brain being an extendible net helped to explain those cases where the intellect remained after the solid substance of the brain was dissolved in water.

That a greater or less development of the forepart of the head is generally coincident with more or less of reasoning power, is certain. The line across the forehead, also denoting musical power, is very common.

Table Talk.

28. HYSTERIA

Hysteria may be fitly called mimosa, from its counterfeiting so many diseases—even death itself.

Table Talk.

29. THE LIMITS OF CONSCIOUSNESS

If any reflecting mind be surprised that the aids of the Divine Spirit should be deeper than our Consciousness can reach, it must arise from the not having attended sufficiently to the nature and necessary limits of human Consciousness. For the same impossibility exists as to the first acts and movements of our own will—the farthest back our recollection can follow the traces, never leads us to the first foot-mark—the lowest depth that the light of our Consciousness can visit even with a doubtful Glimmering, is still at an unknown distance from the Ground: and so, indeed, must it be with all Truths, and all modes of Being that can neither be counted, coloured, or delineated. Before and After, when applied to such Subjects, are but allegories, which the Sense or Imagination supply to the Understanding. The Position of the Aristoteleans, *Nihil in intellectu quod non prius in sensu*, on which Mr. Locke's Essay is grounded, is irrefragable: Locke erred only in taking half the truth for a whole Truth. Conception is consequent on Perception. What we cannot *imagine*, we cannot, in the proper sense of the word, conceive.

Aids to Reflection.

30. ANIMAL MAGNETISM

Whence the contemptuous rejection of animal magnetism before and without examination? How are we to account for this extraordinary antipathy? Had it been a discovery of the same kind with that of the simple magnet, of electricity, above all, of the almost miraculous power (*ex. gr.* that of transferring substances, at indefinite distances) belonging to Galvanism; *then* its apparent contradiction to all the Laws hitherto known, as those of Cohesion, Gravitation, etc., might have justified, at all events, would palliate this preclusive contempt. Or had it been like the discovery of Copernicus, then its broad blank contradiction to the apparent evidence of the senses would make it at once intelligible, or, that men should refuse even to attend to the question and place it (as even so late as the restoration of Charles II. Sir T. Brown did) among the proofs that no absurdity can be so wild, but that some philosopher, or sect of Philosophy will assert it.—A collection of the *a priori* verdicts passed by men of the highest character, and pre-eminent in their generation, from the reign of Elizabeth to that of James the second, against the Copernican System (and in France, Spain, and Italy to a much later period) would be not merely entertaining but highly instructive. For who save those who build cenotaphs, and passed into a reverence of the prophets (as of Jeremiah and etc.) far too near idolatry—the prophets whom their Fore-Fathers had abused, ridiculed, and murdered? 'We' would not have done it! 'No'—but yet these very 'We' were the persons who bellowed out 'crucify him! Crucify him! And loose unto us Barabbas' 'Now Barabbas was a murderer'.

But in the case of Animal Magnetism there is no question concerning a Theory—the whole and sole demand is, to examine with common honesty and inward veracity a series of Facts—and these again not as the evidence of the circumstances that accompanied the first promulgation of Christianity, mere *historical Facts*, the irrecoverable property, and (as it were) the fixtures of the Past; but the reproducible Facts, facts as strictly analogous to those of Galvanism as the difference and the continual changes of organic life of the subjects make possible. The only *position* asserted by Magnetists as Magnetists (and independent of all particular theory, or explanation) as is most evident from its being held in common without the least shade of variation in their facts, in those statements of which their facts are mere generalization, (even as Gravitation in the first and purest sense of the word as solicitiously determined by Sir I. Newton, expressed as a general Term the aggregate of effects—namely, that all Bodies tend to their centers in the direct proportion of their relative masses) the only position, I say, asserted by all Magnetists as Magnetists, is, that the will or (if you prefer it as even less theoric) the *vis vitæ* of Man is not confined in its operations to the Organic Body, in which it appears to be seated; but under certain previously defined Conditions of distance and position, and above all of the relation of the Patient to the Agent and of the Agent to the Patient, is capable of acting and producing certain pre-defined Effects on the living human bodies external to it.—Thus, the *Gymnotus Electricus*, and Two other Fishes, possess a power of acting on bodies at a distance. In them it is true, the power is given to them merely for self-defence and likewise an organic apparatus has been discovered—but these differences are no more than what might have been certainly and securely anticipated from universal analogy.

Every power which man has in common with the Insects, the Bees for instance, is subjected to his Will, and capable of voluntary application—the very faculty of continuing his species in projective reproduction is in his instance only entrusted in a great measure to his Will.—Again no man has yet discovered any organic apparatus for Thought, Passion, Volition—we have discovered the Instrument set in action by them, but not the specific organs—but simply this, that in some way or other the whole nervous system is the organ.—What then is asked of any man? To believe? No! but merely to review the mass of evidence supplied by every variety of witness, from almost every part of Europe—and to show if you can some instances in the past experience of Mankind, of Evidence so concurrent from so many quarters under such very marked and even hostile differences of the attestors themselves, in respect of Country, Religion, Philosophic Sect, Rank, Talent, and even of personal antipathies, in anything afterwards proved to be false. But even on this Ground no faith is demanded, nothing more than the admission that a position as analogous to many known facts of Animal Electricity and Galvanism as two series of facts can be, and so attested, should be put to the test of impartial examination. There is but one demand made—Viz. Try it yourself.

There are but three essential conditions—the first, that the patient should labor under some disturbance of Health. Secondly, that the agent should sincerely and humanely wish to relieve him, if it be in his power to do so—and lastly that he should to the utmost of his power fix his attention and devote his will to this one object. The external manipulations (the necessity of which is not yet demonstrated; but the expedience of which as a means of facilitating the act of *attending* is undeniable; were it only on the same principle that men play with their buttons, watch-chain, or take snuff when they are desirous of attending earnestly to any one object) the external manipulation is far less complex than what is required in the ordinary medical administration of Electricity.—To place yourself face to face with the patient—to lay your left hand on his right shoulder, and your right hand on his left shoulder, to move your hands down his arms to the tips of his fingers, then to hold his thumbs for a few moments, his right thumb between the thumb and forefinger or little finger of your left hand, and his left thumb in the same manner with your right hand—and having repeated this Process half a dozen times, then to draw your hand and arm in a sweep from his head downwards—and if he complain of any local pain, to touch the part repeatedly—and at all events, to draw your hand either with the flat palm, or with the fingers' ends; from the Neck to the Abdomen, either by direct touch or at a distance of one or two inches. Doubtless, the manipulations vary with the case; and every magnetist is led by his own experience, one to prefer one plan, and one another, or to unite all at different times, such as alternating the sweep from the Head downwards by laying one hand on the person's brow and another on his navel—or breathing on the part affected, as in the Eye, in cases of Amaurosis, in the cure of which Animal Magnetism has been found particularly successful—or *flipping*, as it were, the flat of the thumbs with the forefinger at the part—or the placing the one hand on the correspondent region of the back, while the other is employed on the gastric or abdominal region, and during all this no other state of mind is required than what you would think it your duty to produce in yourself, if you were trying over again an experiment (chemical) concerning which you entertained some doubts—as for instance, when Sir H. Davy repeated the experiments of Berzylius with regard to the metal of Barytes, or Mr. Brand Professor Clark's experiments on the fusion of stones, earth, and metals, by Newman's Blowpipe with the condensed Gases——

If it be said that Mesmer was a character who wanted to make his fortune by his secret and that he did so—first of all, he fairly revealed his whole secret to those who bought it, and of the hundred Gentlemen who paid him a hundred louis each, not *one* complained of having been deceived. Secondly, do you not give Dr. James's powders? Was it not the case with Vaccination in the first year of its Introduction—in Germany and Italy? or are there none who *get money* by Medical Electricity and Galvanism? Besides, Mesmer and Mystery are now gone by forever—so far from any secret being made, the cases are published at present in all the respectable foreign Journals, medical and philosophical, as any other cases in Medicine and Physics. Even the sturdy Leader of the matter-of-fact Experimentalists, Gilbert, has at length admitted the subject into his annals, and he himself most reluctantly has been obliged to concede the *facts*. Nearly two years have passed since the Prussian and Austrian Governments have demanded a report on the subject from the Physicians and Eminent Naturalists of Berlin and Vienna, and the report of the French Committee under Dr. Franklin has been subjected to a careful revision, and declared partial. And yet has there arisen one man among all, who has detected falsehood or delusion! Not one . . .

Whence then comes this Incredulity? The English World are against it—and Peter disdains to listen to it because John thinks nothing of it—and John disdains it because Peter does so . . . It is sufficient that men of sense reject it—and who are men of sense? . . . . [*Gaps left in the MS. for insertion of names of eminent scientists and physicians.*] O No! they must be very weak men— they are converts to Animal Magnetism! Consequently there can be no competent evidences—the same sophism has been employed against the credibility of the Christian History—and admirably detected and exposed by Jortin and Lardner——

For myself, I shall even say—I will try it when I have the opportunity, myself—I will endeavour to see it tried by others, when I can—and till then I will be neutral—S. T. Coleridge, July 8th, 1817.

MS.

31. ANIMAL MAGNETISM

I am in the habit of making marginal observations on the books I read—a habit indulged by the partiality of my friends. For the last 20 years there is scarce a book so be-penned or be-penciled but some one or more instances will be found noticed by me of the power of the visual and its substitution for the conceptual. Yet I remember few more striking than the scornful and per- tinacious disbelief of An[imal] Mag[netism] compared with the eager belief of Electricity—the main cause of this difference being, I am persuaded, this only, that the latter exhibited a flash of Light.

MS.

32. ANIMAL MAGNETISM

S. T. C.'s Judgement after a careful and unbiassed Perusal of
this Book. [Kluge on Animal Magnetism.]

Allowing the least possible to Fancy and Exaggeration, I can
yet find nothing in the Cases collected by Dr. Kluge that requires any other conclusion but this—that under certain conditions one human Being may so *act on the body as well as on
the mind of another—as to produce a morbid sleep, from which
the Brain awakes, while the organs of sense remain in stupor. I
speak exclusively of the *intellectual* phaenomena of An[imal]
Mag[netism]. That the same *vis ab extra* may act medically,
there is no reason to doubt—any more than of the effects of
opium. Thus the *modus agendi* in the first instance, the instrument thro' which the Magnetiser operates, is the only mystery:
and on this neither Kluge nor any of his Predecessors have
thrown a ray of Light. Their Somato - or, *brevitatis et euphoniæ
causâ*† Somo- sphere is a mere translation of the Fact into an un-
meaning Image. It is but the substitution of the word, Fluid,
for Dr. Reil or Dr. Kluge. S. T. C.

MS.

33. THE SCIENCE OF MEDICINE

Before the Art of Healing can be made a matter of Common
Sense, the Common Sense must have been itself enlightened by
the Conclusions of Science and the Results of Experience and
experimental Philosophy.

MS.

---

* The act however is a discovery of great importance as well as curiosity:
and it is far from my intention to detract from either.

† A sphere supposed to be filled by a nervous fluid to an undefined
distance round the Body, an *atmosphere* with ʿΣῶμα=body for ἀθμή, Halitus,
or Breathing.

34. A LESSON FROM THE PRIMITIVE

'The possible effect on the imagination, from an idea violently
and suddenly impressed on it.'

I had been reading Bryan Edwards's account of the effects of
the *Oby* witchcraft on the Negroes in the West Indies, and
Hearne's deeply interesting anecdotes of similar workings on
the imagination of the Copper Indians (those of my readers
who have it in their power will be well repaid for the trouble
of referring to those works for the passages alluded to); and I
conceived the design of shewing that instances of this kind are
not peculiar to savage or barbarous tribes, and of illustrating
the mode in which the mind is affected in these cases, and the
progress and symptoms of the morbid action on the fancy from
the beginning.

Preface to *The Three Graves*.

35. DREAMS, VISIONS, GHOSTS AND WITCHCRAFT

I have long wished to devote an entire work to the subject of
dreams, visions, ghosts, and witchcraft, in which I might first
give, and then endeavour to explain, the most interesting and
best attested fact of each, which has come within my knowledge, either from books or from personal testimony. I might
then explain in a more satisfactory way the mode in which our
thoughts, in states of morbid slumber, become at times perfectly *dramatic*, (for in certain sorts of dreams the dullest wight
becomes a Shakespear) and by what law the *form* of the vision
appears to talk to us its own thoughts in a voice as audible as
the shape is visible; and this too oftentimes in connected trains,
and not seldom even with a concentration of power which may
easily impose on the soundest judgments, uninstructed in the
optics and *acoustics* of the inner sense, for revelations and gifts of

prescience. In aid of the present case, I will only remark, that it would appear incredible to persons not accustomed to these subtle notices of self-observation, what small and remote resemblances, what mere hints of likeness from some real external object, especially if the shape be aided by colour, will suffice to make a vivid thought consubstantiate with the real object, and derive from it an outward perceptibility. Even when we are broad awake, if we are in anxious expectation, how often will not the most confused sounds of nature be heard by us as articulate sounds? For instance, the babbling of a brook will appear for a moment the voice of a friend, for whom we are waiting, calling out our own names &c. A short meditation, therefore, on the great law of the imagination, that a likeness in part tends to become a likeness of the whole, will make it not only conceivable but probable, that the inkstand itself, and the dark-coloured stone on the wall, which Luther perhaps had never till then noticed, might have a considerable influence in the production of the fiend, and of the hostile act by which his obtrusive visit was repelled.

A lady once asked me if I believed in ghosts and apparitions. I answered with truth and simplicity: *No, madam! I have seen far too many myself.* I have indeed a whole memorandum book filled with records of these phaenomena, many of them interesting as facts and data for psychology, and affording some valuable materials for a theory of perception and its dependence on the memory and imagination. '*In omnem actum perceptionis imaginatio influit efficienter.*'—Wolff.

Friend.

36. THE CONTAGION OF EXCITEMENT

'It is indisputable that nervous excitation is contagious. The greater part of ghost stories may be traced to this source.'

Allsop.

37. FEAR

It is a most instructive part of my Life the fact, that I have been always preyed on by some Dread, and perhaps all my faulty actions have been the consequence of some Dread or other on my mind, from fear of Pain, or Shame, not from prospect of Pleasure. So in my childhood and Boyhood the horror of being detected with a sorehead; afterwards imaginary fears of having the Itch in my Blood. Then a short-lived Fit of Fears from sex, then horror of *Duns*, and a state of struggling with madness from an incapability of hoping that I should be able to marry Mary Evans (and this strange passion of fervent tho' wholly imaginative and imaginary Love uncombinable by my utmost efforts with any regular Hope—possibly from deficiency of bodily feeling, of tactual ideas connected with the image) had all the effects of direct Fear, and I have lain for hours together awake at night, groaning and praying. Then came that stormy time, and for a few months America really inspired Hope, and I became an exalted Being. Then came Rob. Southey's alienation, my marriage, constant dread in my mind respecting Mrs Coleridge's Temper, &c.—And finally stimulants in the fear and prevention of violent Bowel-attacks from mental agitation; then almost epileptic night-horrors in my sleep, and since then every error I have committed, has been the immediate effect of the Dread of these bad most shocking Dreams—any thing to prevent them—all this interwoven with its minor consequences that fill up the interspaces—the cherry juice running in between the cherries in a cherry pie. Procrastination in dread of this—and something else in consequence of that procrast[ination] &c. And from the same cause the least languor expressed in a Letter from S. H. drives me wild, and it is most unfortunate that I so fearfully despondent should have concentered my soul thus on one almost as feeble in Hope as myself. 11 Jan. 1805.

MS.

38. A 'FANCY'

A shadow, that which subsists in shaped and definite Non-entity. It has often suggested to me the fancy of a Planet without any common atmosphere, but when each Individual has an atmosphere of his own, like a travel-warmed Horse in a winter morning; to receive and communicate, one joins his atmosphere to that of another, and according to the symp[athy] or antipathy of their nature, the refractions and aberrations are less or greater —their Thoughts more or less reciprocally intelligible.

MS.

39. PSYCHOTHERAPY

John Webster in *The Displaying of Supposed Witchcraft*, 1677, refers to 'the effects of healing by the Weapon-salve, the sympathetic Powder, the curing of divers Diseases by Appensions, Amulets, or by Transplantation, and many other most admirable effects both of Art and Nature'.

Coleridge comments: Webster's Belief will be thought by the Learned, yea and by the Unlearned, and above all by the numberless Half-learned of the present day, not less senseless and superstitious, than the Witch-monger Creed which he opposes. I dare confess myself of a different opinion, as far at least, as that I accede to the distinction of Physics into mechanical or mediate, and magical or immediate, agency—not unlike the difference between conducted and radiant Heat. By 'immediate' I do not exclude the possibility of an Intermediate; but mean only that the effect passes from a to b without any known tangible, visible, or ponderable inter-agent. Thus the Act of the Will on the nerves and muscles of my Arm and Fingers I call 'magical' in the original and unsuperstitious use of the term. S. T. Coleridge, 27 Octr. 1819.

MS.

40. AUTO-HYPNOSIS

Webster relates a story from Johannes Baptiste Porta, 'a great Naturalist and a person of competent veracity', of a witch who was observed to anoint herself with an ointment that put her into a deep sleep in which she apparently dreamed of journeys and adventures which she reported, when she woke up, as having really taken place.

Coleridge comments: This of Porta's is not the only well-attested instance of the use, and of the Cataleptic properties of, narcotic Ointments and Potions in the Pharmacy of the poor Self-bewitched. They are a traditional Derivative from Pagan Antiquity (*Pocula Circëia* &c.) and even in the earliest mention of them seem, like most superstitions, to be the *cadaver et putrimenta* of a defunct Natural Philosophy. In many respects the voluntary confessions of Witches would lead one to suppose that an empirical Animal Magnetism was in play; but there is this characteristic difference that the magnetized Cataleptic retain no memory of what they said and imagined during their trance.

Might this difference arise from the Witches remaining un-questioned and unroused, unexcited *ab et ad extra* during the magnetic torpor? Or by the continuance and *Sequelæ* of the Narcotic Influence, so as not to afford any chasm, or abrupt transition into the waking and natural state? That Self-magnetism is in certain conditions, those indeed of the rarest occurrence, possible, has been rendered highly probable, at least. The cases of Behmen, Helmont, Swedenborg, and the assertions of Philo Judæus of himself, and Porphyry both of Plotinus and of himself, might at all events receive a natural solution from the hypothesis. Indeed, the best service which the Mesmerism or Zoomagnetism has yet done is that it enables us to explain the Oracles and a score other superstitions without recourse either to downright self-conscious Lying and Imposture on the one side, or to the Devil and his Works on the other—reducing the

whole of Dæmonology and Diabolography to Neuro-
pathology. S. T. C.

MS.

41. METHODISM AND MAGNETISM

Being called in to another female demoniac at Kingswood, he
set out on horseback. It rained heavily, and the woman, when
he was three miles off, cried out, 'Yonder comes Wesley,
galloping as fast as he can;' a circumstance which it certainly
required no aid from the devil to foresee.

Southey, *The Life of Wesley*, I. 215.

Coleridge comments: A sufficient solution, as far as this particular
case is concerned. But the coincidence throughout of all these
Methodist cases with those of the Magnetists, makes one wish a
solution that would apply to all: now this sense, or appearance
of a sense of the distant, both in time and space, is common to
almost all the Magnetic patients, in Denmark, Germany, France
and North Italy—to many of which the same, or a similar solution could not apply. Likewise, many have been recorded at the
same time in different countries by men who had never heard
of each other's names, and where the simultaneity of publication proves the independence of the testimony—and among the
Magnetizers and Attesters are to be found names of men, whose
competence in respect of integrity and incapability of intentional falsehood is fully equal to Wesley's, and their competence
in respect of physic, and psychological insight and attainments
incomparably greater. Who would dream, indeed, of comparing Wesley with a Cuvier, Hufeland, Blumenbach, Eschenmeyer, Reil, etc.? Were I asked what I think—my answer
would be—that the evidence enforces Scepticism, and a *non
liquet.* Too strong and consentaneous for a candid mind to be
satisfied of its falsehood, or its solvability on the supposition of
imposture, or casual coincidence—too fugacious and infixable
to support any theory that supposes the always potential, and
under certain conditions and circumstances, occasionally actual

existence of a correspondent faculty in the human soul. And nothing less than such an hypothesis would be adequate, to the satisfactory explanation of the facts—though that of a metastasis of specific functions of the nervous energy taken in conjunction with extreme nervous excitement, +some delusion, +some illusion, +some imposition, +some chances, and accidental coincidences might determine the direction in which the Scepticism vibrated. Nine years has the subject of Zoo-magnetism been before me. I have traced it historically—collected a mass of documents in French, German, Italian, and the Latinists of the 16th century—have never neglected an opportunity of questioning eye-witnesses, (*ex. gr.* Tieck, Treviranus, De Prati, Meyer, and others of literary or medical celebrity,) and I remain where I was, and where the first perusal of Kluge's work had left me, without having advanced an inch backward or forward. Treviranus, the famous botanist's reply to me, when he was in London, is worth recording. *Ich habe gesehen was (ich weiss das) ich nicht würde geglaubt haben auf Ihre Erzählung,* etc. 'I have seen what I am certain I would not have believed on your telling; and in all reason, therefore, I can neither expect nor wish that you should believe on mine.'—S. T. C.

42. EMOTION

I have not expressed myself as clearly as I could wish. But the truth of the assertion, that deep feeling has a tendency to combine with obscure ideas, in preference to distinct and clear notions, may be proved by the history of fanatics and fanaticism in all ages and countries. The *odium theologicum* is even proverbial: and it is the common complaint of philosophers and philosophic historians, that the passions of the disputants are commonly violent in proportion to the subtlety and obscurity of the questions in dispute.

Friend.

43. THE WITCHERY OF CHILDHOOD ASSOCIATIONS

Could we emancipate ourselves from the be-dimming influence of custom, and the transforming witchcraft of early associations, we should see as numerous tribes of fetish-worshippers in the streets of London and Paris, as we hear of on the coasts of Africa.

Friend.

44. A DISTINCTION MADE

De Boyer describes a seventeen-year-old girl in a madhouse, born blind, deaf and dumb, and in the class we should now designate by the term idiot, in its technical use: unable to keep clothing on, to walk, or co-ordinate activity in any way.

Coleridge comments: This Girl was evidently not merely blind, deaf and dumb, but had some disease of the Brain or nervous system which made the Body no fit instrument of the development of the Understanding. This disease was the *cause* of the Blindness, &c. &c., for others have been known, whose loss being confined to the Senses, have been instructed and humanized. Let a being born blind, deaf and dumb, yet otherwise healthy, be transplanted to a race of intelligent men who had formed a language of Smell and Touch, and be educated among them.

MS.

45. DISEASE

In the year 1813 I reperuse this dreadful Case, [of a poor and starving weaver, who went mad and attributed his state to the bite of a mad dog twelve years before] communicated to me by Dr. Beddoes—and my humble opinion is, that excessive Distress of Mind and in a less degree, but yet important, the abstraction of needful Stimulation, had, the first called into activity a lurking Poison, and the second deadened those *vires naturae medicatrices* which under happier circumstances would have subdued and quieted it. It only confirms a fearful conjecture of mine, of 20 years standing, that no Disease was ever yet cured, but merely suspended if of the Nature of Poison. *Ex. gr.* I believe, no one who has had the Small Pox, Measles, &c. is as secure in Health, as they would have been, if that Poison had not been absorbed. Good Heavens! if this should be true, what an additional argument for the Vaccine Inoculation! as the Dreams, like a Cathartic, of evacuating, first the Small Pox, and then itself. S. T. Coleridge. 7 Feby. 1813.

71 Berners' Street, London.

MS.

46. EMOTION

OF STATES IN WHICH THE WILL IS THE PREDOMINANT FACTOR: A MEDITATION BY ΕΣΤΗΣΕ

I am inclined to think that the Beginning and the End of all modes, states, and affectments of Being, in which the *Will* is *principally* concerned, are *abrupt*, and by a Vault, as it were. Thus, Liking, Regard, Esteem, are continuous; and the Increase is so gradual as not to destroy the continuity. It is a^1 a^2 a^3 a^4. Liking in the highest degree never *becomes* Love. All in a moment *Love* starts up or leaps in, and *takes place* of *Liking*. And even so it is, I suspect, with *Alienation*. There is a sudden *Death* of Love, or as sudden a Translation. . . . The Dislikes pretended as the Cause are evermore *posthumous*; and the Reasons for the Dislike *invented* or at best *recollected*, in order to pacify the Deserter's own Conscience. In some cases there is no Dislike either before or after. Nay, it may even happen that the Esteem, the Kindness, the Attachment may become stronger. But still the *Love* is gone. Unlike the Nightingale, it may leave the Second Perch, but it never returns to the first. Most commonly, it dies altogether.

The same insulated moment, as the expression *in* time of an act *out* of time—for there are Acts and forms of Being as alien and heterogeneous to *Time*, as our Thoughts, Affections and Passions are to Space*—the same instantaneity I find in the revolutions of Religion and of Moral Conduct. Not St. Paul alone was baptized with Fire—even the Fire-flash of Lightning. We rise from the death of Sin as from the death of the Grave 'in a moment, in the twinkling of an eye'. And (as all religious errors that infect many minds, are grounded on Half or Quarter *Truths*) this is the base of the fanatical notions about Sudden *Conversions*.

MS.

47. JOY

Soother of Absence. Days and weeks and months pass on, and now a year; and the Sun, the Sea, the Breeze has its influence on me, and good and sensible men—and I feel a pleasure upon me, and I am to the outward view of all cheerful, and have myself no distinct consciousness of the contrary; for I use my faculties, not indeed as once, but yet freely. But oh Sara! I am never happy, never deeply gladdened. I know not, I have forgotten, what the *Joy* is of which the Heart is full as of a deep and quiet fountain overflowing insensibly, or the gladness of Joy, when the fountain overflows ebullient. S. T. C.

MS.

48. LOVE

[O Asra! *crossed out*] the strongest antagonist, and at the same time the only Perpetuator of *Desire* is *true Love:* and what is

---

* *Ex. gr.* what should we think of one who said that his Love of his Wife was North West by West of his Passion for Roast Beef?

Love, but to have my enjoyments depend on yours, one being to that of the other reciprocally cause and effect. I am miserable indeed, if you are *un*happy, *whatever* the cause may be; but yet I cannot but be discontented, even when you are happy, unless I have been in part at least, the means and object of your happi ness. O if Love (Love in its [best *crossed out*] own form the fairest Child and tenderest Nurse of Virtue) O! if Love [author- ized *crossed out*] sanctioned Desire (or rather, as the rising Sun shoots thro' and saturates with rich light the Cloud that veils it, took up and transfigured Desire into its own Being) then, then I should appear as such as I should always be—with the genial warmth of Life, not the Heat of Fever, with the tranquil Vigor of Affection fed by Affection, not the paroxysms of Passion disquieted into Appetite by Fear of Transiency, and the un- certainty as to a correspondent attachment. O be assured, that it is for a secure and prosperous Love only to be always unmixed and quiet. S. T. C.

MS.

49. ON GROWING OLD

My dear Green,

One of the many mysteries of Human Nature, of which as inferior to many yet as good as most I take my own to be a pretty fair average, is: the increasing desire of Repose as we grow older, and yet an involuntary Repining at the very events and changes of feeling, which we need only resign ourselves to, to be in possession of the very Repose and wishless Tranquillity, for which we had been sighing. I would fain be independent of any Will that is not one and the same with Reason. I would fain live the short remainder of my Life for God and Universal Interests, and yet I find myself tenaciously clinging to the shadows of past [*unfinished fragment*].

MS.

50. CHANGE OF LIFE

Turn of mind into melancholy and frequent madness and extravagance from the Turn of *Life*—the top of the Hill—at 35 to 40,—different in different men——

MS.

51. A MINUTIA OF EXPERIENCE

O that perilous moment (for such there is) of a half-reconciliation, when the Coldness and the Resentment have been sustained too long! Each is drawing toward the other—but like Glass in the mid-state between fusion and compaction a single sand will splitter it.

MS.

52. FOR AN ESSAY ON THE PASSIONS

INTRODUCTORY PARAGRAPH

Action and Passion, says Descartes, are the same thing contemplated as existing in two [reciprocally opposed *crossed out*] opposite yet corresponding Subjects: and derive their difference from the different relations of the Subjects. An Action in the Mind is a Passion in the Body: and Actions of the Body are reflected as Passions in the Mind. This, however, is a mere logical antithesis of our *Thoughts*—or lower still—a grammatical Antithesis of the Terms, Action and Passion, substituted for a real definition of the Things themselves. That Descartes intended it for such—that it passed for a *real* definition with him—was not owing to any want of logical acumen in this great man, nor even of philosophic Vision; but must be attributed to the influence of a favourite Dogma on his mind *viz.* the *contrariety* of Soul and Body, as Subjects absolutely heterogeneous, each partially definable by negativing the properties of the other. This Hypothesis, by him first asserted in its *absoluteness*, infected

63

the whole mass of his opinions, physical and metaphysical, and is, in fact, the distinguishing and fundamental Principle of the Cartesian Philosophy. . . .

With the Ancients, and with such of the Modern Philosophers before Descartes, as had ventured to propose the question to themselves, Soul and Body were considered as the correspondent Opposites, the Positive and Negative Poles as it were, of which the Man was the Unity. It would lead us too far from our subject, to state the various causes that conspired to procure so ready an admission and so rapid an extension to the new doctrine, of the French philosopher,* according to which Soul and Body are utterly diverse, with no property in common, nay, the constituent attitudes of each incompatible with the essential nature of the other. Suffice it to observe, that the influence of this [notion *crossed out*] Dogma may be traced in sundry opinions, that have survived the School from which they sprung, and have even established themselves, as current phrases, in the different Languages of Europe. Less [obviously *crossed out*] glaringly repugnant to Common Sense, than the Hypothesis of the pre-established† Harmony, i.e. Correspondence of two alien and independent Subjects by the pre-adjustment of their common Creator—which was the first and most obvious inference from the Cartesian Dogma, but for this very reason, more injurious. To enumerate all the mischievous yet legitimate consequences of this utter diversity of Soul and Body, or all the effects of its having passed into a general Belief, would swell an introductory paragraph into a volume. But that the assertion has not been made without grounds, it will be sufficient

* Do not start at this combination of French and Philosopher, hybrid as it now appears. It was not till the latter Half of the reign of Louis the 14th that the Gothic Blood was diluted to evanescence in the Celtic Serum.

† The Historiographers of Philosophy from Brücker to Tennemann have given Spinoza the credit of having afforded the first *Hint* of this bold and brilliant Theory to Leibnitz. But in fact it is plainly asserted by Descartes himself in the 16th Art. of his *De Passionibus* and it would be strange had it been otherwise.

to instance: I. the separation of Psychology from Physiology, depriving the former of all root and objective truth, and reducing the latter to a mere enumeration of facts and phaenomena without copula or living form: II. the gloomy and hopeless opinions concerning Insanity, with the comparatively low state and the empirical character of the Practice in this department which one might fancy to have been thrown off, as a Slough, from the living and waxing Body of Medical Science, or dropt, like a Shed Horn, for Mad-doctors and Madhouse-keepers to make a noise with; and III. in close connection with the IInd, tho' of less immediate importance, the exquisite Superficiality, and *commonplace moral-essay* character of our numerous French, Scotch and English, great and small, Treatises on the *Passions*.

CHAPT[ER] I

Primary sense of the word, from *pati*)(*agere*, to *undergo*)(to act upon. Passion, a state of undergoing. If the word were to be understood in the full extent of its Etymon, the Passions would include every impression made on the Brain and Nerves by external agents or by the Body itself. I need not say that this is not our present use of the word: nor are these impresses, whether black and blue from a Horse-whip, or of all colours from the impinging of Light, or of no colour from the pulses of Air, the subjects of this inquiry into the nature and number of the Passions, instituted for the purpose of satisfying my own and my dear Fellow-students' mind by the formation of somewhat clearer and more distinct conceptions than we have hitherto derived from Books.

Definition of the Word as now used.

Here, however, it may not be amiss to remark, that with the single exception of Geometry a *Definition* as distinguished from a mere verbal explanation [should] find its proper place at the end of a Treatise, and as the Result of the Investigation. And this general Rule is particularly applicable to the Subject in question: for the reasons stated in the concluding sentences of our introductory Paragraph. By a definition therefore we mean no more in the present instance than such an explanation of the word as may suffice to designate the subject and mark the limits of our inquiry. Even for this purpose I find it easier to reject the definitions hitherto given than to provide a substitute. The following is the best that has occurred to me: and if no better strikes you, take it *on tryal*.

By the Passions generally, and described therefore by their generic or common character, we mean—a state of emotion, which tho' it may have its pre-disposing cause in the Body, and its occasion in external Incidents or Appearances, is yet not *immediately* produced by the incidents themselves, but by the person's Thoughts and Reflections concerning them. Or more briefly: A Passion is a state of emotion, having its immediate cause not in Things, but in our Thoughts of the Things—or —A Passion is a state of emotion which, whatever its object or occasion may be, in ourselves or out of ourselves, has its proper and immediate cause not in this, but in our Thoughts respecting it . . . .

. . . Pain not a pure antithesis to Pleasure; because a *total* Pain is not possible. Pain a [general conception *crossed out*] mental generalization—a word; but a total Pleasure may have a real existence. . . .

. . . Tho' Rage is in many cases a Revulsion of Fear, and tho' (if I may borrow the words of the Poet Coleridge—see the poem entitled 'Mad Ox' in the *Sibylline Leaves*)

> Should you a Rat to madness teize,
> Why even a Rat might plague ye—
> There's no Philosopher but sees,
> That Fear and Rage are one Disease:
> Tho' this may burn and that may freeze,
> They're both alike the Ague—

tho' I say Rage and Fear are not seldom seen as the Cold and Hot Fit of the same Fever—yet and notwithstanding, I am strongly inclined to consider *Fear* as an [a accident *crossed out*, product *crossed out*] affection of the Reproductive or first and lowest Function of Life (*vis vitæ vegeta*) and an accident of the assimilative and digestive system—and that the disturbance of the musculo-arterial system is but a consequence—and of the Digestive System I should think the Bowels, and abdominal nerves the principal seat. Mem. the timidity of the herbivorous animals . . .

. . . Fear is cruel and when anger puts on the outward marks of Fear, we are shocked and expect no good from so unnatural a combination. There is always a ground of Fear in premeditative Revenge. . .

. . . Joy and Grief, Hope and Fear, &c. have slipt out their collars, and no longer run in couples, under my whipping-in or from the kennel of my Psycho-somatic Ology. . . .

. . . This experiment [his own attempt to systematize his argument] is a miss . . . And not only a failure—but an impropriety, and an oversight was the introduction of self-impulsions that are merely corporeal, (ψιλο-σωματικά, οὐ μή, [possibly οὐχ?] ὡς ἔδει, ψυχο-σωματικά) and never arrive at Consciousness— psilosomatic, and not, as ought alone to have been mentioned, the psycho-somatic or psycho-zöic.. .

. . . Lastly I take the Mind (φρόνημα σαρκός) and endeavour to refer the remaining Passions to the influence of the Mind. . . whether excited by any of the former Passions, or by outward Agency, or by its own judgement or fancy, on the sensibility. . .

. . . The Final Cause, and the right Discipline of the Passions, whether by control, or prevention, or suppression. . . . This is the Plan. Now then for the execution. . . .

... The *wanting*, the *craving* of Grief (Here quote from Shakespeare's Constance in King John and from the Greek Tragedians —and in all the Passions I purpose to make free use of illustrations from the Poets—especially Dante, Chaucer, Shakespear and Ben Jonson) the characteristic supersession of the Appetite of Hunger—the equally characteristic wasting and marasmus of Grief—all these and there are many more, prove Grief to be a Hunger of the Soul.

53. THE ID, THE EGO, AND THE SUPER-EGO?

Tuesday 19 Oct' 1830——

'As if their whole vocation
Were endless imitation.'

Two things we may learn from little children from 3 to 6 years old—1. that it is a character, an instinct of our human Nature, to pass out of our *self*—i.e. the image (or complex cycle of images) on which act and sensation that by its constant presence and rapidity becomes a stationary *Unity*, a whole of indistinguishable parts, and is the perpetual *represent*ative of our Individuum, and hence by all unreflecting Minds confounded and identified with it. Mem. On this equivocque or double meaning of Self is grounded the Sophism of the Rochefoucauld System. All acts proceed *from Self* (here Self means the *Principium Individualitatis*) therefore all acts *proceed to* Self (here Self means the representative Image). Well! to return—with a *Da Capo*——

The first lesson, that innocent Childhood affords me, is—that it is an instinct of my Nature to pass out of myself, and to exist in the form of others.

The second is—not to suffer any one form to pass into *me* and to become a usurping *Self* in the disguise of what the German Pathologists call a *fixed Idea*. Mem. This is always a *Self*-love— tho' the Conscience may be duped by the alterity and consequent distinct figurableness of the *form*—. As sure as it is cyclical, and forms the ruling *Eddy* in our mind, so surely does it become the representative of our Self, and = Self.

Our best loves and solicitudes may be in excess, and assuredly are so when they are exclusively confined to one Object, or so attached as to distract from the love and care due to others, even [as] the anxious Love of a Mother for a favorite Child. The only exception is the Love of *God*—because the Love of God alone is inclusive of all good and Lovely, and excludes nothing but the *Lust* of Evil, the Solicitude after emptiness.

MS.

II

EXCITING
THE VEGETATING AND
GERMINATING POWERS

'... Education of the Intellect, by awakening
the Method of self-development, ... not any
specific information that can be conveyed into
it from without ... not storing the passive
Mind with the various sorts of knowledge most
in request, as if the Human Soul were a mere
repository or banqueting-room, but to place it
in such relations of circumstance as should
gradually excite its vegetating and germinat-
ing powers to produce new fruits of Thought,
new Conceptions, and Imaginations, and Ideas.'

On Method

EDUCATION

Coleridge's views on education are best seen in the lecture On Education reproduced here (item 65) and in *Coleridge on Logic and Learning*, edited by A. D. Snyder. There are other references in the *Friend* and in the letters and the *Table Talk*. He knew of the work of Pestalozzi on the continent, and in keeping with his dynamic theory of personality, believed in the education of the child first and the teaching of subjects second. His views sound radical enough in some quarters even now. He was interested in the learning process in children; he notes for example the difficulty for a child in 'our lying alphabet', in which the name of a letter does not correspond to the sound: BALL should be Beeāellell. Interest in education became acutely controversial in his day in the rivalry between the Bell and Lancaster schemes for national education. The principles of the two were similar as to educational methods, but the system of Dr. Bell had the support of the Church of England, and in particular of Coleridge's friend the Bishop of Durham, and that was the side he took. The Lancaster party was largely nonconformist and Whig. Progressive in his theories so far as the methods of education of the individual went, he was conservative in his view of its social operation, believing that national education should be in the control of the church, and should proceed by a filtering process from the learned few downwards.

II

EXCITING
THE VEGETATING AND
GERMINATING POWERS

54. THELWALL: EDUCATION

JOHN THELWALL had something very good about him. We were once sitting in a beautiful recess in the Quantocks, when I said to him, 'Citizen John, this is a fine place to talk treason in!'—'Nay! Citizen Samuel,' replied he, 'it is rather a place to make a man forget that there is any necessity for treason!'

Thelwall thought it very unfair to influence a child's mind by inculcating any opinions before it should have come to years of discretion, and be able to choose for itself. I showed him my garden, and told him it was my botanical garden. 'How so?' said he, 'it is covered with weeds.'—'Oh,' I replied, '*that* is only because it has not yet come to its age of discretion and choice. The weeds, you see, have taken the liberty to grow, and I thought it unfair in me to prejudice the soil towards roses and strawberries.'

Table Talk.

55. OF CHILDREN

We are aware that it is with our cognitions as with our children. There is a period in which the method of nature is working for them; a period of aimless activity and unregulated accumulation, during which it is enough if we can preserve them in health and *out of harm's way*. Again, there is a period of orderliness, of circumspection, of discipline, in which we purify, separate, define, select, arrange, and settle the nomenclature of communication. There is also a period of dawning and twilight, a period of anticipation, affording trials of strength. And all these, both in the growth of the sciences and in the mind of a rightly-educated individual, will precede the attainment of a scientific METHOD. But, notwithstanding this, unless the importance of the latter be felt and acknowledged, unless its attainment be looked forward to and from the very beginning prepared for, there is little hope and small chance that any education will be conducted aright; or will ever prove in reality worth the name. . . .

Alas! how many examples are now present to my memory, of young men the most anxiously and expensively be-school-mastered, be-tutored, be-lectured, any thing but *educated*; who have received arms and ammunition, instead of skill, strength, and courage; varnished rather than polished; perilously over-civilized, and most pitiably uncultivated! And all from inattention to the method dictated by nature herself, to the simple truth, that as the forms in all organized existence, so must all true and living knowledge proceed from within; that it may be trained, supported, fed, excited, but can never be infused or impressed.

Friend.

56. AGAINST 'CROCODILES'

I call these strings of school boys or girls which we meet near
London—walking advertisements.

Table Talk.

57. THE TEACHER

But if we hope to instruct others, we should familiarize our
own minds to some fixed and determinate principles of action.
The world is a vast labyrinth, in which almost every one is
running a different way, and almost every one manifesting
hatred to those who do not run the same way. A few indeed
stand motionless, and not seeking to lead themselves or others
out of the maze laugh at the failures of their brethren. Yet with
little reason: for more grossly than the most bewildered wanderer does *he* err, who never aims to go right. It is more honourable to the head, as well as to the heart, to be misled by our
eagerness in the pursuit of truth, than to be safe from blunder-
ing by contempt of it. The happiness of mankind is the *end* of
virtue, and truth is the knowledge of the *means*; which he will
never seriously attempt to discover, who has not habitually
interested himself in the welfare of others. The searcher after
truth must love and be beloved; for general benevolence is
a necessary motive to constancy of pursuit; and this general
benevolence is begotten and rendered permanent by social and
domestic affections.

Essays On His Own Times.

58. THE TEACHING PROFESSION

Teachers of youth are, by a necessity of their present condition,
either unsound or uncongenial. If they possess that buoyancy
of spirit, which *best fits them* for communicating to those under

their charge, the knowledge it is held useful for them to acquire, they are deemed unsound. If they possess a subdued sobriety of disposition, the result of a process compared to which the course of a horse in a mill is positive enjoyment, they of *necessity become ungenial*. Is this a fitting condition, a meet and just return for the class, Instructors? And yet have I not truly described them? Has any one known a teacher of youth who, having attained any repute as such, has also retained any place in society as an individual? Are not all such men "Dominie Sampsons" in what relates to their duties, interests, and feelings as citizens; and, with respect to females, do they not all possess a sort of *mental* odour? Are not all masters, all those who are held in estimation, not scholars, but *always* masters, even in their sports; and are not the female teachers always *teaching* and *setting right*? whilst both not only lose the freshness of youth, both of mind and body, but seem as though they never had been young. *They* who have to teach, can *never afford* to learn; hence their improgression.

To the above remarks, true as they are in themselves, I am desirous to draw your particular attention. Those who have to teach, a duty which if ably discharged is the highest and most important which society imposes, are placed in a position in which they necessarily acquire a general or generic character, and this, for the most part, unfits them for mixing in society with ease to themselves or to others. Is this just, is it for the advantage of the community that those to whom the highest and most responsible trusts are confided, should be rendered unfit to associate with their fellow men, by something which is imposed upon them, or which they are made to acquire, as teachers? Does not Society owe it to this meritorious class, to examine into the causes of these peculiarities with a view to remove ascertained evils, or, by developing them to bring constantly before our eyes the necessity, in *their case*, of results which at present have such evil influences upon the more genial feelings of so large, and every way estimable and intelligent a portion of our fellow men. It is requisite that the conviction now become so self-evident, 'that vice is the effect of error and the offspring of surrounding circumstances, the object of condolence and not of anger', should become a habit of the mind in the daily and hourly occurrences of social life. This consummation, so devoutly to be wished, is now for the first time possible; and, when it shall be fully realized, will lead most assuredly to the amelioration of the human race, and whatever has life or is capable of improvement.

Allsop.

59. POSITIVE DISCIPLINE

The true perfection of discipline in a school is—The maximum of watchfulness with the minimum of punishment.

The Statesman's Manual.

60. THE ART OF METHOD: PLATO'S SYSTEM OF EDUCATION

From Shakespeare to Plato, from the philosophic poet to the poetic philosopher, the transition is easy, and the road is crowded with illustrations of our present subject. For of Plato's works, the larger and more valuable portion have all one common end, which comprehends and shines through the particular purpose of each several dialogue; and this is to establish the sources, to evolve the principles, and exemplify the art of METHOD. This is the clue, without which it would be difficult to exculpate the noblest productions of the divine philosopher from the charge of being tortuous and labyrinthine in their progress, and unsatisfactory in their ostensible results. The latter indeed appear not seldom to have been drawn for the purpose of starting a new problem, rather than that of solving the one proposed as the subject of the previous discussion. But with the clear insight that the purpose of the writer is not so much to establish any particular truth, as to remove the obstacles, the continuance of which is preclusive of all truth, the whole scheme assumes a different aspect, and justifies itself in all its dimensions. We see, that to open anew a well of springing water, not to cleanse the stagnant tank, or fill, bucket by bucket, the leaden cistern; that the EDUCATION of the intellect, by awakening the principle and *method* of self-development, was his proposed object, not any specific information that can be *conveyed* into it from without: not to assist in storing the passive mind with the various sorts of knowledge most in request, as if the human soul were a mere repository or banqueting-room, but to place it in such relations of circumstance as should gradually excite the germinal power that craves no knowledge but what it can take up into itself, what it can appropriate, and re-produce in fruits of its own. To shape, to dye, to paint over, and to mechanize the mind, he resigned, as their proper trade, to the sophists, against whom he waged open and unremitting war.

Friend.

61. HABIT AND MOTIVE

. . . We know too well, that it is not the mere notion however clear that restrains or impels us; but the feelings habitually connected with that notion. The drunkard is convinced that his Drams are poison yet he takes them. For once that a deep conviction is the parent of a Habit, a Habit is an 100 times the parent of the conviction. Hence the immense importance of Education i.e. *training up*. Hence the sophistry may be shewn of Rousseau's Plan of Education in which an intellectual conviction is always to precede the appropriate action. Education is to man what the transmission of Instinct is to animals—entwines Thought with the living Substance, the nerves of sensation, the organ of soul, the muscles of motion, and this, finally, with the *Will*—the total soul energises, unique and unific.

MS.

62. PRESSURE

Touch a door a little ajar, or half open, and it will yield to the push of your finger. Fire a cannon-ball at it, and the Door stirs not an inch: you make a hole thro' it, the door is spoilt for ever, but not *moved*. Apply this to moral Education.

MS.

63. AN ANGRY PARENT

What are you crying for? said an Angry Parent to a Child, whom he had sharply and harshly rebuked. You have snuffed the Candle too close, replied I—and can you wonder, that it *gutters*?

MS.

64. KNOWLEDGE IS NOT EDUCATION

. . . Whatever inconvenience may have arisen from the commonness of education, can only be removed by rendering it universal. But that alone is worthy the name, which does indeed educe the faculties and form the habits; and reading and writing we should place among the *means* of education, instead of regarding it as the *end*. At no time and in no rank of life can knowledge be made our prime object without injury to the understanding, and certain perversion of those moral institutions, to the cultivation of which it must be instrumental and subservient, or, vapour and nothingness as the human intellect is, separated from that better light which lifts and transpierces it, even that which it has will be taken away. The neglect of this truth is the worm at the root of certain modern improvements in the modes of teaching, in comparison with which we have been called on to despise out great public schools

'In whose halls are hung
Armoury of the invincible knights of old,'

and have been instructed how to metamorphose children into prodigies; and prodigies with a vengeance have I known thus produced, prodigies of self-conceit, shallowness, arrogance, and infidelity. Instead of storing the memory, during the period when the memory is the predominant faculty, with facts for the after exercise of the judgment, and instead of awakening by the noblest models the fond and unmixed *love* and *admiration*, which is the natural and graceful temper of early youth, these nurslings of improved pedagogy are taught to dispute and deride, to suspect all but their own and their lecturer's wisdom, and to hold nothing sacred from their contempt but their own contemptible arrogance; boy-graduates in all the technical, and all the dirty passions and impudence of anonymous criticism.

Essays On His Own Times.

65. NEW SYSTEM OF EDUCATION
7TH LECTURE

Bristol, November 18th, 1813.

Mr. Coleridge commenced this lecture by stating that he had from earliest life been accustomed to speak what was uppermost; and he could truly say that the extreme kindness he had experienced during a course of Lectures, not altogether calculated to amuse, had awakened in his mind the most lively gratitude; not that there was any necessity of rendering his feelings intense; for he should never forget that at a time when his heart was above his head, when in the bitterness of party spirit his friends deserted him, he found in Bristol (some of whom were in that room) fathers, protectors, benefactors, and happy should he be, if in the smallest degree, he could repay that kindness by elucidating the most important subject of that night's Lecture— The *application of the New System of Education* to those classes of Society who attended around him.

He should carefully preclude all controversy, God forbid he

should harbour any thought, or divulge any opinion associated with dissention—controversy could not produce love, but still in the progressiveness of our nature, there was an awful duty imperative on every being capable of influencing another, to prove if a new doctrine or a new discovery be founded in fact, or in reason. In his address he hoped nothing would be found to awaken party feeling; if any should occur, it would be forced from him by a sense of duty imposed by the precepts of morality, not by a regard to names and circumstances. He hoped his audience in following him in consequences, would so far falsify their feelings as to forget mistakes on one side and the other, and look at the subject only as men and christians.

To invent was different from to discover—a watch-maker invented a time-piece; but a profound thinker only could discover. Sir Isaac Newton, when he thought upon the apple falling from the tree, discovered but did not invent the law of gravitation; others, following this grand idea, carried elementary principles into particles, and elucidated chemistry. Sir Isaac Newton, having once found that a body fell to the centre, knew that all other appearances of nature would receive a consequence, agreeably to the law of cause and effect; for it was a criterion of science, that when causes were determined, effects could be stated with the accuracy of prophecy.

Of the New System he should first notice the establishment of *Monitors*, or boys teaching boys, under the eye of a Superintendant or Schoolmaster; the latter was necessary not so much to teach, as to observe that there was not a deviation from proper methods; in the simplicity of this one principle, there was a world of richness. This was available by Seminaries adapted to the higher and middle classes, who could not take advantage of public charities; not that he meant to say that any plan would render superfluous (heaven forbid that discovery should reach thus far) the wisest and best of men, who undertook the instruction of youth; but by it labour would be lessened and improvement forwarded.

In bringing a number of children together, and comparing their understandings, a *minimum* of acquirement might be attained—this was of great consequence; by it many of the evils of the old method would be avoided. The Lecturer himself recollected that he was placed in the *Dunce's row*; because he found it easier to be beat than to say his Greek task; with his companions he had nothing to do but to dream; and if it had not been for an accident, he might have continued there; he happened to be musing over the Eclogues of Virgil, which he had been taught to read before he went to school, and was observed by a Clergyman, afterwards an ornament to the bench of Bishops, who asked what he could be doing with Virgil, as he was in the Dunce's row? thus his deliverance was effected.

This reminded him of a friend who said, there might be idiots, but there were no dunces in his school; depend upon it, the master is the dunce, not the boy, for in a state of progression, the art is to begin low enough: if a boy cannot learn three lines, give him two, if not two, one, if not one, half: the level of capacity must be found. He here observed, that he ought, perhaps, before to have noticed the word Education; it was to educe, to call forth; as the blossom is educed from the bud, the vital excellencies are within; the acorn is but educed, or brought forth from the bud. In proportion to the situation in which the individual is likely to be placed, all that is good and proper should be educed; for it was not merely a degradation of the word Education, but an affront of human nature, to include within its meaning, the bare attainment of reading and writing, or of Latin and Greek; as in former Lectures he had placed moral above intellectual acquirements, so in Education its object and its end would only be pernicious, if it did not make men worthy and estimable beings.

One beauty of the system is, that its means call forth the moral energies of action; not merely as relates to acquirement of knowledge, but to fill those scenes which Providence may afterwards place them in. It was a great error to cram the young mind with so much knowledge as made the child talk much and fluently: what was more ridiculous than to hear a child questioned, what it thought of the last poem of Walter Scott? A child should be child-like, and possess no other idea than what was loving and admiring. A youth might devour with avidity without comprehending the excellencies of Young and Gray; the Lecturer himself recollected the innocent and delightful intoxication with which he read them; the feeling was as necessary to a future Poet, as the bud to the flower, or the flower to the seed.

One good effect of children teaching each other was, that it gave the Superintendant a power of precluding everything of a procrastinating nature—the habit of procrastination was early acquired—the Lecturer could trace it in himself, when three hours were allowed at school to learn what he could attain in 15 minutes; the present moment was neglected, because the future was considered as sufficient. It was a great secret in education, that there should not be a single moment allowed a child in which it should not learn something—the moment it had done learning it should play; the doing nothing was the great error; the time that children are rendered passive, is the time when they are led into evil.

A friend of the Lecturer (Mr. Thelwall) at one time was called a traitor, but though he did not deserve that appellation, he was doubtlessly a mistaken man; it was at a period when men of all ranks, tailors and mechanics of various descriptions, thought they had a *call* for preaching politics, as Saints had a *call* for preaching the Gospel—it was Thelwall's continual theme that he kept his mind free from prejudice; the Lecturer had a garden, it was over-run with weeds, it had received no culture; he took Thelwall to it, and told him it resembled his mind, it was free from prejudice, but all that was rank and wild grew in it. It need not be said, that leaving a child to do nothing, was the surest way of exposing him to the ridiculous and foolish notion of

equality; whilst constant employment was the best way of im-
pressing upon his mind the order, extent, and nature of gradua-
tions in society. Never, however, imagine that a child is idle who
is gazing on the stream, or lying upon the earth; the basis of all
moral character may then be forming; all the healthy processes
of nature may then be ripening; but let the standard of action
be, the not leaving that for to-morrow which may be done
to-day.

In the system of appointing children to instruct children, it
must not be supposed that instruction is to come from them, it
must originate with and come from the Master. Another point
is a *minimum of punishment*; let the Master be as humane as he
will, temper will sometimes predominate, therefore certain
punishments should be apportioned to certain faults. It were to
be wished that some mode could be adopted of preserving the
female parental intercession—a mother in giving her instructions to the Tutor, reminds him ''tis but a child'; this ought to
have effect; great schools however know nothing of this; boys
who escape punishment are congratulated on their luck, or if
they bear it with proper fortitude and with a little impudence
too, they are sure of applause; they live in compact, and dare
not betray one another; let boys therefore judge boys; their
Judgment will be honourable; children are much less removed
from men and women, than generally imagined; they have less
power to express their meaning than men, but their opinion of
Justice is nearly the same; this we may prove by referring to
our own experience. Corporal punishment was not less disgraceful if administered as some advertising Coxcomb pretended, with lillies and roses; the substitute was worse than the
original: it were ridiculous to suppose that boys conceived any
great shame attached to it, when they knew that there perhaps
is not a Judge or a bishop on the bench, who has not undergone
the same. The Lecturer held that though it did no good, it never
did harm, but was still preferable to the substitute of selfish re-
wards, which only fed self-love, and excited envy and bad pas-

sion. Nothing should be more impressed on parents and tutors than to make children forget themselves; and books which only told how Master Billy and Miss Ann spoke and acted, were not only ridiculous but extremely hurtful; much better give them Jack the Giant-killer, or the Seven Champions, or anything which, being beyond their own sphere of action, should not feed their self-pride. By the cultivation of our highest faculties we are alone superior to everything around us; and by the power of imagination (of which there was both intellectual and moral) in our present imperfect state, are we enabled to anticipate the glories and honours of a future existence; without these we are inferior to the beast that perishes.

In the division of the *System* already made, Dunces were precluded: from the giving to each child a *minimum*; to this might be added another advantage, the pleasure of getting forward himself in hopes of being appointed to *help others.*—2ndly. The prevention of *procrastination*, so dreadful in its consequences through life.—3rdly. *Emulation* without envy.—Lastly. It enabled a child to learn in one year what usually took three; but above all, it gave an opportunity to boys whilst teaching the lower forms or classes, to divulge all moral and religious ideas whilst in the act of instruction. The worthy propagator of the system (Dr. Bell) on his return from India, held a conversation with the Lecturer on this subject; when he was so struck with its importance that he compared it to gunpowder, which if the friends of one plan did not use, the other would. Of the little quarrel which had arisen, of who first discovered, or who impelled, he should leave to posterity; in all essentials the wise and good agreed; but there was one method in the New System, which he pledged himself would be discarded by all parties in less than ten years—it was the substitution of *positive infamy* for *negative shame*; the latter was consistent with nature; the child at the breast felt it when he hid his face in the neck of his mother: whoever saw anything excellent in a child than [*sic*] was a stranger to fear; the feeling was agreeable to innocency; with

it was combined a sense of what we are with the hope of what
we shall be; the former was a degradation to the species, it
lowered the human mind; it made it callous; to load a boy with
fetters, to hang dying speeches about his neck, to expose him to
the sneers and insults of his peers, because forsooth he reads his
lessons in a *singing tone*, was a pitiful mockery of human nature:
it must be the work of superior grace, if a boy who has suffered
such humiliation, ever afterwards shuddered at a slaveship, or
any other act of barbarity—Children never should be made the
instruments of punishment farther than the taking of one another's place; never should be taught to look with revenge and
hatred on each other; from the goodness of heart of those who
tolerated the system, he was convinced that they need only be
reminded of its ill effects, to explode it. Five minutes confinement from play would have more effect on boys than whipping;
he was not an advocate for that, for he thought it did no good;
but if it were necessary to bring up boys as Britons, who had
and might have again to oppose the world, let them be brought
up to despise pain, but above all to hate *dishonour*; to hold him
who regards only the feeling of the moment, as a wretch and a
coward.

Of the difference of education between the higher and middle
classes, he should speak with the deepest feeling; the ladder of
privileged society in this country was not constituted of disproportionate steps, it was consistent with all order and true freedom. In the first part of education there could be no difference;
all moral and religious truths were essential to all; the middle
classes were not only to be useful, but the higher the same; but
to render the latter so, all that was necessary was a different degree of *acquirement*, a gradation of *acquisition of language and
knowledge;* proportionate to the sphere in which they were to
move.

Returning to general education of children, Mr. C. observed,
there was scarce any being who looked upon the beautiful face
of an infant, that did not feel a strong sensation—it was not

pity, it was not the attraction of mere loveliness; it was a sense of melancholy; for himself, he always when viewing an infant, found a tear a candidate for his eye. What could be the cause of this? It was not that its innocency, its perfectness, like a flower, all perfume and all loveliness, was like a flower to pass away:—or he beheld a being, from the absence or evil of his education, capable of blasting and withering like mildew. To this might be added the thought, doubtlessly felt by everyone—if he could begin his career again, if he could recover that innocency once possessed, and connect it with virtue. With these thoughts who could avoid feeling an enthusiasm for the education of mankind.— Suppose it possible that there was a country, where a great part of its population had one arm rendered useless; who would not be desirous of relieving their distress; but what was a right arm withered, in comparison of having all the faculties shut out from the good and wise of past ages.

The Lecturer concluded with recommending an observance of the laws of nature in the Education of Children; the ideas of a child were cheerful and playful; they should not be palsied by obliging it to utter sentences which the head could not comprehend nor the heart echo; our nature was in every sense a *progress*; both body and mind.

Athenaeum, March 13, 1909, from the *Bristol Gazette*.

66. THE AIM OF EDUCATION: TO KNOW OUR OWN KNOWLEDGE

Readers of my Logic, or the method of legitimate Thinking and Discussing, who yet expect to find short and easy [instruction *crossed out*] Receipts how to think without thinking at all —how to think without thought—how many! Alas! S. T. C.

In order to understand by the Rule you must first understand the Rule and in order to ascertain this, it would be well to know what you mean by Understanding in general. And this is one main object of the present work.

But who does not *know* this? Be it so. I say nothing to the contrary: and therefore I have not required you to *learn* what you ought to mean or should henceforth mean, but to know consciously what you actually, tho' without that reflective attention which constitutes distinct consciousness, always have meant by it. I know much that I do not understand; but to understand what I know (*scire me scire*) is the end of all [speculative *crossed out*] science, (for Instructions, of which this is not the end, may be called Arts, Methods, Rules, Ways, &c., but cannot be named Sciences) and the aim of all liberal Education as far as the Intellect is concerned. The very word implies it— for the mind is educed, drawn forth, or developed, in exact proportion as the consciousness is extended.

MS.

67. A NATIONAL EDUCATION SCHEME

Suppose the Emperor Nicholas an Antonine, sincerely desirous to raise the Russians into a susceptibility of constitutional Government—how could this be most speedily achieved? I should answer, first, by a national education for all the children, according to their different ranks, in Schools where all the forms of a constitutional Government were *enacted*, and acted upon by the Scholars—without reference to politics out of the School: 1. Juries, 2. Parliaments, for the discussion of their by-laws— under the advice of the *Crown*, i.e. the School-Master—if it were only for their Sports and Plays. I am sure that this idea might be worked upon—and that all the most important utilities of Life might be rehearsed in national Schools—horticulture, mechanic arts, &c.

MS.

68. THE DIFFUSION OF KNOWLEDGE

Such are the impediments to the diffusion of knowledge. The means by which Providence seems to be counteracting these impediments are:

First and principally, the progress of the Methodists, and other disciples of Calvinism. It has been a common remark, that implicit faith in mysteries prepares the mind for implicit obedience to tyranny. But this is plausible rather than just. Facts are against it. The most thorough-paced Republicans in the days of Charles the First were religious enthusiasts: and in the present day, a large majority among our sectaries are fervent in their zeal against political abuses. The truth seems to be, that superstition is unfavourable to civil freedom then only, when it teaches sensuality, as among Atheists and Pagans, and Mussulmen; or when it is in alliance with power and avarice, as in the religious establishments of Europe. In all other cases, to forego, even in solitude, the high pleasures which the human mind receives from the free exertion of its faculties, through the dread of an invisible spectator or the hope of a future reward, implies so great a conquest over the tyranny of the present impulse, and so large a power of self-government, that whoever is conscious of it, will be grateful for the existence of an external government no farther than as it protects him from the attacks of others; which when that government omits to do, or when by promoting ignorance and depravity it produces the contrary effects, he is prepared to declare hostilities against it, and by the warmth of his feelings and the gregariousness of his nature is enabled to prosecute them more effectually, than a myriad of detached metaphysical systematizers. Besides, the very act of dissenting from established opinions must generate habits precursive to the love of freedom. Man begins to be free when he begins to examine. To this we may add, that men can hardly apply themselves with such perseverant zeal to the instruction and comforting of the poor, without feeling affection for them; and these feelings of love must necessarily lead to a blameless indignation against the authors of their complicated miseries. Nor should we forget, that however absurd their enthusiasm may be, yet if Methodism produce sobriety and domestic habits among the lower classes, it makes them susceptible of liberty; and this very enthusiasm does perhaps supersede the use of spirituous liquors, and bring on the same pleasing tumult of the brain without injuring the health or exhausting the wages. And although by the power of prejudice these sectaries may deduce from the gospel doctrines which it does not contain, yet it is impossible that they should peruse the New Testament so frequently and with such attention, without perceiving and remembering the precepts which it does contain. Yes! they shudder with pious horror at the idea of defending by famine, and fire, and blood, that religion which teaches its followers,— 'If thine enemy hunger, feed him; if he thirst, give him drink: *for by so doing thou shalt melt him into repentance.*'

Secondly,—the institution of large manufactories; in many of which it is the custom for a newspaper to be regularly read, and sometimes larger publications. Which party they adopt, is of little comparative consequence! Men always serve the cause of freedom by *thinking*, even though their first reflections may lead them to oppose it. And on account of these men, whose passions are frequently inflamed by drunkenness, the friends of rational and progressive liberty may review with diminished indignation two recent acts of parliament, which, though breaches of the constitution, and under pretence of protecting the *head* of the state, evidently passed to prevent our cutting off an enormous *wen* that grows upon it (I mean the system of secret influence,) yet will not have been useless if they should render the language of political publications more cool and guarded, or even confine us for a while to the teaching of first principles, or the diffusion of that general knowledge which should be the basis or substratum of politics.

Thirdly,—the number of book-societies established in almost every town and city of the kingdom; and,

Fourthly, the increasing experience of the dreadful effects of war and corruption.

Essays On His Own Times.

69. PROFESSIONS OR TRADES?

A professor may, if I mistake not, be thus distinguished: that the Services for which a fixed Honorarium is received, are in *form* as well as in substance intellectual, and are not reduced to a marketable and transferable Thing, separable from the person and the particular occasion. A Lawyer, who should sell legal opinions on conceivable and probable Cases, would practise a Trade: a Physician in like manner, who should describe in numerical order two or three hundred varieties of Disease, and sell Prescriptions sealed up, and each with a number correspondent to the disease of which it purported to be the remedy, would sink from a profession to a trade, even tho' both the Diagnostics and the Prescriptions were such as Esculapius himself would countersign. Lastly a Nobleman who puts up his farms to Auction, or in any manner lets out his estate for the exclusive purpose of making the most by each, and who buys and sells land in the same spirit, traffics with his Acres—he drives a Trade.

MS.

III

NO PASSIVE TOOLS

The more *consciousness* in our Thoughts and
Words, and the less in our Impulses and general
Actions, the better and more healthful the state
both of head and heart.

Aids to Reflection

LANGUAGE

On this aspect of Coleridge's work, the excerpts from unpublished manuscripts given by A. D. Snyder in *Coleridge on Logic and Learning* are useful and some items in *Anima Poetae*. Dr. I. A. Richards in *Coleridge on Imagination* stresses the importance of Coleridge as 'the first semasiologist', and there is an essay by J. Isaacs on 'Coleridge's Critical Terminology' in *Essays and Studies by Members of the English Association*, Vol. XXI.

He was not deeply interested in philology and, in fact, his derivations are sometimes so wild as to make one suspect that he approached it in the spirit of fantasy, or at any rate with a pretty light heart. But he was deeply interested in the philosophical implications of language, and sensitive to problems of communication. He was aware of the difference between assertive and emotive power in words, of shades of meaning and the subtleties of context. He could be casual about grammar in the interests of meaning. And his own involved hyper-parenthetical style is the vice of these virtues.

III

NO PASSIVE TOOLS

_____

70. WHAT DOES THE WORD MEAN?
A NOTE HEADED 'SOLGER'S *ERWIN*'

GENERALLY indeed I complain of the German Philo-sophers (as we are most apt to complain of our dearest Friends)—of the Post-Kantians at least—for the precipitance with which they pass to their own determinations of what the *thing* is, without having first enquired what the *word* means when it is used *appropriately*. Whenever I can convince a man that another term would express his meaning far more unexceptionably, the term used was not *appropriate*—but the rule is that the same word should not have heterogeneous or even disparate senses. Thus instead of asking, *Was Schönheit sey?* [What Beauty is?] I would enquire what *schön* properly meant —i.e. what men mean when they use the word *schön* in preference to any other epithet. A rose is a pleasing sight: and so to a hungry man is a Hogspudding. But a Rose is beautiful—ergo, beautiful means something else or something more than pleasing. The difference is not in the *degree*—for add to a keen appetite a long involuntary abstinence from animal food, and a particular predilection, the Hogspudding will become tenfold more pleasing without advancing a single step toward Beauty. In this way I would proceed with all the other phrases that are confounded with beautiful, because perhaps they fare in some common effect or because they are often in juxtaposition &c.: till I had exhausted the meanings of these words, and of course discovered that one meaning which the word, beautiful, and that word alone, peculiarized and expressed. And this, if I mistake not, is the true Socratic Method: assuredly that which best suits the Dialogue form, which only the analytic suits at any time, but this piece of analysis, i.e. desynonymization, best of all—it so naturally arises out of conversation. The Synthetic on the contrary demands the paideutic continuous form. We want a classification of words sadly—into the universals as applying to all the acts of the human Being—2. the generals, subdivided into the sensuous, intellectual, moral, 3. the words appropriate to each particular sense, at least to the imperfect, Taste, Smell, and the organized Touch, Sight, Hearing—&c. &c.

MS.

71. WORDS

A bath at Tophano is described as 'one of the loveliest I have ever seen'.

Coleridge comments: Lovely is a darling word of this Translator, a word that should never be applied except to objects that excite a *moral* feeling of attachment. I may say, 'a lovely Woman' or 'a lovely Infant', but not 'a lovely Diamond, or Topaz'.

MS.

72. CERTAIN SLANG

I regret to see that vile and barbarous vocable *talented*, stealing out of the newspapers into the leading reviews and most respectable publications of the day. Why not *shillinged, farthinged, tenpenced, etc.*? The formation of a participle passive from a noun, is a licence that nothing but a very peculiar felicity can excuse. If mere convenience is to justify such attempts upon the idiom, you cannot stop till the language becomes, in the proper sense of the word, corrupt. Most of these pieces of slang come from America.

Table Talk.

73. A WORD A FOCAL POINT

I do not know whether you are opticians enough to understand me when I speak of a Focus formed by converging rays of Light or Warmth in the *Air*. Enough that it is so—that the Focus exercises a power altogether different from that of the rays not converged—and to our sight and feeling acts precisely as if a solid flesh and blood reality were there. Now exactly such focal entities we are all more or less in the habit of creating for ourselves in the world of Thought. For the given point in the Air take any given *word*, fancy-image, or remembered emotion. Thought after Thought, Feeling after Feeling, and at length the sensations of Touch, and the blind Integer of the numberless number of the Infinitesimals that make up our sense of existing, converge in it—and there ensues a working on our mind so utterly unlike what any one of the confluents, separately considered, would produce, and no less disparate from what any mere Generalization of them all, would present to us, that I do not wonder at the unsatisfactoriness of every attempt to undeceive the person by an analysis, however clear. The focal word has acquired a *feeling* of *reality*—it heats and burns, makes itself be felt. If we do not grasp it, it seems to grasp us, as with a hand of flesh and blood, and completely counterfeits an immediate presence, an intuitive knowledge. And who can reason against an intuition?

MS.

74. WORDS NO PASSIVE TOOLS

... It is indeed never harmless to confound terms: for words are no passive Tools, but organized Instruments, re-acting on the Power which inspirits them. For one fair instance of Logomachy in any controversy of long standing, I will shew a score of Logodædalies—or mental Legerdemain—by first misusing a word for some other, and then drawing the consequences from its proper meaning.

MS.

75. ENTHUSIASM AND FANATICISM: TWO WORDS TWO MEANINGS

In the description of enthusiasm, the author has plainly had in view individual characters, and those too in a light in which they appeared to him; not clear and discriminate ideas. Hence a mixture of truth and error, of appropriate and inappropriate terms, which it is scarcely possible to disentangle. Part applies to fanaticism; part to enthusiasm; and no small portion of this latter to enthusiasm not pure, but as exists in particular men, modified by their imperfections—and bad because not wholly enthusiasm. I regret this, because it is evidently the discourse of a very powerful mind;—and because I am convinced that the disease of the age is want of enthusiasm, and a tending to fanaticism. You may very naturally object that the senses, in which I use the two terms, fanaticism and enthusiasm, are private interpretations equally as, if not more than, Mr. Birch's. They are so; but the difference between us is, that without reference to either term, I have attempted to ascertain the existence and diversity of two states of moral being; and then having found in our language two words of very fluctuating and indeterminate use, indeed, but the one word more frequently bordering on the one state, the other on the other, I try to fix each to that state exclusively. And herein I follow the practice of all scientific men, whether naturalists or metaphysicians, and the dictate of common sense, that one word ought to have but one meaning. Thus by Hobbes and others of the materialists, compulsion and obligation were used indiscriminately; but the distinction of the two senses is the condition of all moral responsibility. Now the effect of Mr. Birch's use of the words is to continue the confusion. Remember, we could not reason at all, if our conceptions and terms were not more single and definite than the things designated. Enthusiasm is the absorption of the individual in the object contemplated from the vividness or intensity of his conceptions and convictions: fanaticism is heat, or accumulation and direction, of feeling acquired by contagion, and relying on the sympathy of sect or confederacy; intense sensation with confused or dim conceptions. Hence the fanatic can exist only in a crowd, from inward weakness anxious for outward confirmation; and, therefore, an eager proselytizer and intolerant. The enthusiast, on the contrary, is a solitary, who lives in a world of his own peopling, and for that cause is disinclined to outward action. Lastly, enthusiasm is susceptible of many degrees, (according to the proportionateness of the objects contemplated), from the highest grandeur of moral and intellectual being, even to madness; but fanaticism is one and the same, and appears different only from the manners and original temperament of the individual. There is a white and a red heat; a sullen glow as well as a crackling flame; cold-blooded as well as hot-blooded fanaticism. . . . I am fully aware that the words are used by the best writers indifferently, but such must be the case in very many words in a composite language, such as the English, before they are desynonymized. Thus imagination and fancy; chronical and temporal, and many others.

> Note on a Sermon on the Prevalence of Infidelity
> and Enthusiasm, by Walter Birch, B.D.

76. ALLEGORY AND SYMBOL

Now an Allegory is but a translation of abstract notions into a picture-language which is itself nothing but an abstraction from objects of the senses; the principal being more worthless even than its phantom proxy, both alike unsubstantial, and the former shapeless to boot. On the other hand a Symbol is characterized by a translucence of the Special in the Individual or of the General in the Especial or of the Universal in the General. Above all by the translucence of the Eternal through and in the Temporal. It always partakes of the Reality which it renders intelligible; and while it enunciates the whole, abides itself as a living part in that Unity, of which it is the representative. The other are but empty echoes which the fancy arbitrarily associates with apparitions of matter.

The Statesman's Manual.

77. READING—AND WRITING

It has been remarked by the celebrated Haller, that we are deaf while we are yawning. The same act of drowsiness that stretches open our mouths, closes our ears. It is much the same in acts of the understanding. A lazy half-attention amounts to a mental yawn. Where then a subject that demands thought, has been thoughtfully treated, and with an exact and patient derivation from its principles, we must be willing to exert a portion of the same effort, and to think with the author, or the author will have thought in vain for us. It makes little difference for the time being whether there be an *hiatus oscitans* in the reader's attention, or an *hiatus lacrymabilis* in the author's manuscript. When this occurs during the perusal of a work of known authority and established fame, we honestly lay the fault on our own deficiency, or on the unfitness of our present mood; but when it is a contemporary production, over which we have been nodding, it is far more pleasant to pronounce it *insufferably dull and obscure*. Indeed, as charity begins at home, it would be unreasonable to expect that a reader should charge himself with lack of intellect, when the effect may be equally well accounted for by declaring the author unintelligible; or accuse his own inattention, when by half a dozen phrases of abuse, as '*heavy stuff, metaphysical jargon*', &c. he can at once excuse his laziness, and gratify his pride, scorn, and envy. To similar impulses we must attribute the praises of a true modern reader, when he meets with a work in the true modern taste, *videlicet,* either in skipping, unconnected, short-winded, asthmatic sentences, as easy to be understood as impossible to be remembered, in which the merest common-place acquires a momentary poignancy, a petty titillating sting, from affected point and wilful antithesis; or else in strutting and rounded periods, in which the emptiest truisms are blown up into illustrious bubbles by help of film and inflation. 'Aye!' (quoth the delighted reader) 'this is sense, this is genius! this I understand and admire! *I have thought the very same a hundred times myself!*' In other words, this man has reminded me of my own cleverness, and therefore I admire him. O! for one piece of egotism that presents itself under its own honest bare face of "I myself I", there are fifty that steal out in the mask of *tuisms* and *ille-isms!*

Essays On His Own Times.

78. A PHILOSOPHER HAS TWO LANGUAGES

A philosopher's ordinary language and admissions, in general conversation or writings *ad populum,* are as his watch compared with his astronomical timepiece. He sets the former by the town-clock, not because he believes it right, but because his neighbours and his cook go by it.

Table Talk.

79. POPULAR AND SCIENTIFIC LANGUAGE

Coleridge has just been writing of number, and of that sense in which the number One is not a number because it is 'the source' of all Number.

N.B. No man can *be,* or can *understand,* a Philosopher, till he has acquired the power and the habit of attaching to words the *generic* sense purely—and unmixed with the accidents of comparative *degrees*. It is this which constitutes the difference between the *proper* Nomenclature of Science and the inevitable language of ordinary life. The latter speaks only of *degrees*. With *quantity* and *quality* it is familiar; but knows nothing of *quiddity* but as a synonyme for worthless subtleties; and only grins wider with more intense self-complacency when it hears the former speak of invisible *Light*, the *Heat* of Ice, &c. The *Uno* nel Più of the Philosopher Saint and Bishop of Geneva (Francesco Sales) would be as senseless to a common Italian, as my 'Multiety in Unity' or 'The One in the Many' could be to a Mr. Wheatley of Oriel or the 'cute Isaacs of the Stock Exchange.

MS.

80. COINING AND USING WORDS

... (*Nota bene.* Not having written my new word lately, I am getting cowardly about it and blush at my own 'Impetite', like a grave smug Elder at a Bastard honestly sworn to him!) in my scheme, I say—O all ye Philo-parenthesists—bless the man that invented *I say*! ...

MS.

81. PUNCTUATION NOT LOGICAL BUT DRAMATIC

Punctuation. Four Stops, two marks of movement, and a stroke, or expression of the indefinite or fragmentary—Comma, Semicolon; Colon: Period. Mark of Interrogation? Note of Admiration! Stroke ——. It appears next to self-evident, that the first four or five characters can never be made to represent all the modes and subtle distinctions of connection, accumulation, disjunction, and completion of sense. It would be quite as absurd as to imagine that the ? and ! should designate all the moods of passion, that we convey by interrogation or wonder, as the simple question for information, the ironical, the impetuous, the ratiocinative &c. No! this must be left to the Understanding of the Reader or Hearer. What then is their use? This will be more easily understood by supposing one person reading what a hundred or more are listening to. Their use is to enable the reader to regulate his *breath* foresightedly, and inclusively his Tones. This will become plain after having considered the use of each stop separately.

The comma is either simply addive, and [synonymous *crossed out*] equivalent to the conjunction 'and'; or it is parenthetic, i.e. marks the insertion of a sentence, between a sentence uncompleted and its completion. He, James, Harry, and I were going =He *and* James and Harry and I. In such cases therefore I deem the comma before the 'and' tautologic. 2. Parenthetic. He and I were going, when we met James, to visit Westminster Abbey.

The semicolon is 1. accumulative, either when it is desired to draw more attention to each member of the cumulus:

'I would urge you to consider long and earnestly, the power of God; the omniscience and wisdom that direct his omnipotence; the ineffable Love, which makes the happiness of creatures a final cause of that self-sufficing Being, where knowledge and might are the efficient causes of all things; and above all, his long-suffering and tender Redemption, of Sinful Creatures who by sin had forfeited all claims on his Justice ever for that only dire demand, which even an unfallen Angel could make on the Justice of a Creator, viz. Annihilation!' This sentence contains likewise the illustration of the second—namely, when the component parts of a cumulus contain more than a simple sentence, consequently, must have a comma, and therefore require a something more than a comma in order to distinguish between the parts of the whole; and the parts of the part. Here therefore in both cases the stop is used not so to express a real logical difference of connection from the comma, for there is none; but to regulate the Breath, so as [to *crossed out*] that the longer pause may mark the limbs of the Period, from the Joints of the Limbs. This use of the Semicolon is far more common in the elder English Classics, from Elizabeth to William the 3rd than in modern writers. See Jeremy Taylor's Works. It was perhaps used in excess by them; but the disuse seems a worse evil. And I am glad to observe, in some of the best articles of our Reviews, and in the later pamphlets of Sir J. Mackintosh, a moderated use of it in this form restored to our Language. Lord Bacon and Jer[emy] Taylor are the two Authors, to be consulted. The second and more admitted use is to express exception or disjunction and therefore commonly precedes *but*. To shew however that this primarily and essentially depends on the regularity of the Breathing, and not on any logical symbolism, it is sufficient to consider, that when we except or disjoin the former sense as it exists in the foresight of the writer or speaker as not compleat, and yet would for the moment appear complete to the Listener—the Speaker therefore naturally goes on more quickly to remove or prevent the misunderstanding, than when the sense is complete in itself; and only requires or permits a confirmation by the addition of the reason. Thence is it that the colon, which precedes the causal connective, *For*, implies a longer pause than the;—and thence too it would be pedantry to place the ; before a *but*, where the shortness and sense of the former sentence rendering its sense wholly incomplete, precludes all misunderstanding. Was it James? No. Not James, but Harry.

I have thus anticipated the use of the Colon—which is distinguished from the full stop by this, that tho' the sense is compleat, yet in that same moment of thought the speaker connects with it and during speaking it foresees the grounds, cause, or reason, or confirmation of it. Here I would use the Colon. But when the sense is completed as far as it existed at that moment in the mind; and then the mind starting a fresh either commences a new train or adds an argument, after a pause of Thought, then tho' the *For* or *But* should be first word, I would use a full stop.—Instances from any good writer.

In short, I look on the stops not as logical Symbols, but rather as dramatic directions representing the process of Thinking and Speaking conjointly—either therefore the regulation of the Breath simply, for in very long periods of exceedingly close reasoning this occurs; or as the movements in the Speaker's Thought make him regulate his Breath, pause longer or shorter, and prepare his voice before the pause for the pause—as for instance—'No good man can contemplate the African Slave-Trade without horror, who has once read an account of the wars and atrocious kidnapping practised in the procuring of the Slaves, the horrors of the middle passage in the conveyance of them, or the outrage to our common nature in the too frequent and always possible final cruelty in employing and punishing them. Then, too, the fearful effect on the oppressor's own mind, the hardness, pride, proneness to frantic anger, sensuality, and the deadening of the moral senses respecting the distinction between Thing and Person will force the Thoughts thro' a fresh Channel to the common Bay and Receptacle, in which the mind floats at anchor upon its accumulated Thoughts, deep and with a sure bottom of Arguments and grounds, yet wary with the passions of honest Indignation.' Now here the latter sense is equally the ground of the preparation with the former; but the former might be, and is gracefully represented as the whole, at the commencement in the Speaker's view. He pauses —then the activity of the mind, generating upon its generations, starts anew—and the pause is not, for which I am contending, at all retrospective, but always prospective, or that is, the pause is not affected by what actually follows, but by what anterior to it was foreseen as following.

It is the first and simplest duty of a Writer to make the pauses, which the movements of his Thought require in order to be intelligible, consistent with an easy regulation of the Breath— not that the Stop depends on the Breath, but that it should prevent the Breath from making a stop from its own necessity.

(Tho' in the modern French Writers and their English Translators one might suppose the necessity of the Breath to be the sole principle of punctuation, and the powers of the Breath averaged from a nation of asthmatic patients). Supposing this therefore (and surely, it would be absurd to lay down rules for punctuating what ought not to have been written) I would say, that Punctuation expresses—say, rather—generally *hints* the sorts of pause which the Speaker makes, and the tones accompanying and leading to them from the Speaker's foresight of his own meaning. Punctuation therefore is always prospective: that is, it is not made according to the actual weight and difference or equality of the logical connections, but to the view which the Speaker is supposed to have at the moment, in which he speaks the particular sentence. Therefore I call them not symbols of Logic, but dramatic directions, enabling the reader more easily to place himself in the state of the writer or original Speaker.[1]

MS.

82. STYLE AND THOUGHT: SHORT PERIODS

We insensibly imitate what we habitually admire; and an aversion to the epigrammatic unconnected periods of the fashionable *Anglo-Gallican* taste has too often made me willing to forget, that the stately march and difficult evolutions, which characterize the eloquence of Hooker, Bacon, Milton, and Jeremy Taylor, are, notwithstanding their intrinsic excellence, still less suited to a periodical essay. This fault I am now endeavouring to correct; though I can never so far sacrifice my judgment to the desire of being immediately popular, as to cast my sentences in the French moulds, or affect a style which an ancient critic would have deemed purposely invented for persons troubled with the asthma to read, and for those to comprehend

[1] Except for the deletion of some dashes, Coleridge's own punctuation is strictly adhered to in this entry.

who labour under the more pitiable asthma of a short-witted intellect. It cannot but be injurious to the human mind never to be called into effort: the habit of receiving pleasure without any exertion of thought, by the mere excitement of curiosity and sensibility, may be justly ranked among the worst effects of habitual novel reading. It is true that these short and unconnected sentences are easily and instantly understood: but it is equally true, that wanting all the cement of thought as well as of style, all the connections, and (if you will forgive so trivial a metaphor) all the hooks-and-eyes of the memory, they are as easily forgotten: or rather, it is scarcely possible that they should be remembered. Nor is it less true, that those who confine their reading to such books dwarf their own faculties, and finally reduce their understandings to a deplorable imbecility. . . . Like idle morning visitors, the brisk and breathless periods hurry in and hurry off in quick and profitless succession; each indeed for the moments of its stay prevents the pain of vacancy, while it indulges the love of sloth; but all together they leave the mistress of the house (the soul, I mean) flat and exhausted, incapable of attending to her own concerns, and unfitted for the conversation of more rational guests.

Friend.

83. ENGLISH AND GERMAN

It may be doubted whether a composite language like the English is not a happier instrument of expression than a homogeneous one like the German. We possess a wonderful richness and variety of modified meanings in our Saxon and Latin quasi-synonyms, which the Germans have not. For 'the pomp and *prodigality* of Heaven', the Germans must have said '*the spend-thriftness*'. Shakespeare is particularly happy in his use of the Latin synonyms, and in distinguishing between them and the Saxon.

Table Talk.

84. GREEK, AND MODERN LANGUAGES

It is hardly possible to conceive a language more perfect than
the Greek. If you compare it with the modern European
tongues, in the points of the position and relative bearing of the
vowels and consonants on each other, and of the variety of
terminations, it is incalculably before all in the former particulars, and only equalled in the last by German. But it is in variety
of termination alone that the German surpasses the other
modern languages as to sound; for, as to position, Nature seems
to have dropped an acid into the language, when a-forming,
which curdled the vowels, and made all the consonants flow
together. The Spanish is excellent for variety of termination;
the Italian, in this particular, the most deficient. Italian prose is
excessively monotonous.

Table Talk.

IV

HARES AND NETTLES

'I not only love Truth, but I have a passion for the legitimate investigation of Truth. The love of Truth conjoined with the keen delight in a strict, skilful, yet impassioned argumentation is my Master passion, and to it are subordinated the love of Liberty and all my public Feelings, and to it whatever I labour under of Vanity, Ambition, and all my inward Impulses.'

MS. note on the 'Letters of Junius'

LOGIC AND PHILOSOPHY

The most important works for a study of Coleridge's philosophical views are the *Friend*, the *Statesman's Manual*, *Aids to Reflection*, *Coleridge On Logic and Learning*, ed. by A. D. Snyder, and the *Philosophical Lectures*. His great philosophical work, the *Opus Maximum*, was never completed, though bulky manuscripts in the hands of the students to whom he dictated it survive in the British Museum and in the Huntington Library in California. His position was Platonic, owing something both to Plato and the Cambridge Platonists, in that he defended the objectivity and authority of the Idea with a capital I; it was Kantian and critical in that he wished to clarify the limits of knowledge. His philosophical thinking, though not systematized, is far more incisive than is frequently suggested by those who have not followed it through; publication of his philosophical marginalia is a *desideratum*, as he would have called it, and would reveal his penetrations in a sharper light than they have yet been seen. He displays a kind of metaphysical reasoning now in disrepute, but it is wrong to call him vague or mystical.

Coleridge as Philosopher, by J. H. Muirhead, is difficult, and written from Platonist hypotheses. In *Kant in England*, Mr. R. Wellek gives Coleridge, of all the writers dealt with, by far the longest treatment, biased in another direction. For those who read German perhaps the best critique is *Coleridge und die Kantische Philosophie*, Leipzig, 1933, by Dr. Elisabeth Winkelmann.

IV

HARES AND NETTLES

---

85. ANALYSIS OF TERMS

WITHOUT any excessive or groundless Refinement I may complain of the too inclusive meaning of $=$ or the mark of equation. For it may be used in three different senses:

1. *One with.* The regenerate Will$=$the Will Divine.
2. *Equivalent to.* 20 Shillings$=$1 Sovereign.
3. *The same as.* $2+2=4$.

The difference in the first might be marked by raising the object above the $=$: thus,

$$\text{Man} = \overset{\text{God}}{}$$

in the second by depressing it: thus, $^{s}20 = \underset{\text{1 sov}^{n}.}{}$

and in the third by retaining both on the same line: $2+2=4$. To which we might perhaps add a 4th:

4. The quotient or product of $5+7=12$, i.e. *is* 12. See Kant on the synthetic character of arithmetical and other processes hitherto supposed analytic—Kant's *Kritik der reinen Vernunft*.

MS.

86. THE POST-KANTIAN NEGLECT OF LOGIC

The Natur-Phil[sophen] are apt to mistake the new-naming of a thing *per antithesim ex. gr. Raumleben* $)($ *Zeitleben*[1], for additional Insight.

The Followers of Fichte, Baader, Schelling, and Steffens, like those of Plotinus, affect to be Eclectic Philosophers—but as you [J. H. Green] truly remarked, they neglect Logic, or rather do not understand what Logic is. Thus what Kant asserted as an assumption for the purposes of a formal Science, Heinroth asserts as matter of fact. It is a necessary fiction of *pure* Logic; just as the very contrary is a necessary fiction of pure Somatology.

MS.

87. 'A RETORT, OR TIT FOR TAT COURTEOUS', AGAINST MATERIALISTS

Grew, in his *Cosmologia Sacra*, 1701, writes: As there is no *Maximum* whereunto we can go, but God only; so there is no *Minimum*, but a Point: which hath no Dimensions, but only a Whereness, and is next to Nothing.

Coleridge answers, in the margin and then on a front flyleaf: Well and happily expressed! But I should like to see the Partition-Wall between Nothing and *Next to* Nothing. *No* Thing, and his next neighbor, Whereness, a strange gentleman who *is* his own empty House—not admitting even his neighbor Nothing's next of kin, Any Thing. Neither of the two, however, the Thisbe nor the Pyramus, is left Anonymous.

Then indeed we might question the *authenticity* of the Narrative. But no! the name of the one is Nothing; and the other was called *Point*—whether as Surname, or by baptism, is not ascertained. It is clear, however, and abundantly descriptive—the first being a No Thing *anywhere* and the second any thing that

[1] $)($ is Coleridge's sign for 'compared with'.

is no thing—or Nothing that is nowhere and where that is Nothing. Hue and Cry, the accused accomplices being—a Nothing that is anywhere, and an anywhere that is Nothing!—N.B. They are next door Neighbour, the one *being* the other's House.

[On the front flyleaf.]

A Nothing that is Nowhere: and a *Where* only, that is Nothing. Ch. III. p.11. Mem.—The Gentleman last mentioned is called Point; whether as Surname, or by individual Christening, I have not learnt;—only, that NOTHING and POINT are next door neighbours: and strange to say, the Latter *is* the other's empty house, (Bedless, however—and therefore even if the *Spelling* had been less irreconcileable, not to be confounded with the Ware so celebrated for its great Bed). This House, which *is* Nothing, tho' punctual in the extreme is so unhospitable as not to admit the next door Neighbor Nothing's next of kin, Any thing!

P.S. *Where only* is Nothing's Landlord inasmuch as He *is* at once his own, and his Neighbour's, house. *Tenementum Merum, quod nihil tenet.*

Mere *Whereness*! Nothing's Landlord and next Neighbour,
Who *art* thy own and *Nothing's* empty house,
Tenentless Tenement!—pinch gut's *only* Where!
Would thou wert No Where! and that thy neighbor, Nothing,
Were Any Thing but what he is and is not!
      From a MSS. Poem, ἀνεκδότου of Athanasius Sphinx.

Mem. Intended as a Retort, or Tit for Tat courteous, if any of the Doctors of the Mechanic corpuscularum Philosophy, the caloric and choleric Atomists of the Daltonist School should, as most probably they will, crow and cachinnate over my *Ens super Ens, Ens verè Ens,* and *Ens ferè non ens.* S. T. C.

[Another note]: It is from admiration of Dr. N. Grew, and my high Estimate of his Powers, that I am almost tempted to say,

that the Reasonings in Chapt. III *ought* to have led him to the perception of the essential phaenomenality of Matter . . .

[*Another note*]: . . . Such must be the sophistic results of every pretence to understand God by the World, instead of the World by God. It is an attempt to see the Sun by Moonlight.

MS.

88. SYLLOGISTIC AND CRITERIONAL LOGIC

There are two kinds of logic: 1. Syllogistic. 2. Criterional. How any one can by any spinning make out more than ten or a dozen pages about the first, is inconceivable to me; all those absurd forms of syllogisms are one half pure sophisms, and the other half mere forms of rhetoric.

All syllogistic logic is—1. Seclusion; 2. Inclusion; 3. Conclusion; which answer to the understanding, the experience, and the reason. The first says, this *ought* to be; the second adds, this *is*; and the last pronounces, this *must* be so. The criterional logic, or logic of premisses, is, of course, much the most important; and it has never yet been treated.

Table Talk.

89. NOT A LOGICAL AGE

This is not a logical age. A friend lately gave me some political pamphlets of the time of Charles I. and the Cromwellate. In them the premisses are frequently wrong, but the deductions are almost always legitimate; whereas, in the writings of the present day, the premisses are commonly sound, but the conclusions false. I think a great deal of commendation is due to the University of Oxford, for preserving the study of logic in the schools. It is a great mistake to suppose geometry any substitute for it.

Table Talk.

90. LOGIC

You abuse snuff! Perhaps it is the final cause of the human nose.

Table Talk.

91. ORIENTAL AND GREEK LOGIC

St. John's logic is Oriental, and consists chiefly in position and parallel; whilst St. Paul displays all the intricacies of the Greek system.

Table Talk.

92. LOGICAL TERMS

I am strongly induced to put the ? whether the term, universal, might not with advantage be done away with in the terminology of Logic, and the term *formal* or essential be substituted. In affirming the equality of the rays of a Circle I affirm an essential form of *the* Circle: or rather the Circle as a total (i.e. seclusive) Form and the equi-radiality as a component (i.e. included) integral part. Even the phrase, *true in all cases*, is preferable to *universal*. . . .

MS.

93. DEDUCTION AND INDUCTION

I do not know whether I deceive myself, but it seems to me that the young men, who were my contemporaries, fixed certain principles in their minds, and followed them out to their legitimate consequences, in a way which I rarely witness now. No one seems to have any distinct convictions, right or wrong; the mind is completely at sea, rolling and pitching on the waves of facts and personal experiences. Mr. —— is, I suppose, one of the rising young men of the day; yet he went on talking, the other evening, and making remarks with great earnestness, some of which were palpably irreconcilable with each other. He told me that facts gave birth to, and were the absolute ground of, principles; to which I said, that unless he had a principle of selection, he would not have taken notice of those facts upon which he grounded his principle. You must have a lantern in your hand to give light, otherwise all the materials in the world are useless, for you cannot find them, and if you could, you could not arrange them. 'But then,' said Mr. ——, '*that* principle of selection came from facts!'—'To be sure!' I replied; 'but there must have been again an antecedent light to see those antecedent facts. The relapse may be carried in imagination backwards for ever,—but go back as you may, you cannot come to a man without a previous aim or principle.' He then asked me what I had to say to Bacon's Induction: I told him I had a good deal to say, if need were; but that it was perhaps enough for the occasion, to remark, that what he was very evidently taking for the Baconian *In*duction, was mere *De*duction—a very different thing.

Table Talk.

94. KANT AND GERMAN PHILOSOPHY

Solger in his *Philosophische Gespräche* contends that Kant and Fichte wrote in the spirit of their own age, and that their works gained their importance from their practical contemporary application.

Coleridge comments: I cannot admit this without serious limitations even of Fichte, still less of Kant: who thought and wrote for his age not *with* it—or *with* it only as far as the *form* and *method* extend. Kant had 1. to overthrow, 2nd. to build the best possible temporary Shed and Tool-house, both for those ejected from the old Edifice, and for the Laborers &c. Lastly, in this Shed to give the Hints and great Ideas for the erection of the new Edifice. What since Kant is not in Kant as a German at least?

[*Another note*]: Of all wearisome Cant this Cant of Action, practical Truth, diese in unserem eigenen Berufe and the like, is the most sickening. What, the Devil! does it mean? We must get our bread and therefore for our own sakes and as honorable men, try to do what we do as well as possible. Who does not know this? And what has it to do with a man's meditations in his leisure Hours? or if he should be a Shoe-maker, &c., even while he is working? Hans Sachs composed 20 folios of Verses, and never made a Shoe the less.

> Solger goes on to say that even men of action in state affairs and on the battlefield have Ideas of higher aim and end.

Coleridge: Whoo!—a Wellington stuffed with *Ideas*!!

MS.

95. SOUTHEY AND METAPHYSICS: THE SUPREME REASON

A NOTE ON SOUTHEY'S 'THE DOCTOR'

Truth and Evidence are distinct terms, the latter implying the former, but not vice versâ. Truths equal in *certainty*, may be of very unequal *Evidence. ex. gr.* Geometry and the Differential Calculus. Would that Southey could be induced to see, that the Light from Metaphysics, that *lumen fatuum,* at which he so triumphantly scoffs, is better than the recollection of the Legends and technical Slang of Common-place Sermons! and then instead of 'the light of mere Reason', he would have said—'the inferences of the sensual *Understanding* imperfectly enlightened by Reason'. There is something shocking to a thoughtful Spirit in the very phrase '*mere* Reason'. I could almost as easily permit my tongue to say, 'mere God'. I am a Christian of the School of John, Paul, Athanasius, Bull and Waterland, a Church of England Christian and therefore do not say, 'God is the Supreme Reason'—but this I will and do say, that the Supreme Reason (ὁ Λόγος, Jehovah, ὁ Ὤν) is God. And are there two *Reasons*, a rational Reason, and an irrational?

MS.

96. THREE SOURCES OF KNOWLEDGE

... There are three distinct sources from one or other of which we must derive our arguments whatever the position may be that we wish to support or overthrow. ... These sources are, 1. transcendental, or anterior to experience, as the grounds without which experience itself could not have been. 2. Subjective, or the experience acquirable by self-observation and composed of facts of inward consciousness, which may be appealed to as assumed to have place in the minds of other[s] but cannot be demonstrated. Each man's experience is a single and insulated Whole. 3. Common and simultaneous Experience, collectively forming *History* in its widest sense, civil, and natural.

MS.

97. TRUTHS AND MAXIMS

The English public is not yet ripe to comprehend the essential difference between the reason and the understanding—between a principle and a maxim—an eternal truth and a mere conclusion generalized from a great number of facts. A man, having seen a million moss roses all red, concludes from his own experience and that of others that all moss roses are red. That is a maxim with him—the *greatest* amount of his knowledge upon the subject. But it is only true until some gardener has produced a white moss rose,—after which the maxim is good for nothing. Again, suppose Adam watching the sun sinking under the western horizon for the first time; he is seized with gloom and terror, relieved by scarce a ray of hope that he shall ever see the glorious light again. The next evening, when it declines, his hopes are stronger, but still mixed with fear; and even at the end of a thousand years, all that a man can feel is, a hope and an expectation so strong as to preclude anxiety. Now compare this in its highest degree with the assurance which you have that the two sides of any triangle are together greater than the third. This, demonstrated of one triangle, is seen to be eternally true of all imaginable triangles. This is a truth perceived at once by the intuitive reason, independently of experience. It is, and must ever be so, multiply and vary the shapes and sizes of triangles as you may.

Table Talk.

98. REAL AND IDEAL

From the beginning I avoid the false opposition of Real and Ideal which embarrasses Schelling. Idea with me is contra-distinguished only from Conception, Notion, Construction, Impression, Sensation.

MS.

99. THE HISTORY OF PHILOSOPHY INTERPRETED

It was of incalculable moment to Philosophy and the best interests of Man, that Occam and his Followers disclosed the unproductive nature of Conceptions and Notions, and the dependence of the Understanding on the Sense and Sensibility, in the broadest light. It was of the greatest importance in order to the regeneration of Realism, and its second triumphant Coming in its genuine form, that Nominalism should obtain a decisive Victory, and possess the philosophic Throne long enough to display its character and consequences without disguise. Then Dialectic was soon left behind, and the Logic swam with the tide; and like the pigs, cut its own throat as it advanced—and soon sunk and gave way to the three other Factors, the Sense, the Sensation, and the Senses as the union of both, i.e. to

Mathematics and Empiricism, the latter subdivided into Observation and Experiment. For the Learned these were enough as long as History and Authority and above all the empassioned Business of detecting Error and *protesting* against the old Usurper, Aristotle, and the Papacy furnished full occupation. But the destruction and negative energies hasten to their own extinction, the more successful the shorter their endurance. And in attempting to survive their rightful Objects [Falsehood *crossed out*] (Error and Imposture) they deteriorated into a heartless Scepticism, and like the Hyena, bit at their own Supports.

Meanwhile for Man as Man, and for the Mass of Society, who were neither Mathematicians, Critics, or Virtuosi, there only remained the Sensations or Sensibility—and there followed an age of Luxury and Dissoluteness—and the names of Vice and Virtue were given to the more or less refined Taste in the same Epicurism.

Then rose the question in the better natures—Surely, these are not all of the Human Being? We have hearts as well as Heads. We can will and act, as well as think, see, and feel. Is there no communion between the intellectual and the moral? Are the distinctions of the Schools separates in Nature? Is there no Heart in the Head? No Head in the Heart? Is it not possible to find a *practical* Reason, a *Light* of Life, a focal power from the union or harmonious composition of all the Faculties? Lastly, there is, it is admitted, a Reason, to which the Understanding must convert itself in order to obtain from within what it would in vain seek for without, the knowledge of necessary and universal conclusion—of that which is because it must be, and not because it had been seen. May there not be a yet higher or deeper Presence, the source of Ideas, to which even the Reason must convert itself? Or rather is not this more truly the Reason, and the universal Principles but the Gleam of Light from the distant and undistinguished community of Ideas—or the Light in the Cloud that hides the Luminary? O! let these questions be once fully answered, and the affirmative

made sure and evident—then we shall have a Philosophy, that
will unite in itself the warmth of the mystics, the definiteness of
the Dialectician, and the sunny clearness of the Naturalist, the
productivity of the Experimenter and the Evidence of the
Mathematician. It was solely from the want of this foundation
that Raymond of Sabunde's grand Attempt was premature, and
abortive. Yet how precious the result! It reminds me of the
fossile animals in the heart of the mountains according to the
bold speculation of Steffens, who holds them for the *first studies*
of [plastic *crossed out*] the organizing Life of Nature, left imperfect, the divine Artist being called off abruptly to quell a new
gathering of the insurgent Titans.

> Where'er I find the Good, the True, the Fair,
> I ask no names. God's Spirit dwelleth there!
> The unconfounded, undivided Three.
> Each for itself, and all in each, to see
> In Man, and Nature is Philosophy.[1]

MS.

100. PLATONISM IN HIS TIME

The gross errors of the Platonists in Physics which tho' they do
not affect the essential meaning, yet seem to do so to impatient
minds—are the secondary cause of the present *supercilium* toward
Platonism. The primary cause is that Impatience itself which
characterizes Europe, and in a growing ratio from the days of
Verulam to Condillac—occasioning and occasioned by the passion for merely sensuous phænomena. Finger-active, brain-lazy
we look with the same arch scorn at ancient philosophy with
which a shrewd Rustic grins at an Astronomer's assertions of
the motion and size of the Earth relatively to the Sun, the poor
Sage having previously mistaken Oats for Barley, or a Plough

[1] I omit a first draft of the lines; in the manuscript Coleridge crossed them
out.

for a Harrow. Commonsense, cry the one, Mother-wit, cries
the other. S. T. C.

MS.

101. GENERAL TRUTH NOT UNIVERSAL LAW: MORAL DOGMA: CALVIN

There is one injurious mistake, that in all ages and countries,
our own not excepted, has come more or less into play; but
which may be said to have been culminant, the Lord of the
Ascendant, from the first appearance of Luther in the Horizon
of History even to the Revolution in 1688. This is, the giving
to a *general* truth, the privileges of a *universal Law*, or in other
words the neglect of that golden Adage, *Summum Jus summa
injuria.* Example. It is a *general* truth, that all Subjects are bound
for conscience's sake to obey the established Powers, passively
by submitting to the penalty where they cannot, from motives
of conscience, religious, or political, obey actively. The abuse
of the sovereignty forms no exception to this general rule,
as to enable a Moralist *a priori* to justify resistance. The *Presumption* must always be against such an Act. The Caesar, to
whom Christ commanded passive obedience, was the Monster,
Tiberius: and 'the Powers that be' for whom St. Paul exacted
submission, were exercised by that Monster, Nero. Neither is
this *general* Rule invalidated, *a priori*, by the mere co-incidence
of *Numbers* in the same resistance. On the contrary, Treason
acquires a worse character when exhibited in *a Mob.* These are
truths. But tho' abstract Reason neither enables or permits us
to allow by *anticipation* any predefinable rebellion, yet History
presents many cases which whoever condemns or does not
extol and honor *in the retrospect* is a slave in soul, a servile Bigot,
and in our own instance of James II a Traitor to the British
Constitution. Now I pray, in what words is it possible that a
Writer should convey this complex position but by affirming
an inherent right of resistance in possible circumstances; by pre-

defining these circumstances to be such, in which each individual acts in the feeling and conviction, that the Spirit of the Whole—not the mere majority of Noses, but the sum total of the Will and the Powers employed in the progressive as well as conservative movements of the Body Politic (or Nation) of which he is a member—is truly represented in himself; and finally, to guard him by all known criteria against mistaking his own fancies, turbulent emotions, and private prejudices, for a public Spirit?

This Calvin has done. But might not any man fancy—so and so? Doubtless. Men have fancied themselves made of glass—and if the falsehood of a moral rule is proveable by its not being able to preclude a fanatic, a fool, or a scoundrel from abusing it, all moral rules are false.

No, Calvin's Error was of the direct contrary kind. . . . His error lay in this, that he too in another *general* rule, universalized, admitting neither exceptions nor limitation. The *general* Rule is: Promote the Truth—and what you *know* to be the Truth, enforce and realize, at whatever sacrifice of private feeling or interest, in proportion to the importance of that truth to the highest Welfare of Mankind. But alas! He forgot, that in order to this rule being *universal*, Omniscience is the pre-requisite, and Omnipotence the necessary accompaniment. He forgot, that a man can only *believe* himself to *know* that any given position is true in each particular form in which he announces it, or that the means which he takes to realize this position, are the right and fit means. And yet if we were to carry this scepticism into our general conduct, if we acted on no occasion with a sense of certainty, we should do nothing—the whole moral world would stagnate. What then is the *reconciling* principle? This:—Take care, that your *act* is proportionate to your faculties, neither forgetting their strength nor their fallibility.

A Surgeon regularly educated performs an amputation, even where only the probability appears to him to be in favor of it, and even tho' the event should be adverse, he yet stands guiltless before God and Man. The act was not merely the result of his best convictions, but it was duly proportioned to his moral sphere, as an Individual. Marat had a conviction amounting in his own mind to a moral certainty that the death of 200,000 of his Countrymen was indispensible to the establishment of the Liberty and ultimate moral and physical Well-being of France, and therein of all Europe. We will even assume, that events should have confirmed the correctness of this belief. And yet Marat was and will remain either execrable as a remorseless Ruffian, or frightful as an Insane Fanatic. And why? The proposal was frightfully disproportionate to the sphere of a poor fallible Mortal. It was a decisive symptom of an inhuman Soul, that, when the lives of myriads of his fellow-men were in question, the recollection of his necessary fallibility, and the probability of mistake where so many myriads of men possessing the same intellectual faculties with himself entertained different convictions with the same sense of positiveness, did not outweigh any confidence arising from his own individual insight.

Nay, a Marat is every man who on the ground of speculative convictions dares authorize the punishment and subversion of all who hold and act on opposite convictions.

This Calvin did—justifying himself by the example of whom? —*Of God:* presumptuously forgetting, that he, Calvin, was not God. But was it Calvin alone? No! No! *Every Sect* of that Age without exception Calvinized in *this respect*; and it is calumnious in Dr. Kenny to seduce the ignorant into the Notion that Calvin, and not the whole Age including Calvin, was the Culprit.

MS.

102. ARISTOTLE'S DEFINITION OF NATURE

It has in its consequences proved no trifling evil to the Christian World, that Aristotle's Definitions of Nature are all grounded on the petty and rather rhetorical than philosophical Antithesis of Nature to Art—a conception inadequate to the demands even of his Philosophy. Hence in the progress of his reasoning, he confounds the Natura *Naturata* (that is, the sum total of the Facts and Phaenomena of the Senses) with an hypothetical Natura *Naturans*, a *Goddess* Nature, that has no better claim to a place in any sober system of Natural Philosophy than the Goddess *Multitudo*; yet to which Aristotle not rarely gives the name and attributes of the Supreme Being. The result was, that the Idea of God thus identified with this hypothetical *Nature* becomes itself but an *Hypothesis*, or at best but a precarious inference from incommensurate premises and on disputable Principles: while in other passages, God is confounded with (and everywhere, in Aristotle's *genuine* works, *included in*) the Universe: which most grievous error it is the great and characteristic Merit of Plato to have avoided and denounced.

Aids to Reflection.

103. NATURAL AND SUPERNATURAL

Whatever is comprized in the Chain and Mechanism of Cause and Effect, of course *necessitated*, and having its necessity in some other thing, antecedent or concurrent—this is said to be *Natural;* and the Aggregate and System of all such things is *Nature.* It is, therefore, a contradiction in terms to include in this the Freewill, of which the verbal definition is—that which *originates* an act or state of Being. In this sense therefore, which is the sense of St. Paul, and indeed of the New Testament throughout, Spiritual and Supernatural are synonymous. . . .

I have already given one definition of Nature. Another, and differing from the former in words only, is this: Whatever is representable in the forms of Time and Space, is Nature. But whatever is comprehended in Time and Space, is included in the Mechanism of Cause and Effect. And conversely, whatever, by whatever means, has its principle in itself, so far as to *originate* its actions, cannot be contemplated in any of the forms of Space and Time—it must, therefore, be considered as *Spirit* or *Spiritual* by a mind in that stage of its Development which is here supposed, and which we have agreed to understand under the name of Morality, or the Moral State: for in this stage we are concerned only with the forming of *negative* conceptions, *negative* convictions; and by *spiritual* I do not pretend to determine *what* the Will *is*, but what it is *not*—namely, that it is not Nature. And as no man who admits a Will at all, (for we may safely presume, that no man ⟨not⟩[1] meaning to speak figuratively, would call the shifting Current of a stream the WILL of the River), will suppose it *below* Nature, we may safely add, that it is super-natural; and this without the least pretence to any positive Notion or Insight.

Aids to Reflection.

104. 'SUPERNATURAL' MUST BE 'SUPERSENSUAL'

The Pretensions to the Supernatural, pilloried by Butler, sent to Bedlam by Swift, and (on their re-appearance in public) *gibbetted* by Warburton, and *anatomized* by Bishop Lavington, one and all have *this* for their essential character, that the Spirit is made the immediate Object of Sense or Sensation. Whether the Spiritual Presence and Agency are supposed cognizable by an indescribable Feeling or in unimaginable Vision by some specific visual energy; whether seen, or heard, or touched, smelt, and tasted—for in those vast Store-houses of fanatical assertion, the volumes of Ecclesiastical History and religious Auto-biography, Instances are not wanting even of the three latter extravagancies . . . the assumption of a something essentially supersensual that is nevertheless the object of Sense, i.e. *not* supersensual.

Aids to Reflection.

[1] Coleridge's manuscript correction.

105. BERKELEY: SPINOZA

Berkeley can only be confuted, or answered, by one sentence. So it is with Spinoza. His premiss granted, the deduction is a chain of adamant.

Table Talk.

106. SPINOZA

Spinoza, at the very end of his life, seems to have gained a glimpse of the truth. In the last letter published in his works, it appears that he began to suspect his premiss. His *unica substantia* is, in fact, a mere notion,—a *subject* of the mind, and no *object* at all.

Table Talk.

107. GERMAN PHILOSOPHY. A NOTE ON HEINROTH'S
ANTHROPOLOGIE

Coleridge objected to 'the tone' of Heinroth's writing on the relation of man to Nature:

It is quite characteristic of that mischmasch of Spinozism, Evangelicalism, and abstract Dynamics generalized from the recent experiments of Electro-magnetic chemistry, which make up the newest German Eclecticism, and pietistic Philosophy. Heinroth is a Philosopher, and must not talk altogether like a common Christian: or rather, I think his Conscience twits him, and so it is *Geist* that works true miracles, and Geist is *gegenüber* Nature, as the positive Pole. . . .

[Then on the front fly-leaf he continues]:
    All that staid and sober Dignity of logical Arrangement, which Wolf had introduced, all that austere beauty of Method, which Kant added, seem to have deserted the present German Philosophers—who are sinking back rapidly into Miscellany,

popular Opinionism, at once superficial and arbitrary; and in short, into the style of oratorical Lectures to [sentimental *crossed out*] blue Ladies and grown up Gentlemen, who have not time for reading. This degeneracy, is, I grieve to say, too apparent in this work on *anthropology*, which might more fitly have been entitled—Sketches of all manner of things about men, women and children, Greeks and Romans, &c. and all of the New Testament with tag ends of sentimental Sermons!

Self-conceit that christens itself *Selb-ständigkeit*, and the Vanity that will be an original Thinker and a Headmaster, and tries to establish its claim by criticism, *i.e.* picking holes in the coat of the Philosopher last in fashion, and lastly that Professorial *Auditorensucht*—these are the Factors to which the exhausted, effort-shunning yet excitement-craving state of men's minds, the vast increase in the number of drest people from Shop, Factory and Counting House, who must know something *about* everything; and the multiscientous Reviewing spirit of Literature generally, are the Co-efficients. The Effects, Detraction—mixtymusty. Shall the cold meats of Sunday, Mon. Tues. Wed. Thurs. Friday, warmed up in the Saturday Squab-pie offer new terms and new schematisms? Add the petty pietistic cant of the Schleiermacher School and you have the present state of philosophizing in Germany! [*last line at bottom of page rubbed out*].

MS.

108. SENSORY, CONCEPTUAL, AND IMMEDIATE KNOWLEDGE

Distinct *notions* do not suppose different things. When I make a threefold distinction in human nature, I am fully aware that it is a distinction, not a division, and that in every act of mind the *man* unites the properties of sense, understanding, and reason. Nevertheless it is of great practical importance, that these distinctions should be made and understood, the ignorance or perversion of them being alike injurious; as the first French constitution has most lamentably proved. It was the fashion in the profligate times of Charles II. to laugh at the Presbyterians, for distinguishing between the person and the king; while in fact they were ridiculing the most venerable maxims of English law;—(the king never dies—the king can do no wrong, &c.)—and subverting the principles of genuine *loyalty*, in order to prepare the minds of the people for despotism.

Under the term 'SENSE', I comprise whatever is passive in our being, without any reference to the question of materialism or immaterialism; all that man is in common with animals, *in kind* at least—his sensations, and impressions, whether of his outward senses, or the inner sense of imagination. This, in the language of the schools, was called the *vis receptiva*, or *recipient* property of the soul, from the original constitution of which we perceive and imagine all things under the forms of space and time. By the 'UNDERSTANDING', I mean the faculty of thinking and forming *judgments* on the notices furnished by the sense, according to certain rules existing in itself, which rules constitute its distinct nature. By the pure REASON, I mean the power by which we become possessed of principle, (the eternal verities of Plato and Descartes) and of ideas, (N.B. not images) as the ideas of a point, a line, a circle, in mathematics; and of justice, holiness, free-will, &c. in morals. Hence in works of pure science the definitions of necessity precede the reasoning, in other works they more aptly form the conclusion.

Friend.

109. THE UNITY OF HUMAN POWERS

I have elsewhere in the present Work, though more at large in the 'Elements of Discourse' which, God permitting, will follow it, explained the difference between the Understanding and the Reason, by Reason meaning exclusively the speculative or scientific Power so called, the *Nous* or *Mens* of the Ancients.

And wider still is the distinction between the Understanding and the Spiritual Mind. But no Gift of God does or can contradict any other Gift, except by misuse or misdirection. Most readily therefore do I admit, that there can be no contrariety between Revelation and the Understanding; unless you call the fact, that the Skin, though sensible of the warmth of the Sun, can convey no notion of its figure, or its joyous light, or of the colours it impresses on the clouds, a contrariety between the Skin and the Eye; or infer that the cutaneous and the optic nerves *contradict* each other.

Aids to Reflection.

IIO. CONSCIENCE—FREEDOM TO WILL AND THINK

I shall hereafter endeavour to prove, how distinct and different the sensation of positiveness is from the sense of certainty;— the turbulent heat of temporary fermentation from the mild warmth of essential life. Suffice it for the present to affirm, to declare it at least, as my own creed, that whatever humbles the heart, and forces the mind inward, whether it be sickness, or grief, or remorse, or the deep yearnings of love, (and there have been children of affliction for whom all these have met and made up one complex suffering,) in proportion as it acquaints us with the thing we are, renders us docile to the concurrent testimony of our fellow men in all ages and in all nations. From Pascal in his closet resting the arm, which supports his thoughtful brow, on a pile of demonstrations, to the poor pensive Indian that seeks the missionary in the American wilderness, the humiliated self-examinant feels that there is evil in our nature as well as good;—an evil and a good, for a just analogy to which he questions all other natures in vain. It is still the great definition of humanity, that we have a conscience, which no mechanic compost, no chemical combination of mere appetence, memory and understanding, can solve; which is indeed an element of our being;—a conscience, unrelenting yet not absolute; which we may stupify but cannot delude; which we may suspend but cannot annihilate; although we may perhaps find a treacherous counterfeit in the very quiet which we derive from its slumber, or its entrancement.

Of so mysterious a phaenomenon we might expect a cause as mysterious. Accordingly, we find this (cause be it, or condition, or necessary accompaniment) involved and implied in the fact, which it alone can explain. For if our permanent consciousness did not reveal to us our free-agency, we should yet be obliged to deduce it, as a necesssary inference, from the fact of our conscience; or rejecting both the one and the other, as mere illusions of internal feelings, forfeit all power of thinking consistently with our actions, or acting consistently with our thought, for any single hour during our whole lives.

Friend.

III. RELIGION THE AIM, SCIENCE THE METHOD OF PHILOSOPHY

Religion therefore is the ultimate aim of philosophy, in consequence of which philosophy itself becomes the supplement of the sciences, both as the convergence of all to the common end, namely wisdom; and as supplying the copula, which, modified in each in the comprehension of its parts in one whole, is in its principles common to all, as integral parts of one system. And this is METHOD, itself a distinct science, the immediate offspring of philosophy, and the link or *mordant* by which philosophy becomes scientific and the sciences philosophical.

Friend.

112. AGAINST CLOUD-CUCKOO-LAND

The expediency even in a moral sense of not carrying speculation above a certain height uninterruptedly; but there to descend to the practical uses of which it might be capable—

like the Indian Fig, which still at a given height declines its branches to earth and takes root anew, forms a new principle.

MS.

113. NOTES ON KANT'S 'VERMISCHTE SCHRIFTEN'

Kant overlooked one fatal difference between the Mathemat: and the Metaphysician, viz. the actual existence of a Mathematical Public, and the non-existence of a Metaphysical—or rather the intrusive existence of an every-body Court of Judicature, the psilosophical Public. I. p. xxxvi.

On the *Allgemeine Naturgeschichte und Theorie des Himmels,* 1755. *Kant: Denn man siehet ihn die Richtung eines Grössten Cirkels . . . einnehmen.* I. p. 331. [One sees it (the Milky Way) follow the line of a huge circle.]

Coleridge comments: My eyes are perhaps different from those of scientific observers—I can only see a sort of Ribbon with ragged edges and of unequal breadth, stretching in the form of an Arch, and ending in a divarication. And as to its extension over the whole cope of Heaven from Horizon to Horizon (if this be implied in the words, *den ganzen Himmel einnehmen,—* all I can say is that I never saw it. S.T.C.

[*And again on the first blank leaf at the end of the volume:*]

Confessio Ignorantiae

p. 331. I am sadly puzzled with this and other descriptions of the Milky Way. I am almost driven to suspect that my eyes are different from other people's—for I have gazed at it a thousand times, but could never see anything but a sort of Hoop that had *sprung* from the nails, that had joined its two ends—or a Ribbon of unequal width and with ragged edges, splitting or divaricating at one end into two unequal Legs or Branches—and as to its extending over the whole Cope of Heaven from one point of the Horizon to the opposite—if this be, as I suppose, the meaning of 'den ganzen Himmel einnehmen'—all I can say, is that *I* never saw it: and I am sure it has not been from want of trying to do so. So again respecting the theory or hypothesis, that the Milky Way forms a system of Suns, each with its dependencies, on the same plane, in the shape of a Platter; and that our Solar System is somewhere near (either on or within) the Rim. How I have *longed* to have that explained to me on the principles of Perspective! I can readily understand how by disappearance of the Interspaces the distant Fixed Stars would be compressed into a ribbon or hoop; but that Gap at one end, where the Strip splits into two straddling thighs—this I cannot account for on the said hypothesis. S. T. Coleridge.

Nay, worse and worse—for there is no end to my stupidity in these matters—it seems to me that if I suppose a city or a vast Cluster of Houses built concircularly on a perfectly level Plain, and myself on the pavement in one of the Circles, the Houses nearest my eye would shut out the rest. Imagine these to be Suns.

★ ★ ★ ★ ★ ★

A B C D E F

How is the light from F to reach me placed near the A? That this is mere stupidity I am well convinced: for it was with no mock humility that I superscribed this, *Confessio Ignorantiae*. Indeed, I now see, where my Blunder lies.

With somewhat greater confidence I dare acknowledge, that this representation of the Starry Universe fails to impress my mind with that super-super[l]ative Sublimity, which Kant (p. 343, and 44) and many other great Men consider it so calculated to inspire. To me it appears an endless repetition of the same Image: nor can I conceive, how the Thought of a blind Mare going round and round in a Mill can derive Sublimity from the assurance, that there are a million of such Mills, each with a dozen or more blind Mares pacing round and round.

The admirable Variety yet Symmetry of a single Moss or Flower would both raise and gratify my imagination in a far higher degree. N.B. I well remember that (some 20 years ago) a valued and most valuable Old Friend, somewhat subject to sudden tho' brief explosions of Anger and Impatience, was nearly for shooting me out of a Coach-door for making this same remark—it was, he swore, such a d——n'd impudent Lie, which the very Dæmon of Paradox and Sophistry could alone have inspired.—No wonder that I had pretended to think that one Shakespeare outweighed a score Sir Isaac Newtons—indeed, he expected to hear me profess Atheism in my next flight of bravado! And yet, dear and honored P[oole]! so I *did* think, and even so I continue to do. S. T. C. 30. Novr 1820.

I. 353. Young as Kant was at the time he composed this work so demonstrative of a grand scientific productive or rather constructive Imagination, still it being posterior to the severely logical critique on the Cartesian and Leibnitzian Controversy, I cannot but be surprized, that he should not have detected the contradiction between his Problem, according to which he engages to construct the system of the material universe out of matter indued merely with the two essential powers, Attraction and Repulsion—and this *unendliche Verschiedenheit* of the primary particles. For not to say, that there is somewhat of trick in the words, *only* Attraction and Repulsion, when yet he intended to bargain for aboriginal difference of *degrees*—by which in fact he includes all possible Powers that can be manifested in the Relations of Space—for what can they be but degrees of retaining, producing and preventing nearness? Yet how is this consistent with primary Atoms? How can we think of comparative Density BUT as paucity of Interspaces in a composite Body?

I. 374. I am really puzzled. In one page K. tells me of endless differences of Density and from this derives his first centers—

and in the next page assumes *all* the matter of *all* the Planets rarified to 30 million times thinner than the Air of our Atmosphere!'

II. *On a blank leaf at the front of Volume II.*

It is an interesting fact in philosophical History i.e. the History of Speculative Philosophy, that the 'De Mundi sensib. et intell. Form et Prin.' that Masterwork of profundity and precision, that model of steady investigation, clear Conception and (as the Cambridge Mathematicians say) *elegant* Demonstration, was published 15 years before the *Critique der reinen Vernunft*— and produced no sensible effect on the philosophic Public. The former work contains all the main principles of the Latter, and often more perspicuously expressed—yet all remained silent. The *Critique der r. V.* appeared—and the Universities of Germany exploded! What was the cause of this difference? *Is it,* that the same Thoughts appeared less strange, less paradoxical, in Latin than in the vernacular Tongue? Or that the ordinary proofs of the higher psychology are exposed more openly and expressly in the *Crit. d. r. V.* than in the former work? Or lastly, that one's mother tongue however philosophized and technical still produces on us a liveliness of impression which a dead Language cannot produce? However this be, the former work should always be studied and mastered previously to the study of the *Critique d. r. V.* and the works that followed it. The student will find it a better auxiliary than 50 Vol. of Comments, from Reinhold, Schmidt, Schulz, Beck, Tieftrunk &c. &c. &c.

II. 344. On the *Träume eines Geistersehers*, 1766.

> *Kant: . . . Enthält das Herz des Menschen nicht unmittelbare sittliche Vorschriften, und muss man um ihn allhier seiner Bestimmung gemäss zu bewegen, durchaus die Maschinen an eine andere Welt ansetzen?* [Does the heart of man contain no direct moral prescripts? Must his moral nature derive its motive power from another world?]

Coleridge comments:

Let the heart answer in silence to these Questions—a cultivated Heart, to which Vice in its ordinary shape is hateful on
its own account. Will it not say—True! What I do, I would
fain do well. It is not any Hope of future Reward that impels
me, nor any Fear of future Punishment which keeps me in the
Road—but the thought, that all I can do is but a dream, and
that not myself only but that all men and all things are but
Dreams, that nothing is permanent—which makes the mortality of man a stupefying thought to me. I cannot conceive a
supreme moral Intelligence unless I believe in my own immortality—for I must believe in a whole system of apparent
means to an end, which end had no existence—my Conscience,
my progressive faculties, &c. But give up this and Virtue wants
all reason. Away with Stoic Hypocrisy! I know that in order
to the idea of Virtue we must suppose the pure good will
or reverence for the Law as excellent in itself—but this very
excellence supposes consequences, tho' not selfish ones. Let my
maxim be capable of becoming the Law of all intelligent
Being—well! but this supposes an *end* possessible by intelligent
Beings. For if the Law be barren of all consequences, what is it
but words? To obey the Law for its own sake is really a mere
sophism in any other sense: you might as well put abracadabra
in its place. I can readily conceive that I have it in my nature
to die a martyr, knowing that annihilation followed Death, if it
were ever possible to believe that all other human Beings were
immortal and to be benefit[t]ed by it; but any benefit that
could affect only a set of transitory Animals, what I could not
deem myself worthy of any exertion in my behalf, how can I
deem others of the same lot? Boldly should I say—O nature! I
would rather not have been—let that which is to come so soon,
come now—for what is all the intermediate space, but sense of
utter Worthlessness? Far, far below animals—for they enjoy a
generic immortality having no individuation. But man is truly

and solely an immortal series of conscious Mortalities, and inherent Disappointments.

II. 426 *f.n.* On the *Beobachtungen über das Gefühl des Schönen und Erhabenen*, 1764.

Kant: *Der Fanaticism muss von Enthusiasmus jederzeit unterschieden werden.* [Fanaticism must be distinguished at all times from enthusiasm. He goes on to say that fanaticism believes it participates in some supernatural power, whereas enthusiasm remains on a human level.]

Coleridge comments:

I dissent from Kant in this, and think that Fanaticism is only a species of Superstition, distinguished by its passion for proselytism—it is born and lives only in a crowd of Sympathists. And what if one gives a false character to an Image, the other to a feeling? This is enough to make a species, not a genus.

114. A HARE IN EVERY NETTLE

There is no way of arriving at any sciential End but by finding it at every step. The End is in the Means: or the Adequacy of each Mean is already its End. Southey once said to me: You are nosing every nettle along the Hedge, while the Greyhound (meaning himself, I presume) wants only to get sight of the Hare, and Flash—strait as a line! he has it in his mouth!—Even so, I replied, might a Cannibal say to an Anatomist, whom he had watched dissecting a body. But the fact is—I do not care two pence for the *Hare*; but I value most highly the excellencies of scent, patience, discrimination, free Activity; and find a Hare in every Nettle I make myself acquainted with. I follow the Chamois-Hunters, and seem to set out with the same Object. But I am no Hunter of *that* Chamois Goat; but avail myself of the Chace in order to [pursue] a nobler purpose—that of making a road across the Mountain in which Common Sense may hereafter pass backward and forward, without desperate Leaps or Balloons that soar indeed but do not improve the chance of getting onward.

MS.

V

NOT A SCALPING KNIFE

'O gentle critic! be advised. Do not trust too much to your professional dexterity in the use of the scalping knife, and tomahawk. Weapons of diviner mould are wielded by your adversary: and you are meeting him here on his own peculiar ground, the ground of Idea, of Thought, and of inspiration.'

On Method

LITERARY CRITICISM

Coleridge's *Biographia Literaria* has been called the best piece of literary criticism in English and the most annoying book in any language. In the *Shakespearean Criticism* and the *Miscellaneous Criticism*, edited by T. M. Raysor, is to be found most of the rest of the literary criticism. The *Anima Poetae*, edited by E. H. Coleridge, is a choice small selection of literary pieces from the notebooks. I reprint here a few items in order to give them more accurately, particularly item 122 (see pp. 155-6) on which so much ink has been needlessly spilt.

Coleridge has received very high praise as a critic but never a full study of his principles and methods of criticism. Yet his theory of the imagination, and his application of it in discussing the dynamic unity of literary works, particularly Shakespeare's plays, his dismissal of the whole paraphernalia of genres and the rules for them, his insistence on the necessity of seeing a work of imagination not by some external standard but in relation to the writer's purposes, and his view of poetry as excluding nothing and involving the harmonious reconciliation of everything, transformed English criticism and helped to transform English literature. Even some anti-romantic poets and critics of our time have been more influenced by him, directly or indirectly, than they appear to recognize.

The best thing about his criticism is that it is not necessary to agree with it in order to be stimulated by it and to find it intelligent.

For a clarifying brief study of Coleridge as critic there is nothing more central than Professor Basil Willey's Warton Lecture on 'Coleridge on Imagination and Fancy' (*Proceedings of the British Academy*, 1946). Mr. Herbert Read's recently published lecture, *Coleridge as Critic*, Faber and Faber, 1949, sketches in some of the philosophical background of Coleridge's criticism, and assigns him a place in the history of existentialism.

V

NOT A SCALPING KNIFE

---

115. SCIENCE AND POETRY

SCIENCE brings about strange revolutions. Already, I suspect, that Thunder and Lightning in Poetry are in danger of becoming School-boyisms, like Phoebus and the Chariot of the Sun. The once tremendous celestial super-human force of Thunder, is audible not beyond 20 miles: the Evening Gun of George Town in Demerara is often heard at lake Batave on the west coast of Essequibo, a distance of about 40 miles, while the explosions during the volcanic eruption of Mount Soufrière were heard at the distance of from 6 to 700 miles.

Yet these changes as they ought not, so they do not, lessen our sense of the Sublime in the Works of the great Poets who wrote under another scheme of Beliefs and Associations—the Psalms for instance. But this supplies no ground of sanction for the repetition of the same—by poets of our times. They would ignorantly *copy* the sentences, when they ought to have imitated the *Poet*, and consequently, have composed, as *he* composed, in the light and with assurance of the Sympathy, of the Age, of which he was the Blossom. The vehement Belief of the Devil and his numberless Army of Rebel Angels was Heroism in Luther—a pitiful anility in Mr. Wilberforce.

MS.

116. EMOTION RECOLLECTED

Ideas may become as vivid and distinct, and the feelings accompanying them as vivid, as original impressions. And this may finally make a man independent of his Senses. One use of poetry.

MS.

117. SOLOMON'S SONG—ALLEGORY

Solomon's Song. There was a time when I thought scorn of this charming Idyll, this prototype of whatever is most beautiful and affecting in Theocritus ... and (as far as the few precious fragments allow the conjecture) in Sappho, having a *spiritual* Sense—in being more than an epithalamium on Solomon's Marriage with a Princess of Egypt. But the more extensive my acquaintance has become with the Persian Poets—and the more attentively I have studied verse by verse the Song itself, and sought either to discover a plan and purpose in the *whole*, or to reduce it to a series of distinct Eclogues or Idylls—the more disposed I find myself to adopt the contrary judgement. The analogous passages in several of the Prophets, especially Isaiah Ch. V, and the Fact, that the Jewish Church before the Birth of Christ interpreted it spiritually, and that Rabbinical Comments which if not themselves of so high antiquity are evidently transcripts or echoes of Teachers before or contemporary with Christ, are in existence and (for we cannot suppose them to have borrowed a hated faith from the hated Christians) demonstrate what indeed Paul's writings seem to me already to prove, that a Spiritual Conception of the Messiah, and of his Communion with the Soul, was entertained by some at least of the Doctors between the Return from the Captivity and the Birth of our Lord. In fact, the lovely Allegory of Cupid and Psyche shews that the Idea was spread among the Gentiles.

MS.

118. BIBLICAL ALLEGORY

It is quite wonderful that Luther who could see so plainly that
Judith was an Allegoric Poem should have been blind to the
Book of Jonas being an Apologue, in which Jonas means the
Israelitesh nation!

MS.

119. POETRY A FREE AND VITAL POWER

To perceive and feel the Beautiful, the Pathetic, and the Sublime in Nature, in Thought, or in Action—this combined with
the power of conveying such Perceptions and Feelings to the
minds and hearts of others under the most pleasurable Forms of
Eye and Ear—this is poetic Genius. A gift of Heaven confined
to no one Race or Period, a ray which penetrates to the Savage
[man *crossed out*] in the [distant recesses of unplanted Forests
crossed out] depth of Wildernesses, and throws a nobler Light, a
glory beyond its own, on the splendor of the Palaces. [If then
there exists no monopoly of poetry as little can there exist
crossed out.] If then Poetry itself be a free and vital power which
never wholly deserts any age or Nation unless it have previously
deserted itself, [and abandoned its own best privilege, that of
fighting up against the hourly influences of Custom and the
pressure of anxieties without Love *crossed out*] that Criticism,
which would bind it down to any one Model, and bid it grow
in a mould is a mere Despotism of False Taste, [a usurpation of
empty [Forms *crossed out*] Rules over Life and Substance] and
would reduce all modern Genius to a state which (if it were not
too ludicrous) might be justly compared to that of the Soldier
Crabs on the Tropical Islands, which wander naked and imperfect till they creep into the cast off Shells of a nobler Race.

To counteract this Disease of long-civilized Societies, and to
establish not only the identity of the Essence under the greatest

variety of Forms, but the congruity and even the necessity of
that variety, is the common end and aim of the present Course.

. . . Beauty, Majesty, Grace and Perspicuity, and before the
Harmony we have described came to its perfection, Vehemence
and Impetuosity—these are the constituents of the Greek Drama
—and the great Rule was the separation, or the removal, of the
Heterogeneous—even as the Spirit of the Romantic Poetry, is
modification, or the blending of the Heterogeneous into an
Whole by the Unity of the Effect. Such were the deeper and
essential contra-distinctions—and to these we must add the more
accidental circumstances, from the origin of the Drama, and the
size, arrangement, and object of the Theatres.

MS.

120. A WORK PROPOSED POSSIBLY AS EARLY AS
1796

Memoranda for a History of English Poetry, biographical, bibli-
ographical, critical and philosophical, in distinct Essays—
 1. English Romances—compared with the Latin Hexameter
Romance on Attila—with the German metrical Romances &c.
 2. Chaucer—illustrated by the Minnesänger, and as in all that
follow an endeavour to ascertain, first, the degree and sort of
the merit of the *Poems* comprized in his Works, and secondly,
what and how much of this belonged strictly *et sibi proprium* to
Chaucer himself, what must be given to his Contemporaries,
and Predecessors. This will be abundantly *more* interesting in
Shakespere; yet interesting and necessary to a philosophical
Critic in all.
 3. Spenser—with connecting Introductions.
 4. English Ballads, illustrated by the Translations of the Volks-
lieder of all countries.—Ossian—Welsh Poets—. Series of true
heroic Ballads from Ossian.

5. Shakespere!!!] Almighty Father! if thou grant me Life, O
6. Milton!!! ∫ grant me Health and Perseverance!

7. Dryden and the History of the witty Logicians, *Butler* (ought he not to have a distinct tho' short Essay?)—B. Johnson, Donne, Cowley —— Pope.—

8. Modern Poetry . . . with introductory (or annexes?) Characters of Cowper, Burns, Thomson, Collins, Akenside, and any real poet, *quod real* poet, and exclusively confined to their own. Faults and Excellencies.—To conclude with a philosophical Analysis of *Poetry*, *nempe ens=bonum*, and the fountains of its pleasures in the Nature of Man: and of the pain and disgust with which it may affect men in a vitiated state of Thought and Feeling; tho' this will have been probably anticipated in the former Essay, Modern Poetry, i.e. Poetry=Not-poetry, *ut lucus a non lucendo*, and *mons a non movendo*, and its badness i.e. impermanence demonstrated, and the sources detected of the pain known to the wise and of the pleasure to the pleasures to the corrupted—illustrated by a History of bad Poetry in all ages of our Literature.——

Milton carefully compared and contrasted with Jerome [*sic*] Taylor—and on occasion perhaps of his Controversy with Hall introduce a philosophical Abstract of the History of English Prose—if only to cut Dr. J. '*to the Liver*'.[1]

MS.

121. FOR 'A NOBLER, FREER AND MORE POWERFUL VERSIFICATION'

The heroic verse of the Italians has been regarded by all Grammarians and Lexicographers hitherto as Paniambic according to its Rule; the deviations from which are to be considered as poetic Licenses, or as Discords introduced into Harmony for

---

[1] I am tempted to read 'Lives', the final letter not being quite beyond doubt; perhaps it is intentionally ambiguous.

Variety or particular Effect. In technical Language we are to describe it as Pan-iambic pentameter hyperacetalectic, in other words (and for those who have no passion for polysyllables or Greek compounds) we are, it seems, to deem the heroic Verse of Dante and Ariosto, as composed of five Iambics, the fifth having a superabundant unaccented Syllable. If this statement be indeed the true one, the loftiest and most learned Italians are licentious beyond all modern precedent, and even among the ancients, who can furnish no legitimate Authority to us, who do not, as they did, *weigh* our [metres *crossed out*] verses by any conscious attention to *Quantity*, who *count* them by the Beat, Pulse, or Accent—yet even among the ancients we shall scarcely find any instance of equal licentiousness, except in the loose Iambics of Latin Comedy, the metre [of] which forms the connecting Link between Verse and the Prose of lively conversation, both the pleasure of which, and the cause of the pleasure, were to be *felt*, not noticed.

It is indeed curious to observe the Prosody invented by the Grammar-writers in order to reduce the Italian Verses to the Possibility of Iambic movement, a Prosody so perfectly arbitrary that whoever read a page of Ariosto according to it would be almost as unintelligible to an Italian, as if he had been reading Chinese. 'Suo', for instance, and 'pria', except at the end of a Line, form but one syllable, and tho' it is admitted on all sides, that in fact the former always *is* two Syllables, and the latter cannot ever be pronounced otherwise than as two. True! it is answered—But such Dissyllables count only as one—a reply, which appears to me to mean neither more or less than this: It is not so, but according to the assertion of Grammarians, it ought to be so. In like manner, the whole doctrine of Elisions, except in the few instances in the Italian in which they actually occur and which in their Poetry are always noted in accurate Printing by the omission of the vowel and by an Apostrophe, is utterly hollow, and borrowed from the Ancient Versification by Quantity, by men of whom it is [not *crossed out and* no more unkind than unjust *substituted*] to say [more unkind than unjust to say?] that they had great and various Learning, but that their Skulls were Magazines, not Manufactures, much less fields or gardens; Magazines sufficiently under the power of their Memory, and wholly undisturbed by any action of philosophic Thought. What indeed can be more incongruous than to admit that in one instance a Vowel shall not be pronounced at all, that in another a Vowel shall be distinctly pronounced, and yet that the latter is to count for as complete a nothing as the actually non-existent former? If this System could be proved false, not only by its inherent Absurdity but by the substitution of a rational System, I deem it more than probable that a nobler, a freer and more powerful Versification (the great menstruum and vehicle of poetic thought and feeling) would gradually [obtain in *crossed out*] win its way in Europe; and then we should feel how much [*fragment incomplete*].

[*f. 52 may or may not be a continuation of f. 51.*] How small effect faults have where there are great Beauties—but then of Beauties there are two senses. 1. mere scattered passages which being selected all is a *Caput Mortuum*—this can render a book valuable to literary men and to the curious in collection, and when a selection has been made and published, not even to them. [2]. But when the Beauties are diffused all over, when the faults as in Milton are only omittable passages—or at best a small part of the Plan—nay, even when they are woven thro' warp and woof, if the Beauties are the same, and in a greater degree—perhaps if even in the same—yet the Book becomes a darling, and we scarcely think of the faults, except as pleasing us less, rather than displeasing.

MS.

122. METAPHYSICAL POETRY

The elder Languages fitter for Poetry because they expressed only prominent ideas with clearness, others but darkly——

Therefore the French wholly unfit for Poetry; because [all] is *clear* in their Language, i.e. Feelings created by obscure ideas associate themselves with the one *clear* idea. When no criticism is pretended to, and the Mind in its simplicity gives itself up to a Poem as to a work of nature, Poetry gives most pleasure when only generally and not perfectly understood. It was so by me with Gray's Bard, and Collins' odes. The Bard once intoxicated me, and now I read it without pleasure. From this cause it is that what *I* call metaphysical Poetry gives me so much delight.

MS.

123. THE IMPROVEMENT IN TASTE SINCE JOHNSON'S DAY

1. Concerning the comparative merit of the present generation (which we would extend to the last 40 or 50 years) and of the preceding period from the Revolution, in point of Genius or productive power, opinions may differ. But we think, that in point of *Taste* in the Fine Arts, and in first principles of Criticism, which can indeed neither create a Taste or supply the want of it but yet may conduce effectively to its cultivation and are perhaps indispensable in securing it from the aberrations of caprice and fashion, there can be little doubt that we have the advantage over our Forefathers. There are, to be sure, Heretics to be met with who would reverse the position in Music, and while in Haydn, Mozart, Cimarosa, and Beethoven, as the Magnates of a whole brilliant constellation, they acknowledge the spirit of Apollo, find in the multitude of musical Critics and dilettanti performers only the ears* and the taste of Midas.

* We fear that grounds for impeachment of Taste might be brought from the works of the great Artists themselves: *ex. gr.* the Rockets, Musquetry, Cavalry, wounded and dying Men that roar, thunder, hiss, crack, tramp, moan, whimper, and howl thro' the *Vittoria* of Beethoven. The address and skill required for the [management *crossed out*] execution of the Artillery

However, *exceptio probat regulam*, and in truth our present purpose would be answered, tho' the position of our superior Taste were Taste in the appreciation of Poetry or even to yet narrower limits, the *art* of Poetry, or the requisite perfections of a Poem. But in proof of this, it might be sufficient to recall the Judgements of Critics of highest name and authority, who had formed their taste in that School, on which the Wartons first adventured a timorous attack, the censure so neutralized by compliments and half-retractions, that it might remind one of a Wasp staggering out of a Honey Pot, with both wing and sting sheathed in the clammy sweetness.

What should we think of a Critic of the present day, who instituting a comparison between the Latin Poems of Milton and Cowley to the advantage of the latter, should gravely assert, that 'Cowley without *much* loss of purity or elegance accommodates the diction of Rome to his own conceptions'. Except the collections of the Italian Latinists of the 15th Century, it would not be easy to name any equal number of Poems by the same author that could be fairly preferred to those of Milton in classical purity on the one hand, or in weight of Thought and unborrowed imagery on the other; while for competitors in barbarism with Cowley's Latin Poem *De Plantis*, or even his *not quite so bad* Davideid Hexameters, we must go I fear to the *Deliciae Poetarum Germanorum* or other [similar *crossed out*] Warehouses of Seal-fat, Whale Blubber and the like Boreal Confectionaries selected by the delicate Gruter.

We may question too with little risk of offence whether even the aweful name of Dr. Johnson will be powerful enough ten years hence to rescue the writer from contempt who should seriously repeat, that without knowledge of the author 'no man could fancy that he read the Lycidas with pleasure'—that in its form it is easy, vulgar and disgusting; and in the whole poem

Notes was such as to call forth the express notice 'that at Vienna, *the great guns* were played by the most eminent *Maestri* di Capella!' Seriously what should we think?

neither nature nor art: or that the metre of the *Par[adise] Lost* is verse to the eye only; or that after half a century of forced thoughts and *rugged metre* some *advances* towards nature and harmony had been made by Waller and Denham; [and yet left to Dryden the honour of having first refined *crossed out*] yet not such as to interfere in any considerable degree with the claims of Dryden as the first who refined the language, improved the *sentiments* (!!) and tuned the numbers, of English Poetry; or lastly that the stanza of Prior in which two elegiac Quatrains are put atop a couplet ending with an Alexandrine, as compared with the Stanza of Spenser (that wonder-work of metrical Skill and Genius! that nearest approach to a perfect Whole, as bringing the greatest possible variety into compleat Unity by the never interrupted interdependence of the parts!—that 'immortal Verse', that 'winding bout

> *Of linked sweetness long drawn out*
> *Untwisting all the chains that tie*
> *The hidden soul of Harmony')*

—that these ten-line Paragraphs into which Prior has divided his ode, and which have about the same claims to be stanzas, as the King and three Fidlers to enter *solus*, should not indeed have been called an *imitation* of the Stanza of the Fairy Queen, but had however avoided its difficulties without losing any of its powers of pleasing!

The revived attention to our elder Poets, which Percy and Garrick had perhaps equal share in awakening, the revulsion against the French Taste which was so far successful as to confine the Usurper within the natural limits of the French Language; the re-establishment of the Romantic and Italian School in Germany and G. Britain by the genius of Wieland, Goethe, Tieck, Southey, Scott, and Byron among the poets, and the Lectures of Coleridge, Schlegel, Campbell and others among the Critics; these, at once aided and corrected by the increased ardor with which the study of ancient literature and especially the Greek

Poets and Dramatists, is pursued, esteemed and encouraged by the Gentry of the Country, and men of the highest rank and office, have given a spread and a fashion to predilections of higher hope and (what is still better) to principles of Preference at once more general and more just.

Still however this Improvement has hitherto, it must be confessed, revealed itself chiefly in the popularity acquired by those works, in which the effort to [extend and vary the measures *crossed out*] introduce into poetry a freer and more various scheme of Diction and Metre: as far as our own language is concerned. And with regard to the measures of the Ancients, we dare not disguise from ourselves, that the improvement is to be inferred from the tendency, as a datum of Hope rather than from any actual progress, if we may be allowed a play of words, rather by the succession than the success of the attempts, to bring the rhythm and metre of the Greek Lyrics into light and order. In the simpler forms of metre, that occur in the dramatic Dialogue, we owe to Porson all that could be achieved by an acute and exact Scholar gifted with a singular fineness of tact thoroughly at home with the [Greek *crossed out*] Attic Drama, and more widely and familiarly acquainted with the Lexicographers and Grammarians than any Philologist that could be said to come near him Φιλόκαλος ὡς or ἐν φιλοκαλίᾳ, *et cui flos nullus apud Ilissi ripas videlebatur,* [*sic*] or something of that sort. . . .

MS.

124. VIRGIL

De Boyer quotes Virgil's panegyric on Marcellus from the *Aeneid*, Book VI, the 23 lines beginning:

> Quis pater, ille virum qui sic comitatur euntem?
> Filius, anne aliquis magna de stirpe nepotum?
> Quis strepitus circa comitum! quantum instar in ipso est?
> Sed nox atra caput tristi circumvolat umbra.

Tum pater Anchises lachrimis ingressus obortis.
O nate, ingentem luctum ne quaere tuorum.
Ostendent terris hunc tantum fata, neque ultra
Esse sinent. Nimium vobis Romana propago
Visa potens, superi, propria haec si dona fuissent.
Quantos ille virum magnam Mavortis ad urbem
Campus aget gemitus? Vel quae, Tyberine, videbis
Funera, cum tumulum praeterlabere recentem!
Nec puer Iliaca quisquam de gente Latinos
In tantum spe tollet avos: nec Romula quondam
Ullo se tantum tellus jactabit alumno.
Heu pietas, heu prisca fides, invictaque bello
Dextera! non illi quisquam se impune tulisset
Obvius armato: seu cum pedes iret in postem,
Seu spumantis equi foderet calcaribus armos!
Heu miserande puer! si qua fata aspera rumpas,
Tu Marcellus eris, manibus date lilia plenis:
Purpureos spargam flores, animamque nepotis.
His saltem accumulem donis et fungar inani
Munere.

[Translation of J. Jackson, O.U.P., 1908.

Who is he my father, that thus attends the warrior's path? A son,
or one of the heroic strain of his children's children? How the retinue
about him murmurs praise! What majesty is in his port! Yet sable
Night hovers round his head with mournful shade. Then father
Anchises began, while his tears welled: 'O my son, seek not to know
the great agony of thy people! Him the fates shall but shew the
earth, nor suffer longer to be. Too great in thy sight, O Heaven, the
power of Rome's children, had this thy guerdon endured! What
moaning of men shall echo from the famed Field to Mavor's queenly
city! What obsequies, O Tiber, shalt thou see, when thou flowest by
his new-raised grave! No child of Ilian blood shall raise his Latin
ancestry so high in hope, nor ever again shall Romulus's land so
vaunt her in any that she fosters. Alas for piety, alas for old-world
faith, and the land unvanquished in war! None scatheless had met
his blade, whether on foot he marched against the foeman, or buried
the spur in the flank of his reeking steed! Ay me, thou child of tears,
if haply thou mayest burst the cruel barriers of fate, thou shalt be
Marcellus! Give me lilies from laden hands; let me scatter purple

blossoms, and shower these gifts—if no more—on the spirit of my child, till the barren service be so discharged.']

Coleridge comments: That the lines are beautiful, especially in the metre and composition, *singultus* quasi numerorum, *sobs* of Harmony,—this I see and feel. But that they are wonderful, super-excellent, &c &c, I deny—for what is there that might not have been said of any other hopeful young Roman who had died in his youth—what one distinct Image? What one deep feeling that goes to the human heart? I see not one.

MS.

125. CHAUCER

I take unceasing delight in Chaucer. His manly cheerfulness is especially delicious to me in my old age. How exquisitely tender he is, and yet how perfectly free from the least touch of sickly melancholy or morbid drooping! The sympathy of the poet with the subjects of his poetry is particularly remarkable in Shakespeare and Chaucer; but what the first effects by a strong act of imagination and mental metamorphosis, the last does without any effort, merely by the inborn kindly joyousness of his nature. How well we seem to know Chaucer! How absolutely nothing do we know of Shakespeare!

I cannot in the least allow any necessity for Chaucer's poetry, especially the Canterbury Tales, being considered obsolete. Let a few plain rules be given for sounding the final è of syllables, and for expressing the termination of such words as *ocëan*, and *natiön*, etc. as dissyllables,—or let the syllables to be sounded in such cases be marked by a competent metrist. This simple expedient would, with a very few trifling exceptions, where the errors are inveterate, enable any reader to feel the perfect smoothness and harmony of Chaucer's verse. As to understanding his language, if you read twenty pages with a good glossary, you surely can find no further difficulty, even as it is; but I should have no objection to see this done:—Strike out those words which are now obsolete, and I will venture to say that I will replace every one of them by words still in use out of Chaucer himself, or Gower his disciple. I don't want this myself: I rather like to see the significant terms which Chaucer unsuccessfully offered as candidates for admission into our language; but surely so very slight a change of the text may well be pardoned, even by black-letterati, for the purpose of restoring so great a poet to his ancient and most deserved popularity.

Table Talk.

126. THUCYDIDES AND TACITUS

The object of Thucydides was to show the ills resulting to Greece from the separation and conflict of the spirits or elements of democracy and oligarchy. The object of Tacitus was to demonstrate the desperate consequences of the loss of liberty on the minds and hearts of men.

Table Talk.

127. EPIC

I have already told you that in my opinion the destruction of Jerusalem is the only subject now left for an epic poem of the highest kind. Yet, with all its great capabilities, it has this one grand defect—that, whereas a poem, to be epic, must have a personal interest,—in the destruction of Jerusalem no genius or skill could possibly preserve the interest for the hero from being merged in the interest for the event. The fact is, the event itself is too sublime and overwhelming.

In my judgment, an epic poem must either be national or mundane. As to Arthur, you could not by any means make a poem on him national to Englishmen. What have *we* to do with him? Milton saw this, and with a judgment at least equal to his genius, took a mundane theme—one common to all mankind. His Adam and Eve are all men and women inclusively.

Pope satirizes Milton for making God the Father talk like a school divine. Pope was hardly the man to criticize Milton. The truth is, the judgment of Milton in the conduct of the celestial part of his story is very exquisite. Wherever God is represented as directly acting as Creator, without any exhibition of his own essence, Milton adopts the simplest and sternest language of the Scriptures. He ventures upon no poetic diction, no amplification, no pathos, no affection. It is truly the Voice of the Word of the Lord coming to, and acting on, the subject Chaos. But, as some personal interest was demanded for the purposes of poetry, Milton takes advantage of the dramatic representation of God's address to the Son, the Filial Alterity, and in *those addresses* slips in, as it were by stealth, language of affection, or thought, or sentiment. Indeed, although Milton was undoubtedly a high Arian in his mature life, he does in the necessity of poetry give a greater objectivity to the Father and the Son, than he would have justified in argument. He was very wise in adopting the strong anthropomorphism of the Hebrew Scriptures at once. Compare the Paradise Lost with Klopstock's *Messiah*, and you will learn to appreciate Milton's judgment and skill quite as much as his genius.

Table Talk.

128. A CHARACTER FOR A DRAMA

The character and conduct of Judas would be an insolvable Enigma, if we had only the three first Gospels. The immediate Disciples of Christ seem indeed to have regarded his act and his whole proceeding with a revulsive horror which made them unwilling to speak of him more than by the hasty statement of the Fact. Even St John does but dart a gleam of Light into the obscurity of the Incident. From him we may probably infer, that Judas had permitted himself to be tampered with by the Pharisaic Faction, possibly from a strange confusion of motives of which he himself could have given no clear account—*ex. gr.*

if he had not the power of rescuing himself, *then* the Pharisees were in the Right, and he was not sent by God—and his [miraculous *crossed out*] magical powers, according to the commonly received opinion, would not avail him after he had been once delivered into the hands of the lawful Authorities—but if he was, then this would only accelerate the open proof of his divine Power, and occasion him to display *the Sign*, which the Pharisees had before tempted him to give—i.e. the signal to a general insurrection against the Romans by the public declaration of his being King of the Jews. We are all too apt to forget the dark and fleshly state of all the Apostles during our Lord's sojourn with them. What were the expectations and imaginations of the Sons of Zebedee when they were quarrelling about the places, they should hold in the new Court—Which should be the Grand Vizier? Hence the character of Judas appears to be far more incomprehensible and strange than in a fair view of all the circumstances it ought to do. But when Judas discovered that our Lord knew what had been going on within him, and the action, with which he had been dallying—then the vindictive anger of a base man unexpectedly detected, and the despair of ever recovering his Lord's esteem and confidence—in short, a morbid chaos of bad and confused thoughts and impulses, a guilty state of somnambulism, supervened—or as St John says, Satan entered into him and he precipitated himself into Guilt as he afterward, as the sequel of the same frightful Dream flung himself headlong into Death. I object from principle to all fictions grounded on Scripture History—and more than all to any introduction of our Lord. Even the *Paradise Regained* offends my mind. Here what is not historic truth, is a presumptuous falsehood. But if I dared dramatize so aweful a part of the Gospel Narrative, I seem to feel that I could evolve the Judas into a perfectly intelligible character.

28 Septr 1829. Monday Night. I will not even in respect of an inward intention hastily determine on such an attempt. But

after writing the preceding page it did strike me, that it might be of use and for edification to compose a sacred Drama, for the purpose of elucidating the character of Judas, and without attributing to our Lord any act or even words not authenticated by the Gospels. One advantage would be, the presenting of a consistent whole by strict adherence to the narrative of John, and availing myself of the other Gospels so far only, as they were evidently consistent and of a piece with it. The first Scene might be a Dialogue between Judas and one of the Leading Pharisees. S. T. C.

MS.

129. SCOTT

'For one person who has remarked or praised a beautiful passage in Walter Scott's works, a hundred have said,—"How many volumes he has written!" So of Matthews: it is not "How admirable such and such parts are!" but "It is wonderful that one man should do *all this*!" '

Allsop.

130. REVIEWERS

Reviewers resemble often the English Jury and the Italian Conclave, that they [are] incapable of eating till they have condemned or crowned.

MS.

131. MILTON

In the Paradise Lost—indeed in every one of his poems—it is Milton himself whom you see; his Satan, his Adam, his Raphael, almost his Eve—are all John Milton; and it is a sense of this intense egotism that gives me the greatest pleasure in reading Milton's works. The egotism of such a man is a revelation of spirit.

Table Talk.

132. SHAKESPEARE AND MILTON

Shakespeare is the Spinozistic deity—an omnipresent creativeness. Milton is the deity of prescience; he stands *ab extra*, and drives a fiery chariot and four, making the horses feel the iron curb which holds them in. Shakespear's poetry is characterless; that is, it does not reflect the individual Shakespeare; but John Milton himself is in every line of the Paradise Lost. Shakespeare's rhymed verses are excessively condensed,—epigrams with the point every where; but in his blank dramatic verse he is diffused, with a linked sweetness long drawn out. No one can understand Shakespeare's superiority fully until he has ascertained, by comparison, all that which he possessed in common with several other great dramatists of his age, and has then calculated the surplus which is entirely Shakespeare's own. His rhythm is so perfect, that you may be almost sure that you do not understand the real force of a line, if it does not run well as you read it. The necessary mental pause after every hemistich or imperfect line is always equal to the time that would have been taken in reading the complete verse.

Table Talk.

133. POLONIUS AND HAMLET

A Maxim is a conclusion upon observation of matters of fact, and is merely retrospective: an Idea, or, if you like, a Principle, carries knowledge within itself, and is prospective. Polonius is a man of maxims. Whilst he is descanting on matters of past experience, as in that excellent speech to Laertes before he sets out on his travels, he is admirable; but when he comes to advise or project, he is a mere dotard. You see, Hamlet, as the man of ideas, despises him.

Table Talk.

134. OTHELLO

I have often told you that I do not think there is any jealousy, properly so called, in the character of Othello. There is no predisposition to suspicion, which I take to be an essential term in the definition of the word. Desdemona very truly told Emilia that he was not jealous, that is, of a jealous habit, and he says so as truly of himself. Iago's suggestions, you see, are quite new to him; they do not correspond with any thing of a like nature previously in his mind. If Desdemona had, in fact, been guilty, no one would have thought of calling Othello's conduct that of a jealous man. He could not act otherwise than he did with the lights he had; whereas jealousy can never be strictly right. See how utterly unlike Othello is to Leontes, in the Winter's Tale, or even to Leonatus, in Cymbeline! The jealousy of the first proceeds from an evident trifle, and something like hatred is mingled with it; and the conduct of Leonatus in accepting the wager, and exposing his wife to the trial, denotes a jealous temper already formed.

Table Talk.

135. HENRY IV. I: HAMLET

The difference between the products of a well-disciplined and those of an uncultivated understanding, in relation to what we will now venture to call the *Science of Method*, is often and admirably exhibited by our great dramatist. I scarcely need refer my readers to the Clown's evidence, in the first scene of the second act of *Measure for Measure*, or to the Nurse in *Romeo and Juliet*. But not to leave the position, without an instance to illustrate it, I will take the 'easy-yielding' Mrs. Quickly's relation of the circumstances of Sir John Falstaff's debt to her:—

FALSTAFF. What is the gross sum that I owe thee?

HOST. Marry, if thou wert an honest man, thyself and the

money too. Thou didst swear to me upon a parcel-gilt goblet, sitting in my Dolphin chamber, at the round table, by a sea-coal fire, upon Wednesday in Whitsun week, when the prince broke thy head for liking his father to a singing-man of Windsor; thou didst swear to me then, as I was washing thy wound, to marry me and make me my lady thy wife. Canst thou deny it? Did not goodwife Keech, the butcher's wife, come in then and call me gossip Quickly?—coming in to borrow a mess of vinegar; telling us she had a good dish of prawns; whereby thou didst desire to eat some; whereby I told thee they were ill for a green wound, etc. *Henry IV. 1st pt. Act ii. sc. 1.*

And this, be it observed, is so far from being carried beyond the bounds of a fair imitation, that 'the poor soul's' thoughts and sentences are more closely interlinked than the truth of nature would have required, but that the connections and sequence, which the habit of Method can alone give, have in this instance a substitute in the fusion of passion. For the absence of Method, which characterizes the uneducated, is occasioned by an habitual submission of the understanding to mere events and images as such, and independent of any power in the mind to classify or appropriate them. The general accompaniments of time and place are the only relations which persons of this class appear to regard in their statements. As this constitutes *their* leading feature, the contrary excellence, as distinguishing the well-educated man, must be referred to the contrary habit. Method, therefore, becomes natural to the mind which has been accustomed to contemplate not *things* only, or for their own sake alone, but likewise and chiefly the *relations* of things, either their relations to each other, or to the observer, or to the state and apprehension of the hearers. To enumerate and analyze these relations, with the conditions under which alone they are discoverable, is to teach the science of Method.

The enviable results of this science, when knowledge has been ripened into those habits which at once secure and evince its possession, can scarcely be exhibited more forcibly as well as more pleasingly, than by contrasting with the former extract from Shakespeare the narration given by Hamlet to Horatio of the occurrences during his proposed transportation to England, and the events that interrupted his voyage:—

HAMLET. Sir, in my heart there was a kind of fighting
That would not let me sleep: methought, I lay
Worse than the mutines in the bilboes. Rashly,
And praised be rashness for it—*Let us know,*
Our indiscretion sometimes serves us well,
When our deep plots do fail: and that should teach us,
There's a divinity that shapes our ends,
Rough-hew them how we will.
　　HOR. That is most certain.
　　HAM. Up from my cabin,
My sea-gown scarf'd about me, in the dark
Grop'd I to find out them; had my desire;
Finger'd their packet; and, in fine, withdrew
To my own room again; making so bold,
My fears forgetting manners, to unseal
Their grand commission; where I found, Horatio,
A royal knavery; an exact command—
Larded with many several sorts of reasons,
Importing Denmark's health, and England's too,
With, ho! such bugs and goblins in *my* life—
That on the supervise, no leisure bated,
No, not to stay the grinding of the axe,
My head should be struck off!
　　HOR. Is't possible?
　　HAM. Here's the commission;—read it at more leisure.
　　　　　　　　　　　　　　　　　　　　Act v. sc. 2.

Here the events, with the circumstances of time and place, are all stated with equal compression and rapidity, not one introduced which could have been omitted without injury to the intelligibility of the whole process. If any tendency is discoverable, as far as the mere facts are in question, it is the tendency to omission: and, accordingly, the reader will observe in the following quotation that the attention of the narrator is called back to one material circumstance, which he was hurrying by, by a direct question from the friend to whom the story is communicated, 'How was this sealed?' But by a trait which is indeed peculiarly characteristic of Hamlet's mind, ever disposed to generalize, and meditative if to excess (but which, with due abatement and reduction, is distinctive of every powerful and methodizing intellect), all the digressions and enlargements consist of reflections, truths, and principles of general and permanent interest, either directly expressed or disguised in playful satire.

> I sat me down;
> Devis'd a new commission; wrote it fair.
> *I once did hold it, as our statists do,*
> *A baseness to write fair, and laboured much*
> *How to forget that learning;* but, sir, now
> It did me yeoman's service. Wilt thou know
> The effect of what I wrote?
>   HOR. Ay, good my lord.
>   HAM. An earnest conjuration from the king,—
> As England was his faithful tributary;
> *As love between them, like the palm, might flourish;*
> *As peace should still her wheaten garland wear,*
> *And many such like As's of great charge—*
> That on the view and knowing of these contents,
> Without debatement further, more or less,
> He should the bearers put to sudden death,
> No shriving time allowed.
>   HOR. How was this seal'd?
>   HAM. Why, even in that was heaven ordinant.
> I had my father's signet in my purse,

Which was the model of the Danish seal:
Folded the writ up in the form of the other;
Subscribed it; gave't the impression; placed it safely,
The changeling never known. Now, the next day
Was our sea-fight; and what to this was sequent,
Thou know'st already.

    HOR. So Guildenstern and Rosencrantz go to't?

    HAM. Why, man, they did make love to this employment.
They are not near my conscience: their defeat
Doth by their own insinuation grow.
'Tis dangerous when the baser nature comes
Between the pass and fell incensed points
Of mighty opposites.

It would, perhaps, be sufficient to remark of the preceding passage, in connection with the humorous specimen of narration,

       Fermenting o'er with frothy circumstance,

in Henry IV, that if, overlooking the different value of the *matter* in each, we considered the *form* alone, we should find both *immethodical*,—Hamlet from the excess, Mrs. Quickly from the want, of reflection and generalization; and that Method, therefore, must result from the due mean or balance between our passive impressions and the mind's own re-action on the same. Whether this re-action do not suppose or imply a primary act positively *originating* in the mind itself, and prior to the object in order of nature, though co-instantaneous with it in its manifestation, will be hereafter discussed. But I had a further purpose in thus contrasting these extracts from our 'myriad-minded bard', (μυριονοῦς ἀνήρ). We wished to bring forward, each for itself, these two elements of method, or, to adopt an arithmetical term, its two main *factors*.

Instances of the want of generalization are of no rare occurrence in real life: and the narrations of Shakespear's Hostess and the Tapster differ from those of the ignorant and unthinking in

general by their superior humour, the poet's own gift and in-
fusion, not by their want of method, which is not greater than
we often meet with in that class, of which they are the dramatic
representatives. Instances of the opposite fault, arising from the
excess of generalization and reflection in minds of the opposite
class, will, like the minds themselves, occur less frequently in
the course of our own personal experience. . . .

Thus exuberance of mind, on the one hand, interferes with
the *forms* of Method; but sterility of mind, on the other, wanting
the spring and impulse to mental action, is wholly destructive
of Method itself. For in attending too exclusively to the relations which the past or passing events and objects bear to
general truth, and the moods of his own thought, the most
intelligent man is sometimes in danger of overlooking that
other relation, in which they are likewise to be placed to the
apprehension and sympathies of his hearers. His discourse appears like soliloquy intermixed with dialogue. But the uneducated and unreflecting talker overlooks *all* mental relations,
both logical and psychological; and consequently precludes all
Method that is not purely accidental. Hence the nearer the
things and incidents in time and place, the more distant, dis-
jointed, and impertinent to each other, and to any common
purpose, will they appear in his narration: and this from the
want of a *staple*, or *starting-post*, in the narrator himself; from
the absence of *the leading thought*, which, borrowing a phrase
from the nomenclature of legislation, I may not inaptly call the
initiative. On the contrary, where the habit of *Method* is present
and effective, things the most remote and diverse in time, place,
and outward circumstance, are brought into mental contiguity
and succession, the more striking as the less expected. But while
I would impress the necessity of this habit, the illustrations adduced give proof that in undue preponderance, and when the
prerogative of the mind is stretched into despotism, the discourse may degenerate into the grotesque or the fantastical.

With what a profound insight into the constitution of the human soul is this exhibited to us in the character of the Prince of Denmark, where flying from the sense of reality, and seeking a reprieve from the pressure of its duties in that ideal activity, the overbalance of which, with the consequent indisposition to action, is his disease, he compels the reluctant good sense of the high yet healthful-minded Horatio to follow him in his wayward meditation amid the graves!

HAM. *To what base uses we may return, Horatio! Why not may imagination trace the noble dust of Alexander till he find it stopping a bung-hole?*

HOR. *'Twere to consider too curiously, to consider so.*

HAM. *No, faith, not a jot; but to follow him thither with modesty enough, and likelihood to lead it; as thus; Alexander died, Alexander was buried, Alexander returneth to dust; the dust is earth; of earth we make loam: And why of that loam whereto he was converted, might they not stop a beer-barrel?*
Imperious Caesar, dead, and turn'd to clay,
Might stop a hole to keep the wind away!

But let it not escape our recollection, that when the objects thus connected are proportionate to the connecting energy, relatively to the real, or at least to the desirable, sympathies of mankind; it is from the same character that we derive the genial method in the famous soliloquy, '*To be, or not to be*' which, admired as it is, and has been, has yet received only the first-fruits of the admiration due to it.

We have seen that from the confluence of innumerable impressions in each moment of time the mere passive memory must needs tend to confusion; a rule, the seeming exceptions to which (the thunder-bursts in Lear, for instance) are really confirmations of its truth. For, in many instances, the predominance of some mighty Passion takes the place of the guiding Thought, and the result presents the method of Nature, rather than the habit of the Individual. For Thought, Imagination, (and I may add, Passion), are, in their very essence, the first connective, the latter co-adunative: and it has been shown, that if the excess lead to Method misapplied, and to connections of the moment, the absence, or marked deficiency, either precludes method altogether, both form and substance; or (as the following extract will exemplify) retains the outward form only.

> *My liege and Madam, to expostulate*
> *What majesty should be, what duty is,*
> *Why day is day, night night, and time is time,*
> *Were nothing but to waste night, day and time.*
> *Therefore—since brevity is the soul of wit,*
> *And tediousness the limbs and outward flourishes,—*
> *I will be brief. Your noble son is mad:*
> *Mad call I it; for to define true madness,*
> *What is't, but to be nothing else but mad!*
> *But let that go.*
>   QUEEN. *More matter with less art.*
>   POL. *Madam, I swear, I use no art at all.*
> *That he is mad, 'tis true: a foolish figure;*
> *But farewell it, for I will use no art.*
> *Mad let us grant him then: and now remains,*
> *That we find out the cause of this effect,*
> *Or rather say the cause of this defect:*
> *For this effect defective comes by cause.*
> *Thus it remains, and the remainder thus*
> *Perpend.*

Does not the irresistible sense of the ludicrous in this flourish of the soul-surviving body of old Polonius's intellect, not less than in the endless confirmations and most undeniable matters of fact of Tapster Pompey or 'the hostess of the tavern' prove to our feelings, even before the word is found which presents the truth to our understandings, that confusion and formality are but the opposite poles of the same null-point?

It is Shakespeare's peculiar excellence, that throughout the whole of this splendid picture-gallery (the reader will excuse the confest inadequacy of this metaphor), we find individuality every where, mere portrait no where. In all his various characters, we still feel ourselves communing with the same nature, which is everywhere present as the vegetable sap in the branches, sprays, leaves, buds, blossoms, and fruits, their shapes, tastes, and odours. Speaking of the effect, that is, his works themselves, we may define the excellence of *their* method as consisting in that just proportion, that union and interpenetration, of the universal and the particular, which must ever pervade all works of decided genius and true science. For Method implies a *progressive transition*, and it is the meaning of the word in the original language. The Greek Μέθοδος is literally a *way* or *path* of *transit*. Thus we extol the Elements of Euclid, or Socrates' discourse with the slave in the Menon of Plato, as *methodical*, a term which no one who holds himself bound to think or speak correctly, would apply to the alphabetical order or arrangement of a common dictionary. But as without continuous transition there can be no Method, so without a preconception there can be no transition with continuity. The term, Method, cannot therefore, otherwise than by abuse, be applied to a mere dead arrangement, containing in itself no principle of progression.

Friend.

136. ON THE JUSTIFIABILITY OF PUBLICATION OF CERTAIN LETTERS

Hartley Coleridge writes in his life of Thomas, Lord Fairfax: It was a most ungentlemanlike act of the weekly-fast-ordaining Parliament or their agents to open Charles's letters to his wife, and all historians who make use of them to blacken his character ought to forfeit the character of gentlemen.

Coleridge comments: How could a faithful historian avoid it? The Parliament had acted *ab initio* on their convictions of the

King's bad faith, and of the utter insincerity of his promises and professions; and surely the justification or condemnation of their acts must depend on, or be greatly modified by the question—were these convictions well grounded, and afterwards proved to be so by evidence, which could without danger to the state be advanced? What stronger presumption can we have of the certainty of the evidences which they had previously obtained, and by the year after year accumulation of which their suspicions had been converted into convictions? And was Henrietta an ordinary *wife*? Was Charles to her as Charles of Sweden to his spouse? The Swedes' Queen was only the man's wife, but Henrietta was notoriously Charles's queen, or rather the He-queen's She-king—a *commander* in the war, meddling with and influencing all his councils. I hold the Parliament fully justified in the publication of the letters; much more the historian. S. T. C.

MS.

137. DON QUIXOTE

Don Quixote is not a man out of his senses, but a man in whom the imagination and the pure reason are so powerful as to make him disregard the evidence of sense when it opposed their conclusions. Sancho is the common sense of the social man-animal, unenlightened and unsanctified by the reason. You see how he reverences his master at the very time he is cheating him.

Table Talk.

138. RABELAIS, SWIFT

Rabelais is a most wonderful writer. Pantagruel is the Reason; Panurge the Understanding,—the pollarded man, the man with every faculty except the reason. I scarcely know an example more illustrative of the distinction between the two. Rabelais had no mode of speaking the truth in those days but in such a form as this; as it was, he was indebted to the King's protection for his life. Some of the commentators talk about his book being all political; there are contemporary politics in it, of course, but the real scope is much higher and more philosophical. It is in vain to look about for a hidden meaning in all that he has written; you will observe that, after any particularly deep thrust, as the Papimania, for example, Rabelais, as if to break the blow, and to appear unconscious of what he has done, writes a chapter or two of pure buffoonery. He, every now and then, flashes you a glimpse of a real face from his magic lantern, and then buries the whole scene in mist. The morality of the work is of the most refined and exalted kind; as for the manners, to be sure, I cannot say much.

Swift was *anima Rabelaisii habitans in sicco*,—the soul of Rabelais dwelling in a dry place.

Yet Swift was rare. Can any thing beat his remark on King William's motto,— *Recepit, non rapuit*,—'that the Receiver was as bad as the Thief?'

Table Talk.

139. THE TRUE IMAGINATIVE STYLE

The Pilgrim's Progress is composed in the lowest style of English, without slang or false grammar. If you were to polish it, you would at once destroy the reality of the vision. For works of imagination should be written in very plain language; the more purely imaginative they are the more necessary it is to be plain.

Table Talk.

140. GENIAL CRITICISM

In the story of Lady Melville of Colville and her three hours prayer—with the sufficient specimen of the 'Gentilwoman in

Culross' Muse, I can find nothing but what is elevating and affecting in the former and in the latter a really striking specimen of smoothness with *strength* in the metre, and of propriety in the Thoughts, so much beyond the average as to surprize a reader unacquainted with the fact of the superior purity and sweetness of the Language used by Women of Rank in ages of Barbarism, whether from immaturity (as in England and Scotland) or from degeneracy, as in Constantinople under the later Greek Emperors, when the Ladies still used a Language which Xenophon and Menander would have acknowledged. Reducing the words to the present fashion of Spelling, and with the alteration of one monosyllable, the application of which in the Lines is now obsolete, I transcribe them, not disguising the wish, I feel, to see the whole Poem.

> Tho' Waters great do compass you about,
> Tho' Tyrants fret; tho' Lions rage and roar;
> Defy them all and fear not to win out—
> Your Guide is near to help you evermore.
> Tho' point of Iron do pierce you wond'rous sore,
> And Lusts more noisome seek your Soul to slay,
> Yet cry on Christ, and he shall go before;
> The nearer Heaven, the harder is the Way.
>
> Rejoice in God! Let not your Courage fail,
> Ye chosen Saints! that are afflicted here:
> Tho' Satan rage, he never shall prevail
> Fight to the end, and stoutly persevere!
> Your God is true: your Blood to him is dear:
> Fear not the way since Christ is your Convoy:
> When Clouds are past, the weather still grow[s] clear:
> Ye sow in tears, but ye shall reap in Joy!

Common-place! Yes! So are the gales of Heaven, yet to the man who after long toiling up the rocky path has just reached the Brow of the Mountain, they are as delightful as tho' they had been prepared by an especial Fiat at that moment.

MS.

141. HACKET'S SERMONS

Did not the Life of Arch[bishop] Williams [by the same divine] prove otherwise. I should have inferred from these Sermons that H[acket], from his first Boyhood had been used to make themes, epigrams, copies of verses, &c. on all the Sundays, Feasts and Festivals of the Church; had found abundant nourishment for this humour of Points, Quirks, and Quiddities in the study of the Fathers and Glossers; and remained an Under-Soph all his life long.

I scarcely know what to say. On the one hand, there is a triflingness, a Shewman or Relique-hawker's Gossip, that stands in offensive Contrast with the momentous nature of the subject, and the dignity of the ministerial office, as if a Preacher, having chosen the Prophets for his theme should entertain his congregation by exhibiting a traditional Shaving Rag of Isaiah's with the Prophet's stubble hair on the dried up soapsuds. And yet on the other hand there is an innocency in it, a security of Faith, a fullness evinced in the play and plash of its overflowing that at other times give me the same sort of pleasure as the sight of Blackberry Bushes, and Children's Handkerchief Gardens on the slopes of a rampart, the Promenade of some peaceful old town, that stood its last siege in the 30 Years War.

MS.

142. CRASHAW

Crashaw seems in his poems to have given the first ebullience of his imagination, unshapen into form, or much of, what we now term, sweetness. In the poem, Hope, by way of question and answer, his superiority to Cowley is self-evident. In that on the name of Jesus equally so; but his lines on St. Theresa are the finest.

Where he does combine richness of thought and diction nothing can excel, as in the lines you so much admire—

> 'Since 'tis not to be had at home,
> She'l travel to a matyrdome.
> No home for her confesses she,
> But where she may a martyr be.
> She'l to the Moores, and trade with them
> For this invalued diadem,
> She offers them her dearest breath
> With Christ's name in't, in change for death.
> She'll bargain with them, and will give
> Them God, and teach them how to live
> In Him, or if they this deny,
> For Him she'll teach them how to die.
> So shall she leave amongst them sown,
> The Lord's blood, or, at least, her own.
> Farewell then, all the world—adieu,
> Teresa is no more for you:
> Farewell all pleasures, sports and joys,
> Never till now esteemed toys—
> Farewell whatever dear'st may be,
> Mother's arms or father's knee;
> Farewell house, and farewell home,
> She's for the Moores and martyrdom.'

These verses were ever present to my mind whilst writing the second part of Christabel; if, indeed, by some subtle process of the mind they did not suggest the first thought of the whole poem.—Poetry, as regards small poets, may be said to be, in a certain sense, conventional in its accidents and in its illustrations; thus Crashaw uses an image:—

> 'As sugar melts in tea away';

which, although *proper then*, and *true now*, was in bad taste at that time equally with the present. In Shakespeare, in Chaucer there was nothing of this.

Allsop.

143. FIELDING AND RICHARDSON

What a master of composition Fielding was! Upon my word, I think the Oedipus Tyrannus, the Alchemist, and Tom Jones the three most perfect plots ever planned. And how charming, how wholesome, Fielding always is! To take him up after Richardson, is like emerging from a sick room heated by stoves, into an open lawn, on a breezy day in May.

Table Talk.

144. GIBBON

The difference between the composition of a history in modern and ancient times is very great; still there are certain principles upon which a history of a modern period may be written, neither sacrificing all truth and reality, like Gibbon, nor descending into mere biography and anecdote.

Gibbon's style is detestable, but his style is not the worst thing about him. His history has proved an effectual bar to all real familiarity with the temper and habits of imperial Rome. Few persons read the original authorities, even those which are classical; and certainly no distinct knowledge of the actual state of the empire can be obtained from Gibbon's rhetorical sketches. He takes notice of nothing but what may produce an effect; he skips on from eminence to eminence, without ever taking you through the valleys between: in fact, his work is little else but a disguised collection of all the splendid anecdotes which he could find in any book concerning any persons or nations from the Antonines to the capture of Constantinople. When I read a chapter in Gibbon, I seem to be looking through

a luminous haze or fog:—figures come and go, I know not how
or why, all larger than life, or distorted or discoloured; nothing
is real, vivid, true; all is scenical, and, as it were, exhibited by
candlelight. And then to call it a History of the Decline and
Fall of the Roman Empire! Was there ever a greater misnomer?
I protest I do not remember a single philosophical attempt made
throughout the work to fathom the ultimate causes of the decline or fall of that empire. How miserably deficient is the
narrative of the important reign of Justinian! And that poor
scepticism, which Gibbon mistook for Socratic philosophy,
has led him to misstate and mistake the character and influence
of Christianity in a way which even an avowed infidel or
atheist would not and could not have done. Gibbon was a man
of immense reading; but he had no philosophy; and he never
fully understood the principle upon which the best of the old
historians wrote. He attempted to imitate their artificial construction of the whole work—their dramatic ordonnance of
the parts—without seeing that their histories were intended
more as documents illustrative of the truths of political philosophy than as mere chronicles of events.

The true key to the declension of the Roman empire—
which is not to be found in all Gibbon's immense work—may
be stated in two words:—the *imperial* character overlaying, and
finally destroying, the *national* character. Rome under Trajan
was an empire without a nation.

Table Talk.

145. S. JOHNSON AND S. JOHNSON: A NOTE ON THE
WORKS OF *MR.* SAMUEL JOHNSON, 1710

The title is modest enough—*Some* Memorials—but they are a
meagre Substitute for a Life of *Mr.* S. J.—a worthier Subject
of Biography than *Dr.* S. Johnson—and this without denying
the worth of the latter—but more thanks to Boswell than to
the Dr's own Works. S. T. C.

Among my countless intentional Works, one was—Biographical Memorials of Revolutionary Minds, in Philosophy, Religion, and Politics. *Mr.* Sam Johnson was to have been one. I meant to have begun with Wickcliff, and to have confined myself to Natives of Great Britain—but with one or two supplementary Volumes, for the Heroes of Germany (Luther and his Company) and of Italy (Vico).

MS.

146. (MR.) SAMUEL JOHNSON

Samuel Johnson, whom to distinguish him from the Doctor, we may call the Whig, was a very remarkable writer. He may be compared to his contemporary Defoe, whom he resembled in many points. He is another instance of King William's discrimination, which was so much superior to that of any of his ministers. Johnson was one of the most formidable advocates for the Exclusion Bill, and he suffered by whipping and imprisonment under James accordingly. Like Asgill, he argues with great apparent candour and clearness till he has his opponent within reach, and then comes a blow as from a sledge-hammer. I do not know where I could put my hand upon a book containing so much sense and sound constitutional doctrine as this thin folio of Johnson's Works; and what party in this country would read so severe a lecture in it as our modern Whigs!

A close reasoner and a good writer in general may be known by his pertinent use of connectives. Read that page of Johnson; you cannot alter one conjunction without spoiling the sense. It is a linked strain throughout. In your modern books, for the most part, the sentences in a page have the same connection with each other that marbles have in a bag; they touch without adhering.

Asgill evidently formed his style upon Johnson's, but he only imitates one part of it. Asgill never rises to Johnson's eloquence. The latter was a sort of Cobbett-Burke.

Table Talk.

147. DR. JOHNSON

Dr. Johnson's fame now rests principally upon Boswell. It is impossible not to be amused with such a book. But his *bow-wow* manner must have had a good deal to do with the effect produced;—for no one, I suppose, will set Johnson before Burke,—and Burke was a great and universal talker;—yet now we hear nothing of this except by some chance remarks in Boswell. The fact is, Burke, like all men of genius who love to talk at all, was very discursive and continuous; hence he is not reported; he seldom said the sharp short things that Johnson almost always did, which produce a more decided effect at the moment, and which are so much more easy to carry off. Besides, as to Burke's testimony to Johnson's powers, you must remember that Burke was a great courtier; and after all, Burke said and wrote more than once that he thought Johnson greater in talking than in writing, and greater in Boswell than in real life.

Table Talk.

148. DR. JOHNSON

Dr. Johnson seems to have been really more powerful in discoursing *viva voce* in conversation than with his pen in hand. It seems as if the excitement of company called something like reality and consecutiveness into his reasonings, which in his writings I cannot see. His antitheses are almost always verbal only; and sentence after sentence in the *Rambler* may be pointed out, to which you cannot attach any definite meaning whatever. In his political pamphlets there is more truth of expression than in his other works, for the same reason that his conversation is better than his writings in general.

Table Talk.

149. DR. JOHNSON AND S.T.C. COMPARED AS CONVERSATIONISTS

Timeless	All Time.
Eolian Harp ✕	Single Drum.[1]

Hence the E.H. pours forth delicious tones, and surges of Tone but which can be neither measured nor retained—the faintest of all memories, the memory, not *of*, but *about* a past sensation, broadly *particularized* by the wide *general*, delightful, sweet, tender, aerial &c. &c.——

Query. As Conversationists is not S. T. C. ✕ Dr J. as Eol[ian] Harp to Single Drum. Hence the stores of remembered Sayings of the latter—while S. T. C. sparks

Sparks that fall upon a River,
A moment bright, then lost for ever.

MS.

150. ALEXANDER POPE

Pope like an old Lark who tho' he leaves off soaring and singing in the heights, yet has his *Spurs* grow longer and sharper, the older he grows.

MS.

151. CRABBE AND SOUTHEY COMPARED

I think Crabbe and Southey are something alike; but Crabbe's poems are founded on observation and real life—Southey's on fancy and books. In facility they are equal, though Crabbe's English is of course not upon a level with Southey's, which is next door to faultless. But in Crabbe there is an absolute defect of the high imagination; he gives me little or no pleasure: yet, no doubt, he has much power of a certain kind, and it is good

[1] ✕ Contrasted or opposed to, a sign frequently used by Coleridge.
✕ Compared with.

to cultivate, even at some pains, a catholic taste in literature. I read all sorts of books with some pleasure except modern sermons and treatises on political economy.

I have received a great deal of pleasure from some of the modern novels, especially Captain Marryat's 'Peter Simple'. That book is nearer Smollett than any I remember. And 'Tom Cringle's Log' in *Blackwood* is also most excellent.

Table Talk.

152. FAUST

Before I had ever seen any part of Goethe's Faust, though, of course, when I was familiar enough with Marlowe's, I conceived and drew up the plan of a work, a drama, which was to be, to my mind, what the Faust was to Goethe's. My Faust was old Michael Scott; a much better and more likely original than Faust. He appeared in the midst of his college of devoted disciples, enthusiastic, ebullient, shedding around him bright surmises of discoveries fully perfected in after-times, and inculcating the study of nature and its secrets as the pathway to the acquisition of power. He did not love knowledge for itself—for its own exceeding great reward—but in order to be powerful. This poison-speck infected his mind from the beginning. The priests suspect him, circumvent him, accuse him; he is condemned, and thrown into solitary confinement: this constituted the *prologus* of the drama. A pause of four or five years takes place, at the end of which Michael escapes from prison, a soured, gloomy, miserable man. He will not, cannot study; of what avail had all his study been to him? His knowledge, great as it was, had failed to preserve him from the cruel fangs of the persecutors; he could not command the lightning or the storm to wreak their furies upon the heads of those whom he hated and condemned, and yet feared. Away with learning! away with study! to the winds with all pretences to knowledge! We *know* nothing; we are fools, wretches, mere beasts. Anon I began to tempt him. I made him dream, gave him wine, and passed the most exquisite of women before him, but out of his reach. Is there, then, no knowledge by which these pleasures can be commanded? That way lay witchcraft, and accordingly to witchcraft Michael turns with all his soul. He has many failures and some successes; he learns the chemistry of exciting drugs and exploding powders, and some of the properties of transmitted and reflected light: his appetites and his curiosity are both stimulated, and his old craving for power and mental domination over others revives. At last Michael tries to raise the Devil, and the Devil comes at his call. My Devil was to be, like Goethe's, the universal humorist, who should make all things vain and nothing worth, by a perpetual collation of the great with the little in the presence of the infinite. I had many a trick for him to play, some better, I think, than any in the Faust. In the meantime, Michael is miserable; he has power, but no peace, and he every day more keenly feels the tyranny of hell surrounding him. In vain he seems to himself to assert the most absolute empire over the Devil, by imposing the most extravagant tasks; one thing is as easy as another to the Devil. 'What next, Michael?' is repeated every day with more imperious servility. Michael groans in spirit; his power is a curse: he commands women and wine; but the women seem fictitious and devilish, and the wine does not make him drunk. He now begins to hate the Devil, and tries to cheat him. He studies again and explores the darkest depths of sorcery for a receipt to cozen hell; but all in vain. Sometimes the Devil's finger turns over the page for him, and points out an experiment, and Michael hears a whisper—'Try *that*, Michael!' The horror increases; and Michael feels that he is a slave and a condemned criminal. Lost to hope, he throws himself into every sensual excess,—in the mid career of which he sees Agatha, my Margaret, and immediately endeavours to seduce her. Agatha loves him; and the Devil facilitates their meetings; but she resists Michael's attempts to ruin her, and implores him not to act so as to forfeit her esteem. Long struggles of passion ensue, in the result of which his affections are called forth against his appetites, and, love-born, the idea of a redemption of the lost will dawns upon his mind. This is instantaneously perceived by the Devil; and for the first time the humorist becomes severe and menacing. A fearful succession of conflicts between Michael and the Devil takes place, in which Agatha helps and suffers. In the end, after subjecting him to every imaginable horror and agony, I made him triumphant, and poured peace into his soul in the conviction of a salvation for sinners through God's grace.

The intended theme of the Faust is the consequences of a misology, or hatred and depreciation of knowledge caused by an originally intense thirst for knowledge baffled. But a love of knowledge for itself, and for pure ends, would never produce such a misology, but only a love of it for base and unworthy purposes. There is neither causation nor progression in the Faust; he is a ready-made conjuror from the very beginning; the *incredulus odi* is felt from the first line. The sensuality and the thirst after knowledge are unconnected with each other. Mephistopheles and Margaret are excellent; but Faust himself is dull and meaningless. The scene in Auerbach's cellars is one of the best, perhaps the very best; that on the Brocken is also fine; and all the songs are beautiful. But there is no whole in the poem; the scenes are mere magic-lantern pictures, and a large part of the work is to me very flat. The German is very pure and fine.

The young men in Germany and England who admire Lord Byron, prefer Goethe to Schiller; but you may depend upon it, Goethe does not, nor ever will, command the common mind of the people of Germany as Schiller does. Schiller had two legitimate phases in his intellectual character:—the first as author of the Robbers—a piece which must not be considered with reference to Shakespeare, but as a work of the mere material sublime, and in that line it is undoubtedly very powerful indeed. It is quite genuine, and deeply imbued with Schiller's own soul. After this he outgrew the composition of such plays as the Robbers, and at once took his true and only rightful stand in the grand historical drama—the Wallenstein; —not the intense drama of passion,—he was not master of that —but the diffused drama of history, in which alone he had ample scope for his varied powers. The Wallenstein is the greatest of his works: it is not unlike Shakespeare's historical plays—a species by itself. You may take up any scene, and it will please you by itself; just as you may in Don Quixote, which you read *through* once or twice only, but which you read *in* repeatedly. After this point it was, that Goethe and other writers injured by their theories the steadiness and originality of Schiller's mind; and in every one of his works after the Wallenstein you may perceive the fluctuations of his taste and principles of composition. He got a notion of re-introducing the characterlessness of the Greek tragedy with a chorus, as in the Bride of Messina, and he was for infusing more lyric verse into it. Schiller sometimes affected to despise the Robbers and the other works of his first youth; whereas he ought to have spoken of them as of works not in a right line, but full of excellence in their way. In his ballads and lighter lyrics Goethe is most excellent. It is impossible to praise him too highly in this respect. I like the Wilhelm Meister the best of his prose works. But neither Schiller's nor Goethe's prose style approaches to Lessing's, whose writings, for *manner*, are absolutely perfect.

Although Wordsworth and Goethe are not much alike to be sure, upon the whole; yet they both have this peculiarity of utter non-sympathy with the subjects of their poetry. They are always, both of them, spectators *ab extra*,—feeling *for*, but never *with*, their characters. Schiller is a thousand times more *hearty* than Goethe.

I was once pressed—many years ago—to translate the Faust; and I so far entertained the proposal as to read the work through with great attention, and to revive in my mind my own former plan of Michael Scott. But then I considered with myself whether the time taken up in executing the translation might not more worthily be devoted to the composition of a work which, even if parallel in some points to the Faust, should be truly original in motive and execution, and therefore more interesting and valuable than any version which I could make; —and, secondly, I debated with myself whether it became my moral character to render into English—and so far, certainly, lend my countenance to language—much of which I thought vulgar, licentious, and blasphemous. I need not tell you that I never put pen to paper as a translator of Faust.

I have read a good deal of Mr. Hayward's version, and I think it done in a very manly style; but I do not admit the argument for prose translations. I would in general rather see verse attempted in so capable a language as ours. The French can't help themselves, of course, with such a language as theirs.

Table Talk.

153. SCOTT AND THE SUPERNATURAL

Tuesday Night, 13 Oct.ʳ 1830.

Sir W. S., a faithful Cosmolater, is always half and half on the subject of the Supernatural in his Novels. The Ghost-seer and the Appearances are so stated as to be readily solved on the commonest and most obvious principles of Pathology; while the exact coincidence of the Events, and thus as in *Guy Mannering*, a complexity of Events with two perfectly coincident predictions so far exceeds our general experience, is so unsatisfactorily accounted for by the doctrine of Chances, as to be little less marvellous than the appearance itself would be, supposing it real. Thus by the latter he secures the full effect of Superstition for the Reader, while by the former he preserves the credit of unbelief and philosophic insight for the Writer—

i.e. himself. I said falsely, the *full* effect: for that discrepance between the Narrator and the Narrative chills and deadens the Sympathy.

MS.

154. THE SUPERNATURAL IN POETRY

Mem.

In poetry, whether metrical or unbound, the super-natural will be impressive and obtain a mastery over the Imagination and feelings, will tend to infect the reader, and draw him to identify himself with, or substitute himself for, the *Person* of the Drama or Tale, in proportion as it is true *to Nature*—i.e. when the Poet of his free will and judgement does what the Believing Narrator of a Supernatural Incident, Apparition or Charm does from ignorance and weakness of mind,—i.e. mistake a *Subjective* product (A saw the Ghost of Z) for an objective fact—the Ghost of Z was there to be seen; or by the magnifying and modifying power of Fear and *dreamy* Sensations, and the additive and supplementary interpolations of the *creative* Memory and the inferences and comments of the prejudiced Judgement slipt consciously into and confounded with the *Text* of the actual experience, exaggerates an unusual Natural event or appearance into the Miraculous and supernatural.

The Poet must always be in perfect sympathy with the Subject of the Narrative, and tell his tale with 'a most believing mind'; but the Tale will be then most impressive for all when it is so constructed and particularized with such [traits ?] and circumstances, that the Psychologist and thinking Naturalist shall be furnished with the Means of explaining it as a possible fact, by distinguishing and assigning the *Subjective* portion to it's true power.

MS.

155. THE HORRIBLE AND UGLY IN ART

The merit of a novellist is in proportion (not simply to the effect but) to the pleasurable effect which he produces. Situations of torment, and images of naked horror, are easily conceived; and a writer in whose works they abound, deserves our gratitude almost equally with him who should drag us by way of sport through a military hospital, or force us to sit at the dissecting table of a natural philosopher. To trace the nice boundaries, beyond which terror and sympathy are deserted by the pleasurable emotions, to reach those limits, yet never to pass them, *hic labor, hic opus est*. Figures that shock the imagination, and narratives that mangle the feelings, rarely discover *genius,* and always betray a low and vulgar *taste.* . . . The romance writer possesses an unlimited power over situations; but he must scrupulously make his characters act in congruity with them. Let him work *physical* wonders only, and we will content to *dream* with him for a while; but the first *moral* miracle which he attempts he disgusts and awakens us. . . . The extent of the powers that may exist, we can never ascertain; and therefore we feel no great difficulty in yielding a temporary belief to any, the strangest of *things.* But that situation once conceived, how beings like ourselves would feel and act in it, our own feelings sufficiently instruct us: and we instantly reject the clumsy fiction that does not harmonise with them.

Review of Lewis's *The Monk* in the
Critical Review for February 1797.

156. WORDSWORTH

Would to heaven I were with you! [Allsop] In a few days you should see that the spirit of the mountaineer is not yet utterly extinct in me. Wordsworth has remarked (in the Brothers, I believe),

The thought of death sits light upon the man
That has been bred, and dies among the mountains.

But I fear that this, like some other few of Wordsworth's *many*
striking passages, means less than it seems, or rather promises, to
mean. Poets (especially if philosophers too) are apt to represent
the effect made upon themselves as general; the geese of Phoebus are all swans; and Wordsworth's shepherds and estates men
are Wordsworths, even (as in old Michael) in the unpoetic
traits of character. Whether mountains have any particular effect
on the native inhabitants by virtue of being mountains exclusively, and what that effect is, would be a difficult problem. If
independent tribes, mountaineers are robbers of the lowlanders;
brave, active, and with all the usual warlike good and bad
qualities that result from habits of adventurous robbery. Add
clanship and the superstitions that are the surviving *precipitate* of
an established religion, both which are common to the uncivil-
ised Celtic tribes, in plain no less than in mountain, and you
have the Scottish Highlanders. But where the inhabitants exist
as states, or civilised parts of civilised states, they appear to be
in mind and character just what their condition and employ-
ments would render them in level plain, the same as amid
Alpine heights. At least the influence acts indirectly only, as
far as the mountains are the *causa causae* or occasion of a *pastoral* life instead of an agricultural; thus combining a lax and
common property, possessed by a whole district, with small
hereditary estates sacred to each, while the properties in sheep
seem to partake of both characters. And truly, to this circumstance, aided by the favourable action of a necessarily scanty
population (for *man* is an oak that wants room, not a *plantation*
tree), we must attribute whatever superiority the mountaineers
of Cumberland and Westmoreland and of the Swiss and Tyrol-
lese Alps possess, as the shocking contrast of the Welsh mountaineers too clearly evinces. But this subject I have discussed,
and (if I do not flatter myself) satisfactorily, in the Literary Life,

and I will not conceal from *you* that this inferred dependency of the human soul on accidents of birth-place and abode, together with the vague, misty, rather than mystic, confusion of God with the world, and the accompanying nature-worship, of which the asserted dependence forms a part, is the trait in Wordsworth's poetic works that I most dislike as unhealthful, and denounce as contagious; while the odd introduction of the popular, almost the vulgar, religion in his later publications (the popping in, as Hartley says, of the old man with a beard), suggests the painful suspicion of worldly prudence—at best a justification of masking truth (which, in fact, is a falsehood substituted for a truth withheld) on plea of expediency—carried into religion. At least it conjures up to my fancy a sort of *Janus* head of Spinoza and Dr. Watts, or 'I and my brother the dean'.

Allsop.

157. WORDSWORTH AND HIMSELF

To W[ordsworth] in the progression of Spirit. Once Simonides, or Empedocles or both in one? O that my Spirit purged by Death of its Weaknesses, which are alas! my *identity*, might flow into *thine*, and live and act in thee, and be Thou.

MS.

158. OF READING AND WRITING

The way to be admired is to tell the reader what he knew before, but clothed in a statelier phraseology, and embodied in apt and lively illustrations. To attempt to make a man wiser is of necessity to remind him of his ignorance, and in the majority of instances, the pain actually felt is so much greater than the pleasure anticipated, that it is natural that men should attempt to shelter themselves from it by contempt or neglect. For a living writer is yet *sub judice*: and if we cannot follow his conceptions or enter into his feelings, it is more consoling to our

NO SCALPING KNIFE

pride, as well as more agreeable to our indolence, to consider
him as lost beneath, than as soaring out of our sight above us.

Friend.

159. GENIUS AND TASTE

A high degree of Taste is, we believe, scarcely compatible with
Genius in its earlier efforts, and only with the highest Genius
even in its maturity.

MS.

160. LE STYLE EST L'HOMME

I do not object to the Thoughts—but it is a *mystical* way of
talking—an *imposing* manner, and whatever is imposing partakes of imposition, and is Second Cousin, if not cousin German,
to Imposture and I don't like such Cozening.

MS.

161. CRITICISMS OF HARTLEY COLERIDGE'S WRITINGS

Hartley Coleridge in his life of Congreve uses the phrase 'old
Heywood, the prose Shakespeare'.

Coleridge comments: This note has less of Hartley's tact and dis-
crimination than, from such a subject, I should have expected.
Surely a prose Shakespeare is not only an over-load for old
Heywood, but something not very unlike a square circle.
S. T. C.

MS.

NOVELS AND PLAYS

Hartley Coleridge writes: 'The thought of confining a novel
to the *unities* was something original . . . and Congreve . . .
might hope to gain a laurel by applying the French rules to a

species of composition never before made amenable to them;
as if one should make tea or brew small beer in chemical
nomenclature.'

Coleridge comments: A most infelicitous illustration! And *might*
not a novel, and a very good one in its kind, be written on such
a plan? I am sure that the 'Pilgrim', 'Beggar's Bush', and several
others of B[eaumont] and F[letcher]'s dramas might be turned
into very interesting novels. Had Congreve said that a good
novel must be so written, then indeed H. might have slapped
him. S. T. C.

MS.

SWIFT

Hartley Coleridge writes: 'With so little of truth or reason
could the man [Swift] write, who, of all his contemporaries,
might have been the greatest philosopher.'

Coleridge comments: That is, if with equal genius he had *not* been
Dean Swift, but almost the very contrary. S. T. C.

MS.

Hartley Coleridge writes: 'It is a rare thing for a serious drama
to be hissed off the stage.'

Coleridge comments: No, only *silenced* and *thin-audienced* off.
S. T. C.

MS.

162. LAWS OF QUOTATION

One of the spurious treatises ascribed to Dionysius the Areopa-
gite was a favourite book among the Moravianized members.
Some extracts were annexed to it, in a style of what Wesley
calls the same superessential darkness. Wesley took the volume
to Fetter Lane, and read these words before the jarring society:
'The Scriptures are good; prayer is good; communicating is
good; relieving our neighbours is good: but to one who is not
born of God, none of these are good, but all very evil. For him

to read the Scriptures, or to pray, or to communicate, or to do
any outward work, is deadly poison. First let him be born of
God. Till then, let him not do any of these things: for if he
does, he destroys himself.'

Southey, *The Life of Wesley.*

Coleridge comments: I strongly suspect either misquotation here,
or misinterpretation. What can be more unfair than to pinch out
a bit of a book this way? Most candid critic, what if I, by way
of joke, pinch out your eye; then holding up the gobbet cry,—
Ha! ha! that men should be dolts!—Behold this slimy dab! and
he, who owned it, dreamt that it could *see*! The idea were
mighty analytic; but should you like it, candid critic? I cannot
help thinking that the biographer has been in several instances
led, by his venial partiality for his hero, into the neighbourhood
of his hero's faults. It was a fault common to Wesley and
Swedenborg to limit the words of their opponents to the worst
possible sense, instead of seeking, as Leibnitz did, the truest
sense, and thus finding the error in the insufficiency and exclu-
siveness of the position. The Moravian leaders, being such as
Southey himself has described them, could not be ignorant, methinks, that the act of restraining and withholding is as much a
positive energy, if not more, as the act of doing this or that
and doubtless for many minds the more profitable. Their error
consisted in universalizing the position, and instead of 'many',
putting 'all'.—S. T. C.

Note on Southey's *The Life of Wesley.*

163. BIOGRAPHY

Robert Southey is an Historian worth his weight in diamonds;
and were he (which Heaven forfend) as fat as myself, and the
diamonds all as big as birds' eggs, I should still repeat the
appraisal. He may err in his own deductions from facts; but he
never deceived by concealing any known part of the grounds

and premises on which he had formed his conclusions. Or if there be any exception,—and pages 227–30 are the only ground or occasion for this 'if',—yet it will be found to respect a complex mass of facts, to be collected from jarring and motley narratives, all as accessible to his readers as to himself. So here, that I am vexed with him for not employing stronger and more impassioned words of reprobation, and moral recoil in this black blotch of Wesley's heart and character, is in another point of view the highest honour to Southey as an historian, since it is wholly and solely from his own statement of the incidents, that my impressions have been received. The manner in which this most delightful of all books of biography has been received by the Wesleyan Methodists demonstrates the justice of the main fault which judicious men charge against the work, viz., partiality towards the sect and its founder; a venial fault indeed, the liability to which is almost a desirable qualification in a biographer.—S. T. C.

Note on Southey's *The Life of Wesley*.

164. THE PHYSIOGNOMY OF TITLE PAGES

Coleridge has referred to 'the almost Pontifical Claims of the fullswoln Dr. Heylyn, D.D. and Chaplain to Charles the First and Charles the Second, Monarchs of Great Britain', and to his '*Necessary Introduction to the History of the Life and Death of the most Reverend and Renowned Prelate William* (Laud) *By Divine Providence, Lord Archbishop of Canterbury, Primate of All England, and Metropolitan; Chancellor of the Universities of Oxon and Dublin, and one of the Lords of the Privy Council to his late Most Sacred Majesty King Charles the First, Second Monarch of Great Britain.*'

He then adds this footnote: I am sensible how dimly this magnificent Title shines in the above Reflex Image, shorn of its Beams, the Types of many sizes, and the fulgency of red-lettered Small, Great, Greater and yet Greater Capitals. It is worthy the

attention of any Philosopher disposed to favor the Public with
The Physiognomy of Title-pages as an appendix to Craniology,
Chiromancy and the like Sciences.

MS.

165. A WILDERNESS OF A WORK

A note on James Hutton's *An Investigation of the Principles of
Knowledge.*

'I cannot walk with them, because I could walk in them,' said a
Wag of a very much too large Pair of Shoes. Something of this
sort might be applied to this Work. There is great metaphysical
Talent displayed in it; and the Writer had made an important
step beyond Locke, Berkeley and Hartley—and was clearly on
the precincts of the Critical Philosophy with which and the
precious Treatises of Kant he appears to have had no acquaintance. In short there is sense, and strong sense; but it loses itself
in its own enormous House, [and a benighted *crossed out*] in the
Wilderness of the multitudinous chambers and Passages. As
poor Sarah Stoddart (afterwards, poor Lass! Mrs. Hazlitt), complained to me of her Brother's Lectures and Remonstrances,
'He drives it *in*, and *in*, and *in* (to my head) till he drives it out,
out, out again. I feel as if there was a Hole thro' my head and
nothing remaining but a Buzz.'

MS.

166. EDINBURGH MAGAZINE

To the Readers of the Edinburgh Magazine, better known by
the name of the Ebony Casket of British Gems, Scotch Pebbles,
to wit, and Bristol Diamonds with *striking* specimens of *Spar*-
work *e podice diaboli, a parte Peak*—i.e. *from party* Pique.

MS.

167. THE DIFFICULTY OF WRITING ON DETACHED SUBJECTS

Doubtless it would visit the Realm of Literature with a plus-quam polar Ink-frost, if a man were bound to write on nothing till he understood everything! Nevertheless, so far I hold it a possible and expedient approximation that, no other person having done it for me, I strive to begin at the Beginning. But independent of the probable unsatisfactory nature of the results, I am yearly more and more sensible of the *difficulty* of writing on detached Subjects (Philosophical subjects I mean, whether physio- theo- or anthropo-logical) and whenever from whatever motive I make the attempt, the importance of this, that, and yet another and another Principle, or Position, which had I proceeded to the Subject as part of the *System*, I should have enunciated a half or a whole Volume before, and from frequent previous applications of the Principle have needed only a few words and a (Vide §— p. —) the sense, I say, of the necessity of some higher *formula* is sure to return and harrass me with its Solicitings, like a night-traveller who every two or three minutes makes a stop and then walks on with his head over his shoulder, because he hears, or fancies that he hears someone behind, panting and calling out his name, some auditual Jack a' Lanthorn, or *Vox Fatua*.

MS.

168. OF HIS OWN WORK—THE 'FRIEND'

My first number bears marks of the effort and anxiety with which it was written, and is composed less happily than I could wish. It assuredly had not the cheerful and winning aspect, which a door-keeper, presenting the bill of fare, ought to possess. Its object, however, was so far answered, as it announced distinctly the fundamental position or grand postulate on which the whole superstructure, with all its supporting beams and pillars, was to rest. I call it a postulate, not only because I deferred the proofs, but because, in strictness, it was not susceptible of any proof from without. The sole possible question was—Is it, or is it not, a fact?—and for the answer every human being must be referred to his own consciousness.

Friend.

169. ON HIS OWN WRITINGS

The Appendix to this Sermon [*The First Lay Sermon*, 1816] is by far the most miscellaneous and desultory of all my writings. It had a right to be such: for it professes to be nothing more than a maniple or handful of loose flowers, a String of Hints and Materials and Materials for Reflection. The Object too was to rouse and stimulate the mind—to set the reader a-thinking—and at least to obtain entrance for the question, whether the truth of the Opinions in fashion is quite so certain as he had hitherto taken for granted—rather than to establish the contrary by a connected chain of proofs and arguments.

And yet let the following words be prefixed as the Common Heading of these Essays. An attempt to fix the true meaning of the Terms, Reason, Understanding, Sense, Imagination, Conscience, and Ideas, with reflections on the theoretical and practical consequences of their perversion from the Revolution (1668) to the present day, 1816, the moral of the whole being that the Man who gives to the Understanding the primacy due to the Reason, and lets the Motives of Expedience usurp the place of the Prescripts of the Conscience, in both cases loses the one and spoils the other—it would not, I dare assert, be easy to find in these Essays as many paragraphs of excursive matter or foreign to the Subjects and Contents annunciated as would fill a couple of Pages. Now surely a series of Essays, the contents and purposes of which are capable of being faithfully and compleatly enumerated in a sentence of 7 or 8 lines, and where all the points treated off [*sic*] tend [to] a common result, cannot justly be regarded as a motley, Patch-work or Farrago of heterogeneous Effusions! even tho' the form and sequence were more aphorismic καὶ ἀσυνάρτητον than is really the case.

Before a just tribunal of Criticism I could apply still more triumphantly the same test—

1st to the Statesman's Manual

2. to the 2nd Lay Sermon

3. to four distinct and entire Disquisitions, each on a several subject, in the three Vol. of the Friend.

4. to two distinct Treatises, in the Literary Life, besides the Essay on authorship as a Trade.

And to these I might add three, if not four, Series of Letters on as many different important Subjects and of permanent interest, morally, politically and historically, in the Morning Post and Courier—with the 24 Lectures on Shakespear, Milton, Spenser, Dante, Ariosto and Don Quixote—and the 12 Lectures on the History of Philosophy, [considered *crossed out*] as the gradual Evolution of the Mind of the World, contemplated as a single Mind in the different successive stages of its development. Here are from 14 to 18 entire and distinct works, produced by my labors—and nevertheless I must be the wild eccentric Genius that has published nothing but fragments and splendid Tirades. S. T. Coleridge.

MS.

170. HIS FLYCATCHERS

It will *seem*, perhaps it may *be*, somewhat fanciful, not to say whimsical, that is, *maggoty*—but there are worse things run in people's heads than maggots, my dear friend! A maggot may catch a Fish, and the Fish may have a Diamond Ring in its Guts (such cases are read of) or the Seal of Solomon. Or it may become a Bee and make honey, or a Silkworm and help adorn Buckingham-house and give bread to Spital-fields. At the worst, it will turn to a Fly, and make a Buz in one of my Flycatchers.

So let it wriggle into Light—into Ink, at least, and end this maggotty digression. . . .

MS.

171. DIGRESSIONS

A blessing, I say, on the inventors of Notes! You have only to imagine the lines between the [   ] to be printed in smaller type at the bottom of the page—and the Writer may digress, like Harris, the Historian, from Dan to Beersheba and from Beersheba in hunt after the last Comet, without any breach of continuity.

> Digress? or not digress? That's now no question
> Do it? Yet do it not! See note* below.

Well! to proceed. . . .

MS.

172. 'AIDS TO REFLECTION' AND THE 'FRIEND'

Coleridge comments: It is matter of earnest thought and deep concernment to me,—and he little knows my heart who shall find the spirit of authorship in what I am about to say,—to think that thousands will read this chapter, [chapter XX of Southey's *Life of Wesley*] or the substance of it, in the writings of Wesley himself, and never complain of obscurity, or that it is, as Hone called my *Aids to Reflection*, a *proper brain-cracker*. And why is this? In the words I use, or their collocation? Not so: for no one has pointed out any passage of importance, which he having at length understood, he could propose other and more intelligible words that would have conveyed precisely the same meaning. No! Wesley first relates his theory as a history: the ideas were for him, and through him for his readers, so many *proper names*, the *substratum* of meaning being supplied by the general image and abstraction, of the human form with the swarm of associations that cluster in it. Wesley *takes* for *granted* that his readers

203

will all understand it, all at once, and without effort. The readers are far too well pleased with this, or rather, this procedure is far too much in accord both with their mental indolence and their self-complacency, that they should think of asking themselves the question. Reflect on the simple fact of the state of a child's mind while with great delight he reads or listens to the story of Jack and the Bean Stalk! How could this be, if in some sense he did not understand it? Yea, the child does *understand* each part of it—A, and B, and C; but not A B C=X. He understands it as we all understand our dreams, while we are dreaming,—each shape and incident, or group of shapes and incidents, by itself— unconscious of, and therefore unoffended at, the absence of the logical copula, or the absurdity of the transitions. He under- stands it, in short, as the READING PUBLIC understands this exposition of Wesley's theology. Now compare this with the manner, and even *obtruded* purpose of the *Friend*, or the *Aids to Reflection*, in which the aim of every sentence is to solicit, nay, tease the reader to ask himself, whether he actually does, or does not, understand distinctly?—whether he has reflected on the precise meaning of the word, however familiar it may be both to his ear and mouth?—whether he has been hitherto aware of the mischief and folly of employing words on questions, to know the very truth of which is both his interest and his duty, without fixing the one meaning which on that question they are to represent? Page after page, for a reader accustomed from childhood either to learn by rote, *i.e.* without understanding at all, as boys learn their Latin grammar, or to content himself with the popular use of words, always wide and general, and expressing a whole county where perhaps the point in discus- sion concerns the difference between two parishes of the same county! (*ex. gr.* MIND, which in the popular use means, some- times *memory*, sometimes *reason*, sometimes *understanding*, some- times *sense* ($αἴσθησις$), sometimes *inclination*, and sometimes all together, confusedly,)—for such a reader, I repeat, page after page is a process of mortification and awkward straining. Will anyone instruct me how this is to be remedied? Will he refer me to any work, already published, which has achieved the objects at which I aim, without exciting the same complaints? But then I should wish my friendly monitor to show me, at the same time, some one of these uncomplaining readers, and convince me that he is actually master of the truth contained in that work—be it Plato's, Bacon's, or Bull's, or Waterland's. Alas! alas! with a poor illiterate, but conscience-stricken, or soul-awakened Haime, or Pawson, I should find few difficulties beyond those that are the price of all momentous knowledge. For while I was demonstrating the inner structure of our spiritual organisms, he would have his mental eye fixed on the same subject, *i.e.* his own mind; even as an anatomist may be dissecting a human eye, and the pupils too far off to see this, may yet be dissecting another eye, closely following the instructions of the lecturer, and comparing his words with the shapes and textures which the knife discloses to them. But in the great majority of our gentry, and of our classically educated clergy, there is a fearful combination of the *sensuous* and the *unreal*. Whatever is *subjective*, the true and only proper *noumenon*, or *intelligibile*, is unintelligible to them. *But all substance ipso nomine* is necessarily *subjective*; of course, an appearance only, which becomes connected with the sense of *reality* by its being common to any number of beholders present at the same moment; but an *apparitio communis* is still but an *apparition*, and can be substantiated for each individual only by his attributing a subject thereto, as its support and *causa sufficiens*, even as the *community* of the appearance is the sign and presumptive proof of its objectivity. In short, I would fain bring the cause I am pleading to a short and simple, yet decisive test. Consciousness, εἰμί, mind, life, will, body, organ)(machine, nature, spirit, sin, habit, sense, understanding, reason: here are fourteen words. Have you ever reflectively and quietly asked yourself the meaning of any one of these, and tasked yourself to return the answer in *distinct* terms, not applicable to any one of the other words? Or have you contented yourself with the vague floating meaning that will just serve to save you from absurdity in the use of the word, just as the clown's botany would do, who knew that potatoes were roots, and cabbages greens? Or, if you have the gift of wit, shelter yourself under Augustine's equivocation, 'I know it perfectly well till I am asked.' Know? Ay, as an oyster knows its life. But do you know your knowledge? If the latter be your case, can you wonder that the *Aids to Reflection* are clouds and darkness for you?—S. T. C.

Note on Southey's *The Life of Wesley.*

173. THE CIRCULATING LIBRARIES

For as to the Devotees of the Circulating Libraries, I may not compliment their Pastime, or rather *Kill time*, with the name of *Reading*. Call it rather a sort of beggarly Day-dreaming in which the mind furnishes for itself only laziness and a little mawkish sensibility, while the whole *Stuff* and Furniture of the Doze is supplied *ab extra* by a sort of spiritual *Camera Obscura*, which (*pro tempore*) fixes, reflects, and transmits the moving phantasms of one man's Delirium so as to people the barrenness of a hundred other brains under the same morbid Trance, or '*suspended Animation*' of Common Sense, and all definite Purpose. We therefore altogether disjoin from the genus '*Reading*' this species of mental Pre-occupation, or rather Preventive Substitutes of occupation, and place it in the class, which has for its common distinctive character the charm of reconciling two contrary yet co-existent propensities of men, the Indulgence of Sloth with the Hatred of Vacancy; and which Class, besides Novels, contains in it, *Gambling*, Swinging or Swaying on a Chair, Spitting over a Bridge, Smoking, Quarrels after dinner between Husband and Wife, when tête a tête, the reading word by word all the advertisements of a Daily Advertiser in a Public House on a rainy Day.

MS.

174. BLOW FOR BLOW: A CRITIC DEMOLISHED

Mr. H[azlitt?] in his lust of Slander and in the rampancy of his malice first commits a rape upon my words, and then arraigns them as unchaste.

Now you have stamped your own image on it, so that it at length became current Depravity and fit to be paid into the Devil's exchequer——

Those critics whose thoughts in working pass at once into the acetous fermentation—a slender-witted Poet [once damn'd *crossed out*] passes as naturally into a sour critic, as thin Must from the vinous to the acetous fermentation.

We may take either way, and the result will be the same—If we say, strong Figures, bold Metaphors, and rapid associations of distinct Images by slight resemblances are appropriate to Poetry, yet these being the natural Language of the Mind in a state of high excitement, Passion must be [the] Soul of Poetry —or if Passion be the Soul of Poetry, then &c.——

MS.

175. OF CRITICS

There is one species of presumption among authors which is truly hateful, and which betrays itself, when writers, who, in their prefaces, have prostrated themselves before the superiority of their readers as supreme judges, will yet, in their works, pass judgments on Plato, Milton, Shakespeare, Spenser, and their compeers, in blank assertions and a peremptory *ipse-dixi*, and with a grossness of censure, which a sensible schoolmaster would not apply to the exercises of the youths in his upper forms. I need no outward remembrances of my own inferiority, but I possess them on almost every shelf of my library; and the very book which I am now using as my writing desk (Lord Bacon's *Novum Organum*) inspires an awe and heartfelt humility, which I would not exchange for all the delight which Buonaparte can enjoy at the moment that his crowned courtiers hail him emperor of emperors, and lord paramount of the West.

Friend.

VI

THE RECONCILEMENT
OF EXTERNAL AND INTERNAL

Art might itself be defined as of a middle
quality between a thought and a thing, or as
. . . the union and reconciliation of that which
is nature with that which is human. It is the
figured language of thought, and is distinguished from nature by the unity of all the
parts in one thought or idea. . . . In every work
of art there is a reconcilement of the external
with the internal.

On Poesy or Art

THE OTHER FINE ARTS

The most useful materials on this subject are the essays 'On the Principles of Genial Criticism concerning the Fine Arts', 'On Poesy or Art', and the fragments on Taste and on Beauty. These are all most conveniently found in Shawcross's edition of the *Biographia Literaria*. Some attention was paid to general aesthetic problems in the lectures on literary subjects, to be found in the three volumes of literary criticism edited by T. M. Raysor. Coleridge projected various works on aesthetics which did not get written.

His experience of painting and music was that of an outsider. 'I accompanied Dr. Callcot [J. W. Callcot, the composer] to a sort of Glee or Catch Club, composed wholly of professional singers and was much delighted,' he writes to friends, in 1808. 'Bartleman, Harrison, Cooke, Greatorex, Smith were the principal singers—Webb, the patriarch of the club, and Father of Catches and Glees in the country, was present and I was much interested by his affectionate cheerfulness under his grievous burthen of Age and infirmities, as well as by the fervent affection payed to him by all the others; and Bartleman and Harrison pleased me as much as men as they did of course as singers. They either were, or were polite enough to be, marvellously delighted with me; and all the musical entertainments of the town are open to me without expenses.' It will be noticed that the human interest predominates over the musical. Similarly with painting, though through his friendship with Hazlitt, the American painter Washington Allston, Sir George Beaumont, Northcote, C. R. Leslie, Thomas Wilkinson (the lake country artist), Mathilda Betham the miniaturist, and Thomas Phillips, he had more opportunity than with musical people, to discuss theory. He was widely read in the aesthetic writings of Lessing, Kant, Schiller, Garve and the Schlegels; and with his contemporaries in Germany in particular, he recognized as important the relations between anthropology and art, and art and religion. At the same time, he considered the primary fact to be the individual's experience of pleasure in a work of art and that this 'calls the whole soul into activity'.

VI

THE RECONCILEMENT
OF EXTERNAL AND INTERNAL

---

176. ROSSINI AND BEETHOVEN

A N ear for music is a very different thing from a taste for music. I have no ear whatever; I could not sing an air to save my life; but I have the intensest delight in music, and can detect good from bad. Naldi, a good fellow, remarked to me once at a concert, that I did not seem much interested with a piece of Rossini's which had just been performed. I said, it sounded to me like nonsense verses. But I could scarcely contain myself when a thing of Beethoven's followed.

Table Talk.

177. HIS TASTE IN MUSIC

Some music is above me; most music is beneath me. I like Beethoven and Mozart—or else some of the aërial compositions of the elder Italians, as Palestrina and Carissimi—And I love Purcell.

The best sort of music is what it should be—sacred; the next best, the military, has fallen to the lot of the Devil.

Good music never tires me, nor sends me to sleep. I feel

physically refreshed and strengthened by it, as Milton says he did.

Table Talk.

178. MUSIC—THIS MIGHTY HOT MAGIC

I have no technical knowledge of Music. I wish, I had. I receive deep sensations, yea, intellectual activities from it; but what it is that so affects me, I know not. I love it, as a Blind man in love who thrills at the touch of her he thinks so beautiful because he feels so dear. Music seems to have an *immediate* communion with my Life; I have no power of tracing it thro' my Ear, no consciousness of it in its' march or passage, except when it ceases to be *music* for me, and becomes mere unpleasant or idle sound. It converses with the *life* of my mind, as if it were itself the Mind of my Life. Yet I sometimes think, that a great Composer, a Mozart, a Beethoven must have been in a state of Spirit much more akin, more analogous, to mine own when I am at once waiting for, watching, and organically constructing and inwardly constructed by, the *Ideas*, the living Truths, that may be re-excited but cannot be expressed by Words, the Transcendents that give the Objectivity to all Objects, the Form to all Images, yet are themselves untranslatable into any Image, unrepresentable by any particular Object than I can imagine myself to be to a Titian, or a Sir C. Wren. Yet I wish I did know something more of the wondrous mystery of this mighty *hot Magic*, were it but to understand why it is that ignorant as I am I should feel so utter, so extreme a difference between the Musical Compositions of Beethoven, Mozart, and our own Purcell for instance, and those of the equally celebrated Russians and others which are just like nonsense verses to me, which I know to be meant for a Poem because I distinguish the rhymes.

But I must be content in this, as in my other vain regret and craving for an insight into and comprehension of the mysteries of the Transcendental Analysis of the great French and German Mathematicians. S. T. Coleridge.

MS.

179. PAINTING NOT COPYING

It is a poor compliment to pay to a painter to tell him that his figure stands out of the canvas, or that you start at the likeness of the portrait. Take almost any daub, cut it out of the canvas, and place the figure looking into or out of a window, and any one may take it for life. Or take one of Mrs. Salmon's wax queens or generals, and you will very sensibly feel the difference between a copy, as they are, and an imitation, of the human form, as a good portrait ought to be. Look at that flower vase of Van Huysum, and at these wax or stone peaches and apricots! The last are likest to their original, but what pleasures do they give? None, except to children.

Table Talk.

180. THE PERISHABILITY OF PAINTING AND POETRY

Poem. Address on W. Alston's larger Landscape sent by sea to England. Threnic on the perishability by accident as well as time, and the narrow Sphere of action of Pictures. Printing: yet even MSS, Homer, &c. &c. &c.—but Apelles, Protogenes, ah where?—Spenser's *Faery Queen*, VI last Books, and his Comedies—but on what authority does this rest?

'Sorrowful yet true Speech of Artists, " *burnt* or gone to England", which is the same as if the Picture were burnt.'

MS.

181. COLOUR

A far more subtle and difficult, yet I would fain believe not hopeless investigation [than an analysis of line and lines] would

215

be respecting the symbolical characters or Significancy of Colors. But for this I am not prepared—I can merely glimpse it from the Mount Pisgah in the distance.

MS.

182. ARCHITECTURAL GENIUS

The architectural genius consists in the power of aptly, becomingly, and proportionally inclosing, subinclosing and applying in all its dimensions a given Space, the place of which remains the same, for a given end or ends; and of producing a unity of the exterior surface, expressing at once the greater or less manifoldness of the Spaces contained and the characteristic purpose of the whole, not without a correspondency and reciprocity of effect to [the object].

MS.

183. 'ARTISTRIAL'

'Artistrial'=concentrated Sense of the Beautiful ✕ the pleasure in Beauty modified by the sense of Propriety, and Rank in Life. See an artist's Room, see a *littery* literary Man's Room! All in disorder—much dirt, more Confusion. But here and there some exquisitely finished Form or Combinations of Form—in the production no less than in the contemplation of which the Painter (whether Poet and likewise technically Painter; or Poet whose Paintings, like those of the *camera obscura*, have only a present endurance to his own eye, and for others can act only as the Sun and Landscape conjoined—i.e. on minds so pre-disposed and pre-harmonized as to be *camerae picturabiles*) annihilates for himself all non-pertinent Objects, which *co-exist* with his compositions only to the Eye of his Visitors. Now a well-attuned and sensitive female mind must have the whole of the given Space *in keeping*; it requires the callus of an extreme stimulation to be able to endure the rags, brushes and broken Gallipots of an Allston, or the scattered Books, fluttering Pamphlets, and dusty Paper-wilderness of a Wordsworth. I know but two individuals who combine both, *viz*—the Ladylike *Wholeness* with creative delight in *particular* forms—and these are Mr. Robert Southey, Poet Laureate, &c. &c. &c., and Mr. Sam. Tayl. Coleridge, whose whole Being has been unfortunately little more than a far-stretched series of *Et Ceteras*.

Calne, Wiltshire. 20 May, 1815.

MS.

VII

THE LOVELY SHAPES
AND SOUNDS INTELLIGIBLE

I am convinced, that for the human soul to
prosper in rustic life a certain vantage-ground
is pre-requisite. It is not every man that is likely
to be improved by country life or by country
labors. Education, or original sensibility, or
both, must pre-exist, if the changes, forms, and
incidents of nature are to prove a sufficient
stimulant.

Biographia Literaria, Chapter XVII

THE NATURAL WORLD: SCIENCE

The poems are of course full of observations of the natural world. Coleridge's physical and aesthetic enjoyment of it is evident in many passages in the letters, in *Anima Poetae*, and in the 'Satyrane Letters' (reprinted from the 1809–10 *Friend* in the *Biographia Literaria*). It stemmed largely from his Devonshire childhood, and was developed through association with the Wordsworths in the brief Quantocks period, and later in the Lakes. Mr. Gordon Wordsworth said that his account of the ascent of Scafell (Item 186) 'is by many years the earliest record of the pleasures of rock-scrambling, or of any ascent of the Scafell group for the mere love of the fells'. He combines a gift for minute observation with a large metaphysical sense of the universe as a whole.

His interest in natural phenomena had a strong scientific component, fostered by his friendship with Humphry Davy, Tom Wedgwood (the first photographer), Blumenbach and others; and the *Theory of Life*, posthumously published by Seth B. Watson in 1848, suggests some of his scientific bearings. The notebooks contain passages on chemistry lectures and chemical books, physiology, anthropology, galvanism and electricity, and medical subjects. A patient himself, as a result of his drug addiction and the physical and mental conditions in which it thrived, he was from Bristol days (1795) onwards always deeply interested in Dr. Crompton and Dr. James Currie and their circle; at Highgate in Joseph Henry Green, a surgeon at Guy's Hospital, John Abernethy, and other leading surgeons and doctors of the time. Though the laboratory he once proposed setting up at Keswick came to nothing, a genuine scientific curiosity persisted to the last weeks of his life and kept him abreast of the latest scientific developments.

VII

THE LOVELY SHAPES
AND SOUNDS INTELLIGIBLE

---

184. ON HIS OWN SUBTLETY

THE finest edge, into which the meditative mind of a
Contemplator was ever ground, is but the back of the
Blade in comparison with the Subtlety of Nature. . . .

MS.

185. PLANT)(INSECT. *πανζωα)(ἐντομοζωα*

1. In the plant each part is capable of passing by metamorphosis, progressive and retrogressive, into every other—while
yet each remaining bears or supports the higher, the root bearing the stem, the stem the leaves, all the calyx and flower. In the
insect each antecedent form makes way for the higher—and
perishes in giving it birth; the Egg is sacrificed that the Larva
may appear, and the Imago, or mature Insect, takes place of the
Larva.

2. The Plant is the nuptial Garland of Earth and Air—their
equation of Carbon, Oxygen and Hydrogen. Or as Carbon as
the negative factor of Life is common to all the realms of organic
Nature, we may better call the Vegetable Tribe the equation of
Oxygen and Hydrogen—not the neutralization, which is water,
and therefore the product of a quantitative combination: but

the *potenziation*, or endlessly varied proportions eliciting the inner spirit of the two Gases by communication of qualities.— Now as in powers the three great Co-efficients of Nature are Gravity and Light with Warmth, as the Indifference, so in bodies, which necessarily contain, each body all three, yet under the predominance of some one, Carbon most represents Gravity, Oxygen Light, and Hydrogen Warmth.

3. Accordingly, in the Flower, the Crown of mature vegetative life, we have the qualitative product of Oxygen=Light in the outness and splendor of Colors, the qualit[ative] prod[uct] of Hydrogen=Warmth in the inwardness and sweetness of Fragrance. All offering that is truly sacrificial, i.e. hallowing, sanctifying, proceeds from and is preceded by and the act of a *Yearning*, desiderium. πόθος, στοργή—what will not the Mother sacrifice when her bowels are yearning for her children. And this constitutes the diversity of Yearning and desire, πόθου καὶ ὀρέξεως. Yearning offers up, resigns itself—passes wholly into another. Desire [catches *crossed out*] seizes hold of, draws to itself, devours, ravishes—and in its fiercest form (*ex. gr.* See a hornet devouring a peach thro' a magnifying glass) *ravages*. Hence in all ages, incense, fragrant steams, have been the accompaniments of Sacrifice. Likewise of gentle Love. (Song of Sol[omon] I. 12. 13. 14—and II. 1. I am the Rose of Sharon, and the Lily of the Valley. III. 6.)

4. The insect is the incarnation of the dissepent [dissepiment?] contractive corrosive power of the Air—the minister of the Antipathy of Air to Earth—Here too therefore we must expect the qualit[ative] product of Oxygen in splendor of colors—but the Warmth becomes external, thermometrical—and the odor either none, or putroid, and marking the ascendancy of a new ingredient, Nitrogen—not unknown indeed in the vegetable world but yet known only as an alien, an antedated Animal in the gluten of Wheat, which is almost an artefact of man and animal manures. As the Plant of Love, Yearning and Sacrifice, so is the Insect the Symbol of [Lust *crossed out*] Appetite, Desire

—Lust hard by hate. Manifold motions making little speed.
And to deform and kill the things whereon they feed.

5. The Plant rests in the products. Its branches, leaves, flowers, seeds, are so many successive Sabbaths ✶ The Insects' products are all working tools, or warnings and wakings to restless activity. The Insect is a *Shop* of Tools.

6. Yet at length both join, the Πόθος (Plant) and the ὄρεξις (Insect) in the submissive love of the female—and with the victory of the former in the στοργή—the hatching and brooding are vegetable processes—and the Bird the Union of Plant and Insect, each glorified by the interpenetration and by the potenziation of ascending intensity of Life. Hence the feathery vegetation of the Birds—the rich colors and a substitute for the fragrancy of the Plants. For as the Bird is the symbol of Air in its emancipation from water, and therefore the continuous and dilative Hydrogen must give way to the contractive distinctive Oxygen, and to the volatile self-projecting dispersive Nitrogen, the Carbon (the Repres[entative] of Gravity)' becomes the mediator—we have Light in the form (under the power) of Gravity in Color, and Gravity sub formâ et ditione Lucis sub ditione. In Sounds and sweet yearning varied by quiet provoking challenging sounds are the surrogates of the Vegetable Odors—and like these, are the celebrations of the Nuptial moments, the hours of Love. Music is to Fragrance, as Air to Water. Milton's *Comus*.

7. The Child, Pocsy, finds a *fall*, a degradation, in the Mammalia.

MS.

186. TOUR IN THE LAKE COUNTRY

FROM SARA HUTCHINSON'S TRANSCRIPT AND NOTEBOOK 2.

Wed, Afternoon 1/2 past 3, Augt 4th 1802—
Wastdale, a mile and a half below the Foot of the Lake, at an Alehouse without a Sign, 20 strides from the Door, under the Shade of a huge Sycamore Tree, without my coat—but that

I will now put on, in prudence—yes here I am and have been for something more than an hour, and have *enjoyed* a good Dish of Tea. I carried my Tea and sugar with me, under this delightful Tree. In the House there are only an old feeble Woman, and a '*Tallyeur*' Lad upon the Table—all the rest of the Wastdale World is a haymaking, rejoicing and thanking God for this first downright summer Day that we have had since the beginning of May. On Sunday Augt. 1st 1/2 after 12, I had a Shirt, cravat, 2 pair of Stockings, a little paper and half a dozen Pens, a German Book (Voss's Poems) and a little Tea and Sugar, with my Night Cap, packed up in my natty green oil-skin, neatly squared, and put into my *net* knapsack, and the knap-sack on my back and the Besom stick in my hand (which for want of a better, and in spite of Mrs C. and Mary, who both raised their voices against it, especially as I left the Besom scattered on the Kitchen Floor) off I sallied—over the Bridge, thro' the hop-Field, thro' the Prospect Bridge at Portinscale, so on by the tall Birch that grows out of the center of the huge Oak, along into Newlands. Newlands is indeed a lovely Place—the houses, each in it's little Shelter of Ashes and Sycamores, just under the Road, so that in some places you might leap down on the Roof, seemingly at least—the exceeding greeness and pastoral beauty of the Vale itself, with the savage wildness of the Mountains, their coves, and long arm-shaped and elbow-shaped Ridges— yet this wildness softened down into a congruity with the Vale by the semicircular Lines of the Crags, and of the bason-like Concavities. The Cataract between Newlands and Kescadale had but little water in it, of course, was of no particular Interest. I passed on thro' the green steep smooth bare Kescadale, a sort of unfurnished Passage or antechamber between Newlands and Buttermere, came out on Buttermere and drank Tea at the little Inn, and read the greater part of the Revelations—the only part of the New Testament, which the Scotch Cobbler read— because why? *Because it was the only part that he understood.* O 'twas a wise Cobbler!

Conceive an enormous round Bason mountain-high of solid Stone, cracked in half and one half gone; exactly in the remaining half of this enormous Bason, does Buttermere lie, in this beautiful and stern Embracement of Rock. I left it, passed by Scale Force, the white downfall of which glimmered thro' the Trees that hang before it like bushy Hair over a Madman's Eyes, and climbed 'till I gained the first Level. Here it was 'every man his own path-maker', and I went directly cross it—upon soft mossy Ground, with many a hop, skip, and jump, and many an occasion for observing the truth of the old saying, 'where Rushes grow, A Man may go'. Red Pike, a dolphin-shaped Peak of a deep red, looked in upon me from over the Fell on my Left; on my right I had, first Melbreak (the Mountain on the right of Crummock, as you ascend the Lake) then a Vale running down with a pretty Stream in it, to Loweswater, then Heck Comb, a Fell of the same height and running in the same direction with Melbreak, a Vale on the other side too, and at the bottom of both these Vales the Loweswater Fells running abreast. Again I reached an ascent, climbed up, and came to a ruined Sheep-fold—a wild green view all around me, bleating of Sheep and noise of Waters. I sate there near 20 minutes, the Sun setting on the Hill behind with a soft watery gleam; and in front of me the upper Halves of huge deep-furrowed Grasmere (the mountain on the other side of Crummock) and the huge Newland and Buttermere Mountains, and peeping in from behind, the Top of Saddlcback. Two Fields were visible, the highest cultivated Ground on the Newland side of Buttermere, and the Trees in those Fields were the only Trees visible in the whole prospect.

I left the Sheepfold with regret—for of all things a ruined Sheepfold in a desolate place is the dearest to me, and fills me most with Dreams and Visions and tender thoughts of those I love best.

Well! I passed a bulging roundish-headed green Hill to my Left, (and to the left of it was a frightful crag) with a very high round-head right before me; this latter is called Ennerdale-Dodd, and bisects the ridge between Ennerdale and Buttermere and Crummock. I took it on my right hand, and came to the top of the bulging green Hill, on which I found a small Tarn, called Flatern [?Floutern] Tarn, about 100 yds. in length, and not more than 7 or 8 in breadth, but O! what a grand Precipice it lay at the foot of! The half of this Precipice (called Herdhouse) nearest to Ennerdale was black, with green moss-cushions on the Ledges; the half nearest to Buttermere a pale pink, and divided from the black part by a great streamy Torrent of crimson Shiver, and Screes, or Skilly (as they call it). I never saw a more heart-raising Scene. I turned and looked on the Scene which I had left behind, a marvellous group of Mountains, wonderfully and admirably arranged—not a single minute object to interrupt the oneness of the view, excepting those two green Fields in Buttermere—but before me the glorious Sea with the high Coast and Mountains of the Isle of Man, perfectly distinct—and three Ships in view. A little further on, the Lake of Ennerdale (the lower part of it) came in view, shaped like a clumsy battle-dore—but it is, in reality, exactly *fiddle-shaped*. The further Bank of the higher part, steep, lofty, bare bulging Crags; the nether Bank green and pastoral, with Houses in the shelter of their own dear Trees. On the opposite Shore in the middle and narrow part of the Lake there bulges out a huge Crag called Angling Stone, being a famous Station for Anglers—and the reflection of this Crag in the Water is admirable—pillars or rather it looks like the pipes of some enormous Organ in a rich golden Color.

I travelled on to Long Moor, two miles below the foot of the Lake, and met a very hearty welcome from John Ponsonby, a Friend of M^r. Jackson's—here I stayed the night, and the greater part of Monday—the old Man went to the head of the Lake with me. The mountains at the head of this Lake and Wast-dale are the Monsters of the Country, bare bleak Heads, evermore doing deeds of Darkness, weather-plots, and storm-conspiracies in the Clouds. Their names are Herdhouse, Bowness, Wha Head, Great Gavel, the Steeple, the Pillar, and Seat Allian.

I left Long Moor after Tea, and proceeded to Egremont, 5 miles—thro' a very pleasant Country, part of the way by the River Enner, with well wooded Banks, and nice green Fields, and pretty houses with Trees, and two huge Sail-cloth Manufactories. Went to Girtskill, a mercer, for whom I had a Letter, but he was at Workington, so I walked on to S^t. Bees, 3 miles from Egremont. When I came there could not get a Bed—at last got an apology for one, at a miserable Pot-house; slept or rather dozed, in my Clothes—breakfasted there—and went to the School and Church ruins. Had read in the history of Cumb-[erlan]d that there was an 'excellent Library presented to the School by Sr James Lowther', which proved to be some 30 odd Volumes of Commentaries on the Scripture utterly worthless, and which with all my passion for ragged old Folios I should certainly make serviceable for fire-lighting. Men who write Tours and County Histories I have by woeful experience found out to be *damned Liars*, harsh words, but true! It was a wet woeful oppressive Morning. I was sore with my bad night. Walked down to the Beach, which is a very nice hard Sand for more than a Mile, but the St Bees Head which I had read much of as a noble Cliff, might be made a song of on the Flats of the Dutch Coast—but in England 'twill scarcely bear a looking-at. Returned to Egremont, a miserable walk, dined there, visited the Castle, the Views from which are uncommonly interesting. I looked thro' an old wild Arch—slovenly black Houses, and gardens, as wild as a Dream, over the Hills beyond them, which slip down in one place making a noticeable gap. Had a good Bed, slept well—and left Egremont this morning after Breakfast.

Had a pleasant walk to Calder Abbey—an elegant but not very interesting Ruin, joining to a very handsome Gentleman's House built of red free-stone, which has the comfortable warm Look of Brick without it's meanness and multitude of puny squares. This place lies just within the Line of circumference of *a Circle* of woody Hills—the area, a pretty Plain half a mile perhaps in diameter—and completely cloathed and hid with wood, except one red hollow in these low steep hills, and except behind the Abbey, where the Hills are far higher, and consist of green Fields almost (but not quite) to the Top. Just opposite to Calder Abbey, and on the Line of the Circumference, rises Ponsonby Hill, the Village of Calder Bridge, and it's interesting Mill, all in Wood, some hidden, some roofs just on a line with the Trees, some higher, but Ponsonby Hall far higher than the rest. I regained the Road, and came to Bonewood, a single Ale-house on the top of the Hill above the Village, Gosforth—drank a pint of Beer (I forgot to tell you that the whole of my expenses at St Bees, a glass of Gin and Water, my Bed, and Breakfast amounted to 11^d). From this Bonewood is a noble view of the Isle of Man on the one side, and on the other side all the bold dread tops of the Ennerdale and Wastdale Mountains. Indeed the whole way from Egremont I had beautiful Sea Views, the low hills to my right dipping down into inverted Arches, or Angles, and the Sea, often with a Ship seen thro'; while on my left the Steeple and Sca' Fell facing each other, far above the other Fells, formed in their interspace a great Gap in the Heaven. So I went on, turned Eastward, up the Irt, the Sea behind and Wastdale Mountains before[1]—and here I am. And now I must go and see the Lake, for immediately at the Foot of the Lake runs a low Ridge so that you can see nothing of the Water till you are at it's very Edge.

Between the Lake and the Mountains on the left, a low ridge of hill runs parallel with the Lake, for more than half it's length; and just at the foot of the Lake there is a Bank even and smooth and low like a grassy Bank in a Gentleman's Park. Along the hilly Ridge I walked thro' a Lane of green Hazels, with hay-fields and Hay-makers on my Right, beyond the River Irt, and on the other side of the River, Irton Fell with a deep perpen-

[1] N.B. 2: Mem. beautiful shadow of the Fern upon the lichened Stone which it over-canopied.

dicular Ravine, and a curious fretted Pillar of Clay, crosier-shaped, standing up on it. Next to Irton Fells and in the same line are the Screes, and you can look at nothing but the Screes tho' there were 20 quaint Pillars close by you. The Lake is wholly hidden 'till your very Feet touch it', as one may say, and to a Stranger the Burst would be almost overwhelming. The Lake itself seen from it's Foot appears indeed of too regular shape; exactly like the sheet of Paper on which I am writing, except it is still narrower in respect of it's length. (In reality however the Lake widens as it ascends and at the head is very considerably broader than at the foot). But yet, in spite of this it is a marvellous sight: a sheet of water between 3 and 4 miles in length, the whole or very nearly the whole of it's right Bank formed by the Screes, or facing of bare Rock of enormous Height, two-thirds of it's height downwards absolutely perpendicular; and then slanting off in *Screes*, or Shiver, consisting of fine red Streaks running in broad Stripes thro' a stone colour —slanting off from the Perpendicular, as steep as the meal newly ground from the Miller's spout. So it is at the foot of the Lake; but higher up this streaky Shiver occupies two-thirds of the whole height, like a pointed Decanter in shape, or an out-spread Fan, or a long-waisted old maid with a fine prim Apron, or—no, other things that would only fill up the Paper. When I first came the Lake was a perfect Mirror; and what must have been the Glory of the reflections in it! This huge facing of Rock *said* to be half a mile in perpendicular height, with deep Ravines the whole *wrinded* [*sic*] and torrent-worn, except where the pink-striped Screes come in, as smooth as Silk, all this reflected, turned into Pillars, dells, and a whole new-world of Images in the water! The head of the Lake is crowned by three huge pyramidal Mountains, Yewbarrow, Sca' Fell, and the Great Gavel; Yewbarrow and Sca' Fell nearly opposite to each other, yet so that the Ness (or Ridge-line, like the line of a fine Nose,) of Sca' Fell runs in behind that of Yewbarrow while the Ness of great Gavel is still further back, between the two others, and of course, instead of running athwart the Vale it directly falls

thus \\// The Lake and Vale run nearly from East to West

and this figure below will give you some idea of it (But the Transcriber has not ingenuity enough to copy it, nor the full length Portrait of the Author—so they must be dispensed with).[1]

Melfell (lying South of the Lake) consists of great mountain Steps decreasing in size as they approach the Lake.

My Road led along under Melfell and by Yewbarrow—and now I came in sight of it's other side called Keppel Crag and then a huge enormous bason-like Cove called Green Crag—as I suppose, from there being no single Patch of green to be seen on any one of it's perpendicular sides—so on to Kirk Fell, at the foot of which is Thomas Tyson's House where W[ordsworth] and I slept Novr will be 3 years, and there I was welcomed kindly, had a good Bed, and left it after Breakfast.

Thursday Morning, Augt 5th—went down the Vale almost to the Water Head, and ascended the low Reach between Sca' Fell and the Screes, and soon after I had gained it's height came

in sight Burnmoor Water, a large Tairn ⟨○⟩ nearly of that

shape,[2] it's Tail towards Sca' Fell, at its head a gap forming an inverted arch with Black Coomb and a peep of the Sea seen thro' it. It lies directly at the Back of the Screes, and the stream that flows from it down thro' the gap, is called the Mite, and runs thro' a Vale of it's own called Miterdale, parallel with the lower part of Wastdale, and divided from it by the high Ridge called Irton Fells. I ascended Sca' Fell by the side of a torrent, and climbed and rested, rested[3] and climbed, 'till I gained the very summit of Sca' Fell—believed by the Shepherds here to be

[1] N.B. 2 contains a rough diagram of the topography, but alas! no self-portrait. 'The transcriber' was Sara Hutchinson.

[2] N.B. 2: Flounder-shaped.

[3] Another account of this expedition now all but illegible in the faded pencil jottings in Notebook 2, gives us some of his thoughts while he rested: 'A gentle madman that would wander still over the Mountains by the

higher than either Helvellyn or Skiddaw. Even to Black Coomb, before me all the Mountains die away running down westward to the Sea, apparently in eleven ridges and three parallel Vales with their three Rivers, seen from their very Sources to their falling into the Sea, where they form (excepting their Screw-like flexures) the *Trident* of the Irish Channel at Ravenglass. O my God! what enormous Mountains these are close by me, and yet below the Hill I stand on, Great Gavel, Kirk Fell, Green Crag, and behind, the Pillar, then the Steeple, then the Hay Cock, on the other side and behind me, Great End, Esk Carse, Bow-fell and close to my back two huge Pyramids, nearly as high as Sca' Fell itself, and indeed parts and parts of Sca' Fell known far and near by these names, the hither one of Broad Crag, and the next to it (but divided from it by a low Ridge) Doe Crag, which is indeed of itself a great Mountain of stones from a pound to 20 Ton weight embedded in woolly Moss. And here I am *lounded*—so fully lounded—that tho' the wind is strong, and the Clouds are hasting hither from the Sea—and the whole air Seaward has a lurid Look—and we shall certainly have Thunder—yet here (but that I am hunger'd and provision-less) *here* I could lie warm, and wait methinks for tomorrow's Sun, and on a nice Stone Table am I now at this moment writing to you—between 2 and 3 o'Clock as I guess—surely the first Letter ever written from the Top of Sca' Fell! But O! what a look down just under my Feet! The frightfullest Cove that might ever be seen, huge perpendicular Precipices, and one

lonely Tairns—the like never seen since the crazy Shepherd, who having lost all his sheep in a long hard snow and now was repulsed or thought himself treated coldly by his Sweetheart—and so went a wanderer seeking his Sheep forever—in storm and snow especially. . . . Bear witness for me, what thoughts I wandered about with—if ever I imagined myself a conqueror, it was always to bring peace—but mostly turned away from these thoughts to more humane and peaceable Dreams.

'One plan for one book the Genius of some place appearing in a Dream and upbraiding me for omitting *him*.

'. . . Love to all the Passions and Faculties as Music to all the varieties of Sound.'

Sheep upon it's only Ledge, that surely must be crag! Tyson told me of this place, and called it Hollow Stones. Just by it and joining together, rise two huge Pillars of bare lead-colored Stone. I am no measurer, but their height and depth is terrible. I know how unfair it is to judge of these Things by a comparison of past Impressions with present—but I have no shadow of hesitation in saying that the Coves and Precipices of Helvellin are nothing to these! From this sweet lounding Place I see directly thro' Borrowdale, the Castle Crag, the whole of Derwent Water, and but for the haziness of the Air I could see my own House. I see clear enough where it stands——

Here I will fold up this Letter. I have Wafers in my Inkhorn, and you shall call this Letter when it passes before you the Sca' Fell Letter. I must now drop down how I may into Eskdale— that lies under to my right, the upper part of it the wildest and savagest surely of all the Vales that were ever seen from the Top of an English Mountain and the lower part the loveliest.

Eskdale, Friday, Augt. 6th at an Estate House called Toes

There is one sort of Gambling, to which I am much addicted; and that not of the least criminal kind for a Man who has Children and a Concern. It is this. When I find it convenient to descend from a Mountain, I am too confident and too indolent to look round about and wind about 'till I find a track or other symptom of safety; but I wander on, and where it is first *possible* to descend, there I go, relying upon fortune for how far down this possibility will continue. So it was yesterday afternoon. I passed down from Broad Crag, skirted the Precipices, and found myself cut off from a most sublime Crag-summit, that seemed to rival Sca' Fell Man in height, and to outdo it in fierceness. A Ridge of Hill lay low down, and divided this Crag (called Doe-Crag) and Broad-crag—even as the hyphen divides the words broad and crag. I determined to go thither; the first place I came to, that was not direct Rock, I slipped down, and went on for a while with tolerable ease—but now I came (it was midway down) to a smooth perpendicular Rock about 7 feet high—this was nothing—I put my hands on the Ledge, and dropped down. In a few yards came just such another. I *dropped* that too. And yet another, seemed not higher—I would not stand for a trifle, so I dropped that too—but the stretching of the muscle of my hands and arms, and the jolt of the Fall on my Feet, put my whole Limbs in a *Tremble*, and I paused, and looking down, saw that I had little else to encounter but a succession of these little Precipices—it was in truth a Path that in a very hard Rain is, no doubt, the channel of a most splendid Waterfall. So I began to suspect that I ought not to go on; but then unfortunately tho' I could with ease drop down a smooth Rock of 7 feet high, I could not *climb* it, so go on I must; and on I went. The next 3 drops were not half a Foot, at least not a foot, more than my own height, but every Drop increased the Palsy of my Limbs. I shook all over, Heaven knows without the least influence of Fear. And now I had only two more to drop down—to return was impossible—but of these two the first was tremendous, it was twice my own height, and the Ledge at the bottom was exceedingly narrow, that if I drop down upon it I must of necessity have fallen backwards and of course killed myself. My limbs were all in a tremble. I lay upon my Back to rest myself, and was beginning according to my Custom to laugh at myself for a Madman, when the sight of the Crags above me on each side, and the impetuous Clouds just over them, posting so luridly and so rapidly to northward, overawed me. I lay in a state of almost prophetic Trance and Delight and blessed God aloud for the powers of Reason and the Will, which remaining no Danger can overpower us! O God, I exclaimed aloud, how calm, how blessed am I now. I know not how to proceed, how to return, but I am calm and fearless and confident. If this Reality were a Dream, if I were asleep, what agonies had I suffered! what screams! When the Reason and the Will are away, what remain to us but Darkness and Dimness and a bewildering Shame, and Pain that is utterly

Lord over us, or fantastic Pleasure that draws the Soul along swimming through the air in many shapes, even as a Flight of Starlings in a Wind.—I arose, and looking down saw at the bottom a heap of Stones which had fallen abroad and rendered the narrow Ledge on which they had been piled doubly dangerous. At the bottom of the third Rock that I dropt from, I met a dead Sheep quite rotten. This heap of stones, I guessed, and have since found that I guessed aright, had been piled up by the Shepherd to enable him to climb up and free the poor Creature whom he had observed to be crag-fast, but seeing nothing but rock over rock, he had desisted and gone for help and in the mean time the poor Creature had fallen down and killed itself. As I was looking at these I glanced my eye to my left, and observed that the Rock was rent from top to bottom. I measured the breadth of the Rent, and found that there was no danger of my being *wedged* in, so I put my knap-sack round to my side, and slipped down as between two walls, without any danger or difficulty. The next Drop brought me down on the Ridge called the How. I hunted out my Besom Stick, which I had flung before me when I first came to the Rocks, and wisely gave over all thought of ascending Doe-Crag, for now the Clouds were again coming in most tumultuously. So I began to descend, when I felt an odd sensation across my whole Breast—not pain nor itching—and putting my hand on it I found it all bumpy—and on looking saw the whole of my Breast from my Neck—to my Navel, exactly all that my Kamell-hair Breast-shield covers, filled with great red heat-bumps, so thick that no hair could lie between them. They still remain but are evidently less and I have no doubt will wholly disappear in a few Days. It was however a startling proof to me of the violent exertions which I had made. I descended this low Hill which was all hollow beneath me—and was like the rough green Quilt of a Bed of waters. At length two streams burst out and took their way down, one on [one] side a high Ground upon this Ridge, the other on the other. I took that to my right

236

(having on my left this high ground, and the other Stream, and beyond that Doe-crag, on the other side of which is Esk Halse, where the head-spring of the Esk rises, and running down the Hill and in upon the Vale looks and actually deceived me, as a great Turnpike Road—in which, as in many other respects the Head of Eskdale much resembles Langdale) and soon the Channel sank all at once, at least 40 yards, and formed a magnificent Waterfall—and close under this a succession of Waterfalls 7 in number, the third of which is nearly as high as the first. When I had almost reached the bottom of the Hill, I stood so as to command the whole 8 Waterfalls, with the great triangle-crag looking in above them, and on the one side of them the enormous and more than perpendicular Precipices and *Bull's-Brows*, of Sca' Fell! And now the Thunder-Storm was coming on, again and again! Just at the bottom of the Hill I saw on before me in the Vale, lying just above the River on the side of a Hill, one, two, three, four Objects; I could not distinguish whether Peat-hovels, or hovel-shaped Stones. I thought in my mind, that 3 of them would turn out to be stones—but that the fourth was certainly a Hovel. I went on toward them, crossing and recrossing the Becks and the River and found that they were all huge Stones—the one nearest the Beck which I had determined to be really a Hovel, retained its likeness when I was close beside. In size it is nearly equal to the famous Bowder Stone, but in every other respect greatly superior to it—it has a complete Roof, and that perfectly *thatched* with weeds, and Heath, and Mountain-Ash Bushes. I now was obliged to ascend again, as the River ran greatly to the Left, and the Vale was nothing more than the Channel of the River, all the rest of the interspace between the Mountains was a tossing up and down of Hills of all sizes—and the place at which I am now writing is called—*Te-as*, and spelt, *Toes*—as the Toes of Sca' Fell. It is not possible that any name can be more descriptive of the Head of Eskdale. I ascended close under Sca' Fell, and came to a little Village of Sheep-folds—there were 5

together—and the redding Stuff, and the Shears, and an old
Pot, was in the passage of the first of them. Here I found an
imperfect Shelter from a Thunder-shower accompanied with
such Echoes! O God! what thoughts were mine! O how I
wished for Health and Strength that I might wander about for
a Month together, in the stormiest month of the year, among
these Places, so lonely[1] and savage and full of sounds! After the
Storm I passed on and came to a great Peat-road, that wound
down a Hill, called Maddock How, and now came out upon
the first cultivated Land which begins with a Bridge that goes
over a Stream, a Waterfall of considerable height and beauti-
fully wooded above you, and a great water-slope under you.
The Gill down which it falls, is called Scale Gill and the Fall
Scale Gill Force. (The word Scale and Scales is common in this
Country—and is said by [*blank*] to be derived from the Saxon
Sceala; the wattling of Sheep; but judging from the places
themselves, *Scale Force* and this Scale Gill Force, I think it as
possible that it is derived from Scalle—which signifies a deafen-
ing Noise.) Well, I passed[2] thro' some sweet pretty Fields, and
came to a large Farm-house where I am now writing. The
place is called Toes or *Te*-as—the Master's name John Vicars
Towers. They received me hospitably. I drank Tea here and
they begged me to pass the Night—which I did and supped of
some excellent Salmonlings, which Towers had brought from
Ravenglass whither he had been, as holding under the Earl of
Egremont, and obliged 'to ride the Fair'—a custom introduced
during the time of Insecurity and piratical Incursion for the
Protection of Ravenglass Fair. They were a fine Family—and
a Girl who did not look more than 12 years old, but was nearly
15, was very beautiful, with hair like vine-tendrils. She had
been long ill and was a sickly child. 'Ah poor Bairn!' (said the
Mother) 'worse luck for her, she looks like a Quality Bairn, as
you may say.' This Man's Ancestors have been time out of mind

---

[1] G. H. B. C. read: lovely.   [2] G. H. B. C. read: peeped.

in the Vale, and here I found that the common Names, Towers and Tozers are the same; *er* signifies 'upon'—as Mite-er-dale the Dale upon the River Mite, Donnerdale, a Contraction of Duddon-er-dale, the Dale upon the River Duddon. So Towers, pronounced in the Vale *Te*-ars—and Tozers is those who live on *the Toes*—i.e. upon the *Knobby* feet of the Mountain. M^r. *Te*ars has mended my pen. This morning after breakfast I went out with him, and passed up the Vale again due East, along a higher Road, over a heathy upland, crossed the upper part of Scale Gill, came out upon Maddock How, and then ascending turned directly Northward, into the Heart of the Mountains; on my left the wild Crags under which flows the Scale Gill Beck, the most remarkable of them called Cat Crag (a wild Cat being killed there) and on my right hand six great Crags, which appeared in the mist all in a file, and they were all, tho' of different sizes, yet the same shape, all triangles. Other Crags far above them, higher up the Vale, appeared and disappeared as the mists passed and came—one with a waterfall, called Spout Crag—and another most tremendous one, called Earn Crag. I passed on a little way, till I came close under a huge Crag, called Buck Crag, and immediately under this is Four-foot Stone—having on it the clear marks of four foot-steps. The Stone is in its whole breadth just 36 inches, (I measured it exactly) but the part that contains the marks is raised above the other part and is just 20 1/2 Inches. The length of the Stone is 32 1/2 Inches. The first foot-mark is an Ox's foot—nothing can be conceived more exact; this is 5 3/4 Inches wide. The second is a Boy's shoe in the Snow, 9 1/2 Inches in length; this too is the very Thing itself, the Heel, the bend of the Foot, &c. The third is the Foot-step, to the very Life of a Mastiff Dog—and the fourth is *Derwent's very own first little Shoe*, 4 Inches in length and O! it is the sweetest Baby Shoe that ever was seen. The wie-foot in Borrowdale is contemptible; but this really does work upon my imagination very powerfully and I will try to construct a Tale upon it. The place too is so very, very wild.

I delighted the Shepherd by my admiration, and the Four Foot
Stone is my own Christening, and Towers undertakes it shall
hereafter go by that name for hitherto it has been nameless.
And so I returned and have found a Pedlar here of an interesting Physiognomy—and here I must leave off—for Dinner is
ready——

After the Thunder-storm I shouted out all your Names[1] in
the Sheep-fold—when Echo came upon Echo, and then Hartley
and Derwent and then I laughed and shouted Joanna. It leaves
all the Echoes I ever heard far far behind, in number, distinct-
ness and *humanness* of Voice; and then not to forget an old
Friend, I made them all say Dr. Dodd &c.——

Keswick Augt. 25th 1802

All night it rained incessantly and in a hard storm of Rain this
morning, at 1/2 past 10, I set off, and drove away toward
Newlands. There is a Waterfall that divides Great Robinson
from Buttermere Halse Fell, which when Mary, and Tom, and
I passed, we stopped and said—what a wonderful Creature it
would be in a hard Rain. Dear Mary was especially struck with
it's latent greatness and since that time I have never passed it
without a haunting wish to see it in it's fury. It is just 8 miles
from Keswick. I had a glorious Walk—the rain sailing along
those black Crags and green Steeps, white as the woolly Down
on the underside of a Willow Leaf, and soft as Floss Silk and
silver Fillets of Water down every Mountain from top to bottom that were as fine as Bridegrooms. I soon arrived at the
Halse and climbed up by the waterfall as near as I could, to the
very top of the Fell but it was so craggy, the Crags covered with
spongy soaky Moss, and when bare so jagged as to wound one's
hands fearfully, and the Gusts came so very sudden and strong,
that the going up was slow, and difficult and earnest and the
coming down, not only all that, but likewise extremely dangerous. However, I have always found this *stretched* and *anxious*

[1] Cf. Item 16.

state of mind favorable to depth of pleasurable Impressions in the resting Places and *lownding* Coves.

The Thing repaid me amply. It is a great Torrent from the Top of the Mountain to the Bottom; the lower part of it is not the least Interesting, where it is beginning to slope to a level. The mad water rushes thro' its *sinuous* bed, or rather prison of Rock, with such rapid Curves as if it turned the Corners not from the mechanic force but with foreknowledge, like a fierce and skilful Driver: great Masses of Water, one after the other, that in twilight one might have feelingly compared them to a vast crowd of huge white Bears, rushing, one over the other, against the wind—their long white hair scattering abroad in the wind. The remainder of the Torrent is marked out by three great Waterfalls, the lowermost Apron-shaped, and though the Rock down which it rushes is an inclined Plane, it shoots off in such an independence of the Rock as shews that its direction was given it by the force of the Water from above. The middle which in peaceable times would be two tinkling Falls formed in this furious Rain one great *Water-wheel* endlessly revolving and double the size and height of the lowest. The third and highest is a mighty one indeed. It is twice the height of both the others added together, nearly as high as Scale Force, but it rushes down an inclined Plane, and does not *fall*, like Scale Force; however, if the Plane has been smooth, it is so near a Perpendicular that it would have *appeared* to fall, but it is indeed so fearfully savage, and black, and jagged, that it tears the flood to pieces. And one great black Outjutment divides the water, and overbrows and keeps uncovered a long slip of jagged black Rock beneath, which gives a marked *Character* to the whole force. What a sight it is to look down on such a Cataract! The wheels, that circumvolve in it, the leaping up and plunging forward of that infinity of Pearls and Glass Bulbs, the continual *change* of the *Matter*, the perpetual *Sameness* of the *Form*—it is an awful Image and Shadow of God and the World. When I reached the very top, where the Stream flows level, there were feeding three darling Sheep, with their red ochre Letters on their sides, as quiet as if they were by a Rill in a flat meadow, flowing clear over smooth tressy water-weeds, and thro by long Grass. Bless their dear hearts, what darlings Mountain Sheep are! A little above the summit of the Waterfall I had a very striking view. The Lake and part of Keswick in a remarkably interesting point of view seen at the end of the Vista formed by the vale of Newlands—this was on my right—and as I turned to my left, the Sun burst out and I saw close by me part of the Lake of Buttermere, but not an inch of any one of it's Shores or of the Vale—but over away beside Crummock a white shining dazzling view of the Vale of Lorton and the Sea beyond it.

I went to Lodore on Sunday.[1] It was finer than I had ever seen it before. Never were there three Waterfalls so different from each other, as Lodore, Buttermere Halse Fall, and Scale Force. Scale Force is a proper Fall between two very high and narrow Walls of Rock, well tree'd—yet so that the Trees rather add to, than lessen the precipice Walls. Buttermere Halse Fall is a narrow, open, naked Torrent with three great Water-slopes individualized in it one above another, large, larger, largest. Lodore has it's Walls, but they are scarcely Walls, they are wide apart, and not upright, and their beauty and exceeding Majesty take away the Terror—and the Torrent is broad and wide, and from top to bottom it is small Waterfalls, abreast and abreast. Buttermere Halse Fall is the War-song of a Scandinavian Bard. Lodore is the Precipitation of the fallen Angels from Heaven, Flight and Confusion, and Distraction, but all harmonized into one majestic Thing by the genius of Milton, who describes it. Lodore is beyond all rivalry the first and best Thing of the whole Lake Country. Indeed (but we cannot judge at all from Prints) I have seen nothing equal to it in the Prints and Sketches of the Scotch and Swiss Cataracts.

MS.

[1] August 8, 1802.

187. GENIUS

.... Pindar's remark on sweet Music holds equally true of Genius; as many as are not delighted by it are disturbed, perplexed, irritated. The Beholder either recognizes it as a projected Form of his own Being, that moves before him with a Glory round its head, or recoils from it as from a Spectre.

Aids to Reflection

Coleridge comments: This refers to a curious phaenomenon which occurs occasionally when the air is filled with fine particles of frozen Snow, constituting an almost invisibly subtle Snow-mist, and a Person is walking with the Sun behind his Back. His Shadow is projected and he sees a figure moving before him with a glory round its Head. I have myself seen it twice: and it is described in the first or second Volume of the Manchester Philosophical Transactions.

MS.

188. BEES

Scales, Stipulae, Chaff, from the bases of the leaves of the Beech Tree on May 23, 1825, on the rich dark green Moss carpet.

> The glossy Scales that gay as living things
> Dance in the Winnow of the Moss-bees' wings
> That hovers o'er the Moss beneath the Beech
> Then renews his *routing* toil
> Delving and tearing up
> With head and sturdy thighs——
>
> *Bombyx Muscorum.*

N.B. What do the humblebees do in those small hollow funnels they make? Often they put their hind Half and orange plush small-clothes in these funnels and move backward and forward ovi-position. I, however, could never find any the least speck even with a glass in the bottom of the funnel.

MS.

189. HABIT AND INSTINCT

SOME NOTES ON WHITE'S 'SELBORNE'

White writes: Thus is instinct in animals, taken the least out of it's [sic] way an undistinguishing, limited faculty; and blind to every circumstance that does not immediately respect self-preservation, or lead at once to the propagation or support of their species.

Coleridge comments: This is an inadequate explanation. I would rather say, that Instinct is the wisdom of the species, not of the Individual; but that let any circumstance occur regularly and thro' many generations, that then its *every-time-felt* inconvenience would by little and little act thro' the blind sensations on the organic frame of the animals, till at length they were *born* wise in that respect. And by the same process do they lose their not *in*nate but *con*nate wisdom: thus Hens hatched in an artificial oven, as in Egypt, in 3 or 4 generations (the same process having been repeated in each) lose their instinct of Brooding. I trust that this Note will not be considered as lessening the value of this sweet delightful Book. S. T. Coleridge, July 7, 1810. Keswick.

MS.

White refers to 'these cobweb-like appearances called *gossamer*'.

Coleridge comments: Permit me to observe as a certain yet hitherto unnoticed, etymology of this word, that it is 'God's Dame's Hair', and in monkish Latin (where I found it) called *Fila Mariæ, capilla matris Dei.* Thus Gossip, i.e. *God's Sib.*

White, discussing gypsies with a Greek name, then in the south of England writes: It would be matter of some curiosity could one meet with an intelligent person among them, to inquire whether in their jargon they still retain any Greek words.

Coleridge comments: This has been done by a learned German (Grellman) who has made it evident, that they are the remains of an expelled nation from between Persia and Hindostan.

White: Thus far it is plain that the deprivation of *masculine vigour* puts a stop to the growth of those parts or appendages that are looked upon as its insignia. But the ingenious Mr. Lisle in his book on husbandry carries it much farther; for he says that the loss of these insignia alone has sometimes a strange effect·on the ability itself.

Coleridge comments: Blumenbach told me, that the abscission of the Horns of the Stag and Male Deer had the effect of Castration.

MS.

White in Letter XLII describes the flight of various birds.

Coleridge comments: This letter has disappointed me. I have myself made and collected a better table of characters of Flight and Motion.

White describes 'honey-dews'.

Coleridge comments: This is now known to be saccharine excrement of the Aphides. It is a true *sugar*. No wonder therefore that, tho' not directly vegetable, the Bees arc fond of it.

White describes the summer of 1783, 'an amazing and portentous one, and full of horrible phenomena; for, besides the alarming meteors and tremendous thunderstorms that affrighted and distressed the different counties of this kingdom, the peculiar haze or smoky fog ... was a most extraordinary appearance.'

Coleridge comments: occasioned by the eruption of four tremendous Rivers of Fire in Iceland.

MS.

190. ONE BREEZE OF LIFE?

Wonderful, perplexing divisibility of Life. It is related by D. Unzer, an authority wholly to be relied on, that an Ohrwurm (Earwig?) cut in half eat its' own hinder half. Will it be the reverse with G. Britain and America? The Head of the rattlesnake severed from the body bit at, and squirted out its poison.

Related by Beverley in his Hist[ory] of Virginia. Lyonnet in his Insect-theol[ogy] tore a wasp in half, and 3 days after the fore-half bit whatever was presented to it of its' former food, and the hind-half darted out its' sting on being touched. *Boyle mentions a female butterfly that when beheaded not only admitted the male but lay eggs in consequence of the impregnation.* But a Turtle has lived six months with his Head off and wandered about, yea, six hours after it's heart and bowels (all but the Lungs) were taken out. How shall we think of this compatible with the *monad* Soul? If I say what has Spirit to do with space, what odd dreams it would suggest? Or is every animal a republic *in se*? Or is there one Breeze of Life, at once the soul of each and God of all? Is it not strictly analogous to generation, and no more contradictory to unity than *it*? But *it*? Aye! there's the Twist in the Logic. Is not the reproduction of the Lizard a complete generation! O it is easy to dream, and surely better of these things than of a 20,000 £ Prize in the Lottery, or of a Place at Court! 13 Dec. 1804. Malta.

MS.

191. BOTANY, CHEMISTRY, POETRY

All that can be done by the most patient and active industry, by the widest and most continuous researches; all that the amplest survey of the vegetable realm, brought under immediate contemplation by the most stupendous collections of species and varieties, can suggest; all that minutest dissection and exactest chemical analysis, can unfold; all that varied experiment and the position of plants and of their component parts in every conceivable relation to light, heat, (and whatever else we distinguish as imponderable substances), to earth, air, water, to the supposed constituents of air and water, separate and in all proportions—in short, all that chemical agents and re-agents can disclose or adduce;—all these have been brought, as conscripts, into the field, with the completest accoutrement, in the best discipline, under the ablest commanders. Yet after all that was effected by Linnaeus himself, not to mention the labours of Gesner, Caesalpinus, Ray, Tournefort, and the other heroes who preceded the general adoption of the sexual system, as the basis of artificial arrangement;—after all the successive toils and enterprises of Hedwig, Jussieu, Mirbel, Sir James Smith, Knight, Ellis, &c. &c.,—what is botany at this present hour? Little more than an enormous nomenclature; a huge catalogue, *bien arrangé*, and yearly and monthly augmented, in various editions, each with its own scheme of technical memory and its own conveniences of reference! A dictionary in which (to carry on the metaphor) an Ainsworth arranges the contents by the initials; a Walker by the endings; a Scapula by the radicals; and a Cominius by the similarity of the uses and purposes! The terms system, method, science, are mere improprieties of courtesy, when applied to a mass enlarging by endless appositions, but without a nerve that oscillates, or a pulse that throbs, in sign of *growth* or inward sympathy. The innocent amusement, the healthful occupation, the ornamental accomplishment of *amateurs* (most honourable indeed and deserving of all praise as a preventive substitute for the stall, the kennel, and the subscription-room), it has yet to expect the devotion and energies of the philosopher.

So long back as the first appearance of Dr. Darwin's *Phytologia* the writer, then in earliest manhood, presumed to hazard the opinion, that the physiological botanists were hunting in a false direction, and sought for analogy where they should have looked for antithesis. He saw, or thought he saw, that the harmony between the vegetable and animal world, was not a harmony of resemblance, but of contrast; and that their relation to each other was that of corresponding opposites. They seemed to him, (whose mind had been formed by observation, unaided, but at the same time unenthralled, by partial experiment) as two streams from the same fountain indeed, but flowing the one due west, and the other direct east; and that consequently, the resemblance would be as the proximity, greatest in the first and rudimental products of vegetable and animal organization. Whereas, according to the received notion, the highest and most perfect vegetable, and the lowest and rudest animal forms, ought to have seemed the links of the two systems, which is contrary to fact. Since that time, the same idea has dawned in the minds of philosophers capable of demonstrating its objective truth by induction of facts in an unbroken series of correspondences in nature. From these men, or from minds enkindled by their labours, we may hope hereafter to receive it, or rather the yet higher idea to which it refers us, matured into LAWS of organic nature, and thence to have one other splendid proof, that with the knowledge of LAW alone dwell Power and Prophecy, decisive Experiment, and, lastly, a scientific method, that dissipating with its earliest rays the gnomes of hypothesis and the mists of theory may, within a single generation, open out on the philosophic seer discoveries that had baffled the gigantic, but blind and guideless, industry of ages.

Such, too, is the case with the assumed indecomponible substances of the laboratory. They are the symbols of elementary powers, and the exponents of a law, which, as the root of all these powers, the chemical philosopher, whatever his theory may be, is instinctively labouring to extract. This instinct, again, is itself but the form, in which the idea, the mental correlative of the law, first announces its incipient germination in his own mind: and hence proceeds the striving after unity of principle through all the diversity of forms, with a feeling resembling that which accompanies our endeavours to recollect a forgotten name; when we seem at once to have and not to have it; which the memory feels but cannot find. Thus, as 'the lunatic, the lover, and the poet', suggest each the other to Shakespeare's Theseus, as soon as his thoughts present to him the ONE FORM, of which they are but varieties; so water and flame, the diamond, the charcoal, and the mantling champagne, with its ebullient sparkles, are convoked and fraternized by the theory of the chemist. This is, in truth, the first charm of chemistry, and the secret of the almost universal interest excited by its discoveries. The serious complacency which is afforded by the sense of truth, utility, permanence, and progression, blends with and ennobles the exhilarating surprise and the pleasurable sting of curiosity, which accompany the propounding and the solving of an enigma. It is the sense of a principle of connection given by the mind, and sanctioned by the correspondency of nature. Hence the strong hold which in all ages chemistry has had on the imagination. If in Shakespeare we find nature idealized into poetry, through the creative power of a profound yet observant meditation, so through the meditative observation of a Davy, a Wollaston, or a Hatchett;

————————'By some connatural force,
Powerful at greatest distance to unite
With secret amity things of like kind,'

we find poetry, as it were, substantiated and realized in nature, —yea, nature itself disclosed to us, *geminam istam naturam, quae fit et facit, et creat et creatur,* as at once the poet and the poem.

Friend.

192. THEORETICAL AND PRACTICAL CHEMISTRY

A NOTE ON OERSTED'S 'ANSICHT DER CHEMISCHEN
NATURGESETZE'

It is of the highest importance in all departments of knowledge to keep the Speculative distinct from the Empirical. As long as they run parallel, they are of the greatest service to each other: they never meet but to cut and cross. This is Oersted's fault, the rock of offence on which this Work strikes. Davy is necessarily right: for he follows the established *Regula recta* of empirical chemistry, *viz.* that all Bodies shall be considered as simple, till they shall have been *shewn* to be compound. On this Rule, Chlorine, and Iodine claim the title of Simple Bodies (*Stoffen*) with the same right as Oxygen, or the Metals, while the Speculative Chemist sees *a priori*, that all alike must be composite.

MS.

193. MATTER NOT INERT

... I cannot suppress the suggestion that the Qualitative Energies, the *inside* of the metallic Bodies must be looked to, in order to discover the most proper character of Metallity, and that one great purpose of the Noun Adjectives Oxygen+Chlorine+Iodine and Hydrogen is to *express* their qualities— by destroying or exhausting their quantitative and outside power of Cohesion—or appropriate Attraction! That this the *C*ontractive and the *D*ilative restore the conditions under which the Qualities can be called from potence into Act. The Twymetal, Iron, must be slightly oxydated in order to reveal its magnetic life. Even mechanic Divisions, as in filings, by overpowering the cohesion enabled metal to *communicate* its astringency: its tonic Virtue is the force of Cohesion as changed into a transitive or causative Quality.

MS.

194. NEWTON, GOETHE, OKEN

Oken, writing about Newton's theory of light, says he speaks harshly but not unjustly, and that he will, in what follows, '*ganz ruhig*' refute it.

Coleridge comments: Good Heaven! how much more would Oken have done, how much more both wit and wisdom would he have displayed, if instead of this rough Railing and d-n-your-eyes-you-lie Ipse-dixits, he had *begun* with this '*quite-quiet* confutation of the Newtonian Doctrine', especially it being so very easy a task! Goethe (not indeed '*ganz ruhig*') had attempted it in detail both by impeachment of Newton's Experiments, and by Counter-experiments of his own. And yet, G. himself confesses, that he had not succeeded in convincing or converting a single Mathematician, not even among his own friends and Intimates.

That a clear and sober confutation of Newton's [*Optics* as far
as *crossed out*] Theory of Colors [are concerned *crossed out*] is
practicable, the exceeding unsatisfied state, in which Sir I.
Newton's first Book of *Optics* leaves my mind—strongly per-
suades me. And it is Oken's mountebank Boasting and Threat-
ening that alone make me sceptical as to his own ability to
perform the promise, here given by him. S. T. C.

P.S. I readily admit, that the full exhibition of another Theory
adequate to the Sum of the Phaenomena, and grounded on
more safe and solid principles, would be virtually the best confutation—but no one who knows [note unfinished].

MS.

Oken writes: Yellow is the span of red turned to white; blue is
the span of red turned to black, or yellow is a white, blue is a
black red.

Coleridge comments: These, even these, are the passages that annoy
me in the *Natur-philosophen*! Yellow a white, and Blue a black
Red!! It is true, I know what Oken means by the words—but
why Oken chose such words to convey such meanings, I do not
know—tho' Vanity is so common a foible, a Quackery so
ordinary a symptom and effect of that so common Foible, that
I can pretty well guess. Goethe, and then Schelling and Steffens,
had opposed to the Newtonian optics the ancient doctrine of
Light and Shadow on the ground principle of Polarity—Yellow
being the positive, Blue the negative, Pole, Red the Culmina-
tion and Green the Indifference. Oken follows them—but stop!
He waits till they are out of sight. Hangs out a new Banner
(i.e. metaphor) and becomes a Leader himself. S. T. C.

MS.

195. HIS NEGLECTED 'TOOLS OF REASON'

Next to that, to which there is no Near, the γυιλτ [guilt] and
the avenging Daemon of my Life, I must place the neglect of

Mathematics, under the strongest motives, and the most favorable helps and opportunities for acquiring them. Not a week passes in which I do not regret this Oversight of my Youth with a sort of remorse that turns it to a Sin.—This day I read the account of Faraday's Microphone and instantly recognized a fond and earnest dream-project of my own of 30 years' standing—with sundry other imaginations respecting what might be effected in the only embryo Science of Acoustics. The Walls of Jerico were to fall before my War-trumpet[s]. But where were the Hands, where the Tools of my Reason? I had not the *Organ* of all Sciences that respect Space and Quantity. My Dreams were akin to Reason: but I could not awake out of my prophetic Sleep, to effectuate their objectivization—for I was ignorant of the Mathematics! S. T. C.

MS.

196. GEOMETRY

In the *Kabbalistische Briefe* of Jean Baptiste de Boyer, Benkiber writes to Abukibak on the inadequacy of geometry to application in physics, arguing that Newton as a geometrician believed in the infinite divisibility of matter, and as a physicist denied it with his solid atoms.

Coleridge comments: What philosophic Mathematician ever supposed Geometry to be anything else, than a system of the conceivable and inconceivable in the mind's constructive Intuitions? It is wholly *ideal*. Newton's solid atoms are utter aliens from Geometry, in which the mind exclusively contemplates its own energies: and *applies* them not otherwise than hypothetically. Newton erred by introducing *Dogmatic Realism* into the *Ideal World*.—Solid atoms are not an *hypothesis*, as Geometry is; but a mere Hypo-pœsis.

MS.

197. IMAGINATIVE CHEMISTRY

August 1817.

Q[uer]y. The sulphurous smell noticeable even in the air after great heats immediately before Storms with Thunder and the forked zig-zag Lightning—and intensely strong in rooms that have been struck with Lightning (as in the late Tempest at Lueben [? Quebec]—does it proceed from Sulphur? If so, whence does the Sulphur come?

If there exist in Nature a power converting Nitrogene into Hydrogen, the latter being *supposed* the Protoxide, the former a Deutroxide of the supposit[it]ious Ammonium or in a more philosophic Language, Nitrogene being the Base X in the condition of + Magnetism, and Hydrogen the same Base under the condition of + Electricity, an intermediate or transitional state is conceivable, namely, that in which X is indifferently Base and Spirit, Base to A, Spirit or Modifier to B. And what [if] Sulphur were this product?

Q[uer]y. Is it within my present Quantum of Light to construct imaginatively a product or series of products that in their very nature shall be componible, yet not decomponible? i.e. Indecomponible compounds.

If all primary Numbers, *ex. gr.* 5 = 1, in all the simple proportions of the five forces of the One Power, be such, then what are the *primary* Numbers—namely, in how many several forms of predominance, varied by the relations of co- and subordination in the four powers predominated, can the one be multiplied—

$$B\ C\ D\ F\ G = 1$$
$$B\ C\ D\ F\ G$$
$$c\ b\ b\ b\ b$$
$$d\ d\ c\ c\ c$$
$$f\ f\ f\ d\ d$$
$$g\ g\ g\ g\ f$$
$$1 = 5$$

But it may be B.f.g.c.d, B d f g c &c. A School-boy in Cube
Root would tell me in a few minutes.
B=attraction. D=Repulsion. C=contraction. F=Dilution.
G=Centrality.

MS.

198. HISTORY OF SCIENCE

It is a wonderful property of the human mind, that when once
a momentum has been given to it in a fresh direction, it pursues
the new path with obstinate perseverance, in all conceivable
bearings, to its utmost extremes. And by the startling consequences which arise out of these extremes, it is first awakened
to its error, and either recalled to some former track, or receives some fresh impulse, which it follows with the same
eagerness, and admits to the same monopoly. Thus in the 13th
century the first science which roused the intellects of men from
the torpor of barbarism, was, as in all countries ever has been,
and ever must be the case, the science of Metaphysics and
Ontology. We first seek what can be found at home. ... For
more than a century men continued to invoke the oracle of
their own spirits, not only concerning its own forms and modes
of being, but likewise concerning the laws of external nature.
All attempts at philosophical explication were commenced by
a mere effort of the understanding, as the power of abstraction;
or by the imagination, transferring its own experiences to every
object presented from without. By the former, a class of
phenomena were in the first place abstracted, and fixed in some
general term; of course this could designate only the impressions
made by the outward objects, and so far, therefore, having been
thus metamorphosed, they were effects of these objects; but
then made to supply the place of their own causes, under the
name of occult qualities. Thus the properties peculiar to gold,
were abstracted from those it possessed in common with other
bodies, and then generalized in the term Aureity: and the

254

inquirer was instructed that the Essence of Gold, or the cause which constituted the peculiar modification of matter called gold was the power of aureity. By the latter, i.e. by the imagination, thought and will were superadded to the occult quality, and every form of nature had its appropriate Spirit, to be controlled or conciliated by an appropriate ceremonial. This was entitled its SUBSTANTIAL FORM. Thus, physics became a sort of poetry, and the art of medicine (for physiology could scarcely be said to exist) was a system of magic, blended with traditional empiricism. Thus the forms of thought proceeded to act in their own emptiness, with no attempt to fill or substantiate them by the information of the senses, and all the branches of science formed so many sections of logic and metaphysics. And so it continued, even to the time that the Reformation sounded the second trumpet, and the authority of the schools sank with that of the hierarchy, under the intellectual courage and activity which this great revolution had inspired. Power, once awakened, cannot rest in one object. All the sciences partook of the new influences. The world of experimental philosophy was soon mapped out for posterity by the comprehensive and enterprising genius of Bacon, and the laws explained by which experiment could be dignified into experience. But no sooner was the impulse given, than the same propensity was made manifest of looking at all things in the one point of view which chanced to be of predominant attraction. Our Gilbert, a man of genuine philosophical genius, had no sooner multiplied the facts of magnetism, and extended our knowledge concerning the property of magnetic bodies, but all things in heaven, and earth, and in the waters beneath the earth, were resolved into magnetic influences.

Shortly after a new light was struck by Harriott and Descartes, with their contemporaries, or immediate predecessors, and the restoration of ancient geometry, aided by the modern invention of algebra, placed the science of mechanism on the philosophic throne. How widely this domination spread, and how long it continued, if, indeed, even now it can be said to have abdicated its pretensions, the reader need not be reminded. The sublime discoveries of Newton, and, together with these, his not less fruitful than wonderful application, of the higher mathesis to the movements of the celestial bodies, and to the laws of light, gave almost a religious sanction to the corpuscular system and mechanical theory. It became synonymous with philosophy itself. It was the sole portal at which truth was permitted to enter. The human body was treated of as an hydraulic machine, the operations of medicine were solved, and alas! even directed by reference partly to gravitation and the laws of motion, and partly by chemistry, which itself, however, as far as its theory was concerned, was but a branch of mechanics working exclusively by imaginary wedges, angles, and spheres. Should the reader chance to put his hand on the 'Principles of Philosophy', by La Forge, an immediate disciple of Descartes, he may see the phenomena of sleep solved in a copper-plate engraving, with all the figures into which the globules of the blood shaped themselves, and the results demonstrated by mathematical calculations. In short, from the time of Kepler to that of Newton, and from Newton to Hartley, not only all things in external nature, but the subtlest mysteries of life and organization, and even of the intellect and moral being, were conjured within the magic circle of mathematical formulæ. And now a new light was struck by the discovery of electricity, and, in every sense of the word, both playful and serious, both for good and for evil, it may be affirmed to have electrified the whole frame of natural philosophy. Close on its heels followed the momentous discovery of the principal gases by Scheele and Priestley, the composition of water by Cavendish, and the doctrine of latent heat by Black. The scientific world was prepared for a new dynasty; accordingly, as soon as Lavoisier had reduced the infinite variety of chemical phenomena to the actions, reactions, and interchanges of a few elementary substances, or at least excited the expectation that this would speedily be effected,

the hope shot up, almost instantly, into full faith, that it had
been effected. Henceforward the new path, thus brilliantly
opened, became the common road to all departments of knowledge: and, to this moment, it has been pursued with an eagerness and almost epidemic enthusiasm which, scarcely less than
its political revolutions, characterise the spirit of the age. Many
and inauspicious have been the invasions and inroads of this
new conqueror into the rightful territories of other sciences;
and strange alterations have been made in less harmless points
than those of terminology, in homage to an art unsettled, in the
very ferment of imperfect discoveries, and either without a
theory, or with a theory maintained only by composition and
compromise. Yet this very circumstance has favoured its encroachments, by the gratifications which its novelty affords to
our curiosity, and by the keener interest and higher excitement
which an unsettled and revolutionary state is sure to inspire.
He who supposes that science possesses an immunity from such
influences knows little of human nature.

Theory of Life.

199. SCIENCE ANONYMOUS

The truths of Reason, as distinguished from Truths of History,
are all anonymous. There is no heraldry in Science. Not a
Quis Dixit? but *Quid dixit?* is the question here.

MS.

200. IN THE SWIFTIAN MODE

Grew, in his *Cosmologia Sacra*, 1701, suggests that 'the Moon
may be inhabited but has . . . perhaps a different Furniture of
Animals'.

Coleridge comments: But why, of necessity, any? Must all possible Planets be lousy? None exempt from the *Morbus pedicularis*
of our verminous man-becrawled Earth?

MS.

201. A DRY INK

Desideratum—A dry Ink, that will write smoothly, and with virtual fluency, neither slurring, scratching, nor stamping the Paper.

MS.

202. PHYSICS—ELECTRICITY—MAGNETISM—
IMAGINATION

But in experimental philosophy, it may be said how much do we not owe to accident? Doubtless: but let it not be forgotten, that if the discoveries so made stop there; if they do not excite some master IDEA; if they do not lead to some LAW (in whatever dress of theory or hypotheses the fashions and prejudices of the time may disguise or disfigure it):—the discoveries may remain for ages limited in their uses, insecure and unproductive. How many centuries, we might have said millennia, have passed, since the first accidental discovery of the attraction and repulsion of light bodies by rubbed amber &c. Compare the interval with the progress made within less than a century after the discovery of the phaenomena that led immediately to a THEORY of electricity. That here as in many other instances, the theory was supported by insecure hypotheses; that by one theorist two heterogeneous fluids are assumed, the vitreous and the resinous; by another, a plus and minus of the same fluid; that a third considers it a mere modification of light; while a fourth composes the electrical aura of oxygen, hydrogen, and caloric; this does but place the truth we have been evolving in a stronger and clearer light. For abstract from all these suppositions, or rather imaginations, that which is common to, and involved in them all; and we shall have neither notional fluid or fluids, nor chemical compounds, nor elementary matter,— but the idea of *two—opposite—forces*, tending to rest by equilibrium. These are the sole factors of the calculus, alike in all the theories. These give the *law*, and in it the *method*, both of arranging the phaenomena and of substantiating appearances into facts of science; with a success proportionate to the clearness or confusedness of the insight into the law. For this reason, we anticipate the greatest improvements in the *method*, the nearest approaches to a *system* of electricity, from these philosophers, who have presented the law most purely, and the correlative idea as an idea: those, namely, who, since the year 1798, in the true spirit of experimental dynamics, rejecting the imagination of any material substrate, simple or compound, contemplate in the phaenomena of electricity the operation of a law which reigns through all nature, the law of POLARITY, or the manifestation of one power by opposite forces; who trace in these appearances, as the most obvious and striking of its innumerable forms, the agency of the positive and negative poles of a power essential to all material construction; the second, namely, of the three primary principles, for which the beautiful and most appropriate symbols are given by the mind in the three ideal dimensions of space.

The time is, perhaps, nigh at hand, when the same comparison between the results of two unequal periods, the interval between the knowledge of a fact, and that from the discovery of the law,—will be applicable to the sister science of magnetism. But how great the contrast between magnetism and electricity at the present moment! From remotest antiquity, the attraction of iron by the magnet was known and noticed; but, century after century, it remained the undisturbed property of poets and orators. The fact of the magnet and the fable of the phoenix stood on the same scale of utility. In the thirteenth century, or perhaps earlier, the polarity of the magnet, and its communicability to iron, were discovered; and soon suggested a purpose so grand and important, that it may well be deemed the proudest trophy ever raised by accident in the service of mankind—the invention of the compass. But it led to no idea, to no law, and consequently to no Method: though a variety of phaenomena, as startling as they are mysterious, have forced on us a presentiment of its intimate connection with all the great agencies of nature; of a revelation, in ciphers, the key to which is still wanting. I can recall no event of human history that impresses the imagination more deeply than the moment when Columbus, on an unknown ocean, first perceived one of these startling facts, the change of the magnetic needle.

In what shall we seek the cause of this contrast between the rapid progress of electricity and the stationary condition of magnetism? As many theories, as many hypotheses, have been advanced in the latter science as in the former. But the theories and fictions of the electricians contained an *idea*, and all the same idea, which has necessarily led to METHOD; implicit indeed, and only regulative hitherto, but which requires little more than the dismission of the imagery to become constitutive like the ideas of the geometrician. On the contrary, the assumptions of the magnetists (as for instance, the hypothesis that the planet itself is one vast magnet, or that an immense magnet is concealed within it, or that of a concentric globe within the earth, revolving on its own independent axis) are but repetitions of the same fact or phaenomenon looked at through a magnifying glass; the *reiteration* of the problem, not its solution. The naturalist, who cannot or will not see, that one fact is often worth a thousand, as including them all in itself, and that it first *makes* all the others facts, who has not the head to comprehend, the soul to reverence, a central experiment or observation (what the Greeks would perhaps have called a *protophaeno-menon*),—will never receive an auspicious answer from the oracle of nature.

Friend.

VIII

LANDMARKS IN
THE MAP OF HUMAN NATURE

Assuredly the great use of History is to acquaint us with the nature of Man. This end is best answered by the most faithful portrait. But Biography is a collection of portraits. At the same time there must be some mode of grouping and collecting the individuals who are themselves the great landmarks in the Map of Human Nature.

Friend

Unless a man understand his own heart, it is impossible that he should have insight into the hearts of other men.

Notebook 51

HIS CONTEMPORARIES

Coleridge's comments on men and women of his time are to be found in *Essays on His Own Times*, the *Table Talk* and the letters. He hated and would not endure gossip for gossip's sake; but a sociable inclination, newspaper work, an interest in public causes, and in the different pursuits in which men engage, brought him into touch with many interesting and some prominent persons. *Coleridge at Highgate*, by Mrs Lucy [Gillman] Watson, and, more recently, *Coleridge the Talker* by Armour and Howes, a collection of contemporary reports on his conversation, give a lively impression of a wide circle of acquaintance. Towards those he did not know personally his attitude was inclined to be positive even when he did not agree with them. His attitude towards women, in general and particular, was interested and considered, and the many references to children are observant, dignified and respectful.

On the whole his judgements of persons are less marred by partisan prejudice, whether religious or political or national, than those of most people; he did suffer, in relation to his closer associates, from the persecution feelings to which drug addicts are prone, thought the strongest of these relations survived the difficulties. Indeed his life was rich in friendships, and any attempt to measure his intellectual influence must take almost as much account of his friends and admirers as of his written works.

VIII

LANDMARKS IN
THE MAP OF HUMAN NATURE

203. GEORGE IV AND WILLIAM IV

Saturday, Night, 26 June 1830. This morning $\frac{1}{2}$ past Three the King, George IV, died, and about Noon William IVth was proclaimed. A most impressive Lesson for Princes will be read by some youthful Historian, when the distance of Time from the event shall render it fit and decent. The series of brilliant successes from the commencement of the Regency to the end of the Reign, contrasted with the impolitic and calamitous measures and events during the reign of George the Fourth—and the reverse Contrast in the feelings, affections and regrets of the Nation (of every Man deserving the name of Englishman) towards the one and the other. I have never heard from Man or Woman a simple sentiment of Regret, except that derived from the too probable apprehensions and bodements respecting the character &c. of the 4th *William*! I pray with unfeigned Heart, that the Successor who of his two names Henry and William has chosen the latter, may direct his mind and honorable ambition to the third William instead of the 8th Henry. If his ascension should be the occasion of checking the plan of the last 20 years to force the *Military* on us as the Premier Class, and their obtrusion on all situations of public

Trust, at home and in the Colonies, we shall have reason to be thankful for the Changes.

MS.

204. ANONYMOUS

—— is one of those men who go far to shake my faith in a future state of existence; I mean, on account of the difficulty of knowing where to place him. I could not bear to roast him; he is not so bad as all that comes to: but then, on the other hand, to have to sit down with such a fellow in the very lowest pot-house of heaven, is utterly inconsistent with the belief of that place being a place of happiness for me.

Table Talk.

205. BURKE

Burke was, indeed, a great man. No one ever read history so philosophically as he seems to have done. Yet, until he could associate his general principles with some sordid interest, panic of property, jacobinism, etc., he was a mere dinner bell. Hence you will find so many half truths in his speeches and writings. Nevertheless, let us heartily acknowledge his transcendant greatness. He would have been more influential if he had less surpassed his contemporaries, as Fox and Pitt, men of much inferior minds in all respects.

Table Talk.

206. BURKE

It is bad policy to represent a political system as having no charm but for robbers and assassins, and no natural origin but in the brains of fools or mad men, when experience has proved, that the great danger of the system consists in the peculiar fascination it is calculated to exert on noble and imaginative spirits; on all those, who, in the amiable intoxication of youthful benevolence, are apt to mistake their own best virtues and choicest powers for the average qualities and attributes of the human character. The very minds, which a good man would most wish to preserve or disentangle from the snare, are by these angry misrepresentations rather lured into it. Is it wonderful that a man should reject the arguments unheard, when his own heart proves the falsehood of the assumptions by which they are prefaced; or that he should retaliate on the aggressors their own evil thoughts? I am well aware, that the provocation was great, the temptation almost inevitable; yet still I cannot repel the conviction from my mind, that in part to this error, and in part to a certain inconsistency in his own fundamental principles, we are to attribute the small number of converts made by BURKE during his life time. Let me not be misunderstood. I do not mean, that this great man supported different principles at different aeras of his political life. On the contrary, no man was ever more like himself. From his first published speech on the American colonies to his last posthumous Tracts, we see the same man, the same doctrines, the same uniform wisdom of *practical* counsels, the same reasoning and the same prejudices against all abstract grounds, against all deduction of practice from theory. The inconsistency to which I allude, is of a different kind: it is the want of congruity in the principles appealed to in different parts of the same work; it is an apparent versatility of the principle with the occasion. If his opponents are theorists, then every thing is to be founded on prudence, on mere calculations of expediency; and every man is represented as acting according to the state of his own immediate self-interest. Are his opponents calculators? *Then* calculation itself is represented as a sort of crime. God has given us feelings, and we are to obey them;—and the most absurd prejudices become venerable, to which these feelings have given consecration. I have not forgotten, that Burke himself defended these half contradictions, on the pretext of balancing the too much on the one side by a too much on the other. But never can I believe but that the straight line must needs be the nearest; and that where there is the most, and the most unalloyed truth, there will be the greatest and most permanent power of persuasion. But the fact was, that Burke in his public character found himself, as it were, in a Noah's ark, with a very few men and a great many beasts. He felt how much his immediate power was lessened by the very circumstance of his measureless superiority to those about him: he acted, therefore, under a perpetual system of compromise—a compromise of greatness with meanness; a compromise of the philosopher (who, armed with the twofold knowledge of history and the laws of spirit, as with a telescope, looked far around and into the remote distance) with the mere men of business, or with yet coarser intellects, who handled a truth, which they were required to receive, as they would handle an ox, which they were desired to purchase. But why need I repeat what has been already said in so happy a manner by Goldsmith of this great man:—

... Who too deep for his hearers, still went on refining,
And thought of convincing, while they thought of dining.

And if in consequence it was his fate to 'cut blocks with a razor', I may be permitted to add, that in respect of *truth*, though not of *genius*, the weapon was injured by the misapplication.

The FRIEND, however, acts and will continue to act under the belief, that the whole truth is the best antidote to falsehoods which are dangerous chiefly because they are half-truths: and that an erroneous system is best confuted, not by an abuse of theory in general, nor by an absurd opposition of Theory to Practice, but by a detection of the errors in the particular theory. For the meanest of men has his theory, and to think at all is to theorize.

Friend.

207. PITT

William Pitt was the younger son of Lord Chatham; a fact of no ordinary importance in the solution of his character, of no mean significance in the heraldry of morals and intellect. His father's rank, fame, political connections, and parental ambition were his mould;—he was cast, rather than grew. A palpable election, a conscious predestination controlled the free agency, and transfigured the individuality of his mind; and that, which he *might have been*, was compelled into that, which he *was to be*. From his early childhood it was his father's custom to make him stand up on a chair and declaim before a large company; by which exercise, practised so frequently, and continued for so many years, he acquired a premature and unnatural dexterity in the combination of words, which must of necessity have diverted his attention from present objects, obscured his impressions, and deadened his genuine feelings. Not the *thing* on which he was speaking, but the praises to be gained by the speech, were present to his intuition; hence he associated all the operations of his faculties with words, and his pleasures with the surprise excited by them.

But an inconceivably large portion of human knowledge and human power is involved in the science and management of *words*; and an education of words, though it destroys genius, will often create, and always foster, talent. The young Pitt was conspicuous far beyond his fellows, both at school and at college. He was always full grown: he had neither the promise nor the awkwardness of growing intellect. Vanity, early satiated, formed and elevated itself into a love of power; and in losing this colloquial vanity he lost one of the prime links that connect the individual with the species, too early for the affections, though not too early for the understanding. At college he was a severe student; his mind was founded and elemented in words and generalities, and these too formed all the super-structure. That revelry and that debauchery, which are so often fatal to the powers of intellect, would probably have been serviceable to him; they would have given him a closer communion with realities, they would have induced a greater presentness to present objects. But Mr. Pitt's conduct was correct, unimpressibly correct. His after-discipline in the special pleader's office, and at the bar, carried on the scheme of his education with unbroken uniformity. His first political connections were with the Reformers, but those who accuse him of sympathising or coalescing with their intemperate or visionary plans, misunderstand his character, and are ignorant of the historical facts. Imaginary situations in an imaginary state of things rise up in minds that possess a power and facility in combining images.— Mr. Pitt's ambition was conversant with old situations in the old state of things, which furnish nothing to the imagination, though much to the wishes. In his endeavours to realise his father's plan of reform, he was probably as sincere as a being, who had derived so little knowledge from actual impressions, could be. But his sincerity had no living root of affection; while it was propped up by his love of praise and immediate power, so long it stood erect and no longer. He became a member of the Parliament—supported the popular opinions, and in a few years, by the influence of the popular party, was placed in that high and awful rank in which he now is. The fortunes of his country, we had almost said, the fates of the world, were placed in his wardship—we sink in prostration before the inscrutable dispensations of Providence, when we reflect in whose wardship the fates of the world were placed!

The influencer of his country and of his species was a young man, the creature of another's pre-determination, sheltered and weather-fended from all the elements of experience; a young man, whose feet had never wandered; whose very eye had never turned to the right or to the left; whose whole track had been as curveless as the motion of a fascinated reptile! It was a young man, whose heart was solitary, because he had existed always amid objects of futurity, and whose imagination too was unpopulous, because those objects of hope, to which his habitual wishes had transferred, and as it were *projected*, his existence, were all familiar and long established objects!—A plant sown and reared in a hot-house, for whom the very air that surrounded him, had been regulated by the thermometer of previous purpose; to whom the light of nature had penetrated only through glasses and covers; who had had the sun without the breeze; whom no storm had shaken; on whom no rain had pattered; on whom the dews of heaven had not fallen!—A being, who had had no feelings connected with man or nature, no spontaneous impulses, no unbiassed and desultory studies, no genuine science, nothing that constitutes individuality in intellect, nothing that teaches brotherhood in affection! Such was ⸀he man—such, and so denaturalised the spirit, on whose wisdom and philanthropy the lives and living enjoyments of so many millions of human beings were made unavoidably dependent. From this time a real enlargement of mind became almost impossible. Pre-occupations, intrigue, the undue passion and anxiety, with which all facts must be surveyed; the crowd and confusion of those facts, none of them seen, but all communicated, and by that very circumstance, and by the necessity of perpetually classifying them, transmuted into words and generalities; pride, flattery, irritation, artificial power; these, and circumstances resembling these, necessarily render the heights of office barren heights, which command indeed a vast and extensive prospect, but attract so many clouds and vapours, that most often all prospect is precluded. Still, however, Mr. Pitt's situation, however inauspicious for his real being, was favourable to his fame. He heaped period on period; persuaded himself and the nation, that extemporaneous arrangement of sentences was eloquence; and that eloquence implied wisdom. His father's struggles for freedom, and his own attempts, gave him an almost unexampled popularity; and his office necessarily associated with his name all the great events, that happened during his Administration. There were not however wanting men, who saw through this delusion; and refusing to attribute the industry, integrity, and enterprising spirit of our merchants, the agricultural improvements of our land-holders, the great inventions of our manufacturers, or the valour and skilfulness of our sailors to the merits of a minister, they have continued to decide on his character from those acts and those merits, which belong to him and to him alone. Judging him by this standard, they have been able to discover in him no one proof or symptom of a commanding genius. They have discovered him never controlling, never creating, events, but always yielding to them with rapid change, and sheltering himself from inconsistency by perpetual indefiniteness. In the Russian war, they saw him abandoning meanly what he had planned weakly, and threatened insolently. In the debates on the Regency they detected the laxity of his constitutional principles, and received proofs that his eloquence consisted not in the ready application of a general system to particular questions but in the facility of arguing for or against any question by specious generalities, without reference to any system. In these debates, he combined what is most dangerous in democracy, with all that is most degrading in the old superstitions of monarchy; and taught an inherency of the office in the person, in order to make the office itself a nullity, and the Premiership, with its accompanying majority, the sole and permanent power of the State. And now came the French Revolution. This was a new event; the old routine of reasoning, the common trade of politics were to become obsolete. He appeared wholly unprepared for it: half favouring, half condemning, ignorant of what he favoured, and why he condemned, he neither displayed the honest enthusiasm and fixed principle of Mr. Fox, nor the intimate acquaintance with the general nature of man, and the consequent *prescience* of Mr. Burke.

After the declaration of war, long did he continue in the common cant of office, in declamation about the Scheldt and Holland, and all the vulgar causes of common contests! and when at last the immense genius of his new supporter had beat him out of these *words* (words signifying *places* and *dead objects*, and signifying nothing more), he adopted other words in their places, other generalities—Atheism and Jacobinism—phrases, which he learnt from Mr. Burke, but without learning the philosophical definitions and involved consequences, with which that great man accompanied those words. Since the death of Mr. Burke, the forms and the sentiments, and the tone of the French have undergone many and important changes: how, indeed, is it possible that it should be otherwise, while man is the creature of experience! But still Mr. Pitt proceeds in an endless repetition of the same *general phrases*. This is his element; deprive him of general and abstract phrases, and you reduce him to silence. But you cannot deprive him of them. Press him to specify an *individual* fact of advantage to be derived from a war, and he answers, Security! Call upon him to particularize a crime, and he exclaims—Jacobinism! Abstractions defined by abstractions! Generalities defined by generalities! As a minister of finance, he is still, as ever, the man of words and abstractions! Figures, custom-house reports, imports and exports, commerce and revenue—all flourishing, all splendid! Never was such a prosperous country, as England, under his administration! Let it be objected, that the agriculture of the country is, by the overbalance of commerce, and by various and complex causes, in such a state, that the country hangs as a pensioner for bread on its neighbours, and a bad season uniformly threatens us with famine—This (it is replied) is owing to our prosperity—all *prosperous* nations are in great distress for food!—still PROSPERITY, still GENERAL PHRASES? unenforced by one *single image*, one *single fact* of real national amelioration; of any one comfort enjoyed, where it was not before enjoyed; of any one class of society becoming healthier, wiser, or happier. These are *things*, these are realities; and these Mr. Pitt has neither the imagination to body forth, nor the sensibility to feel for. Once indeed, in an evil hour, intriguing for popularity, he suffered himself to be persuaded to evince a talent for the Real, the Individual; and he brought in his POOR BILL! ... When we hear the minister's talent for finance so loudly trumpeted, we turn involuntarily to his POOR BILL—to that acknowledged abortion—that unanswerable evidence of his ignorance respecting all the fundamental relations and actions of property, and of the social union!

As his reasonings, even so is his eloquence. One character pervades his whole being. Words on words, finely arranged, and so dexterously consequent, that the whole bears the semblance of argument, and still keeps awake a sense of surprise; but when all is done, nothing rememberable has been said; no one philosophical remark, no one image, not even a pointed aphorism. Not a sentence of Mr. Pitt's has ever been quoted, or formed the favourite phrase of the day—a thing unexampled in any man of equal reputation. But while he speaks, the effect varies according to the character of his auditor. The man of no talent is swallowed up in surprise; and when the speech is ended, he remembers his feelings, but nothing distinct of that which produced them—(how opposite an effect to that of nature and genius, from whose works the idea still remains, when the feeling is passed away—remains to connect itself with the other feelings, and combine with new impressions!) The mere man of talent hears him with admiration—the mere man of genius with contempt—the philosopher neither admires nor contemns, but listens to him with a deep and solemn interest, tracing in the effects of his eloquence the power of words and phrases, and that peculiar constitution of human affairs in their present state, which so eminently favours this power.

Such appears to us to be the prime minister of Great Britain, whether we consider him as a statesman or as an orator. The same character betrays itself in his private life; the same coldness to realities, and to all whose excellence relates to reality. He has patronised no science, he has raised no man of genius from obscurity; he counts no one prime work of God among his friends. From the same source he has no attachment to female society, no fondness for children, no perceptions of beauty in natural scenery; but he is fond of convivial indulgences, of that stimulation, which, keeping up the glow of self-importance and the sense of internal power, gives feelings without the mediation of ideas.

These are the elements of his mind; the accidents of his fortune, the circumstances that enabled such a mind to acquire and retain such a power, would form a subject of a philosophical history, and that too of no scanty size. We can scarcely furnish the chapter of contents to a work, which would comprise subjects so important and delicate, as the causes of the diffusion and intensity of secret influence: the machinery and state intrigue of marriages; the overbalance of the commercial interest; the panic of property struck by the late revolution; the short-sightedness of the careful; the carelessness of the far-sighted; and all those many and various events which have given to a decorous profession of religion, and a seemliness of private morals, such an unwonted weight in the attainment and preservation of public power. We are unable to determine whether it be more consolatory or humiliating to human nature, that so many complexities of event, situation, character, age, and country, should be necessary in order to the production of a Mr. Pitt.

Essays on His Own Times.

208. PITT—AND IRELAND

I am quite sure that no dangers are to be feared by England from the disannexing and independence of Ireland at all comparable with the evils which have been, and will yet be, caused to England by the Union. We have never received one particle of advantage from our association with Ireland, whilst we have in many most vital particulars violated the principles of the

British constitution solely for the purpose of conciliating the Irish agitators, and of endeavouring—a vain endeavour—to find room for them under the same government. Mr. Pitt has received great credit for effecting the Union; but I believe it will sooner or later be discovered that the manner in which, and the terms upon which, he effected it, made it the most fatal blow that ever was levelled against the peace and prosperity of England. From it came the Catholic Bill. From the Catholic Bill has come this Reform Bill! And what next?

Table Talk.

209. ROBESPIERRE AND THE GIRONDISTS: POWER
DEPRAVES

The Girondists, who were the first republicans in power, were men of enlarged views and great literary attainments; but they seem to have been deficient in that vigour and daring activity, which circumstances made necessary. Men of genius are rarely either prompt in action or consistent in general conduct: their early habits have been those of contemplative indolence; and the day-dreams, with which they have been accustomed to amuse their solitude, adapt them for splendid speculation, not temperate and practicable counsels. Brissot, the leader of the Gironde party, is entitled to the character of a virtuous man, and an eloquent speaker; but he was rather a sublime visionary, than a quick-eyed politician; and his excellences equally with his faults rendered him unfit for the helm, in the stormy hour of revolution. Robespierre, who displaced him, possessed a glowing ardour that still remembered the *end*, and a cool ferocity that never either overlooked, or scrupled, the *means*. What the *end* was, is not known: that it was a wicked one, has by no means been proved. I rather think, that the distant prospect, to which he was travelling, appeared to him grand and beautiful; but that he fixed his eye on it with such intense eagerness as to neglect the foulness of the road. If however his first intentions were pure, his subsequent enormities yield us a melancholy proof, that it is not the character of the possessor which directs the power, but the power which shapes and depraves the character of the possessor. In Robespierre, its influence was assisted by the properties of his disposition.— Enthusiasm, even in the gentlest temper, will frequently generate sensations of an unkindly order. If we clearly perceive any one thing to be of vast and infinite importance to ourselves and all mankind, our first feelings impel us to turn with angry contempt from those, who doubt and oppose it. The ardour of undisciplined benevolence seduces us into malignity: and whenever our hearts are warm, and our objects great and excellent, intolerance is the sin that does most easily beset us. But this enthusiasm in Robespierre was blended with gloom, and suspiciousness, and inordinate vanity. His dark imagination was still brooding over supposed plots against freedom—to prevent tyranny he became a tyrant—and having realized the evils which he suspected, a wild and dreadful tyrant.—Those loud-tongued adulators, the mob, overpowered the lone-whispered denunciations of conscience—he despotized in all the pomp of patriotism, and masqueraded on the bloody stage of revolution, a Caligula with the cap of liberty on his head.

Essays on His Own Times.

210. BONAPARTE: CHANGING ATTITUDES

(1) *January 10, 1800*

Besides, whom does Bonaparte hope to deceive? . . . But it is a common weakness with men in power, who have used dissimulation successfully, to form a passion for the use of it, dupes to the love of duping! A pride is flattered by these lies. He who fancies that he must be perpetually stooping down to the prejudices of his fellow creatures, is perpetually telling himself how much higher he is than they.—But no real greatness can long coexist with deceit.—The whole faculties of man must be exerted in order to noble energies; and he who is not in earnest, self-mutilated, self-paralysed, lives in but half his being.

Essays On His Own Times.

(2) *March 11, 1800*

It is too common to mistake for the causes of the late revolution in France the accidents which determined the manner and moment of its explosion. The arrival of Bonaparte from Egypt, his ambition, his temerity, and his good luck, were indeed indispensable as occasions and subordinate agents; but would of themselves have been as powerless and of as rapid extinction, as the sparks from a sky-rocket let off in a storm of rain. The real causes of the usurpation must be sought for in the general state of the public feeling and opinion; in the necessity of giving concentration and permanence to the executive government; and the increasing conviction that it has become good policy to exchange the forms of political freedom for the realities of civil security, in order to make a real political freedom possible at some future period. The reasons for preferring a new power under a new title to the restoration of monarchy were many and irrefragable.

First, the attempt could be realized without any approximation to that most dreadful of all revolutions, a revolution of property; a fact, the knowledge, and deep feeling of which, attach all the new rich men to the Chief Consulate. Now in all great cities in all countries, much more therefore in a revolutionary country, the possessors of wealth newly acquired will be more powerful than men of hereditary wealth, because they are more pliant, because they are more active, and because, in consequence of having experienced a greater variety of scene and circumstance, they have, collectively, more talent and information. Add to this, that in France, the men of hereditary wealth are of very various creeds respecting the restoration of monarchy; but the new rich men *can* have but one creed on that subject, and of that one creed they are not only unwavering believers, but likewise zealous apostles.

Secondly, a Chief Consulate admitted a choice of person; a circumstance of incalculable significance in the present affairs of France. It is, we confess, a grievous error to calculate on the virtue and wisdom of any nation; but still we cannot, with ministers, expect such excess of folly in the French, as to believe (however as Englishmen we may wish it), that (menaced as France now is by the boundless ambition of Austria, and stripped of her navy, her commerce, and her colonies, by the monopolising marine of England), the majority of the French nation will consent to entrust the supreme power to a weak man, the puppet of priests and irritated nobles, and bound by an unnatural weight of obligation to the natural enemies of his country. In conniving at the usurpation of Bonaparte, they have seated on the throne of the republic a man of various talent, of commanding genius, of splendid exploit, from whose policy the peaceful adherents of the old religion anticipate toleration; from whose real opinions and habits the men of letters and philosophy are assured of patronage; in whose professional attachment and individual associations the military, and the men of military talent, look confidently for the exertions of a comrade and brother; and, finally, in whose uninterrupted felicity the multitude find an object of superstition and enthusiasm. . . . Thirdly, a Chief Consulate was the only conceivable means of uniting the parties in France, or at least of suspending their struggles. Even if we should concede (what appears to us an absurdity), that the majority in that kingdom are as decidedly in favour of Louis XVIII. as in the first years of our revolution the majority in this kingdom were in favour of the Pretender; still, however, the restoration of the monarch would leave the minority irreconcileable. It would leave no possibility, it would permit no hope, of the realization of their projects at some more distant period. But the Chief Consulate is a much more malleable thing. It pretends to no sacredness;

it is no Nile, made mysterious by the undiscoverableness of its fountain-head; it exists, because it is suitable to existing circumstances; and when circumstances render it unnecessary, it is destructible without a convulsion. The Republicans, the Jacobins and even the *patriotic* Royalists, can still hope, can still contemplate the usurpation, as only the transient means of a permanent end. How well this delusion is adapted to human nature, how quietly a suspension and re-suspension of our freedom is submitted to, where a *formal* repeal would be resisted with life and property, we in this country are now suffering under the proof. It is well known, that a considerable part of the submission to William the Third was owing to the hopes, which the Jacobites conceived from his successor. In all innovations in human affairs, that change bids fairest to be permanent, which permits to the discontented a hope of further change; still more so, when, as in the present case, it may be made appear even as the means of that further change.

These seem to us the causes, which placed Bonaparte in the Chief Consulate. Of his own share in that event we have repeatedly declared our abhorrence; but it is required of us by truth and common justice to admit, that since then, his interests, and those of his country and of Europe, have run completely parallel. The first and chief article of the test required of those whom Bonaparte employs in the service of the republic is, not that they shall have such or such opinions, but that they assent to the necessity of suspending the operation of such and such opinions, wherein they run counter to the existing circumstances. By this toleration he has collected around his immediate interests all the talent of France; and as man is a placable being; as abstract notions give way to surrounding realities; as assumed opinions soon become real ones; and the *suspension* of a tenet is a fainting-fit, that precedes its death; it is probable, that by this toleration he may really reconcile those whom he has brought together, and convert this armistice of factions into a permanent peace. Meantime, it is undeniable, that already his commanding genius has introduced a new tone of morality into France, and that it is now fashionable to assume the rigid and simple character of the Great Consul. Vice cannot now perpetrate its orgies under a gauze cover, as during the monarchy; or in the open air, as during the dynasty of the Jacobins. It must now shut the door, and draw the curtains. This may be hypocrisy; but let it be remembered, that however execrable hypocrisy may be in the individual, yet in a nation at large it is a symptom of convalescence. Perhaps even in individuals, in every reform from vice there is a middle, a transient, and half conscious state of hypocrisy. Now for the first time since the revolution, neither the savage sansculotterie of the Jacobins, nor the intensely selfish frivolity, so fashionable during the weak government of the Directory, is tolerated—but a composed and serious manner is demanded from men, even as a test of good breeding, in the present awful pressure of France upon all the world, and of all the world upon France. In his individual character and conduct, the Chief Consul has hitherto supported the part of a man ambitious of greatness: too intensely pre-occupied to be otherwise than austere in morals; too confident in his predestined fortune to be suspicious or cruel; too ambitious of a new greatness for the ordinary ambition of conquest or despotism. He has opened the prisons and the churches; he has recalled the zealots, if only they were lovers of their country; and the priests, if only they were quietists; and both by consular edict, and private example, has endeavoured to persuade his fellow-citizens not to yield themselves up to their dissensions as politicians, till they had first submitted themselves to the kindly operation of their common sympathies, as men. In this usurpation, Bonaparte stabbed his honesty in the vitals; it has perished—we admit, that it has perished—but the mausoleum, where it lies interred, is among the wonders of the world.

Essays On His Own Times.

(3) *April 21, 1800*

But while we state our objections to the means by which Bonaparte has arrived at his present power, we must acknowledge that he has made a wise and moderate use of it. He is a despot indeed, but not a tyrant. This is the distinction which we take upon his conduct; and it may be necessary for our readers to mark it, that they may detect those who, accusing us of inconsistency, have no other rule themselves, than that of censuring or approving in the lump all political men, of advocating the cause of a party, and justifying its errors with the same zeal as its wisest proceedings. Bonaparte is endeavouring to heal the wounds of the revolution; he has associated in his government all the men of abilities and moderation; he has repressed public vice, tolerated religion, and relaxed the severe laws against emigrants and other unfortunate persons of that description: he has forborne from any measures of terror or extortion in finance; and if he has not been so successful as he wished in recruiting the armies, it is a proof that he has not used cruel or tyrannical measures for that purpose: he has sought peace in the spirit of peace with humbleness and conciliatory language. The whole system he has adopted is that of a mild despotism in respect to the interior of France, and of a wary and moderate government in respect to her foreign affairs.—The wisdom of his proceedings induces men to submit in France, though they feel no spirit of enthusiasm in his favour.—The emigrants speak of his genius with admiration, and of his views with hope: Englishmen the most alarmed at the French revolution, and the most friendly to the war, feel their fears subside in consequence of his conduct. He has given repose to men's minds, if not to the armies directed by governments. Every man can perceive that the public apprehension of danger from France exists no more now than it ever did in any common war. Bonaparte has buried under his new constitution the principles of revolutionists; but he excites the hopes of almost all descriptions of men; even the royalists do not despair of some amelioration of their condition. He has palsied the hostility of all parties, if he has gained the enthusiastic support of none. His is a government of experiment rather than of popularity. His object is to give tranquillity, and gain the confidence of temperate, wise men, rather than to fanaticise factions, and to rule by public delirium. It was that mode of government which exhausted France, and rendered the revolution an object of terror both at home and abroad; and Bonaparte must maintain himself without having recourse to it, in order to succeed in the system he has begun.

It is unnecessary to speculate upon the duration of the government of France, or upon the changes it may undergo. Our present object is to draw a distinction between the detestable means by which Bonaparte has obtained power, and the wise and mild use he has made of it. Whether he will act with true greatness, and make the happiness of the nation, rather than personal power, his object, is a question which time alone can decide. Upon that question depends the character of his present conduct. If it be necessary for the public welfare to deposit the whole authority of the state in the hands of one man, Bonaparte is the person of all others to whom such a trust should be confided. He is without a rival in renown; no one can attempt to cope with him in personal influence; his great genius points him out as the man who is best able to restore to France peace and prosperity; and to give repose and confidence to Europe. If his virtues be as great as his genius, he may do for the old world what Washington has done for the new.

Essays On His Own Times.

(4) *Sept. 21, 1802*

It would be too great a digression to inquire, at present, which of the three first Caesars we mean, when, in imitation of his late addresses, we style Bonaparte the new Caesar. His character comprises in it many of the good, and some of the bad, traits of all the three. If in courage, splendour of military fame, in military success and conduct, and the love of science, he recall Julius to our memory; if he remind us of Augustus in his close application to public business, and his encouragement of the liberal arts and great public works, we must at the same time admit, that he has likewise the imperious, irritable, and ostentatious mind of the former, with the constitutional coldness and politic craft of the latter. But if reserve, if darkness, if the employment of spies and informers, if dread and hatred of all political discussions, if vindictive hatred of all bold political writings, if an indifference to all religions, except as instruments of state policy, with a certain strange and dark superstition respecting fate, a blind confidence in his destinies—if these be any parts of the Chief Consul's character, they would force upon us, even against our own will, the name and history of Tiberius—*Vide* Suetonius, lib. 3. Tib. Caesar, *passim. Non modo morosus, sed praetrepidus quoque, is qua famosa de se ac suis carmina, imo, versiculi facti, animadversum est statim in auctores, scriptaque abolita.—Nemini delatorum fides abrogata.—Circa Deos ac Religiones negligentior, persuasionisque plenus cuncta Fato agi.*

Essays On His Own Times.

December 21, 1809

Bonaparte.

The error, which of all others most besets the public mind, and which yet of all others is the most degrading in its nature, the most tremendous in its consequences, is an inward prostration of the soul before enormous Power, and a readiness to palliate and forget all iniquities to which prosperity has wedded itself; as if man were only a puppet without reason and free will, and without the conscience which is the offspring of their union, a puppet played off by some unknown power! as if success were the broad seal of the divine approbation, and tyranny itself the Almighty's inauguration of a Tyrant!

> Planned merely, 'tis a common felony;
> Accomplished, an immortal undertaking!

And with success comes Pardon hand in hand:
For all event is God's arbitrement.—*Wallenstein.*

The main strength of Bonaparte, Sir, is in the imaginations of
men, which are dazzled and blinded by the splendid robes and
gaudy trappings which have been purchased by guilt for its
own disguise. Is it to be borne by good men without an attempt
on their part to stem or counteract the delusion, that the power
and prosperity, which derive their very being from excess of
wickedness, should secure for that wickedness an immunity
from our hate and execration? But if the detestation be right,
can the utterance of it be culpable? Is it not the nature of man,
that all inward feelings will languish and go out, if not fanned
and fuelled by their outward and visible signs? Has Providence
given us our senses and sensitive nature as the means of Imposture only, and to be exclusively the tools of villains? There
is a book, Sir, which we have not yet learnt to treat with contempt, that abounds with examples of words and phrases that
seem on fire with anger, and indignant reprobation, and these
used by inspired Wisdom itself to scare the vicious as with
thunders, and to kindle the hearts of good men like the blast of
a trumpet calling them to battle against the giants that war
against Heaven. For assuredly against Heaven doth that man
wage war, whose whole career is in defiance of all the principles
which alone give a meaning to our erect form, and entitle us
to look toward Heaven as to our natural and destined country.
I have styled the present Ruler of France a Wretch and a
Monster, but on what occasion? Were these phrases provoked
by his Veni-vidi-vici victories over the armies of Russia,
Prussia, and Austria? No! I have denounced him as a remorseless Tyrant, and the enemy of the human race. But was it
because he had sworn the ruin of Great Britain, and had exhausted all the resources of his stupendous power in prepara-
tions for its invasion? No! I exulted, indeed, that his army of
England lay encamped on his coasts like wolves braying at the

moon, and that he is condemned to behold his vast flotillas as worthless and idle as the sea-weed that rots around their keels. I exulted, indeed, as became a Briton; but I neither reviled nor even blamed him. But that in order to gratify his rage against one country, he made light of the ruin of his own subjects; that to undermine the resource of one enemy, he would reduce the Continent of Europe to a state of barbarism, and by the remorseless suspension of the commercial system, destroy the principal source of civilization, and abolish a middle class throughout Christendom; for this, Sir, I declared him the common enemy of mankind! For this, Sir, and for the murder of Palm, and for the torture and private assassination of Wright, of Pichegru, and Toussaint, (the latter a hero as much his superior in genius as in goodness); for his remorseless behaviour to the Swiss and to the Tyrolese, and for his hatred of liberty everywhere; and lastly for his ingratitude, perfidy, baseness, and fiend-like cruelty, for this amalgam of all vices, in the one vice of his conduct towards Spain. I have spoken of him, and of his power with abhorrence, because it is only by a clear conception of its foul and dark foundations that this power can be effectually resisted. In what other terms, than those of execration, could I describe a power, which subsists, for the greater part, in the consistency and systematic perfection of its possessor's vices; crime corresponding to crime, villainy entrenched and barricaded by villainy? An additional motive was supplied by the necessity of directing the public attention to the moral consequences of his tyranny, and that these are far more to be dreaded than the worst of those outward and calculable evils, which chiefly shock the imaginations of men. What good will the Tyrolese do themselves by their heroic resistance? exclaims one man. What are the Spaniards fighting for? exclaims another—as if man were made only to eat above ground, and be eaten; as if we had no dignity to preserve, no conscience to obey, no immortality to expect. . . .

There is a class of men, Sir, who make a point of rejecting or disregarding all arguments that are enforced with warmth of feeling and illustrated by the lights of imagination. (The latter is indeed the effect of the former; for the boldest figures of speech are the natural language of profound feeling and a heart affected in good earnest.) These persons seem to rank wisdom and truth among the Alpine flowers, which can flourish only amid ice and snow, and where all other qualities of intellect are notoriously wanting, they charitably clothe the naked with the substantial praises of judgment and calm good sense. But woe to that man, who on circumstances which vitally affect the weal and woe of the whole human race in time and for eternity, can reason in as cold-blooded a tone, as if he were demonstrating a problem in geometry. The warmth, which the development and disclosure of such truths occasions, is altogether different from the heat of passion; and by the frivolous and unfeeling alone will the earnestness of a deep conviction be confounded with the irritability of self-mistrusting positiveness. A complete tranquillity, a cold self-possession, in the contemplation and defence of man's highest interests and most awful concerns, is the commencement of that depraved indifference, that deadness of the moral and religious sense, which (a morbid accumulation being the usual consequence of an unnatural obstruction) so easily passes into the brutal and stupid revolution-phrenzy, and then having raved out its hour of madness, sinks to sleep in the strait-waistcoat of military despotism. For myself, both in the intercourse of private life, and in the performance of my public duties as the Editor of a Work, the main object of which is to refer the opinions of men to their proper objects, I shall always deem myself acting most judiciously when I employ those feelings, which the Supreme Wisdom has interwoven with my existence, in the enforcement of those truths and duties, the acknowledgment and performance of which the same Wisdom ordained to be the characteristic of our nature, and the end and object of our being.

O Friend and Father of the human mind,
Whose Art for noblest ends our frame design'd!
If I, though fated to the studious shade,
Which party-strife, nor anxious power invade—
If I aspire in public virtue's cause
To guide the Muses by sublimer laws:
Do thou the authority of truth impart,
And give my labours entrance to the heart!
Perhaps my voice may rouse the smother'd flame,
And snatch the fainting Patriot back to fame;
Perhaps by worthy thoughts of human kind
To worthy deeds exalt the conscious mind,
Or dash corruption in her proud career,
And teach her Slaves that Vice was born to fear.

S. T. Coleridge

Grasmere.

Essays On His Own Times.

211. NELSON

Lord Nelson was an admiral every inch of him. He looked at every thing, not merely in its possible relations to the naval service in general, but in its immediate bearings on his own squadron; to his officers, his men, to the particular ships themselves his affections were as strong and ardent as those of a lover. Hence though his temper was constitutionally irritable and uneven, yet never was a commander so enthusiastically loved by men of all ranks from the captain of the fleet to the youngest shipboy. Hence too the unexampled harmony which reigned in his fleet year after year, under circumstances that might well have undermined the patience of the best balanced dispositions, much more of men with the impetuous character of British sailors. Year after year, the same dull duties of a wearisome blockade of doubtful policy—little if any opportunity of taking prizes; and the few prizes, which accident might throw in the way, of little or no value—and when at last the occasion presented itself which would have compensated for all, then a disappointment as sudden and unexpected as it was unjust and cruel, and the cup dashed from their lips!—Add to these trials the sense of enterprizes checked by feebleness and timidity else-where, not omitting the tiresomeness of the Mediterranean sea, sky, and climate; and the unjarring and cheerful spirit of affec-tionate brotherhood, which linked together the hearts of that whole squadron, will appear not less wonderful to us than admirable and affecting. When the resolution was taken of com-mencing hostilities against Spain, before any intelligence was sent to Lord Nelson, another admiral, with two or three ships of the line, was sent into the Mediterranean, and stationed before Cadiz, for the express purpose of intercepting the Spanish prizes. The admiral dispatched on this lucrative service gave no information to Lord Nelson of his arrival in the same sea, and five weeks elapsed before his lordship became ac-quainted with the circumstance. The prizes thus taken were immense. A month or two sufficed to enrich the commander and officers of this small and highly-favoured squadron: while to Nelson and his fleet the sense of having done their duty, and the consciousness of the glorious services which they had per-formed were considered, it must be presumed, as an abundant remuneration for all their toils and long-suffering! It was indeed an unexampled circumstance, that a small squadron should be sent to the station which had been long occupied by a large fleet, commanded by the darling of the navy, and the glory of the British empire, to the station where this fleet had for years been wearing away in the most barren, repulsive, and spirit-trying service, in which the navy can be employed; and that this minor squadron should be sent independently of, and with-out any communication with, the commander of the former fleet, for the express and solitary purpose of stepping between it and the Spanish prizes, and as soon as this short and pleasant service was performed, of bringing home the unshared booty with all possible caution and despatch. The *substantial* advantages of naval service were perhaps deemed of too *gross* a nature for men already rewarded with the grateful affections of their own country-men, and the admiration of the whole world! They were to be awarded, therefore, on a principle of compensation to a commander less rich in fame, and whose laurels, though not scanty, were not yet sufficiently luxuriant to hide the *golden* crown which is the appropriate ornament of victory in the bloodless war of commercial capture. Of all the wounds which were ever inflicted on Nelson's feelings (and there were not a few), this was the deepest—this rankled most. 'I had thought,' (said the gallant man, in a letter written in the first sense of the affront) 'I fancied—but nay, it must have been a dream, an idle dream—yet I confess it, I *did* fancy, that I had done my country service—and thus they use me. It was not enough to have robbed me once before of my West India harvest; now they have taken away the Spanish; and under what circumstances, and with what pointed aggravations! Yet, if I know my own thoughts, it is not for myself, or on my own account chiefly, that I feel the sting and the disappointment. No! it is for my brave officers; for my noble-minded friends and comrades—such a gallant set of fellows! such a band of brothers! My heart swells at the thought of them!'

This strong attachment of the heroic admiral to his fleet, faithfully repaid by an equal attachment on their part to their admiral, had no little influence in attuning their hearts to each other; and when he died it seemed as if no man was a stranger to another: for all were made acquaintances by the rights of a common anguish. In the fleet itself, many a private quarrel was forgotten, no more to be remembered; many, who had been alienated, became once more good friends; yea, many a one was reconciled to his very enemy, and loved, and (as it were) thanked him, for the bitterness of his grief, as if it had been an act of consolation to himself in an intercourse of private sympathy. The tidings arrived at Naples on the day that I returned to that city from Calabria: and never can I forget the sorrow and consternation that lay on every countenance. Even to this day there are times when I seem to see, as in a vision, separate groups and individual faces of the picture. Numbers stopped and shook hands with me, because they had seen the tears on my cheek, and conjectured that I was an Englishman; and several, as they held my hand, burst themselves into tears. And though it may excite a smile, yet it pleased and affected me, as a proof of the goodness of the human heart struggling to exercise its kindness in spite of prejudices the most obstinate, and eager to carry on its love and honour into the life beyond life, that it was whispered about Naples that Lord Nelson had become a good Catholic before his death. The absurdity of the fiction is a sort of measurement of the fond and affectionate esteem which had ripened the pious wish of some kind individual, through all the gradations of possibility and probability, into a confident assertion believed and affirmed by hundreds.

Friend.

212. DUKE OF WELLINGTON

I sometimes fear the Duke of Wellington is too much disposed to imagine, that he can govern a great nation by word of command, in the same way in which he governed a highly disciplined army. He seems to be unaccustomed to, and to despise, the inconsistencies, the weaknesses, the bursts of heroism followed by prostration and cowardice, which invariably characterise all popular efforts. He forgets that, after all, it is from such efforts that all the great and noble institutions of the world have come; and that, on the other hand, the discipline and organization of armies have been only like the flight of the cannon-ball, the object of which is destruction.

Table Talk.

213. CANNING

The stock-jobbing and moneyed interest is so strong in this country, that it has more than once prevailed in our foreign councils over national honour and national justice. The country gentlemen are not slow to join in this influence. Canning felt this very keenly, and said he was unable to contend against the city train-bands.

Table Talk.

214. CANNING

Canning is very irritable, surprisingly so for a wit who is always giving such hard knocks. He should have put on an ass's skin before he went into parliament. Lord Liverpool is the single stay of this ministry; but he is not a man of a directing mind. He cannot ride on the whirlwind. He serves as the isthmus to connect one half of the cabinet with the other. He always gives you the common sense of the matter, and in that it is that his strength in debate lies.

Table Talk.

215. BROUGHAM ON THE 'COLONIAL POLICY OF THE EUROPEAN POWERS'

Again and again and again, I am made to feel that the disease of Brougham's mind is the mistaking the *contingent* for the *necessary*—the defining of an *universal term* by all the properties of one particular Instance—as if, *ex. gr.* a mineralogist should include in his definition of Gold all the matters found in a particular Lump of *Gold Ore*. A colony with him means an oppressed, or at least, unfraternized *Wen* of a distant Country with checks and counter-checks in the government that destroy all vigor and promptness, and laws for the exclusive advantage of the distant Mother—or Step-mother—State, that preclude all patriotism and natural Enthusiasm in the Inhabitants.

p. 60. 'other things being equal'! *hm! hm!*—but other things never are equal. For instance, if the Negroes form an independent State in St. Domingo, this will admit of no general reasoning, of any great importance, that is deducible from the nature of Colonies *in genere.* . . .

. . . Mr. B's Logic is a perfect See-saw and like a Conjurer who has ill-learnt the black Art, he often raises up Spirits that he cannot lay again.

MS.

216. HORNE TOOKE

Horne Tooke was pre-eminently a ready-witted man. He had that clearness which is founded on shallowness. He doubted nothing; and, therefore, gave you all that he himself knew, or meant, with great completeness. His voice was very fine, and his tones exquisitely discriminating. His mind had no progression or development. All that is worth any thing (and that is but little) in the *Diversions of Purley* is contained in a short pamphlet-letter which he addressed to Mr. Dunning; then it was enlarged to an octavo, but there was not a foot of progression beyond the pamphlet; at last, a quarto volume, I believe, came out; and yet, verily, excepting *Morning Chronicle* lampoons and political insinuations, there was no addition to the argument of the pamphlet. It shows a base and unpoetical mind to convert so beautiful, so divine, a subject as language into the vehicle or make-weight of political squibs.

Table Talk.

217. TOOKE AND GODWIN

Horne Tooke was always making a butt of Godwin; who, nevertheless, had that in him which Tooke could never have understood. I saw a good deal of Tooke at one time: he left upon me the impression of his being a keen, iron man.

Table Talk.

218. KEAN

Kean is original; but he copies from himself. His rapid descents from the hyper-tragic to the infra-colloquial, though sometimes productive of great effect, are often unreasonable. To see him act, is like reading Shakespeare by flashes of lightning. I do not think him thorough-bred gentleman enough to play Othello.

Table Talk.

219. MACKINTOSH

Sir James Mackintosh is the king of the men of talent. He is a most elegant converser. How well I remember his giving break-fast to me and Sir Humphry Davy, at that time an unknown young man, and our having a very spirited talk about Locke and Newton, and so forth! When Davy was gone, Mackintosh said to me, 'That's a very extraordinary young man; but he is gone wrong on some points.' But Davy was, at that time at least, a man of genius; and I doubt if Mackintosh ever heartily appreciated an eminently original man. He is uncommonly powerful in his own line; but it is not the line of a first-rate man. After all his fluency and brilliant erudition, you can rarely carry off anything worth preserving. You might not improperly write on his forehead, 'Warehouse to let!' He always dealt too much in generalities for a lawyer. He is deficient in power in applying his principles to the points in debate. I remember Robert Smith had much more logical ability; but Smith aimed at conquest by any gladiatorial shift; whereas Mackintosh was uniformly candid in argument. I am speaking now from old recollections.

Table Talk.

220. GARRICK

The warmest admirers of histrionic merit would not willingly be supposed to overlook the difference, both in kind and degree, between an excellence that in its very nature is transient, or continuing only as an echo, in the memory of a single generation, while the name alone remains for posterity, and a power, enduring as the Soul of Man and commensurate with the human language.

But, without dreading the imputation of a wish to balance weights so unequal, we may assert that if ever two great men might seem to have been made for each other, we have this correspondency presented to us in the instance of Garrick and Shakespeare. It will be sufficient for me to direct attention to one peculiarity, the common and exclusive characteristic of both,—the union of the highest Tragic and Comic Excellence in the same Individual. This indeed supersedes the necessity of mentioning the particular merits which it implies and comprehends, while it is eminently and in the exactest sense of the word *characteristic*, inasmuch as this transcendant power sprung from the same source in both,—from an insight into human nature at its fountain head, which exists in those creations of Genius alone, in which the substance and essential forms are the Gifts of Meditation and self-research, and the individualising accidents, and the requisite drapery are supplied by observation and acquaintance with the world. We may then hope for a second Garrick or of an approach to a Shakespeare where we find a knowledge of Man united to an equal knowledge of Men, and both co-existing with the power of giving Life and Individuality to the Products of both. For such a Being possesses the rudiments of every character in himself, and acquires the faculty of *becoming*, for the moment, whatever character he may choose to represent. He combines in his own person at once the materials and the workman. The precious proofs of this rare excellence in our Greatest Dramatic Poet are in the hands of all men. To exhibit the same excellence in our greatest actor, we can conceive no more lively or impressive way than by presenting him in the two extreme Poles of his Creative and almost Protean Genius—in his Richard the Third and his Abel Drugger.

Allsop.

221. WORDSWORTH

Of all the men I ever knew, Wordsworth has the least femineity in his mind. He is *all* man. He is a man of whom it might have been said,—"It is good for him to be alone."

Allsop.

222. JEFFREY

Clarkson (the moral steam engine, or Giant with one idea) had recently published his book, and being in a very irritable state of mind, his wife expressed great fears of the effect of any severe review in the then state of his feelings. I wrote to Jeffrey, and expressed to him my opinion of the cruelty of any censure being passed upon the work as *a composition.* In return I had a very polite letter, expressing a wish that I should review it. I did so; but when the Review was published, in the place of some just eulogiums due to Mr. Pitt, and which I stated were upon the best authority (in fact, they were from Tom Clarkson himself), was substituted some abuse and detraction. Yet Clarkson expressed himself gratified and satisfied with the effect of the review, and would not allow me to expose the transaction. Again, Jeffrey had said to me that it was hopeless to persuade men to prefer Hooker and Jeremy Taylor to Johnson and Gibbon. I wrote him two letters, or two sheets, detailing, at great length, my opinions. *This* he never acknowledged; but in an early number of the Review he inserted the whole of my communication in an article of the Review, and added at the conclusion words to this effect: "We have been anxious to be clear on this subject, as much has been said on this matter by men who evidently do not understand it. Such are Wordsworth, Southey, Coleridge, and Miss Baillie."

Allsop.

223. GODWIN AND TOBIN

I used to be much amused with Tobin and Godwin. Tobin would pester me with stories of Godwin's dulness; and upon his departure Godwin would drop in just to say that Tobin was more dull than ever.

Allsop.

224. MALTHUS

Is it not lamentable—is it not even marvellous—that the monstrous practical sophism of Malthus should now have gotten complete possession of the leading men of the kingdom! Such an essential lie in morals—such a practical lie in fact as it is too! I solemnly declare that I do not believe that all the heresies and sects and factions which the ignorance and the weakness and the wickedness of man have ever given birth to, were altogether so disgraceful to man as a Christian, a philosopher, a statesman, or citizen, as this abominable tenet. It should be exposed by reasoning in the form of ridicule. Asgill or Swift would have done much; but, like the Popish doctrines, it is so vicious a tenet, so flattering to the cruelty, the avarice, and sordid selfishness of most men that I hardly know what to think of the result.

Table Talk.

225. EDWARD IRVING

The two most uncommon things in the world are the Love of the Good, *as* good, and the Love of the True, *as* Truth—each *absolutely* and only for itself. And of these two uncommon things the latter is the more uncommon. I do not mean Veracity, or the man's abhorrence of Falsehood or of saying what he does not think—that he does so think must be grounded on no other interest but the desire of thinking the Truth. Again, I do not mean partially, or generally, but as a principle, operating without exception.

The former rare excellence I could confidently attribute to my Friend Edward Irving: but not with equal confidence, or so unexceptionally, the latter. For instance, I cannot help believing, that his imagination that the XXth Chapter of the Revelations favors the doctrine of a future Millennium prevents him from seeing, that it is a mere imagination; and that the passage was actually intended to evacuate this favorite fancy of the Jews and Jewish Converts by substituting under the same name the anticipation of the Establishment of Christianity as the Religion of the Empire. S. T. C.

MS.

226. EDWARD IRVING

I have no faith in his prophesyings; small sympathy with his fulminations; and in certain peculiarities of his *theological* system as distinct from his religious principles, I cannot see my way.

But I hold withal, and not the less firmly for these *discrepances* in our moods and judgements, that *Edward Irving* possesses more of the spirit and purposes of the first Reformers, that he has more of the Head and Heart, the Life, the Unction, and the genial Powers of *Martin Luther*, than any man now alive; yea than any man of this and the last Century.

MS.

IX

SOCIAL CONFIDENCE

All our happiness and the greater part of our virtues depend on social confidence.

Conciones ad Populum.

SOCIETY

The most important works for this part of a study of Coleridge are the *Friend, Essays on His Own Times, On the Constitution of the Church and State,* and the *Table Talk.* The early periodical the *Watchman* should not be overlooked. A selection from these and other writings has been usefully brought together in *The Political Thought of S. T. Coleridge* by R. S. White.

Coleridge is often remembered as a foolish pantisocrat in his French Revolutionary youth and a regenerate Tory in his old age. Both extremes have been exaggerated in report, and both elements were in him from the beginning to the end, never completely harmonized. His opposition to the Reform Bill of 1832 was no more conservative than socialist; it was not from opposition to the extension of the franchise so much as from a desire to see the standard of living raised instead, and the extension of education first and votes second. He suspected that the vote was a soporofic which would only postpone the real reckoning and lead to the poor laws. On the other hand, he felt that the national culture demanded the maintenance of privileged classes, landed and learned, and a high evaluation of tradition. Society, like the individual, was more than the sum of the parts; it was a living organism, though humanly constructed and to be changed at need. He never fully reconciled, in his social theory, what he recognized to be the claims of expediency on the one side and of the ideal state on the other.

IX

SOCIAL CONFIDENCE

227. OF MEN AND WOMEN

A manuscript note on the front flyleaf and title-page of [Henry More's] *Observations upon Anthroposophia Theomagica, and Anima Magica Abscondita*, by Alagonomastix Philalethes, 1650.

THIS is an exquisite specimen of *university* Wit and Manners in 1650—or rather of that style which is sure to prevail among Cælibates and in works destined for the exclusive Reading of Cælibates, whether Young—or old—Bachelors! Gri[pping] even to emetical.

I fear that the same Remark will apply no less to the other Sex in Harems, Nunneries and English Girls-Boarding Schools. Each sex is necessary to even the *special* Virtues of the other. Man (whether male or female) was not made to live alone. S. T. C.

MS.

228. MARRIAGE

Men are not more generous than women. Men desire the happiness of women apart from themselves, chiefly, if not only, *when and where* it would be an imputation upon a woman's affections for her to be happy; and women, on their part, seldom cordially carry their wish for their husband's happiness and enjoyment beyond the threshold. Whether it is that women have a passion for nursing, or from whatever cause, they invariably discourage all attempts to seek for health itself, beyond their own abode. When balloons, or these new roads upon which they say it will be possible to travel fifteen miles an hour, for a day together, shall become the common mode of travelling, women will become more locomotive;—the health of all classes will be materially benefitted. Women will then spend less time in attiring themselves—will invent some more simple head gear, or dispense with it altogether.

Thousands of women, attached to their husbands by the most endearing ties, and who would deplore their death for months, would oppose a separation for a few weeks in search of health, or assent so reluctantly, and with so much dissatisfaction, as to deprive the remedy of all value—rather make it an evil. I speak of affectionate natures and of the various, but always selfish, guises of self will.

Caresses and endearment on this side of sickening *fondness*, and affectionate interest in all that concerns himself, from a wife freely chosen, are what every man loves, whether he be communicative or reserved, staid or sanguine. But affection, where it exists, will always prompt or discover its own most appropriate manifestation. All men, even the most surly, are influenced by affection, even when little fitted to excite it. I could have been happy with a servant girl had she only in sincerity of heart responded to my affection.

Allsop.

229. EDUCATION AND EQUALITY OF SEXES

The education of the Germans gave them strength and stature, and their strength was preserved by the remarkable continence that so peculiarly and honorably distinguished them; 'but there,' says Tacitus, 'no one laughs at vice, nor is it called the fashion to corrupt and be corrupted.' They looked upon women as their equals and companions, and whoever wished for the love of a woman, first made himself worthy of her esteem. They deemed them favoured by the gods, and we find frequent mention of Prophetesses attending upon their armies. Nor is this wonderful, for they constantly employed themselves either in war or hunting. They left the study of simples and the art of healing to the women; and the art was as mysterious as the occasion was frequent. The women were respected, and therefore they became respectable.

It has been observed, 'that the refinements of life corrupt, while they polish, the intercourse of the sexes;' and the rude poverty of Germany has been assigned as one cause of the German continence. If refinement consist in 'luxurious entertainments, midnight dances, and licentious spectacles', we may agree with Gibbon, that they at once present temptation and opportunity to frailty: but that only can with propriety be styled refinement, which, by strengthening the intellect, purifies the manners. All else enervates and depraves. If a mind skilled in the routine of etiquette, and the nothingness of *politesse*, and a body enfeebled by the delicate languor of fashion, constitute refinement, I must turn to contemplate the dignity of woman in the tent of a barbarian.

'But (says the historian) heroines of such a cast may claim our admiration; but they were most assuredly neither lovely, nor very susceptible of love. Whilst they affected to emulate the stern virtues of *man*, they must have resigned that attractive softness in which principally consists the charm and weakness of *woman*.' Of this I must say with Mary Woolstonecraft, 'that it is the philosophy of sensuality'. The women of Germany were the free and equal companions of their husbands: they were treated by them with esteem and confidence, and consulted on every occasion of importance. What, then, is this love which woman loses by becoming respectable?

Essays on His Own Times.

230. MARRIAGE RELATIONS

I sometimes think I shall write a book on the duties of women, more especially to their husbands. If such a book were *well written*, I cannot doubt but that its results would be most salutary. I am inclined to think that both men and women err in their conduct and demeanour towards each other, quite as much from ignorance and unconsciousness of what is displeasing, as from selfishness or disregard. But to the execution of such a work, or rather such works (for A New Duty of Man is quite as much required, and this must be written by an affectionate and right-minded woman), the present sickly delicacy, the over-delicacy (and therefore essential indelicacy) of the present taste would be opposed. To be of any use it should be a plain treatise, the results of experience, and should be given to all newly married couples by their parents, not in the form of admonition, but rather as containing much important information which they can no where else obtain.

Allsop.

231. MARRIAGE

Marriage has, as you say, no *natural* relation to love. Marriage belongs to society; it is a social contract. It should not merely include the conditions of esteem and friendship, it should be the ratification of their manifestation. Still I do not know how it can be replaced; *that* belongs to the future, and it is a question which the future only can solve. I however quite agree that we can now, better than at any former time, say what *will not*, what *cannot* be.

Allsop.

232. MARRIAGE—PARENTAL DUTY

On the subject of parental authority in respect of marriage, I observed that we too often in such cases had the Daughters in view rather than the Sons, and I contended, that after a *certain Age* and a certain fair time for consideration, a Son or Daughter retaining the same conviction became morally free Agents. For that there was this difference between Law and Morality: in Law I may have a Right which it is not my Duty to exercise, which it may be me Duty NOT to exercise, but in Morality my Rights grow out of my Duties, and are bounded, i.e. determined by them. Prove it a Parent's *Duty* to refuse his consent, and you will have proved his *Right* so to do.

MS.

233. WOMEN

Southey in *The Doctor* quotes Thomas Fuller on daughters, as being in a family 'silent strings' sending no sound to posterity, but 'losing their own surnames in their matches'.

Coleridge comments: This evil in genealogy the French and Germans endeavour, if not to prevent yet in fact to remedy, by affixing the maiden or paternal to the married Name— thus: *Frances Pattison, née Coleridge.* Catherine Pappenheissen, gebohrne Von Axen, an heraldic usage worthy of adoption in England, where the disruption of the married Daughter from her parent Stock, and absorption into the name and family of the Husband, is not to be praised. It is a *discontinuity* in descents —and a Nothingizing of the Female.

MS.

234. DOMESTIC RELATIONS

I have shown in the *Biographia Literaria* the great evil of too entire domestication. My after-experience would confirm, nay even extend, this. I incline to think that, unless the husband is abroad the whole day, and therefore only a partaker of his wife's social parties, that in the choice of their associates they should be independent. To exclude all that a woman or a man might wish to exclude from his or her help-mate's society, might leave the rest of little value, and lead to mutual discomfort. The Turkish method is good: they have no difference of opinion in that fine country; but, as our own habits and customs are different, we should seek to make arrangements in harmony with them; and this I think may be accomplished. Why insist upon a married pair—paired not matched—agreeing in the choice of their visitors. The less the independence of married people, especially that of man, is trenched upon, the better chance of happiness for both. Are there any men to whom the wife has a dislike? why should she be annoyed with their presence? Are there women amongst his wife's acquaintance who to him are un-genial, why force them upon the husband's distaste or dislike. I have known permanent aversions, and, what is the same thing, permanent alienations proceed from this cause, all which might have been avoided by each of the parties simply agreeing to see their own friends without the presence or intervention of the other. In the one case the range of the more kindly sym-pathies may appear to be circumscribed, in the other, dislike is quickly ripened into aversion.

Allsop.

235. REVERENCE THE INDIVIDUALITY OF YOUR FRIEND !

Throughout all Nature we find evidences of a Will and a Reason, and the Will is *deeper* than Reason. It can no more be called *above* Reason than you would describe the Tap-root of an Oak as *above* the Trunk; and it can as little oppose or contradict Reason, as the Foot-sole can go contrary to the Limb—or than the Stuff or matter can contradict the Form. The Stuff is pre-supposed in order to the Form. Now Will is the Stuff and Reason the Form. In every creature, the Will appears in Reason and by Reason—it acts in the form of Reason. But likewise in every creature the Will shews itself, i.e. the Will manifests itself as Will. That same Principle which we had seen in the Reason as the power and reality of Reason, makes itself known as a real Power, remaining underneath all that is resolvable into Reason, as the Bason water of a Fountain is seen distinct from the salient watry column, in which it rises, shapes, and blossoms. Hence it is, that in every product of Nature from Comet and Coral up to Man and Woman there is that which can be understood, and a somewhat that cannot be understood —some things, arrangements, relations, that can be reduced to a Law, accounted for and on which we may calculate, and a somewhat that cannot be accounted [for] or even described intelligibly, because it has its source in that which is deeper than Intelligence, and which lies underneath all assignable Reasons and Causes, as their common Ground.

Take two lovely and interesting Faces—Mrs. Gillman's for instance, and Mrs Aders's (and to my notion there are few finer ones). You will find no difficulty in stating this and that feature, proportion, shade of color, in which the two faces differ, and by which you might enable a Stranger to distinguish the one from the other. But will you allow, that these contain the whole difference, or that these taken in conjunction with the points common to both faces, would give you the whole impression of either face, either singly or comparatively? Would the Sum total of all the describable or even visible differences produce in you that sense of the *individual* character of either face, which the Face itself gave you? Certainly not.

Now from this uncommon Metaphysics, there may be drawn a sound common-sense and practical moral. Laugh, if you please, at oddities that are contrary to Reason, and condemn Caprices that are the eruptions of a feverish Selfishness: for both are results and symptoms of a *want* of Will—of a will too scanty to rise, too imbecile to shape itself into forms of Reason. To respect the free-agency of our Neighbor is a duty of common Honesty. It is his Castle, the strong-hold retreat when field and forest have changed their owner. Nay, it is his Treasurevault, sunk into the foundations of the House, and holds the Title-deeds of his Humanity. In the code of conscience it is aggravated Burglary to break into it. But a noble mind will do more than abstain from doing wrong. We should impose on ourselves a higher Rule. Reverence the *Individuality* of those you live among. Laugh if you like at Oddities, that are contrary to Reason, and condemn Caprices, that are most often no better than eruptions of a feverous Selfishness. For these are the results and symptoms of a want of Will, Marks of a Will too scanty and lifeless to spring up and shape itself in the forms of Reason. But then be sure that what you call Odd and Capricious may not be a Peculiarity connected with the individuality of the Person's Being and Character—and unintelligible to you, because its source lies deeper than Intelligence.

Reverence the Individuality of your friend! It is the religion of a delicate Soul—and to ensure or facilitate the performance of the duty, it is no unimportant part of moral discretion to provide for this in every plan of co-habitation or of Intimacy next to domestic Familiarity, in the original sense of the word. To the eye of the World your Establishment may appear a concentric Circle— ◎ with many circumferential lines but only one center. But in itself it must be a [union of *crossed out*] close neighborhood of centers within a swelling outline formed by the segments of the outer circles. And the scheme then only promises success, when room is allowed for every point to have a small circumference of its own, so that the contraction to which each must consent in order to give space for the others, shall yet in no instance bring the circumferential line so close to the center for any radii [not?] to be describable in the interspaces.

Even to two Lovers on the point of becoming Man and Wife I would say—would you wish that year after year your wedding should every day commence anew? Agree beforehand, nay, if in the fullness of your love, and oneheartedness it should require invention and contrivance, yet invent, contrive that there shall be some points, some things respecting which you are to continue single. Be assured that these exceptions will strengthen the rule—and that this abstinence, these interposed Fasts of Sympathy are more favorable to its longevity—*a fortiori* in all looser ties.

MS.

236. DISAGREEMENTS BETWEEN FRIENDS

If you suffer your conduct to be actuated (be it more or less) by a feeling or belief which you cannot avow—first of all, remember that a little self-complacency in your own shrewdness and observation (as shown in the nod of the head, and the 'I *saw* what was going on') may make the grounds of this belief appear far stronger and more plausible to yourself, than you could make them appear to an indifferent person, much more to the party on the opposite side. Secondly, such feeling or belief being neither known or suspected by the other party, and you not having reckoned it among the reasons that actuated you, can you wonder that the reasons which you do avow, should be thought insufficient to account of it, and your conduct therefore be felt as strange and unkind?

Another common error I have noticed in disagreements between Friends: especially where there are three Parties, each [composing *crossed out*] including a family—say, A. B. and C. C. conceives himself slighted or unkindly used by A, and appeals to the common Friend, B. whether *B*. if it were his own case, would not have felt himself wronged. B. asks himself the question, and his Heart answers it in the affirmative. Now the error to be avoided in this instance consists in confounding two very different things—'If it were my own case, I should feel, and (I daresay) act so and so'—and 'It not being my own case, I yet ought to feel so and so'. Now the former may be very true, and yet the latter be altogether false and contrary to your duty. Do *you* reason thus: Were this my case, as it is C.'s I should feel as C. feels; but it is *not* my case, and it is for *that* reason, that C. appeals to me as to a dispassionate Arbiter and Adviser. Therefore *I ought not* to feel as C. does; but to *soften* matters, and not to judge by the mere Right and Wrong of the Point but by its comparative importance or triflingness. 'Treat it as a *Tiff* of temper, and pass it over. If it should *prove*, as I daresay it will, a mere Tiff, it is not to be thought of with such an old friend as A.—and the less you resent or retort his unkindness, the more he will feel it himself. But if it *should* be more than temper, it will soon shew itself in other things: and you may safely wait till then—for this is one of the very few cases, in which Procrastination is virtuous.'

MS.

237. JEALOUSY

Hatred of superiority is not, alas! confined to the ignorant. The best informed are most subject to jealousy, and to unfair representations of new views and doctrines.

Allsop.

238. CRIME AND PUNISHMENT

We have just read in a provincial paper a list of the petty culprits who had received sentence at a County Sessions—We do not mention names: for our remarks apply to the laws, and not to the individuals who exercised their discretion within the bounds permitted by them. In this list we see one man imprisoned twelve months for stealing a sack of coals; a young woman, for stealing six loaves, sentenced to six months' imprisonment, *and to be whipped*; and three other females for petty thefts, one to six, and the others to three months' imprisonment, *and to be whipped*; while a man and a woman, convicted of having long kept an *infamous brothel* in a *country town*, were sentenced to two months' imprisonment, and to be fined ONE SHILLING.

Now let any thinking head and feeling heart consider the nature and consequences of the offence last mentioned. Think of such a house in such a place, as a small swamp, whose pestilential vapours extend as far as the remotest habitation of those who attend its weekly markets. Think of the early corruption and *heart-hardening* of the apprentices and other youths of the town and vicinity; of the recruits for prostitution raised from the servant maids, and other still more unprotected females; of the diseases, sapping manhood, and alas! so often carried into families, and re-appearing in the second and third generation in the form of scrofula, consumption, and mania!—and then weigh in the balance of reason a hundred petty thefts with the guilt of this one crime! We well know, that laws cannot be proportioned to the moral guilt of actions, but must take in, as a most important guide, the difficulty and necessity of prevention; but we likewise know, that laws can never *outrage* the proportions established by the conscience without either baffling themselves or degrading the public morals.

This, however, is not all that pained us. We were in hopes, that with the progressive refinement and increased tenderness of private and domestic feelings (in which we are doubtless superior to our ancestors, whatever the average of virtue may be), this unmanly practice of scourging females had gradually become obsolete, and placed among the *Inusitata* of the law dictionary. It is not only the female herself, who yet, if not already a miscreant, must needs (to use a far softer phrase than our feelings would prompt) be grievously injured in the first sources and primary impulses of female worth—for, who will deny, that the infamy which would attend a young woman from having been stripped naked under the lash of a townsman, would be incomparably greater, and have burnt deeper in, than what would accrue from her having been detected in stealing half a dozen loaves? We are not shocked for the female only, but for the inflictor, and at the unmanliness of the punishment itself. Good God! how is it possible, that man, *born of woman*, could go through the office? O never let it be forgotten either by the framers or dispensers of criminal law, that the stimulus of shame, like some powerful medicines, if administered in too large a dose, becomes a deadly narcotic poison to the moral patient! Never let it be forgotten, that every human being bears in himself that indelible something which belongs equally to the whole species, as well as that particular modification of it which individualizes him; that *the* woman is still *woman*, and however she may have debased herself, yet that we should still shew some respect, still feel some reverence, if not for her sake, yet in awe of that Being, who saw good to stamp in her his own image, and forbade it ever, in this life at least, to be utterly erased.

Essays on His Own Times.

239. BARBARISM, ANCIENT AND MODERN

Barbarism)([as distinguished from] Savage State is the Effect or Result of Moral Corruption, False Religion, Priestcraft and Despotism, whether it be the Despotism of one, of few, or of the Many, i.e. whether it be a monarchical, an aristocratical or a democratical Despotism. It (Barbarism, I mean) consists in the absence of the means of National and individual Progression by the accumulation of Knowledge and Experience from age to age, and of the disposition thereto—Letters, Books, Printing, Men of Learning, Men of Science, Artists ;* Schools for the different Ranks of Society, and the oppotunities of *moral* education and *religious* instruction for all in all ranks, and last but not least the equality of Women to men in social and domestic Life, and the unconditional sovereignty of *Law* over individual Will, these are the characters of a State that is both civilized and culti-vated, when they are *all* found, and are organized by mutual inter-dependence into a System of Society. But where only the six first, which I have marked off by a ; and * are found, as in Russia, for instance, such a Nation or Empire does not cease to be in a state of Barbarism, tho' it may be partially civilized. Nay, a Nation may be in a state of Civility or Civilization throughout, as China seems to be; and yet if the Characters mentioned after the ; * are wanting, *viz.* the development of the 3 principles, by which Human Nature is distinguished from the Brute, and which therefore ought to be developed in all men alike,—1. the *Rational*, the *Moral*, and the *Religious* Principles; 2. Respect and reverential Tenderness toward Women, [and *crossed out*] or the equal rights, reciprocal Benefits, and mutual Dependence of the Sexes; 3, the exclusive Sovereignty of Law, so that every Individual at the age of reason has a sphere for the exercise of his Free-agency, into which no other Individual is permitted to intrude in all points necessary to his Well-being and Progressive Improvement as a responsible Creature destined for a State after Death—where these three, I say, are wanting in a Nation, let it be as civilized as Taylors, Milliners, Friseurs, Dancing-Masters, Drill-Serjeants, Cooks, Upholsterers &c. can make it, that Nation is still in a state of *Barbarism*, tho' the Inhabitants may be civilized Barbarians.

Whatever state is improgressive, so that any regular and constituent Portion of that state (the class of Tillers of the Earth, or the class of Artisans, for instance) remain on the same Grade of Knowledge, Morality and social Comfort in the year 1800 that their Forefathers were in the year 800—much more if this is the case with all classes—that state is Barbarian. . . .

MS.

240. THE IDEA OF A SOCIAL CONTRACT

Reflect on an original Social Contract, as an *incident*, or historical *fact*: and its gross improbability, not to say impossibility, will stare you in the Face. But an ever-originating Social Contract *is* an Idea, which exists and works continually and efficaciously in the Moral Being of every free Citizen, tho' in the greater number unconsciously or with a dim and confused consciousness. And what *a Power* it is! As the vital power compared with the mechanic, as a Father compared with a Moulder in wax or clay, such is the Power of Ideas compared with the Influence of Conceptions and Notions! S. T. C.

MS.

241. TOLERATION

Mendelssohn writes in his *Jerusalem*, that if religious people disturb the peace, they should be punished for their deeds, not for their opinions.

Coleridge comments: But is not the propagation of principles Subversive of Society itself an *Act*? Are there none but *manual* notions? I am convinced that no Theory of Toleration is possible; but. that the Practice must depend on Expedience and Humanity. S. T. C.

MS.

242. HOW LAW WORKS ON THE MIND

Strength may be met with strength; the power of inflicting pain may be baffled by the pride of endurance; the eye of rage may be answered by the stare of defiance, or the downcast look of dark and revengeful resolve; and with all this there is an outward and determined object to which the mind can attach its passions and purposes, and bury its own disquietudes in the full occupation of the senses. But who dares struggle with an *invisible* combatant? with an enemy which exists and makes us know its existence—but *where* it is, we ask in vain. No space contains it—time promises no control over it—it has no ear for my threats—it has no substance, that my hands can grasp, or my

weapons find vulnerable—it commands and cannot be commanded—it acts and is insusceptible of my re-action—the more
I strive to subdue it, the more am I compelled to think of it—
and the more I think of it, the more do I find it to possess a
reality out of myself, and not to be a phantom of my own imagination; that all, but the most abandoned men, acknowledge its
authority, and that the whole strength and majesty of my
country are pledged to support it; and yet that for *me* its power
is the same with that of my own permanent self, and that all the
choice, which is permitted to me, consists in having it for my
guardian angel or my avenging fiend! This is the spirit of law!
the lute of Amphion, the harp of Orpheus! This is the true
necessity, which compels man into the social state, now and
always, by a still-beginning, never-ceasing, force of moral
cohesion.

Thus is man to be governed, and thus only can he be
governed.

Friend.

243. FREEDOM: AN ARGUMENT AGAINST STEFFENS

But ask of Italy, and Sicily whether a bad and wicked constitution may not prevent Freedom and all the virtues of Free Men!
I respect the Negative Pull-down and Clear-away Principle as
little as Steffens. But it does appear to me a strange objection to
one who calls aloud for the removal of a river [?] of pestilence
or a fever-marsh, that he aims at nothing positive. A nation,
that wants to have a weight taken off, and is striving up against
it, proves in the very effort the existence of elastic power, *einer
Federkraft.*

To hear Steffens talk, one would imagine that by some pre-
established harmony, some new refinement of predestination, a
boorly soul was born a Boor—and that all calm and lofty souls
entered into the foetuses of future Serene Highnesses.

Oh fie! fie! What other Equality but that which Steffens

himself demands, p. 217, l. 15, do the German patriots require
—the equality of power to develop powers, subject to no other
checks than the necessity of unequal possessions brings with it.
These God knows! are numerous enough and powerful enough
—without any wanton additions on the part of the Laws and
Governments. In short, I do not know what or whom Steffens
is combatting. A Peasant does not wish to be a Lord—no, nor
perhaps does he wish to be a Parson or a Doctor, but he would
have the soul of a Slave if he did not desire that there should be a
possibility of his children or Grand-children becoming such.

MS.

244. FREEDOM AND SECURITY *vs.* DESPOTISM

Tetens, in his *Philosophische Versuche*, in the chapter XIV on
human perfectibility argues that there can be despotism enough
in 'free states', and conversely, freedom enough under an absolute monarchy.

Coleridge comments: If by Monarchies here be meant the union
of the legislative and executive supremacy in one only person,
this being a mortal and not an angel, I say with regret, and contrary to my custom write it with Ink, that is a Slave's Sentiment.
For political 'true Freedom' consists not merely in the enjoyment
but in such *security* of the enjoyment of equal Laws, as human
Wisdom can plan and adopt, and human Courage and Patriotism realize. This may be defective; no absolute security may be
possible; but the greatest possible has been procured, and what
is still more, man has done his Duty. This is the creed of a
Freeman, all else is cowardly and slothful Selfishness—a 'what
have I to do with Posterity? What has Posterity done for me?'
Augustus+Tiberius, Nero, Caligula, still better, the Antonines
+Caracalla &c!

MS.

245. PRELIMINARY REPRESENTATION

Is the House of Commons to be re-constructed on the principle of a representation of interests, or of a delegation of men? If on the former, we may, perhaps, see our way; if on the latter, you can never, in reason, stop short of universal suffrage; and in that case, I am sure that women have as good a right to vote as men.

Table Talk.

246. MORAL INDIGNATION AND SELF-INTEREST

There is observable among the many a false and bastard sensibility that prompts them to remove those evils and those evils alone, which by hideous spectacle or clamorous outcry are present to their senses, and disturb their selfish enjoyments. Other miseries, though equally certain and far more horrible, they not only do not endeavour to remedy—they support, they fatten on them. Provided the dunghill be not before their parlour window, they are well content to know that it exists, and that it is the hot-bed of their pestilent luxuries.—To this grievous failing we must attribute the frequency of wars, and the continuance of the Slave-trade. The merchant finds no argument against it in his ledger: the citizen at the crowded feast is not nauseated by the stench and filth of the slave-vessel—the fine lady's nerves are not shattered by the shrieks! She sips a beverage sweetened with human blood, even while she is weeping over the refined sorrows of Werther or of Clementina. Sensibility is not benevolence. Nay, by making us tremblingly alive to trifling misfortunes, it frequently prevents it, and induces effeminate and cowardly selfishness. Our own sorrows, like the Princes of Hell in Milton's Pandemonium, sit enthroned 'bulky and vast': while the miseries of our fellow-creatures dwindle into pigmy forms, and are crowded, an innumerable multitude, into some dark corner of the heart. There is one criterion by which we may always distinguish benevolence from mere sensibility—benevolence impels to action, and is accompanied by self-denial.

Essays On His Own Times.

247. DIGNITIES AND SLAVERIES

Wherein am I made worse by my ennobled neighbour? Do the childish titles of aristocracy detract from my domestic comforts, or prevent my intellectual acquisitions? But those institutions of society which should condemn me to the necessity of twelve hours' daily toil, would make my *soul* a slave, and sink the *rational* being in the mere animal. It is a mockery of our fellow creatures' wrongs to call them equal in rights, when by the bitter compulsion of their wants we make them inferior to us in all that can soften the heart, or dignify the understanding. Let us not say that this is the work of time—that it is impracticable at present, unless we each in our individual capacities do strenuously and perseveringly endeavour to diffuse among our domestics those comforts and that illumination which far beyond all political ordinances are the true equalizers of men.

We turn with pleasure to the contemplation of that small but glorious band, whom we may truly distinguish by the name of thinking and disinterested patriots. These are the men who have encouraged the sympathetic passions till they have become irresistible habits, and made their duty a necessary part of their self-interest, by the long-continued cultivation of that moral taste which derives our most exquisite pleasures from the contemplation of possible perfection, and proportionate pain from the perception of existing *depravation*. Accustomed to regard all the affairs of man as a process, they never hurry and they never pause. Theirs is not that twilight of political knowledge which gives us just light enough to place one foot before the other; as they advance the scene still opens upon them, and they press right onward with a vast and various landscape of existence around them. Calmness and energy mark all their actions. Convinced that vice originates not in the man, but in the surrounding circumstances; not in the heart, but in the understanding; he is hopeless concerning no one—to correct a vice or generate a virtuous conduct he pollutes not his hands with the scourge of coercion; but by endeavouring to alter the circumstances would remove, or by strengthening the intellect, disarms, the temptation.

Essays On His Own Times.

248. WE GET THE GOVERNMENT WE DESERVE

A Tyrant is only a monstrous Phantasm up-streaming from the grave and corruption of the huddled corses of the self-murdered Virtue and inner freedom of the People, *i.e.* the Majority of the Citizens of the State. July 6, 1822.

MS.

249. STUART KINGS

What a world of Love and Bee-like Loyalty and Heart-adherence did the Stuarts trick and tyrannize away!

MS.

250. DESPOTISM, POLITICAL AND ECONOMIC: SECURITY AND FREEDOM

It is security which distinguishes liberty from a virtuous despotism: and this security never exists unless when the legislative power is in the hands of those, whose worldly self-interests manifestly preponderate in favour of the incorrupt use of it. It has indeed been affirmed, that we are secure with the wealthy:

since in impoverishing their country they must injure themselves most of all, and that their wealth lifts them above the
reach of temptation. We might quote in answer every page of
the history of England for these last hundred years: but supposing the assertion not to have been confuted by facts, we yet deny
the probability of it. For first, the taxes are not levied in equal
proportions, so that without directly injuring himself a legisla-
tor may vote away the pittance of the poor: secondly, where
the actual, efficient, independent legislators are so few, and the
revenues of government so immense, the administration can
always put into a great man's pocket incalculably more than
they take from his estate: thirdly, his wealth so far from lifting
him above temptation exposes him to it. A man of large fortune
lives in a splendour and luxury, which long habit makes him
consider essential to happiness. He has perhaps a number of
children, all of whom share his affection equally. He wishes that
all his children should continue to live in the style in which they
have been brought up, but by the law of primogeniture the
eldest only will possess the means of so doing. Hence, he seeks
fortunes for the rest in the enormous patronage of the crown.
A man of moderate wealth is not exposed to this temptation.
His rank does not make industry disgraceful, and by industry
all his children may be as well off as their father. Besides
(though we would not dispeople St. Stephen's by such an
exclusion-bill, as was passed in the days of Cromwell) yet while
gaming is so much the rage, no man can be safely called
wealthy, or supposed to be armed against temptation. Thus the
actual possessors of power are few, and independent of the
people: which is despotism. And the manners of the great
are depraved, the sources of corruption incalculable, and consequently the temptations to private and public wickedness
numerous and mighty: all which unite in precluding the
probability of its proving a *virtuous* Despotism.

Essays on His Own Times.

251. GREAT AND SMALL STATES

When I first heard from Stewart of the Courier that Buonaparte had declared that the interests of small states must always succumb to great ones, I said, "Thank God! he has sealed his fate: from this moment his fall is certain."

Allsop.

252. THE NEW FRENCH CONSTITUTION

Except that it is convenient for Buonaparte to have eighty places of a thousand a year each at his disposal, we remain wholly in the dark concerning the intention, or possible utility of this new conservative [constitution]. It *makes* the whole of the political machine, and it can suspend its operations. Other occupation it has none. Like the god of the mechanic materialists, it has no other attributes but those of creation and miracle. The people have no promise or security that it will possess wisdom, talent, or integrity, and no appeal if it possess them not.

It were wasting our readers' attention to direct it particularly to the other branches of the legislature, the hundred tribunes who are to talk and do nothing, and the three hundred legislators whom the constitution orders to be silent. What a ludicrous Purgatory for three hundred Frenchmen! The shamelessness of calling that a legislature which can neither propose nor reason, and whose acts are annullable *ad arbitrium*, can only be equalled by the exquisite absurdity involved in the very notion of splitting the intellectual faculties, and subdividing the business of thought, almost as curiously as that of a pin manufactory. However, all these different law-manufacturers are well salaried; yet not so as to place them out of the temptation of corruption. Even the chief consul must find it necessary to bribe high to secure his re-election, by influence, by promises, and not improbably by taking the pay of foreign governments. Indeed, never was a government framed which lay so open to corruption, both in itself, and from external powers! There exists no appearance of a preventive, in a nominal legislature, for which no property is requisite, in which no talent can be exerted, and where no popularity can be gained. The whole constitution betrays a rooted contempt of the people, and a distrust of human virtue in general, yet leaves to none, whom it invests with power, any of those common assistants to well doing which the most virtuous man does not profess to deem useless. It has indeed divisions and sub-divisions even to superfluity; but how, under any circumstances these could be a check on each other, or on the consulate, no where appears. It is indeed mere fraud and mockery. Checks and counterpoises can only be produced by real diversity of interests, of interests existing independent of legislative functions; but these chambers are all alike filled with the creatures of the dictator, by him chosen, feeding on his stipends, and acting under his controul. But it cannot last: for to what body of men or species of interest can it appeal for love or protection? Property, talent, popular spirit, the prejudices of the royalist, the priest, and the jacobin, are all injured, insulted, trodden under foot by it. And what are idle promises of individual liberty in a constitution which recognises in the chief consul the right of suspending it *ad arbitrium*, and which does not recognise in the nation that which is worth a thousand tribunates, that without which no nation can be free or happy under the wisest government, the LIBERTY OF THE PRESS?

Essays On His Own Times.

253. REPRESENTATIVES AS WELL AS LEADERS

No individual, Sir, or handful of individuals, whether a regent, a general, or a junta, can be the representative of a public cause in a season of peril and uncertainty—Least of all a general. It is unnatural for individuals to sustain any higher character than that of public functionaries, each in his own department the executor of the national will. As an individual, his character will, however reason and justice may object to this criterion, be affected by the event of his measures, and therefore if he appears as the sole outward representative of the cause, as its visible fountain-head, and yet at the same time the responsible agent in the measures for its protection and promotion, the cause will inevitably be confounded with the measures; and as these will be judged of according to the event, so will the cause likewise. But where there exists a parliament, a congress, or a cortes, the things which are most subject to the caprice of fortune, and the accidents of treason or incapacity, as military expeditions, battles, sieges, &c. are referred to the responsible individuals; while the public body elected by the public will, and the representative of the public cause, remaining distinct from the particular measures, remains aloof from the influence of their results. Nay, the existence of such a body, preserves or recalls the public mind from despondency by presenting always an object of hope to which the people turn for the remedy of calamity and the punishment of misconduct.

During the American war, there was a period of universal consternation; the militia broke up and retired each man to his home, and Washington was almost abandoned. Had there not been a congress, to which the people had delegated the power of the state, whose *right* to be obeyed their consciences compelled them to admit, a congress whom they had already accustomed themselves to obey; or if that congress had then deserted its post, little would the influences of Washington's own character have availed in dispelling the panic, or rallying the Americans once more round the standard of independence. The same fortune which suspended his success could have paralysed his authority; those whom he could not induce to remain with their colours, while they were yet embodied under him as their *general*, he could never have brought back again from their separate homes and hiding-places, as an individual *citizen*.

Washington would probably have perished as the ring-leader of a rebellion, and thousands, who afterwards fought and conquered under the auspices of the ASSEMBLED FATHERS OF THE LAND, thousands, whom he, as servant of the congress, himself afterwards led on to victories, would have anxiously detached their names from him and from the cause, by early submission and compensatory acts of loyalty.

It is not possible, Sir, that any small number of individuals should possess equal means of inspiring the general enthusiasm, of guiding the public opinion, of counteracting the proclamations of the enemy, or the insidious reports of its agents, of rousing, informing, and undeceiving the people, which a large body of representatives will possess, both collectively and as individuals, having each his own sphere of additional influence.

Why need I add the facility which a national assembly affords to the disclosure of great talents, the stimulus it supplies to their exertion, and the opportunity it gives to stirring spirits of reconciling ambition with patriotism and with virtue? or why mention, that their very debates, becoming of necessity the topic of general conversation, and the constant incitement and nourishment of public curiosity, will at length blend the interests of the state with the feelings and concerns of private life, and give the *country* a place at each domestic fireside? Suffice it to say, Sir, that it is with a national assembly as it is with the common air of heaven. If it be corrupted, it is the sorest visitation of offended Providence: if its equipoise be suddenly and violently destroyed, its tempests are terrifying, and every man has a tale to tell of their fury; but they are purifying likewise, and of *that* few men think! But in its ordinary and natural state, Sir, it is food to our food, and life to our life: and the very inequalities of its temperature, and the struggles to preserve or restore its balance, are the breezes that fill the sails of the country, and speed the vessel onward in its voyage of industry, or its chase of glory and of vengeance.

Essays on His Own Times.

254. REPRESENTATIVE GOVERNMENT?

In that imperfect state of society in which our system of representation began, the interests of the country were pretty exactly
commensurate with its municipal divisions. The counties, the
towns, and the seaports, accurately enough represented the only
interests then existing, that is to say,—the landed, the shop-
keeping or manufacturing, and the mercantile. But for a
century past, at least, this division has become notoriously imperfect, some of the most vital interests of the empire being
now totally unconnected with any English localities. Yet now,
when the evil and the want are known, we are to abandon the
accommodations which the necessity of the case had worked
out for itself, and begin again with a rigidly territorial plan of
representation! The miserable tendency of all is to destroy our
nationality, which consists, in a principal degree, in our representative government, and to convert it into a degrading delegation of the populace. There is no unity for a people but in
a representation of national interests; a delegation from the
passions or wishes of the individuals themselves is a rope of
sand.

Undoubtedly it is a great evil that there should be such an
evident discrepancy between the law and the practice of the
constitution in the matter of the representation. Such a direct,
yet clandestine, contravention of solemn resolutions and established laws is immoral, and greatly injurious to the cause of
legal loyalty and general subordination in the minds of the
people. But then a statesman should consider that these very
contraventions of law in practice point out to him the places in
the body politic which need a remodelling of the law. You
acknowledge a certain necessity for indirect representation in
the present day, and that such representation has been instinctively obtained by means contrary to law; why then do you
not approximate the useless law to the useful practice, instead

of abandoning both law and practice for a completely new system of your own?

Table Talk.

255. THE REFORM BILL OF 1832

I am afraid the Conservative party see but one half of the truth. The mere extension of the franchise is not the evil; I should be glad to see it greatly extended;—there is no harm in that *per se*; the mischief is that the franchise is nominally extended, but to such classes, and in such a manner, that a practical disfranchisement of all above, and discontenting of all below, a favoured class are the unavoidable results.

Table Talk.

256. PARTY *VS.* PRINCIPLE

Under the title, 'The Thoughts of an Honest Tory, of 1821', Coleridge transcribed the following:

'You have here my free Thoughts. I have this peculiarity in my temper, that I am more affected and angry at the Vices and Evil Practices of my own Party, than of the contrary, and I hold myself more obliged to declare against them. And I cannot but think there never was such ground as there is at this time. We used to complain of the Methods and Arts of the Whigs. And we are now combating them with more infamous Weapons than they ever, in my Memory, used against us. We are lamenting the *profaneness* of others. What greater profaneness is there than to be wicked [in defence of Religion *crossed out*] for the *Church*; and to shew our regard for the Church by suffering it to be degraded, I will not say, into a tool of State-policy, but into a *play-thing* of Passion, a means of announcing and gratifying the personal antipathy and vindictive feelings of an Individual? And what seems a fate upon us, our Wit is dwindled with our Honesty, and our Sense has forsaken us together with our Plain-dealing. I profess to you, I can hardly meet with any one thing writ on our side during the late and present struggle, but what is either noisomely *dull*, or inhumanly *abusive*; what is enough to make either the *Man* very sick or the *Christian* very melancholy. God help a cause that is supported by such methods!

Thoughts of an Honest Tory of 1710'.

He comments: Were a wise man asked, why he valued History beyond a well-written Romance, the *Anabasis, Hellenics*, &c. of Xenophon to the *Cyropaedia* of the same Author, or the *Relations* of Thuanus to the *Argenis* of Barclay, he would find himself at a loss to assign any other cause but this: that History, as entitled to the casting Vote in the strife of probabilities, affords an antidote to the delusive influence of the Present on the affections and judgements of men, a standard of admeasurement for supposed Interests, by demonstrating as the one Central Fact, in which all the Lines of Experience meet, the dependence of national Welfare on the fidelity, with which the state has adhered to *Principles* against the temptations of apparent temporary expedience. I should think the battle half won, were I sure that the very word *Principles* would be understood.

MS.

257. THEORY *VS*. EXPERIENCE IN POLITICS

But if a readiness to act on mere presumptions of Theory be the error, that most easily besets thinking minds, a blind Faith in false analogies of the Past is often a still worse snare to the unthinking, who are too willing to consider what they chuse to call Experience as a cheap Substitute for the necessity of Thought altogether.

MS.

258. TORY AND WHIG

The ideal Tory and the ideal Whig (and some such there have really been), agreed in the necessity and benefit of an exact balance of the three estates: but the Tory was more jealous of the balance being deranged by the people; the Whig, of its being deranged by the Crown. But this was a habit, a jealousy only; they both agreed in the ultimate preservation of the balance; and accordingly they might each, under certain circumstances, without the slightest inconsistency, pass from one side to the other, as the ultimate object required it. This the Tories did at the Revolution, but remained Tories as before.

I have half a mind to write a critical and philosophical essay on Whiggism, from Dryden's Achitophel (Shaftesbury), the first Whig, (for, with Dr. Johnson's leave, the devil is no such cattle) down to ——, who, I trust, in God's mercy to the interests of peace, union, and liberty in this nation, will be the last. In it I would take the last years of Queen Anne's reign as the zenith, or palmy state, of Whiggism in its divinest *avatar* of common sense, or of the understanding, vigorously exerted in the right direction on the right and proper objects of the understanding; and would then trace the rise, the occasion, the progress, and the necessary degeneration of the Whig spirit of compromise, even down to the profound ineptitudes of their party in these days. A clever fellow might make something of this hint. How Asgill would have done it!

Table Talk.

259. PARTY

Party men always hate a slightly differing friend more than a downright enemy. I quite calculate on my being one day or other holden in worse repute by many Christians than the Unitarians and open infidels. It must be undergone by every one who loves the truth for its own sake beyond all other things.

Table Talk.

260. IF WE COULD BUT LEARN FROM HISTORY

If men could learn from history, what lessons it might teach us! But passion and party blind our eyes, and the light which experience gives, is a lantern on the stern, which shines only on the waves behind us!

Table Talk.

261. COMMERCE, AND THE CONDITION OF ENGLAND

But on the supposition that by a perpetual continuance of the war, or by a restoration of despotism, or by any other means, we could be and remain the monopolists of the commerce of Europe, is it quite ascertained, that it would be a real *national* advantage? Is it quite certain, that the condition and morals of the lower and more numerous classes would not be progressively deteriorated? Is it quite certain, that it would not give such a superiority to the moneyed interest of the country over the landed, as might be fatal to our constitution? Has not the hereditary possession of landed estate been proved, by experience, to generate dispositions equally favourable to loyalty and established freedom? Has not the same experience proved that the moneyed men are far more malleable materials? that ministers find more and more easy ways of obliging them, and that they are more willing to go with a minister through evil and good? Our commerce has been, it is said, nearly trebled since the war; is the nation at large the happier? Have the schemes of internal navigation, and of rendering waste lands useful, proceeded with their former energy? Or have not loans and other ministerial job-work created injurious and perhaps vicious objects for moneyed speculations?—And what mean these Committees for the labouring poor? These numerous soup-establishments? These charities so kindly and industriously set on foot through the whole kingdom? All these are highly honourable to the rich of this country! But are they equally honourable to the nation at large?—Is that a genuine prosperity, in which healthy labourers are commonly styled 'the labouring *poor*', and industrious manufacturers obliged to be fed, like

Roman clients, or Neapolitan Lazzaroni? It was well said of revolutions,

> In principatu commutando civium
> Nil praeter domini nomen mutant pauperes.

And other goodly names, besides that of Liberty, have had still *worse* effects.

Finally, commerce is the blessing and pride of this country. It is necessary, as a stimulus to the agriculture which sustains, and as the support of the navy which defends, us; but let us not forget that commerce is still no otherwise valuable than as the means to an end, and ought not itself to become the end, to which nobler and more inherent blessings are to be forced into subserviency.

Essays on His Own Times.

262. CLEANLINESS AND PROGRESS

L'Estrange translates from the French of Thevenot: The Turks shave their heads, and think it strange that the Francks suffer their Hair to grow; for they say that the Devil nestles in it; so that they are not subject to that filth and nastiness which breed among our Hair, if we be not careful to comb it well.

Coleridge comments: This is worth the notice of a Writer who should wish to give the History of the Progress of Civilization. —This was written about 160 years from the present Date, 1814. England at *that* time even, had advanced beyond all other nations, as may be proved by the Disgust manifested by the English at the Lousiness of the Scotch who came with James I. Yet even now Portugal, Naples, Sicily, are little better.

MS.

263. THE CORN LAWS: PROTECTION

Those who argue that England may safely depend upon a supply of foreign corn, if it grow none or an insufficient quantity of its own, forget that they are subjugating the necessaries of life it-self to the mere luxuries or comforts of society. Is it not certain that the price of corn abroad will be raised upon us as soon as it is once known that we must buy?—and when that fact is known, in what sort of a situation shall we be? Besides this, the argu-ment supposes that agriculture is not a positive good to the nation, taken in and by itself, as a mode of existence for the people, which supposition is false and pernicious; and if we are to become a great horde of manufacturers, shall we not, even more than at present, excite the ill will of all the manufacturers of other nations? It has been already shown, in evidence which is before all the world, that some of our manufacturers have acted upon the accursed principle of deliberately injuring foreign manufactures, if they can, even to the ultimate disgrace of the country and loss to themselves.

Table Talk.

264. ENGLISH INSOLENCE

There exists in England a *gentlemanly* character, a *gentlemanly* feeling, very different even from that, which is the most like it, the character of a well-born Spaniard, and unexampled in the rest of Europe. This feeling probably *originated*, in the fortunate circumstance, that the titles of our English nobility follow the law of their property, and are inherited by the eldest sons only. From this source, under the influences of our constitution and of our astonishing trade, it has diffused itself in different modifica-tions through the whole country. The uniformity of our dress among all classes above that of the day labourer, while it has authorized all classes to assume the appearance of gentlemen, has at the same time inspired the wish to conform their manners, and still more their ordinary actions in social intercourse, to their notions of the gentlemanly, the most commonly received attribute of which character is a certain generosity in trifles. On the other hand, the encroachments of the lower classes on the higher, occasioned and favoured by this resemblance in exteriors, by this absence of any cognizable marks of distinction, have rendered each class more reserved and jealous in their general communion, and far more than our climate, or natural temper, have caused that haughtiness and reserve in our outward demeanor, which is so generally complained of among foreigners. Far be it from me to depreciate the value of this gentlemanly feeling: I respect it under all its forms and varieties, from the House of Commons to the gentlemen in the one shilling gallery. It is always the ornament of virtue, and oftentimes a support; but it is a wretched substitute for it. Its *worth*, as a moral good, is by no means in proportion to its *value*, as a social advantage. These observations are not irrelevant: for to the want of reflection, that this diffusion of gentlemanly feeling among us is not the growth of our moral excellence, but the effect of various accidental advantages peculiar to England; to our not considering that it is unreasonable and uncharitable to expect the same consequences, where the same causes have not existed to produce them: and, lastly, to our proneness to regard the absence of this character (which, as I have before said, does, for the greater part, and, in the common apprehension, consist in a certain frankness and generosity in the detail of action) as decisive against the sum total of personal or national worth; we must, I am convinced, attribute a large portion of that conduct, which in many instances has left the inhabitants of countries conquered or appropriated by Great Britain, doubtful whether the various solid advantages which they derived from our protection and just government were not bought dearly by the wounds inflicted on their feelings and prejudices, by the contemptuous and insolent demeanor of the English as individuals.

Friend.

265. AMERICANISM AND JOHN BULLISM

I must say I cannot see much in Captain B. Hall's account of the Americans, but weaknesses—some of which make me like the Yankees all the better. How much more amiable is the American fidgettiness and anxiety about the opinion of other nations, and especially of the English, than the John Bullism, which affects to despise the sentiments of the rest of the world.

Table Talk.

266. AMERICANS

I deeply regret the anti-American articles of some of the leading reviews. The Americans regard what is said of them in England a thousand times more than they do any thing said of them in any other country. The Americans are excessively pleased with any kind or favourable expressions, and never forgive or forget any slight or abuse. It would be better for them if they were a trifle thicker-skinned.

The last American war was to us only something to talk or read about; but to the Americans it was the cause of misery in their own homes.

I, for one, do not call the sod under my feet my country. But language, religion, laws, government, blood,—identity in these makes men of one country.

Table Talk.

267. THE AMERICAN REVOLUTION: VISION OF A COMMONWEALTH

It required all the frenzy and all the stupidity of Madness and Ideotcy conjoined [in 'our miserable Ministry'] to have separated the American States from us. Good Heavens! read the history of that war! But more of this at some future time. I am deeply convinced that as soon as a Colony can maintain itself, the Mother Country ought to make it an equal, true, integral part of herself and give to it all the privileges, it could enjoy as an independent State. That we do not do so, arises entirely from mistaken views on the Subject of Revenue. . . . Americans ought to have been as independent as Members of the B[ritish] Emp[ire], as they now are. They are now members of a department, which is a component part of a State, which is a component part of an Empire: and even so ought they to have been, and so they might have been tho' there had been no disjunction from G[reat] Britain.

MS.

268. ENGLAND AND THE UNITED STATES

The possible destiny of the United States of America,—as a nation of a hundred millions of freemen,—stretching from the Atlantic to the Pacific, living under the laws of Alfred, and speaking the language of Shakspeare and Milton, is an august conception. Why should we not wish to see it realized? America would then be England viewed through a solar microscope; Great Britain in a state of glorious magnification! How deeply to be lamented is the spirit of hostility and sneering which some of the popular books of travels have shown in treating of the Americans! They hate us, no doubt, just as brothers hate; but they respect the opinion of an Englishman concerning themselves ten times as much as that of a native of any other country on earth. A very little humouring of their prejudices, and some courtesy of language and demeanour on the part of Englishmen, would work wonders, even as it is, with the public mind of the Americans.

Table Talk.

269. THE UNION WITH IRELAND

If any modification of the Union takes place, I trust it will be a total divorce *a vinculo matrimonii*. I am sure we have lived a cat and dog life of it. Let us have no silly saving of one crown and two legislatures; that would be preserving all the mischiefs without any of the goods, if there are any, of the union.

I am deliberately of opinion, that England, in all its institutions, has received injury from its union with Ireland. My only difficulty is as to the Protestants, to whom we owe protection. But I cannot forget that the Protestants themselves have greatly aided in accelerating the present horrible state of things, by using that as a remedy and a reward which should have been to them an opportunity.

If the Protestant Church in Ireland is removed, of course the Romish Church must be established in its place. There can be no resisting it in common reason.

How miserably imbecile and objectless has the English government of Ireland been for forty years past! Oh! for a great man—but one really great man,—who could feel the weight and the power of a principle, and unflinchingly put it into act! But truly there is no vision in the land, and the people accordingly perisheth. See how triumphant in debate and in action O'Connell is! Why? Because he asserts a broad principle, and acts up to it, rests all his body on it, and has faith in it. Our ministers—true Whigs in that,—have faith in nothing but expedients *de die in diem*. Indeed, what principles of government can they have, who in the space of a month recanted a life of political opinions, and now dare to threaten this and that innovation at the huzza of a mob, or in pique at a parliamentary defeat?

I sometimes think it just possible that the Dissenters may once more be animated by a wiser and nobler spirit, and see their dearest interest in the church of England as the bulwark and glory of Protestantism, as they did at the Revolution. But I doubt their being able to resist the low factious malignity to the church, which has characterized them as a body for so many years.

Table Talk.

270. THE POPEDOM

What a grand subject for a history the Popedom is! The Pope ought never to have affected temporal sway, but to have lived retired within St. Angelo, and to have trusted to the superstitious awe inspired by his character and office. He spoiled his chance when he meddled in the petty Italian politics.

Table Talk.

271. ENGLISH IN FRANCE

Well-fermented wine carried into a place where new wine is ferment[ing], will ferment afresh. English in France.

MS.

272. GÖTTINGEN

Göttingen had been a considerable town long before George the Second made it a university—So early as 1475 there was calculated to be 800 Master Manufacturers of Cloth and Stuffs. Before the year 1400 it had been admitted into the Hanseatic League, and remained in it till the year 1572. But both town and manufactory received injuries in the famous Thirty Years War, from which it has never recovered. A Sovereign Prince in order to establish a University in his Dominions must receive the imperial Privilege: this privilege George the IInd received from the Emperor Charles VIth; Jan. 13th 1733. The university commenced in October 1731 and having been presented with complete rights of Jurisdiction distinct from the civil power and dependent only on the Government, it was solemnly consecrated 17th Sept. 1737. From the name of its founder it is called The Georgia Augusta University; and the King of England is always the *Rector Magnificentissimus*.

The Prorector is elected annually from out of the ordinary Professors—or rather they take it by turns. During this office he is an Imperial Count Palatine, and as such has the right (I quote from the charter) 'to nominate notaries and laureate Poets, to legitimate Bastards, restore their honour to the Infamous', &c &c. . . .

A Professor is one who has received from the Government and University that especial Degree—which authorizes him to teach publicly in the particular department or faculty, of which he is a professor. The ordinary Professors, (*Professores Ordinarii*) are not only authorized to read lectures, but are salaried by the Government to do so. Since the founding of this University it has had a succession of the most eminent men in Germany as its ordinary Professors—among which the names of Mosheim, Gesner, Haller, Michaelis, Pütter, Kästner, Heyne, Letz or Less, Blumenbach, Lichtenburg, Planck, Eichhorn, Meiners and Jacobi are as well known to the Literati throughout Europe, as to their own countrymen.

The Professors are divided into four Faculties,—the theological, consisting of 3 and sometimes 4 members, 2 The Jurists, of 4 members, The Medicinists of 3 and the Philosophers of 8— sum total 18 or 19. These are the Professors *ordinarii*—the number of those who can teach but are not appointed to do so, is in each faculty indefinite. The *Professores ordinarii* of the first faculty in all processions &c wear a black *robe*, of the second a light Scarlet, of the third a deep Red—and the Philosophers march in Purple—with drum, fife and trumpet too! too! too! . . . [*Unfinished, and page torn.*]

MS.

273. NATIONAL CHARACTERISTICS

FRENCH, ENGLISH, GERMAN AND SCOTCH

I have been in the habit of considering the qualities of intellect, the comparative eminence in which characterizes individuals and even countries, under four kinds—GENIUS, TALENT, SENSE, and CLEVERNESS. The first I use in the sense of most general acceptance, as the faculty which *adds* to the existing stock of power and knowledge by new views, new combinations; (by discoveries not accidental but anticipated, or resulting from anticipation[1]). In short, I define GENIUS, as originality in intellectual construction: the moral accompaniment, and actuating principle of which consists, perhaps, in the carrying on of the freshness and feelings of childhood into the powers of manhood.

By TALENT, on the other hand, I mean the comparative facility of acquiring, arranging, and applying the stock furnished by others and already existing in books or other conservatories of intellect.

By SENSE I understand that just balance of the faculties which is to the judgment what health is to the body. The mind seems to act *en masse* by a synthetic rather than an analytic process: even as the outward senses, from which the metaphor is taken, perceive immediately, each as it were by a peculiar tact or intuition, without any consciousness of the mechanism by which the perception is realized. This is often exemplified in well-bred, unaffected, and innocent women. I know a lady, on whose judgment, from constant experience of its rectitude, I could rely almost as on an oracle. But when she has sometimes proceeded to a detail of the grounds and reasons for her opinion, then, led by similar experience, I have been tempted to interrupt her with—'I will take your advice,' or, 'I shall act on your opinion: for I am sure you are in the right. But as to the *fors* and

---

[1] Inserted from manuscript corrections by Coleridge.

becauses, leave them to me to find out.' The general accompaniment of Sense is a disposition to avoid extremes, whether in theory or in practice, with a desire to remain in sympathy with the *general mind* of the age or country, and a feeling of the necessity and utility of *compromise.* If Genius be the initiative, and Talent the administrative, Sense is the *conservative,* branch in the intellectual republic.

By CLEVERNESS (which I dare not with Dr. Johnson call a *low* word, while there is a sense to be expressed which it alone expresses) I mean a comparative readiness in the invention and use of means, for the realizing of objects and ideas—often of such ideas, which the man of genius only could have originated, and which the clever man perhaps neither fully comprehends nor adequately appreciates, even at the moment that he is prompting or executing the machinery of their accomplishment. In short, Cleverness is a sort of genius for instrumentality. It is the brain in the hand. In literature Cleverness is more frequently accompanied by wit, Genius and Sense by humour.

If I take the three great countries of Europe, in respect of intellectual character, namely, Germany, England, and France, I should characterize them thus—premising only that in the first line of the first two tables I mean to imply that Genius, rare in all countries, is equal in both of these, the instances equally numerous; (not, therefore, contra-distinguishing either from the other, but both from the third country. We can scarcely avoid considering a Cervantes and Calderon as in some sort characteristic of the nation which produced them. In the last war we felt it in the hope, which the recollection of these names inspired. But yet it cannot, equally with the qualities placed as second and third in each table, be called a *national* characteristic; though, in the appropriation of these likewise, we refer exclusively to the intellectual portion of each country[1]).

[1] *Ibid.*

GERMANY.	ENGLAND.	FRANCE.
GENIUS,	GENIUS,	CLEVERNESS,
TALENT,	SENSE,	TALENT,
FANCY.*	HUMOUR.	WIT.

So again with regard to the forms and effects, in which the qualities manifest themselves intellectually.

GERMANY.	ENGLAND.	FRANCE.
IDEA, or LAW anticipated,	LAW discovered,	THEORY invented,
TOTALITY,	SELECTION,	PARTICULARITY,
DISTINCTNESS.	CLEARNESS.	PALPABILITY.

Lastly, we might exhibit the same qualities in their moral, religious, and political manifestations: in the cosmopolitism of Germany, the contemptuous nationality of the Englishman, and the ostentatious and boastful nationality of the Frenchman. The craving of sympathy marks the German: inward pride the Englishman: vanity the Frenchman. So again, enthusiasm, visionariness seems the tendency of the German: zeal, zealotry of the English; fanaticism of the French. But the thoughtful reader will find these and many other characteristic points contained in, and deducible from the relations which the mind of the three countries bears to TIME.

GERMANY.	ENGLAND.	FRANCE.
PAST and FUTURE.	PAST and PRESENT.	THE PRESENT.

A whimsical friend of mine, of more genius than discretion, characterizes the Scotchman of literature (confining his remark, however, to the period since the union) as a dull Frenchman and a superficial German. But when I recollect the splendid exceptions of Hume, Robertson, Smollett, Reid, Thompson (if this last instance be not objected to as favouring of geographical pedantry, that truly amiable man and genuine poet having been

*The latter chiefly as exhibited in wild combination and pomp of ornament. N.B. *Imagination* is implied in Genius.

born but a few furlongs from the English border), Dugald Stewart, Burns, Walter Scott, Hogg and Campbell—not to mention the very numerous physicians and prominent dissenting ministers, born or bred beyond the Tweed—I hesitate in recording so wild an opinion, which derives its plausibility, chiefly from the circumstance so honourable to our northern sister, that Scotchmen generally have more, and a more learned, education than the same ranks in other countries, below the first class; but in part likewise, from the common mistake of confounding the general character of an emigrant, whose objects are in one place and his best affections in another, with the particular character of a Scotchman: to which we may add, perhaps, the clannish spirit of provincial literature, fostered undoubtedly by the peculiar relations of Scotland, and of which therefore its metropolis may be a striking, but is far from being a solitary, instance.

Friend.

274. INTERNATIONALISM: THE HUMANITIES

Monday Night, 20 Dec. 1810.

Mem. A Society for opposing National Antipathies, and the discouragement of all writings (*ex. gr. Quarterly Review*) tending to kindle or feed hostile and contemptuous feelings between the Members of the same Christendom and for the promotion of mutual Love, esteem and instruction. The maxim of the Society to be:—It is impossible, that any Nation in that state of advancement, in which France, N. America and G. Britain exist, can have any true interest which is not the interest of the other and of the whole civilized world. Likewise, that the better time will come, when a different Government will no longer be supposed to constitute or imply a different Nation or Country —but Laws, Manners, Religion and Language. And further, that the three first are all tending to become more and more one and the same throughout Christendom, with no greater or more essential differences than now prevail in different Districts of the same Country, not so great as the differences between different Counties of England were in the reign of Elizabeth. And even with Language it will be as with Money: there will be a Gold and Silver, that however stamped, will pass according to its weight in all countries, tho' each nation will retain paper and the baser metals for their every day marketing.

Likewise, a British and Foreign Human Society of Science and Literature, whose Duty it would be to watch over, record, and make known Works and Discoveries, where ever published, and as soon as published to form a center [sic] of Correspondence for the Man of Genius and Science in all countries &c. With such a Society it would not have been possible for the French to have so successfully and systematically palmed the labors and discoveries of Sweden, Denmark and Germany as their own new Lights.

Their Proceedings would form a Review or Magazine. But no mere Review-Editor or Publisher can be equal to the functions of a respectable Society. I see at present no reason why this latter should not be one with the former—or one of Bureaus. The Human Society for the Defence, Extension and Advancement of the Humanities—i.e. of whatever being common to cultivated Man, and the ground-work and precondition of his rights and duties, as the Member of a particular State, contra-distinguish Man from the [irrational *crossed out*] Animals and in Man himself his human from his animal Nature. *Vide* J. H. Green's concluding Lectures of his great course of philosophical Zoology, Zoography and Zoogony.

MS.

275. DIPLOMACY

The sure way to make a foolish ambassador is to bring him up to it. What can an English minister abroad really want but an

honest and bold heart, a love for his country and the ten com-
mandments? Your art diplomatic is stuff—no truly great man
now would negotiate upon any such shallow principles.

Table Talk.

276. INTERNATIONAL RELATIONS

The nature of a government, considered simply and in itself, is
no argument either for or against the possibility of peace with it.
Let the Emperor of Russia be as wise, as righteous, as heroic a
monarch as our minister has chosen to paint him, still, however,
no Englishman but would shudder at the Russian form of
government, if it were introduced into England. Yet, who is
mad enough to deem this an objection against our alliance with
the Emperor of Russia? The French tolerate atheism and
deism; the Emperor of China tolerates both, and idolatry to
boot—and yet we send flattering embassies to him. We have
made treaties with the Arch-pirate of Algiers, and with the
Delai Lama of Thibet. And why? Because we have nothing to
do with the wickedness or absurdity of a government, except as
far as they are dangerous to ourselves. What are the present
principles of the French government? Those of a military oligarchy, equally abhorred by every party in this country, and
concerning the propagation of which it were idiotcy to entertain any alarm. It were a paradox too bold even for ministerial
sophistry, that Jacobinism in England is to be destroyed by
making war on a government which is itself exerting a tyranny
to destroy it in France. The truth is, that whatever nomenclature
the French Executive may adopt, France itself has fallen back
into its ancient character of an ambitious, intriguing military
power; and its ambition is to be guarded against by this country
equally under a monarchy as a republic. But ambition forms no
reason against fair negotiations for peace, which, if once concluded, would be found the securest provision against it.

Essays On His Own Times.

277. INTERNATIONAL QUESTIONS

The French have broken treaties; we, therefore, can make no treaties with the French. But did not all our allies, at the commencement of the war, enter into solemn treaties not to lay down arms but by mutual consent? And did they not all break this treaty? What is the whole history of modern Europe, but a succession of wars, originating in broken treaties? It is absurd to apply that against a treaty of peace with one country, which does not apply against even a treaty of alliance with all other countries; and yet, as Mr. Fox well observed, the moral character of our friends and fellow labourers is assuredly of more importance to us than that of those whom we wish only not to be our enemies. Let any man mention any act of folly, treachery, or oppression in the French Republic, and we pledge ourselves to find a *fellow* to it in our own allies, or in the history of the line of princes, upon the restoration of whom an honourable peace is now made to depend. To us the turn of the debate on Monday is matter of hope and exultation. The harangues of the ministers were absolute confessions of weakness. Long and tedious details of French aggressions, which, if they had been as fair and accurate as they were false and partial, would still prove nothing; violent personalities on Bonaparte, and as violent panegyrics on the superior science, talents, and humanity of the conqueror of Warsaw and Ismail; and the old delusive calculations about French resources, calculations always accompanied by prophecies, which prophecies have been always, even to a laughable degree, falsified: these formed the substance and contents of the ministerial orations. More than one half of Mr. Pitt's speech was consumed in the old re-repeated tale of the origin of the war. This can be nothing more than an appeal to passion. For let us suppose for a moment, that we and not the French were the aggressors, the unprovoked aggressors; that they were innocent, and we guilty—yet how would this affect the subject of peace? Is any man so contemptibly ignorant of the rules and first foundations of State morality, as to affirm that because our Ministers had entered into a war knavishly, that therefore the people were bound in honour or honesty to conclude a peace ruinously? The interest of nations, the true interest, is and ought to be the sole guide in national concerns; and all besides is puerile declamation, only serviceable as covering a defeat, and preventing the appearance of an absolute rout, such as would have been implied in silence. What two nations were ever at war, and did not obstinately charge the aggression, each on the other? Has not this been matter of course since the time that the introduction of the Christian religion has made the governors of mankind afraid to state conquest or glory as their motives? And to adduce this as a political reason against the propriety of concluding a peace, or even of entering on a negotiation!

Essays On His Own Times.

278. WAR

The Crusades were as favourable in their effects, as they were honourable in their causes. Then first did Europe feel, and become conscious of the blessing of a common religion, and of civil institutions, differing only as the branches of one family, '*qualis decet esse sororum*'. The warriors brought back from the holy land imaginations highly excited, minds enlarged by the contemplation of a scenery and of customs so new to them, and manners polished beyond the experience of former ages. A new aera commenced in the world; a new sun rose on our social habits, on the tone of governments, and on the nature of our literature. The monkish legend and obsolete miracle gave way to Knights, and Giants, and Genii; and enthusiasm and imagination, mutually feeding each other, were brought to act on the side of gentleness and public justice. Unless therefore it shall be admitted, that Suwarrow and his Russians have returned home poets and gentlemen; or that our Bond-street officers have been transmuted, by the alchemy of our expeditions, into the chaste, gentle, and sober knights of ancient chivalry; let us call the present war anything: ONLY NOT A CRUSADE.

These Crusades were likewise the parents of all the freedom which now exists in Europe. The pecuniary distresses of the monarchs and nobles compelled them to part with many and various privileges; the anarchy, which prevailed during their absence, procured to the lower classes many others. Commerce was diverted from the Venetian and Genoese monopolisers; and there began to arise in all countries, but more especially in England, that greatest blessing and ornament of human nature, an important and respectable middle class. The monarch became more an officer, and less a person; the nobility were seen gradually to draw nearer to the class of the people; and long before the first dawn of religious reformation, the poetic genius imported from the last had prepared the way for it, by continued and successful satires on the absurdities and crimes of the Priesthood. Unless therefore it be admitted that the *direct* object of the present war is to lay the foundations of a greater freedom than we before enjoyed; unless it be admitted, that it has tended to prevent commerce from being a monopoly of one nation; unless it be granted, that it, *viz.* this present war, spite of the assessed and income taxes, is peculiarly favourable to the increase and permanence of a middle class; that it militates against all attachment to kings as persons, and nobles as *privileged* classes; and to the Roman Catholic superstitions, as absurdities; unless all this be conceded by the friends of Freedom let them call the present war any thing: ONLY NOT A CRUSADE.

Essays On His Own Times.

279. WAR AND 'THE POOR'

In former wars the victims of ambition had crowded to the
standard from the influence of national antipathies; but this
powerful stimulant has been so unceasingly applied, as to have
well nigh produced an exhaustion. What remains? Hunger.
Over a recruiting place in this city I have seen pieces of beef
hung up to attract the half-famished mechanic. It has been said
that government though not the best preceptor of virtue procures us security from the attack of the lower orders.—Alas!
why should the lower orders attack us, but because they are
brutalized by ignorance and rendered desperate by want? And
does government remove this ignorance by education? And
does not government increase their want by taxes?—Taxes
rendered necessary by those national assassinations called wars,
and by that worst corruption and perjury, which a reverend
moralist has justified under the soft title of 'secret influence!'
The poor infant born in an English or Irish hovel breathes
indeed the air and partakes of the light of Heaven; but of its
other bounties he is disinherited. The powers of intellect are
given him in vain: to make him work like a brute beast he is
kept as ignorant as a brute beast. It is not possible that this
despised and oppressed man should behold the rich and idle,
without malignant envy. And if in the bitter cravings of hunger
the dark tide of passions should swell, and the poor wretch rush
from despair into guilt, then the government indeed assumes
the right of punishment though it had neglected the duty of
instruction, and hangs the victim for crimes, to which its own
wide-wasting follies and its own most sinful omissions had supplied the cause and the temptation. And yet how often have the
fierce bigots of despotism told me, that the poor are not to be
pitied, however great their necessities: for if they be out of
employ, the king wants men! They may be shipped off to the
slaughter-house abroad, if they wish to escape a prison at home!

—Fools! to commit robberies and get hung, when they might fight for their king and country,—yea, and have sixpence a day into the bargain!

Essays On His Own Times.

280. POOR-LAWS

Poor-laws are the inevitable accompaniments of an extensive commerce and a manufacturing system. In Scotland, they did without them, till Glasgow and Paisley became great manufacturing places, and then people said, 'We must subscribe for the poor, or else we shall have poor-laws.' That is to say, they enacted for themselves a poor-law in order to avoid having a poor-law enacted for them. It is absurd to talk of Queen Elizabeth's act as creating the poor-laws of this country. The poor-rates are the consideration paid by, or on behalf of, capitalists for having labour at demand. It is the price, and nothing else. The hardship consists in the agricultural interest having to pay an undue proportion of the rates; for although, perhaps, in the end, the land becomes more valuable, yet, at the first, the landowners have to bear all the brunt. I think there ought to be a fixed revolving period for the equalization of rates.

Table Talk.

281. SUNDAY, FOR RICH AND POOR

I sincerely wish to preserve a decent quiet on Sunday. I would prohibit compulsory labour, and put down operas, theatres, etc., for this plain reason—that if the rich be allowed to play, the poor will be forced, or, what comes to the same thing, will be induced, to work. I am not for a Paris Sunday. But to stop coaches, and let the gentleman's carriage run, is monstrous.

Table Talk.

282. TWO PAMPHLETS

REMARKS . . . ON SIR ROBERT PEEL'S BILL

In drawing up the following considerations, which we now respectfully submit to you, we have been most anxious to avoid every unnecessary encroachment on your time and attention. For this reason we offer no reply to the assertion hazarded by the opponents of Sir R. Peel's Bill, that Children from six to sixteen years of age, who are kept at work, standing, from thirteen to fifteen hours in the twenty-four, in a heated and polluted atmosphere, are healthier and happier than those who are employed in trades where the said grievances do not exist; and in a still greater degree 'better off', than Children who remain at home, or follow their fathers into the fields. It appears superfluous to confute a statement, the truth of which would imply one or the other of two things. Either all the opinions, concerning the laws of animal life, which have been hitherto received by mankind as undoubted truths, must be false: or else there is a continued interference of a miraculous power suspending and counteracting those laws, in mark of God's especial favour toward the Cotton Factories. In fact, some of our opponents themselves seem disposed to abandon their own assertions. If, however, any reply be required, it has been already given in the numerous testimonials in proof of the very contrary, from the most respectable medical men, clergymen, disinterested visitors of the Sunday Schools, and other residents of the town and neighbourhood of Manchester. These, whose veracity as witnesses none dare impeach, whose competence as judges, the interested only will have the hardihood to question, have attested the actual existence of certain facts, with a force and minuteness which would have sufficed to establish the same, had they been improbable—how much more then of the facts, on which the present measure is grounded! Facts, which on the first hearing of the circumstances, under which the children are placed, would be foretold as the inevitable results of such circumstances without hesitation and previous to any testimony.

Of a far more formidable character (if not in themselves, yet on account of the impression, they appear to have made) are the objections to the measure, drawn from the impropriety of legislative interference with free labour; from the danger of beginning a course of innovation, without any certainty at what point it may stop, and thus of encouraging an endless succession of claims; from the inadequacy of the measures proposed to the removal of the evil, while by attracting attention to the same, and by the excitement of hopes that are incompatible with the present state of society, and with the indispensable conditions of a commercial and manufacturing nation, they are calculated to increase discontent in a greater degree than they can be expected to palliate the grievance; and lastly that what can be done toward the removal of the evil can be best brought about by the master manufacturers themselves, as the individuals, and that from the humane spirit of this enlightened age, and the consequent growth and increasing influence of an enlightened self-interest, we may rest assured, that the said individuals will gradually more and more attempt to do what they alone can do effectually.

In these four objections, we apprehend, the whole strength of our opponents' reasonings is comprised; and we flatter ourselves that we have not detracted from their full force in the above recapitulation. Now in reply to the first, namely, the impropriety of legislative interference with free labour, we might fairly enquire on what grounds is this impropriety presumed? Certainly not on past experience, or the practice of the British Constitution; the Statute Books are (perhaps too much) crowded with proofs to the contrary. The first institution, by law, of Apprenticeships was an interference with free labour, and still more so the various clauses that regulate the time, privileges, etc., of the individuals, in many cases controlling the power of masters, as well as the employment of the free labour of adults, however skilful, who had not been previously bound to the trade. The recent regulations of the labour to be required from the apprentices are still more unfavourable to the presumption. For these regulations do in many instances directly interfere with the free labour of the journeymen employed with the apprentices. Whether this is desirable or no, is not the question. Yet we live in an age the events of which may pardonably suggest the recollection that the states and countries which have been most prosperous in trade and commerce, and at the same time most remarkable for the industry, morality and public spirit of the inhabitants, as Great Britain, Holland, the Hanseatic and other free towns of Germany, have been governed and regulated by a system of law and policy in almost direct opposition to the so-called Physiocratic Principles of more modern Political Economists. The result of their adoption in France under all the revolutionary schemes, but with more especial predilection under the last Government, does not tend to weaken any doubts which our historic recollections may have excited.

But if this objection to interference in free labour can derive no sanction from the *practice* of the Legislature, still less can it appeal to the *principles* and *spirit* of the British Constitution: and pardon us, if we add, God forbid, that it should! Only under a military despotism, entitled to dispense with it at all times for its own purposes, could such a principle be even partially realized; and then only when it was the object of the Government to reduce all classes to insignificance but those of soldiers and agriculturists. The *principle* of *all* constitutional law is to make the claims of each as much as possible compatible with the claims of all, as individuals, and with those of the commonweal as a whole; and out of this adjustment the claims of the individual first become *Rights*. Every Canal Bill proves that there is no species of property which the legislature does not possess and exercise the right of controlling and limiting, as soon as the right of the individuals is shown to be disproportionately injurious to the community. But that the *contra bonos mores*, the subversion of morals, is deemed in our laws a public injury, it would be superfluous to demonstrate.

But *free* Labour!—in what sense, not utterly sophistical, can the labour of children, extorted from the want of their parents, 'their poverty, but not their will, consenting', be called *free*? A numerous body of these very parents are among the petitioners for the measure though at the foreseen diminution of their profits. In what fair sense then can this be called *free* Labour? The argument comes to this point. Has it or has it not been proved that the common results of the present system of labour in the Cotton Factories is disease of the most painful and wasting kinds, and too often a premature death? This, we repeat, *has* been *fully* proved. Would that the opponents of the measure were confined to those who still pretend to doubt the truth of the facts. We are anxious to avoid every invidious remark; but we dare not on so awful a subject soften truth down into falsehood. It is our duty to declare aloud, that if the labour were indeed free, the employer would purchase, and the labourer sell, what the former has no right to buy, and the latter no right to dispose of: namely, the labourer's health, life and well-being. These belong not to himself *alone*, but to his friends, to his parents, to his King, to his Country, and to God. If the labour were indeed free, the contract would approach, on the one side, too near to suicide, on the other to manslaughter. The objection therefore would far better suit those who maintain the existence of rights, self-originated and independent of duties, than English subjects who pretend to no *rights* that do not refer to some *duty* as their origin and true foundation.

But the main ground of opposition to the Bill, it is said, rests on its interference with the labour of the adults, which cannot go on without that of the Children. But it has been shown, by a reference to the acts regulating the employment of apprentices, which acts forbid the period of their labour to exceed a limited time, that this objection has been laid before Parliament already, and over-ruled as invalid. And at *whose* request, and in behalf of *whom* is it again brought forward? Is it that of the adults themselves? So far from it, these very *adults* are among the most earnest petitioners that the Bill should pass. Their hearts, their prayers, their convictions derived from their own daily experience, are all with us. No small number of the petitioners are themselves parents of the children. Their profits therefore are exposed to a double diminution. Yet they are prepared, they are *eager* to incur this risk, rather than continue eye-witnesses of the children's sufferings during the latter hours of their daily labour, rather than have to watch their decay and forebode their too probable perdition. VOLENTI NULLA FIT INJURIA. The adults solicit a boon: and is the very contrary to be *forced* upon them as a benefit? Are the objectors certain that these clients of their own making are at all ambitious for the privilege of having their labour protected against all legislative protection?

To the second objection there needs no better reply than that of Sir Robert Peel, the more than mere *disinterested* originator of the Bill in question. What are these claims, with an endless succession of which you threaten us, as the consequence of conceding the present? If they are equally just, if the grievances that justify them are as heavy, and if the proposed remedy be attended with no greater inconvenience, in God's name let them be conceded! And if they are not such, the passing of the present Bill can form no *precedent*. To this plain and manly argument we can add nothing. But we may properly carry on the question. From what quarters are these apprehended claims to proceed? What trades are there in which children from six to sixteen years of age are kept at work, standing, from thirteen to fifteen hours, in a foul air artificially heated? But we ask in vain. Here as elsewhere we are left in the dark, menaced by generalities to which each man's fancy is to assign 'a local habitation and a name'.

This our reply to the second objection is equally valid as applied to the third—namely, that the proposed plan is a mere palliative better calculated to excite discontent in the sufferers, than to effect any considerable diminution of the evil. This plea has been, we repeat, confuted for the greater part by anticipation. It deserves however some distinct notice as being one of the approved means of reconciling indolence and selfishness with the warmest pretensions not only to humanity but to sensibility. But we feel convinced that the objectors themselves would shrink back from so weak and wicked a doctrine, as:— that we are to do nothing of what we can, because we cannot do all that we would wish. Who, we would ask, are to be the judges whether the proposed measures will or will not be a serious diminution of the sufferings and evils complained of? Whether it will or will not be received as a boon from their highest earthly guardian, for which the receivers not only are *bound*, but are *disposed*, to be most grateful? Surely, either the sufferers or their parents and nearest relatives. But the latter are among the most earnest petitioners for this Bill: and if the tender age of the former precludes, or would throw suspicion on, any petition from themselves, we have here too as in the intrepid assertions of their superior health and happiness, a safe appeal to common sense. Who does not know that in a journey too long for the traveller's strength, it is the last few miles that torment him by fatigue and injure him by exhaustion? Must not the anticipation of the recurrence weigh on his spirits at every recommencement of the same task? Must not the sufferings, which the close of the day are sure to bring with it, cast a gloom over the morning and noon? Suppose him suddenly informed that his journey was shortened by a fourth of the length. Will he not move forward with a brisk step like a man renovated? But this, though a fair illustration, is a tame and most inadequate analogy. The traveller still enjoys the pure air, is refreshed by the breezes, amused by the succession of objects, every change of the muscles called into action is a species of

356

repose, and the very activity itself tends in some measure to suspend the consciousness and counteract the effects of the action. Substitute a child employed on tasks the most opposite to all its natural instincts, were it only from their improgressive and wearying uniformity—in a heated stifling impure atmosphere, fevered by noise and glare, both limbs and spirits outwearied—and that, at the tenth hour, he has still three, four, or five hours more to look forward to. Will he, will the poor little *sufferer*, be brought to believe that these hours are mere trifles—or the privilege of going home not worth his thanks? Generalities are apt to deceive us. Individualise the sufferings which it is the object of this Bill to remedy, follow up the detail in some one case with a human sympathy, and the deception vanishes.

But we hasten to the fourth and last objection, namely, that the reform of all these grievances may be safely trusted in these enlightened times to the good sense and humanity of the masters themselves. This is, doubtless, highly flattering to the present age, and still more so to that which is to follow. It is, however, sufficient for us to have proved that it remains a mere assertion, and that up to this very hour the asserted increase of humane feeling and enlightened self-interest has produced no such effects as are here so confidently promised, have exerted no adequate counteraction to the keen stimulants of immediate profit, and the benumbing influences of custom and example. Nay, it is notorious that within the last twenty years the time and quantum of the labour extorted from the children has been increasing. The growth of the sciences among the few, and the consequent increase of the conveniences of life among the people at large, are, however, far from necessarily implying an *enlightened* age in that sense which alone applies to the case in question. There are few who are not enlightened enough to understand their duties, few but must *wink hard* not to see the path laid out for them. Something else is wanted here, the warmth to impel, and not the knowledge to guide. The age had been complimented with the epithets of enlightened, humane, etc., years before the abolition of the Slave Trade. And was that Trade abolished at last by the increasing humanity, the enlightened self-interest, of the slave owners? As far as the parties immediately interested are concerned, dare our Legislators even now trust to these influences? The Bills passed and the one now before the House, concerning the Slave Trade, are the best reply.

Anxiously have we wished to avoid every invidious remark. But we should be treacherous to the measure, of which we are the earnest, though humble, advocates, if we left wholly unnoticed the singular coincidence between the present Bill and that for the abolition of the Slave Trade, in the order and progress of the arguments adopted by the opponents of each. The defence of the Slave Trade, exactly as the attempted defence of the system of the Cotton Factories, *began* with the bold declaration that the Negro Slaves were happy and contented: nay, that they were far *better off* in every respect than the labouring poor and the peasantry in England. This, however, was found to be too strong a dose, and even before this assertion was overwhelmed by evidence to the contrary, it was felt to be dangerous. It was, indeed, fully equivalent to the assertion that the peasantry, and the labouring classes of Great Britain, *i.e.*, the majority of its inhabitants, were worse off than Negro Slaves, a position suited only to the sowers of sedition and the advocates for insurrection. This having been abandoned, the defenders rested their argument on the impropriety and inefficiency of all legislative interference with the freedom of Commerce. The Legislature had nothing to do with traders but to levy the duties, and then grant their only request—'Let us alone'. And truly in the instance of the Slave Trade this objection was very far from being groundless, in respect to the apprehended inefficiency of such interference. So strong, indeed, was it, that little less than the united power of all the governments of the Christian World was and is requisite to remove it. But praise be to God, who never fails to supply what is wanting to us, as long as we are earnest in doing *our* best, the Powers of the Christian World *have* united. But let it not be forgotten that this union never could have taken place had the British Legislature yielded to apprehension. The two remaining objections to the present Bill were urged repeatedly in the very same words in support of the Slave Trade; and we conclude this Address, for the length of which we must seek our best apologist in the reader's own humanity, with the observation, that the argument founded on the danger of establishing a precedent for other claims is so far realised, that we, in the present instance, are appealing to a precedent instead of making one; and that every argument of any force, which the opponents of the Bill have urged against it, has been declared invalid, as applied to the continuance of any system *admitted* to be cruel and unjust, and solemnly negatived by the British Parliament, in the glorious precedent of the Abolition of the Slave Trade.

In conclusion we take leave to subscribe ourselves,

SINCERE FRIENDS OF INDUSTRY,

TO THE MUTUAL ADVANTAGE OF

MASTER AND LABOURER.

London, 18th April, 1818.[1]

THE GROUNDS OF SIR ROBERT PEEL'S BILL VINDICATED BY
S. T. COLERIDGE

It has been objected to Sir Robert Peel's Bill that its grounds are not borne out by the evidence before the Select Committee in 1816. In reply, we refer, first, to the examination of the most eminent medical authorities, Dr. Baillie, Mr. Ashley Cooper,

[1] *Manuscript note on his own copy, in the British Museum:*
I ought to have made a collection of Papers of this kind, written by me on various Subjects brought before Parliament. This is not one of the best; and yet I do not think it below par. S. T. Coleridge.

Dr. Pemberton, Mr. A. Carlisle, Dr. Tuthill, and Sir Gilbert
Blane, gentlemen unconnected with the Factories and of course
not examined concerning the truth of the facts, but as to the
probable results on the *supposition* of the truth. Now the
warmest friends of suffering humanity could not have wished
for opinions more decisive, more consistent with each other,
or in more perfect coincidence with the positive testimony
adduced in support of the Bill. It was affirmed by them all, that
whatever exceptions might arise from particular strength of
constitution, yet according to all their experience and in conformity with all the laws of animal life, universally received by
the profession at large, the *general* results of the employment of
children, in the manner stated to them, must be greatly and
radically detrimental to their health: that the consequences to be
expected would be—stinted growth, debility, rickets, scrofula,
mesenteric obstructions, in short, all the various diseases that
arise from impaired digestion and pulmonary derangement, in
many; but diminished vigor and the seeds of future ill-health in
a great *majority*, of the children exposed daily to such influences
during such a number of hours. Evidence more decisive, more
satisfactory in itself, or more respectable from the characters of
the gentlemen examined, it would be difficult to imagine and
suspicious to require. What then remained but to prove, first,
that the circumstances had been faithfully stated to them; and
next, that the actual results did in every respect verify the
opinions delivered on that supposition? Now as to the first
point, the opposers of the Bill have themselves furnished the
proof. It is found in their own evidence. We need refer to no
other testimony than their own admissions. (See the collected
testimonies of more than forty Master Spinners, delivered
before the Select Committee, in pages 374 and 375, of the
printed evidence.) It is scarcely necessary to add that the
grievances are not likely to have been *exaggerated* in these admissions. But in proof of the second point, *viz.*, the actual state
of the children resulting from the time and circumstances of

their employment, we refer (see pages 286, 287) to the decisive testimony, the full and circumstantial statements, of Mr. Simmons, the senior surgeon of the Manchester Infirmary, and who had been then surgeon of that institution for five and twenty years. We refer also to the accurate and minute information contained in the answers of Mr. Kinder Wood, likewise a medical practitioner, whose examination will be found in the printed evidence, pages 191–208. Both these attest what they have themselves seen, speak to facts into which they have themselves examined, record the results of long and careful observation: and does a shade of suspicion rest on their characters as men or as professional men, on their competence as observers, or on their veracity as witnesses? By all, who know them, the very question would scarcely be tolerated. And does not their evidence bear out the utmost that has been stated in behalf of the necessity of the Bill? But there is other and more extensive evidence (*weightier* there scarcely can be), now before the House and officially in its possession. We can refer to at least twenty Petitions, containing the most solemn attestations as to the existence of the facts, and to the kind and degree of the sufferings resulting from them, the greater number from the adult labourers themselves, many of whom are parents or relatives of the children, and the remainder from persons not otherwise interested in the Bill, than as having before their eyes the afflicting proofs of its expediency. With especial confidence we refer to the Petition from more than seventeen hundred of the principal inhabitants of the towns and neighbourhood of Manchester and Salford, among whom are found *seven magistrates, nine physicians, twenty-one surgeons*, and *twenty clergymen*, seventeen of whom are of the Established Church. In the list of medical gentlemen who undersigned it we find the names of Dr. Bardsley, senior physician of the Manchester Infirmary, who has been a physician of the same for twenty-seven years; Mr. Simmons, senior surgeon, who has in like manner been a surgeon there for twenty-seven years; Dr. Winstanley, a physician of the Infirmary ten years; Dr. Ward a surgeon of the same for fourteen years; Mr. Hamilton, a surgeon of the same for twenty-seven years; Mr. Thorpe, ditto, fourteen years; Dr. Hull, who has practised in Manchester upwards of twenty years; Mr. Wood, as a surgeon, twenty-eight years; Mr. Boutflower and Mr. Bellott, each twenty-five years; and Mr. G. Tomlinson, for thirty years! All these, in common with the other highly respectable residents of the same and other professions whose names we are prevented from noticing by their number alone, bear solemn testimony to the existence and extent of '*the sufferings, which they feelingly deplore*'. They attest the '*fatally injurious consequences*' of the present system, especially to the delicate frame and strength of the children; and finally declare their conviction that 'from the generality of the practice and the natural competitions of the trade, *such evils cannot be removed without the aid of legislative authority*'.

We have purposely abstained from referring to any evidence not officially before Parliament, nor can we bring ourselves to believe that for an impartial judgment any additional evidence can be necessary. For what, it may be asked, can be opposed to that which is already in the possession of the House, so far as the *Facts* themselves are concerned? What efficient counterweight can there be to the testimonies in affirmation of the *grounds* of the Bill; whether the numbers, the respectability, or the disinterestedness, of the witnesses, their competence to distinguish, or their opportunities of knowing, the truth, should be brought into comparison? In reply to this natural question it is sufficient to say that the evidence on the contrary side is almost exclusively that of the Master Spinners themselves or their dependents!

We disclaim everything that borders on an invidious or personal reflection; but with regard to the assertions of men interested (or rather who believe themselves interested) in bringing about the failure of the measure in question, we have to observe that there is a wide difference between the *sensation* of *positiveness* which is the ordinary growth of passion from prejudice and imagined self-interest, and the *sense* of *certainty* which is the result and reward of tranquil and disinterested examination. A man must be strangely inexperienced in the history of his own heart, who is not aware that we as often unconsciously deceive ourselves as we (intentionally or otherwise) deceive our neighbours. In suspecting the accuracy of statements made under the strongest predilections of (*supposed*) self-interest, we do not necessarily impeach the veracity of the staters. We are far from wishing to accuse them of insincerity, of a conscious intention to assert falsehood or suppress truth: but we *do* wish to impress the necessity of being on our guard in receiving the testimony of men (as for instance, of Master Spinners in the present question) on a point in which they can only be regarded as witnesses in their own cause. For as their own cause do our opponents appear to consider every attempt to frustrate the measure. In their own cause do they come forward as witnesses. Now in proof that such testimony ought not to be received without caution, that it requires to be *looked into*, we again refer to the printed evidence, pages 374 and 375. Here we find it observed by Mr. Sandford, a delegate from the *Master Spinners* of Manchester, and himself a Master Spinner, that in more than forty factories there is, in each, one hour at least in the day allowed 'for Meals out of the Mill'. Now in the Minutes of the Committee, it is on evidence that in one* of these very factories enumerated by Mr. Sandford, namely Messrs. Birley and Hornby's, there is but *one* day in the week on which children regularly go home to their dinners, being detained on the other five to clean the machinery. It also

* *This* is not the only factory noticed in the Minutes of Evidence where Children are detained five days in the week during the dinner time to clean the machinery. It is further on evidence that at one mill the people are detained during the dinner hour *every* day; that they are employed fourteen hours a day without intermission, the steam engine never stopping during that time; consequently whatever refreshment they get is taken as the works go on.

appears on the same Minutes, that *no* time is allowed for the breakfast or the afternoon meals, which must be taken while the work is going on: as if the food earned by the toil were to be made a part of the toil.

Of these factories Mr. Sanford gave in a scale under a variety of heads. And in this scale it is affirmed that out of the whole number (with the exception of one, from which no report had been received), that is, out of Eleven Thousand Seven Hundred and Twenty-five Persons employed, there were at that period only Forty Persons sick; and that Thirty-six only of the Eleven Thousand Seven Hundred and Twenty-five had died in the course of the last twelve months: that is, little more than THREE IN A THOUSAND!!—And this in *Cotton Factories*! A strange result, and such as might well justify the exclamation of the great medical authorities examined; *if* so, it is *very* extraordinary! An expression of surprise (might we not say, almost of incredulity) which will appear highly natural when it is considered that in no age or country is there recorded anything like so small a proportion of deaths, even under the most favourable circumstances. To such assertions the astonishment of those who live in the neighbourhood of cotton factories supersedes the necessity of a verbal answer which could not indeed be satisfactory without becoming invidious. Instead of it we content ourselves with the following general remarks on the fallacy —we had almost said, the disingenuity—of all such statements respecting the health of the Children. First, these statements respect only the Children actually at work in the factories at the time the statements were made: whereas common sense would require that they should comprehend the whole number of those who had worked in the factories during some given period, noticing the sickly and diseased, who had been discharged, and the Children who had been taken in their place. This is about as fair as it would be to decide on the healthiness of a Surinam Swamp by the number of slaves alive at any one moment, without distinguishing the new importations and without striking the balance between those who had perished and those who had stood the seasoning—or the dangers to which a regiment in active service had been exposed, by the existing numbers on the muster roll, without any reference to the numbers that had been killed off and filled up by fresh recruits. Secondly, the deleterious effects of the time, etc., of the labour in the Cotton Factories, consist for the greater part in a slow, insensible, undermining of the constitution. The diseases to which the Children are most liable are such as presuppose a long preceding period of decaying inward strength, the outward signs of which evade the notice of a chance spectator.

As to the other arguments circulated by the opponents of the Bill as—that men after working eleven or twelve hours in the day are to be deemed *idle* during the remaining hours—that in consequence of this *idleness* they must necessarily rush into riot and profligacy—that the diminution in their wages, from the limitation of their hours of labour, instead of checking these vicious propensities, will only hurry them into the perpetration of crimes in order to procure the means of gratifying them; which is equivalent to the assertion that all labourers whose daily work does not exceed twelve hours, their meal hours included, must be idle and profligate; (for strange to say, such are the assertions in a pamphlet just published by the opponents of the Bill)—these we regard as outrages on human nature and mere struggles of conscious weakness. But against these, and against all former attempts to justify the employment of Children from thirteen to fifteen hours in the day, under the most deleterious influences, and who are thus, in contradiction of all the instincts of nature, compelled 'to attend early in the morning and continue their toil till late at night'—we make our confident appeal to Conscience and to Common Sense.

S. T. Coleridge.

London, 24th April, 1818.

283. 'THE POOR'

One of the ominous characteristics of this reforming age, the Custom of addressing '*The Poor*', as a permanent Class, assumed to consist ordinarily of the same individuals. Just as in Jamaica I might address myself to '*the Negros*'. Now if this have a sound foundation in the fact, it assuredly marks a most deplorable State of Society. The Ideal of a Government is that which under the existing circumstances most effectually affords Security to the Possessors, Facility to the Acquirers, and *Hope* to all. Poverty, whatever can justify the designation of 'the Poor' ought to be a transitional state—a state to which no man ought to admit himself to belong, tho' he may find himself *in* it because he is passing *thro'* it, in the effort to leave it. Poor men we must always have, till the Redemption is fulfilled, but *The Poor*, as consisting of the *same* Individuals! O this is a sore accusation against any society! And to address an Individual as having *his* interest merged in his character as one of *the Poor*, his *abiding* interest! O as well ought you to appeal to an individual with an eruption from Cold as one of the *Scabby faced*, without reference to his Being, as in Health! The Poor can have, ought to have, one interest only—*viz*. to cease to be *poor*. But to call the man who by labor maintains himself under *human* conditions and comforts, who by labor procures himself what is needful for him and his essential affections a Pauper—to *designate* the sum total of such Laborers *the Poor*! O if this be not a foul misuse of words, if there be a ground in fact for it, it is in the same proportion a dire impeachment of both Church and State, such as would warrant a Revolution. For that Country must have a canker at the Core.

How *does* the case stand? *I* believe thus. There is enough of *truth* to furnish a too plausible pretext for the language and far too little to justify it. O when will the Tories, the so called *Conservative* Party, learn to address their *country*, their neighbors, tenants, dependants, &c. instead of addressing each other, and convincing the already convinced! Alas! the *vanity* engendered in our Gentry, even in our landed Gentry, by the Newspaper Press, and the lust of having their names mentioned! Men of estate and family are thus *bribed* by their desire to be puffed in the Papers to become accomplices in a conspiracy against all estate, all family, whatever has the nature of permanence, and of reason, instead of chance, passion, appetite, the Mob, and the To Day!!

MS.

284. PHILOSOPHY AND SOCIETY

In every state, not wholly barbarous, a philosophy, good or bad, there must be. However slightingly it may be the fashion to talk of speculation and theory, as opposed (sillily and non-sensically opposed) to practice, it would not be difficult to prove, that such as is the existing spirit of speculation, during any given period, such will be the spirit and tone of the religion, legislation, and morals, nay, even of the fine arts, the manners, and the fashions. Nor is this the less true, because the great majority of men live like bats, but in twilight, and know and feel the philosophy of their age only by its reflections and refractions.

Essays On His Own Times.

285. PILGRIM'S PROGRESS: HISTORY

Take from History its impertinences and it differs from the Pilgrim's Progress only in the co-incidences of the Proper Names with those of the Parish Registers of the particular Time and Country.

MS.

286. A REVIEW OF CLARKSON'S 'HISTORY OF THE ABOLITION OF THE SLAVE TRADE'

It contains the history of the rise and progress of an evil the most pernicious, if only because the most criminal, that ever degraded human nature. The history of a war of more than two centuries, waged by men against human nature; a war too carried on, not by ignorance and barbarism against knowledge and civilization; not by half-famished multitudes against a race blessed with all the arts of life, and softened and effeminated by luxury; but, as some strange nondescript in iniquity, waged by unprovoked strength against uninjuring helplessness, and with all the powers which long periods of security and equal law had enabled the assailants to develop,—in order to make barbarism more barbarous, and to add to the want of political freedom the most dreadful and debasing personal suffering. Thus, all the effects and influences of freedom were employed to enslave; the gifts of knowledge to prevent the possibility of illumination; and powers, which could not have existed but in consequence of morality and religion, to perpetuate the sensual vices, and to ward off the emancipating blow of Christianity; and, as if this were not enough, positive laws were added by the best and freest nation of Christendom, and powers entrusted to the basest part of its population, for purposes which would almost necessarily make the best men become the worst.

Nor are the effects of this strange war less marvellous than its nature. It is a war in which the victors fall lower than the vanquished; in which the oppressors are more truly objects of pity than the oppressed; while, to the nation which had most extensively pursued and most solemnly authorized it, it was an eating ulcer into the very vitals of its main resources as to defence, and a slow poison acting on that constitution which was the offspring, and has continued to be the protection, of its freedom and prosperity. In short, the present work is the history of one great calamity,—one long continuous crime, involving every possible definition of evil: for it combined the wildest physical suffering with the most atrocious moral depravity. . . .

. . . The author commences his history by an eloquent and dramatic representation of the evils belonging to the slave trade, with respect to the Africans, in its three principal stages. First, on the continent of Africa; secondly, in the middle passage; thirdly, in the West Indies and the adjoining colonies. This is followed by a well reasoned and affecting counterpart of the evil, in the grievous effects of this trade on those who are employed in carrying it on. First, on the masters and men of the slave ships; next, on the factors and those employed in purchasing or seizing the unhappy victims; and, lastly, on the planters and owners of slaves, and on the countries in general in which slavery is established. We have, indeed, always been of opinion, that too little stress has been laid on *this* part of the subject. The sufferings of the Africans were calculated, no doubt to make a more rapid and violent impression on the imaginations and bodily sympathies of men; but the dreadful depravity that of necessity was produced by it on the immediate agents of the injustice; the almost universal corruption of manners which at the present day startles reflecting travellers on passing from the Northern States of America into those in which slavery obtains; and the further influence of such corruption on the morals of countries that are in habits of constant commercial intercourse, and who speak the same language; these, though not susceptible of colours equally glaring, do yet form a more extensive evil,—an evil more certain, and of a more measurable kind. These are evil in the form of guilt; evil in its most absolute and most appropriate sense; that sense to which the sublimest teachers of moral wisdom, Plato, Zeno, Leibnitz, have confined the appellation; and which, therefore, on a well disciplined spirit, will make an impression deeper than could have been left by mere agony of body, or even anguish of mind; in proportion as vice is more hateful than pain, eternity

more awful than time. To this may be added, the fatal effects on
national morals, from the public admission of principles *pro-
fessedly* incompatible with justice, and from the implied dis-
avowal of any obligation paramount to that of immediate expediency, compared with which even state-hypocrisy may not
have been without its good effects. Those who estimate all
measures, institutions and events, exclusively by their palpable
and immediate effects, are little qualified to trace, and less inclined to believe, the ceaseless agency of those subtler causes to
which the philosopher attributes the deterioration of national
character. Yet history will vouch for us, if we affirm, that no
government ever avowedly acted on immoral principles (as,
for instance, the Prussian, since the accession of their Frederic
the unique, as the Germans style him, and the court of France
from the administration of Richelieu), without inducing a pro-
portional degradation in the virtue and dignity of the individuals who form the mass of the nation. . .

   A majority of the [British] cabinet, it is believed, were hostile
to the abolition; but the nation, throughout city, town, and
village, was only not unanimous: and though the almost
weekly explosion of new events, all of them more .or less
directly affecting the interests of Great Britain, drew away their
attention, or deadened their zeal, for a time, as to this great subject, yet is was only necessary to proclaim the same facts anew,
and the same zeal was rekindled, the same sense of duty felt
and expressed by all classes. In France, on the contrary, the most
eminent characters were deeply interested for a little moment
in the abolition; but the people throughout France were either
ignorant of the horrors of the trade, or unaffected by them.
This is that which constitutes the true, the fundamental strength
of our empire. Great Britain is indeed a *living body politic*: the
chain of interests extends in unbroken links from the great city
to the far extremities of the empire; and thoughts and feelings
are conducted by it with the rapidity of an electric charge. At

the commencement of the Revolution, a temporary enthusiasm seems indeed to have shed one and the same spirit on the great majority of the French people; but (wanting both the continuous gradation of ranks which exists in our landed property, and that unbroken connexion of interests produced by insular situation; our national debt; our established commercial pre-eminence; and that unbounded confidence between man and man, which is the consequence of these) the enthusiasm was transient; and the first victorious soldier, who dared act the traitor, gave proof to all Europe, that France had indeed an immense *populace*, but not a *people; Plebem, non populum*. The republican legislators had laboured, by a variety of evolutions and schemes of arrangement, to give to the people the means of acting on, and influencing, the conduct of their governors. But conventional statutes, neither harmonizing with old customs, nor arising out of the state and circumstances of the country, could weave only a rope of sand: they could not supply that true link of interests, which law may protect and encourage, but which individuals must have previously created. London is *the* chief city of Great Britain; Paris *a* vast city in France. London is the true *heart* of the empire. No pulse beats there, which is not corresponded to proportionally through the whole circulation. Paris is a wen; and the existence of such an excrescence was not the least powerful cause of the failure of every effort to give France a free constitution.

We have heard indeed, the prosperity of America declared by Lord Sidmouth, when he was Minister of State, to be an awful warning to Great Britain, never hereafter to colonize a new country. Merciful Heaven! that the brethen of our ancestors should have founded a mighty empire, indefinite in its increase,—an empire, which retains and is spreading all that constitutes 'Country' in a wise man's feelings, *viz.* the same laws, the same customs, the same religion, and above all the same language; that, in short, to have been the mother of prosperous empires, is to *be a warning to* Great Britain! And whence this dread? Because, forsooth, our eldest born, when of age, had set up for himself; and not only preserving, but, in an almost incalculable proportion, increasing the advantages of former reciprocal intercourse, had saved us the expense and anxiety of defending, and the embarrassment of governing a country three thousand miles distant! That this separation was at length effected by violence, and the horrors of a civil war, is to be attributed solely to the ignorance and corruption of the many, and the perilous bigotry of a few. . . .

The Africans are more versatile, more easily modified than perhaps any other known race. A few years of strict honesty and humane attention to their interests, affections, and prejudices, would abolish the memory of the past, or cause it to be remembered only as a fair contrast. The Legislature of Great Britain having once decreed that no territorial conquest shall be made in Africa, this law having been made public there, and enforced by correspondent conduct on the part of our mercantile agents, there would be less difficulty in buying up the tributes hitherto levied by the African chieftains on the great rivers, than William Penn found in purchasing the more important possession of Pennsylvania from the American Indians. Permission would in time be gained to raise commercial magazines, so armed and manned, as should be found necessary for the security of our countrymen. Privileges, both useful and flattering, should be held forth to such of the African tribes as would settle round each of these forts: still higher honours should be given to the individuals among such settlers as should have learnt our language, and acquired our arts of manufacture or cultivation. Thus, each fort, instead of being, as hitherto, a magazine of death and depravity, would finally become a centre of civilization, with diverging lines, the circumference of which would join or pass through similar circles. The intercourse with every part of Africa would not only be rendered secure in relation to the natives, but, from their friendly dispositions, rendered less dangerous to the health of European adventurers, no longer compelled to remain unsheltered, exposed to the vertical sun by day, or the destructive dews of the night. How valuable the productions of Africa already known are, may be learnt by consulting either Mr Clarkson's work on the Impolicy, or the volumes now before us, (vol. II, p. 14, &c.) or the Evidence before the Committee of the House of Commons. That these bear but a small proportion, both in number or value, to what would be hereafter discovered in consequence of our being masters of the great rivers, is most probable: and we are certain, that if African industry were awakened, few indeed are the articles necessary for our manufactures or consumption, which might not be raised in Africa, and come to us more cheaply, including the first cost and the freightage, than from any other part of the world.

Africa holds out no temptations, either to conquest or individual rapacity. The timid statesman will have to contemplate no independent American republic in its germ: the philosopher no future East Indian empire, to render peace short and insecure, and war more costly and anxious. It cannot be denied that the superstitions of the Africans will occasion great difficulties and embarrassments; but, by a systematic repression of all religious proselytism, except indeed that most effective instrument of conversion, the Christian conduct of our agents; by a prudent and affectionate attention to the wishes and comforts of the chieftains, and the Mandingo priests; and by sedulous endeavours to enlighten them as *men*; this obstacle might gradually be removed,—at all events greatly lessened. Every individual employed in the different forts or settlements, should act under the conviction, that knowledge and civilization must, in the first instance, form the foundation, not the superstructure, of Christianity.

The African character is strikingly contrasted with that of the North American Indians; and the facility with which the Africans are impressed, the rapidity with which they take the colours of surrounding objects, oftentimes place them in a degrading light, as men, but are most auspicious symptoms of what they may hereafter become, as citizens. A crowd of slaves shouting in triumph at the proclamation of the reestablishment of slavery, (we allude to Villaret's letter,) or fighting with desperate fury against their own countrymen, who had escaped from a common tyrant, will not indeed bear a comparison, in moral dignity, with the stern, unbending warriors of the interior of North America; and yet present far better *data* of hope, regarded prospectively, and as the materials of a future nation. The American Indians are savages: the Africans (to speak classically) barbarians. Of the civilization of savages, we know no certain instance, the actual origin of Mexico and Peru, the only cases that have any claim at all to be adduced, not having been preserved even by the rudest tradition. But of the progress from barbarism to civilization, through its various stages, the history of every nation gives a more or less distinct example, in proportion to our opportunity of tracing it backward.

This distinction between the savage and barbarous state, which is indeed fruitful in consequences, bears upon the present question in one important point, the willingness, we mean, with which barbarous tribes adopt, as it were at command, the changes in laws or religion, dictated to them by their leaders. Let no alarming zeal be betrayed: rather let the initiation into Christianity be held up as a distinction,—as a favour to be bestowed; and it need not be doubted that natural curiosity will prompt the chieftains, and most intelligent of the African tribes, to inquire into the particulars of a religion professed by a race confessedly so superior to them, and that the sense of this superiority will act as a powerful motive toward their adoption of it. At all events, a long trial has been given to injustice and cruelty: surely justice and benevolence may claim, that one experiment should be made of their influence, and in their favour.

Edinburgh Review, July 1808.

X

THE SPIRIT OF OBEDIENCE
IN OURSELVES

From a spirit of fear . . . to a spirit of love, from
a spirit of bondage to a filial spirit.
                    Note on Southey's *Wesley*

RELIGION

The works that deal most with Coleridge's opinions on religious matters are: *The Statesman's Manual*, 1816, 1817; the *Aids to Reflection*, 1825 (comments on passages from Leighton, Jeremy Taylor, Hooker and other English divines); *On the Constitution of the Church and State*, 1830, (on the Catholic Bill, and the need for a national church); and the *Confessions of an Inquiring Spirit*, (for a spiritual and imaginative reading of the Bible and against text-bandying), posthumously published in 1840. There are many references in the *Table Talk*, and the notebooks after 1827 are largely theological.

In 1827, after a serious illness, Coleridge took communion for the first time since Cambridge days, and it is clear that he looked more and more for personal and national spiritual sustenance in an established national church. But John Stuart Mill was hardly correct in labelling him a High Churchman. Nor was he, as is sometimes suggested, a religious mystic, greatly though he admired the Quakers and the Moravian Church. It was just as difficult for him to find a religious affiliation to meet his complicated views, as to find a satisfactory political party.

The best and fullest modern treatment of this aspect of Coleridge is *Coleridge and the Broad Church Movement* by C. R. Sanders.

X

THE SPIRIT OF OBEDIENCE
IN OURSELVES

---

287. RELIGION OF THE ANCIENTS

OBSERVE the remarkable contrast between the religion of the tragic and other poets of Greece. The former are always opposed in heart to the popular divinities. In fact, there are the popular, the sacerdotal, and the mysterious religions of Greece, represented roughly by Homer, Pindar, and Aeschylus. The ancients had no notion of a fall of man, though they had of his gradual degeneracy. Prometheus, in the old mythus, and for the most part in Aeschylus, is the Redeemer and the Devil jumbled together.

Table Talk.

288. PRAYER

No. 19. Homily on Prayer

Observe: we must not worship God, as if *his* Ways were as *our* Ways. We must not apply to him, neither, as tho' God were the same with Sensible Nature, or the sum total of the Objects of our bodily Senses. For Nature in this sense must of necessity appear to us but as a more subtle and exquisite sort of Machine —and so to think of God is a deathly Superstition. And to speak

379

aloud to God and by the sound and meaning of our words to suppose ourselves influencing him as we in this way influence our fellow-men, this is a *delirious* Superstition. O in that, which comprizing both transcends both, what precious Mysteries lie hid.

Means+intreaty—O miraculous indeed hath been and would be such Prayer!

MS.

289. FAITH—A TOTAL ACT OF THE SOUL

Just and generous actions may proceed from bad motives, and both may, and often do, originate *in parts*, and, as it were, *fragments* of our nature. A lascivious man may sacrifice half his estate to rescue his friend from prison, for he is constitutionally sympathetic, and the better part of his nature happened to be uppermost. The same man shall afterwards exert the same disregard of money in an attempt to seduce that friend's wife or daughter. But faith is a *total* act of the Soul: it is the *whole* state of the mind, or it is not at all! and in this consists its power, as well as its exclusive worth.

Friend.

290. UNITARIANISM

I make the greatest difference between *ans* and *isms*. I should deal insincerely with you, if I said that I thought Unitarianism was Christianity. No; as I believe and have faith in the doctrine, it is not the truth in Jesus Christ; but God forbid that I should doubt that you, and many other Unitarians, as you call yourselves, are, in a practical sense, very good Christians. We do not win Heaven by logic.

By the by, what do you mean by exclusively assuming the title of Unitarians? As if Tri-Unitarians were not necessarily Unitarians, as much (pardon the illustration) as an apple-pie must of course be a pie! The schoolmen would, perhaps, have called you Unicists; but your proper name is Psilanthropists—believers in the mere human nature of Christ.

Upon my word, if I may say so without offence, I really think many forms of Pantheistic Atheism more agreeable to an imaginative mind than Unitarianism as it is professed in terms: in particular, I prefer the Spinosistic scheme infinitely. The early Socinians were, to be sure, most unaccountable logicians; but, when you had swallowed their bad reasoning, you came to doctrine on which the *heart*, at least, might rest for some support. They adored Jesus Christ. Both Laelius and Faustus Socinus laid down the adorability of Jesus in strong terms. I have nothing, you know, to do with their logic. But Unitarianism is, in effect, the worst of one kind of Atheism, joined to the worst of one kind of Calvinism, like two asses tied tail to tail. It has no covenant with God; and looks upon prayer as a sort of self-magnetizing—a getting of the body and temper into a certain *status*, desirable *per se*, but having no covenanted reference to the Being to whom the prayer is addressed.

Table Talk.

291. HISTORY, NATURAL AND MORAL

In natural history, God's freedom is shown in the law of necessity. In moral history, God's necessity or providence is shown in man's freedom.

Table Talk.

292. PROOFS OF THE EXISTENCE OF GOD

Assume the existence of God,—and then the harmony and fitness of the physical creation may be shown to correspond with and support such an assumption;—but to set about *proving* the existence of a God by such means is a mere circle, a delusion.

It can be no proof to a good reasoner, unless he violates all syllogistic logic, and presumes his conclusion.

Kant once set about proving the existence of God, and a masterly effort it was. But in his later great work, the 'Critique of the Pure Reason', he saw its fallacy, and said of it—that *if* the existence could be proved at all, it must be on the grounds indicated by him.

Table Talk.

293. REASON AND UNDERSTANDING

The unspeakable importance of the Distinction between the Reason and the Human Understanding, as the only Ground of the Cogency of the Proof *a posteriori* of the existence of a God from the order of the known Universe. Remove or deny this distinction, and Hume's argument from the Spider's proof that Houses &c were spun by Men out of their Bodies becomes valid.

MS.

294. WHETHER MIRACLES CAN, OF THEMSELVES, WORK A TRUE CONVICTION IN THE MIND

There are spiritual truths which must derive their evidence from within, which whoever rejects, 'neither will he believe though a man were to rise from the dead' to confirm them. And under the Mosaic law a miracle in attestation of a false doctrine subjected the miracle-worker to death: and whether the miracle was really or only seemingly supernatural, makes no difference in the present argument, its power of convincing, whatever that power may be, whether great or small, depending on the fulness of the belief in its miraculous nature. *Est quibus esse videtur.* Or rather, that I may express the same position in a form less likely to offend, is not a true *efficient* conviction of a moral truth, is not the creating of a new heart, which collects

the energies of a man's whole being in the focus of the conscience, the one essential miracle, the same and of the same
evidence to the ignorant and the learned, which no superior
skill can counterfeit, human or dæmoniacal? Is it not emphatic-
ally that leading of the Father, without which no man can come
to Christ? Is it not that implication of doctrine in the miracle
and of miracle in the doctrine, which is the bridge of communication between the senses and the soul?—That predisposing
warmth which renders the understanding susceptible of the
specific impression from the historic, and from all other outward seals of testimony? Is not this the one infallible criterion
of miracles, by which a man can know whether they be of
God? The abhorrence in which the most savage or barbarous
tribes hold witchcraft, in which however their belief is so intense
as even to control the springs of life,—is not this abhorrence of
witchcraft under so full a conviction of its reality a proof, how
little of divine, how little fitting to our nature, a miracle is,
when insulated from spiritual truths, and disconnected from
religion as its end? What then can we think of a theological
theory, which adopting a scheme of prudential legality, common to it with 'the sty of Epicurus,' as far at least as the *springs*
of moral action are concerned, makes its whole *religion* consist
in the belief of miracles! As well might the poor African prepare
for himself a fetish by plucking out the eyes from the eagle or
the lynx, and enshrining the same, worship in them the power
of vision. As the tenet of professed Christians (I speak of the
principle not of the men, whose hearts will always more or less
correct the errors of their understandings) it is even more
absurd, and the pretext for such a religion more inconsistent
than the religion itself. For they profess to derive from it their
whole faith in that futurity, which if they had not previously
believed on the evidence of their own consciences, of Moses and
the Prophets, they are assured by the great Founder and Object
of Christianity, that neither will they believe it, in any spiritual
and profitable sense, though a man should rise from the dead.

For myself, I cannot resist the conviction, built on particular and general history, that the extravagancies of Antinomianism and Solifidianism are little more than the counteractions to this Christian paganism: the play, as it were, of antagonist muscles. The feelings will set up their standard against the understanding, whenever the understanding has renounced its allegiance to the reason: and what is faith but the personal realization of the reason by its union with the will? If we would drive out the demons of fanaticism from the people, we must begin by exercising the spirit of Epicureanism in the higher ranks, and restore to their teachers the true Christian *enthusiasm*, the vivifying influences of the altar, the censer, and the sacrifice. They must neither be ashamed of, nor disposed to explain away, the articles of prevenient and auxiliary grace, nor the necessity of being born again to the life from which our nature had become apostate. They must administer indeed the necessary medicines to the sick, the motives of fear as well as of hope; but they must not withhold from them the idea of health, or conceal from them that the medicines for the sick are not the diet of the healthy. Nay, they must make it a part of the curative process to induce the patient, on the first symptoms of recovery, to look forward with prayer and aspiration to that state, in which *perfect love shutteth out fear*. Above all, they must not seek to make the mysteries of faith what the world calls *rational* by theories of original sin and redemption borrowed analogically from the imperfection of human law-courts and the coarse contrivances of state expedience.

Friend.

295. GOD, AND THE NATURE OF THE REVELATION OF DIVINE GOODNESS

Stillingfleet writes: But there is this vast difference between them [God and the sun], that though God is essentially and necessarily good, yet the communications of this goodness are the effect of his Will and not merely of his nature.

Coleridge comments: Well! but is not the *Will* of God identical with his nature? Is it not naturally good or beneficent? Is there in Eternity a distinguishable moment, that one moment should possibly be preferred to another? And where is the danger to Religion, if we make preservation a perpetual creation, and interpret the first words of Genesis as we must do (if not Socinians) the first words of St. John, 'From all eternity God created the Universe—And the Earth became waste and void' &c. It might have been a comet—it might have been as to its whole surface, ruined by a comet. It is a rule of infinite importance, that the Scriptures always speak not *ad rem in se ipsâ, sed quoad hominem.* It is a moral and religious, not a physical revelation, and in order to render us good moral agents, not accurate natural speculators, to make us know ourselves and our relations both present and future, not to make us knowing in nature— without industry or intellectual exercitation. S. T. C.

MS.

296. PHILOSOPHY AND CHRISTIANITY

Stillingfleet writes: And how inefficacious the precepts of Philosophy were, appears by the Philosophers themselves, who were far from having command by them over their Masterless passions, and were fain sometimes to confess that nature was too headstrong to be kept in by such weak reins as the precepts of Philosophy were.

Coleridge comments: Cannot the philosophers quote as many instances as can reasonably be expected from men who did not make plebeian Sects? And are not the lives of nominal Christians as offensive to Christianity, as those of nominal Philosophers to Philosophy? And is not the number in each proportionate to that of the Professors? Nay! are there not more bad Christians in proportion? Why? because the very habits of Speculation remove men farther from Temptation, or disarm it. This is not meant as an argument in favor of Philos. against Christianity, but to overthrow its dangerous enemy, false Reasoning, in its favor. And why is Philosophy for ever to be set up as the Rival rather than the Friend and natural Companion, of Christianity? What is Christianity but a divine and pre-eminent Philosophy? A stream, in whose depths the Elephant may *swim*, and in whose practical and saving Truths the Lamb may *ford*? Besides, who shall dare say of your river, such and such a wave came from such a fountain? What Scholar (and by scholars the vulgar are taught) shall say—Such a conviction, such a moral feeling, I received from St. John, such and such from Seneca, or Epictetus? S. T. C.

MS.

297. ROMAN CATHOLIC AND PROTESTANT

A Beech rises in a columnal Trunk to the height of 20 feet from the Ground and there it divides into two, diverging as the Samian Y. A River flows from its fountain in one widening stream over a vast tract of Country and thro' various soils, till it reaches a bed of rocks, over and between which it twists, foams, roars, eddies for a while,

'Shatters its waters abreast, and in many tumult bewilder'd

‒ ◡ ◡ ‒ ◡ ◡ ‒ ‒ ‒ ◡ ◡ ◡ ‒ ◡ ◡ ‒ ‒

Rushes dividuous all, all rushing impetuous onwards,'

till it is met by a vast compact breast-work of Rock, which divides the stream into two diverging channels—and obtains the name of the Rock of Separation. Which of the two Limbs shall call itself the Beech-tree and retain the name of Trunk? Which of the two streams, the South-West, or the South-East, shall call itself *the* River? Is not the question palpably absurd? What if the *Genie* or Naiad of the one Channel should with an angry sneer ask the Sister Naiad, 'Where were you and your Stream before Rock Separation?' Might not the latter reply, 'Exactly where you were, Sister. To be sure, I have deposited a good deal of the mud and the filth which our waters had contracted during their long journey. I wish, Sister! you would make use of my Filtring Machine!' To the same purpose was the answer of —— to his Catholic Neighbour who had asked him, 'Where was your Religion before Luther?'—'Where was your Face before you washed it this morning?' S. T. C.

MS.

298. CHRISTIANITY AND TRUTH

The poltroonery of our clergy in their anxiety to suppress the arguments of Infidels or Heretics. *Ex. gr.* I was speaking of Eichhorn's Theory of the three first Gospels, and his View of the Apocalypse, to an Oxford and lettered Clergyman—and the answer was—'I don't wish to hear anything about [that]. Let them keep it to themselves.' And recommended silence to me, lest some busybody may translate it. As if Truth were to be prized because and as far as it happened to be Christianity, and not Chr[istianity] because it is the Truth.

MS.

299. THE NATURALNESS OF CHRISTIAN ORDINANCES

Whether it may be expedient or even consistent with the duties of Charity to the Weak in Faith to publish the maxim, I have not decided—but of the maxim itself I have no doubt, viz. That nothing having a primary relation to the present State, whether moral, or prudential or gubernamental, is ordained in the New Testament which would not have been, according to the nature of the case, binding on the Conscience, true for the Reason, or apt for the Understanding, independent of the Ordinance. *In relationibus humanis e statu mundano et sociali sive politico ortis, nihil religat Religio Christiana quod non ante ligatum erat.* The Ignorance of this great Truth, in application to the government and discipline of Christian Communities, led the first and second Generation of Reformers into grievous Errors, on both sides. Had they but asked themselves what would naturally arise, what would be dictated by prudence and good sense, and what the Graces of Humility, brotherly Affection, and Zeal in a common cause would have impelled and realized, under the known state and circumstances of the Apostolic Age and then compared the Result with the Apostolic Precepts and Ordinances, recorded or resting on a constant Tradition, and found the coincidence perfect, they would in like manner have begun to consider calmly all the state and circumstances of their own Age and Country, each in his own Land and from these would with Christian Confidence have inferred, what under such circumstances, the same Apostles would have ordained. The Lauds would not have quarreled with the Genevan and Scottish Frames, nor the Leightons (*Senr*) and Melvills have entangled the two Nations with Covenants against the English Frame.

MS.

300. METAPHORS AND SIMILES: RELIGION AND MORALS

Similes and Metaphors judiciously used serve not only for illustration and refreshment. To inventive and thoughtful minds they are often the suggesters of actual analogies—the apparent Likeness being referred to a common Principle, *ex. gr.* the likeness between animal life and flame to the vital air present for both. But they have a third use—namely, that on many occasions they present a far more perfect, both a fuller [and yet less equivocal *crossed out*] and a more precise and accurate language than that of abstract or general words.

For instance, I suppose myself to say 'I have known many instances of men who are religious because they are good but not one of whom the person was good because he was religious, and I wonder not that it startles and offends. For first, it may be

388

understood as asserting a goodness divided and even contra-distinguished from Religion, both of which positions are false, and dangerous Falsehoods. But let me begin with explaining the identity or co-inherence of Morality and Religion, as the Transcendent containing both *in* one, and *as* one, that which our elder Divines meant by the Seed of Election in the Soul, and which St. Paul calls the Root (*Vide* the aphorism on the equivocal meaning of the term, 'Consciousness') and let it be premised that by moral and religious I mean only two different forms and states in the development or gradual unfolding of this principle into distinct existence and outward Manifesta-tion, so as to become severally the object of a distinct Con-sciousness—I may then safely speak of Morality proceeding from the Root of obedience as the Stem, with its sprays and leaves, and Religion from the summit of the Stem, as the Crown and Flower of the Plant. But this Flower with its Petals, which differ from the leaves by a more refined Sap, and a more transparent membrane, in their more harmonious arrange-ment, and in a more intimate communion with the Light, is not only the Seat of its especial Beauty and Fragrancy, but the Seat and Organ of its reproductive Powers, and giving birth to new growths, both Stem and Flower. To make the Image adequate and to give it a full spiritual propriety, we have only to conceive this process as proceeding in a succession of Acts in the same Individual, instead of its being carried on, as in the vegetable Creation,·in a succession of Individuals. (For we may say with the old Schoolmen, to whom the cause of Truth and reformed Religion is under far greater obligations than the shallow and contemptuous Spirit of the Philosophy in fashion will allow itself to suspect, each immortal Soul is at once an Individual and a Species: or rather, an Individual containing its Species and co-extended and co-enduring with it and in it.) We may likewise pursue the Likeness on to another point. That as wherever the Crown or Corolla is conspicuous, the whole Plant is called a Flower, and all numerous sorts of Plants thus distinguished have this for their common or family Name, naturally and were it not for the mournful frequency of Pharisaical Hypocrisy, as universally would we express the *whole* of Goodness, the moral no less than the devotional Requisites, by the appellation, 'Religious',—as, 'He is a religious Man', or 'the Religious of all ranks and denominations'.

MS.

301. MORE MOUNTAINS OF ICE: OUR MUTUAL LIFE

Our mutual life a Stoppage in the Blood—an eddy in the Ocean of pure Activity, from concourse of Currents—Pyramids—Alps, and Andes, giant Pyramids the work of Fire, Fire who like a generous Victor raises Monuments over the Conquered, Tombstones of a World destroyed—yet these, even these, float toward the great Equator, like Mountains of Ice, melting as they float.

Life knows only its product, and beholds itself only as far as it is visible in its offspring. Yea, the Ground and Cause of All comprehends itself only because the Logos in its co-eternal offspring, its Product, is at the same time its adequate Idea. No Word, no God.

MS.

302. SOME DOUBTS ABOUT DUTY

Yes, my dear Mrs. W.

That is indeed the one great Paramount, without whose countenance nothing dare be even held indifferent—*Duty*, the Voice of God to all, the Presence of God in each, more than Human, and yet the very Essence of Humanity. Let us do our Duty: all else of mortal Life is but a Dream. But then what is Duty? What ought we to mean by the word? Is it but a general term, comprizing an aggregate of particular acts defined and described beforehand? The Name of a Dictionary or Catalogue, in which the Things to be done or not done are to [be] looked out for, with the ways and means of doing each? Is it a magic Scroll, which read forwards dictates one [long series *crossed out*] linked chain of Self-sacrifice?

MS.

303. THE EARTH IS THE LORD'S

Thomas Adam, in *Private Thoughts on Religion*, writes: The world slides into our hearts by the avenues of sense, in cases we think little of. There may be danger in giving ourselves up fully to a warm sunshine, or the pleasures of a beautiful landscape.

Coleridge comments: To certain characters this is true, but unfortunately those are most likely to act upon it to whom it is not true—those, to whom a quiet Subjacence to sunshine and natural beauty would be often medicinal. S. T. C.

And again in the same work Adam says: What is it to me whether the Americans are in a state of rebellion or not? Why do I not advert more to the rebellion of my own heart and will against God?

Coleridge comments: Have we then no duties to mankind? Or is it the Monk or Hermit only that performs them? Did not Christ weep over Jerusalem, even as over Lazarus? He wept twice, once in justification of public, and once of private affections. I can easily conceive that such a reflection may arise virtuously from the sense of unchristian excess and of worldly Bustle in the Heart—and may act medicinally on the reflector—but there is danger in propounding such reflections as general Truths, in præscribing my medicine for every man's food. S. T. C.

MS.

304. AN 'ENCYCLOPAEDIA BIBLICA' PROPOSED

Encyclopaedia Biblica—to be published in monthly Numbers, each containing 12 Sheets Quarto=96 Pages, with maps and plates chiefly illustrative and explanatory of Plants, animals, costume, Architecture &c.

CONTENTS

1. The sacred Scriptures in a fair large Type in three Columns, i.e. first the original Text, the Hebrew from Buxtorf's Edition with the latest universally admitted Corrections, the Greek of the Apocrypha from Grabe, of the N.T. from Griesbach: the second, the common authorized Version: the third, a new Version, in which no alteration is made not rendered necessary by errors in the sense of the original, and all words, phrases, and collocation of words and phrases not found in the Church Bible are carefully avoided.

2. The various Readings, the variations of [the] Septuagint from the Hebrew Text, and of the present from the elder English Versions, with the most plausible conjectural emendations.

3. An elaborate Commentary, philo-chrono-phyto-zoo-geo-etho-theological, historical and geographical—and the Interpretations that have at any rate obtained currency chronologically arranged from the Fathers to the School-men, from the School-men to the Reformers and their learned Opponents of the Roman Church, and then the systematic Divines to the Latitudinarian, even to the present Day, including the comments of Eichhorn, Paulus, &c.—and of the English Unitarians, accurately stated, and the Tenets and Interpretations common to the Reformed Protestant Churches explained and defended.

4. Original comments by the Editor, theological and critical.

5. The Texts best fitted for Sermons, with numerous Skeletons of Sermons illustrating the manner in which the Text may

be aptly divided, and the most instructive and affecting deductions be naturally drawn.

MS.

305. SERMONS NOT TO BE READ

As many notes, memoranda, cues of connection and transition, as the Preacher may find expedient or serviceable to him. But to read *in* a MSS Book, as our Clergy now do, is not to *preach* at all. Preach *out of* a Book if you must, but do not read *in* it—or even *from* it. A read Sermon of 20 minutes will seem longer to the Hearers than a free Discourse of an Hour. S. T. C.

MS.

306. CHAOS AND CREATION

... And the capacious and capable *Ether* was the work of God the Spirit, as the Spirit singly. It was the Breath of God breathed on the closed Eye-lids of the Darkness, the Brooding and Hush that smoothing the convulsive Death-throe into the smooth Sleep made Death and the Darkness parturient at the voice of the heavenly Lucina.

MS.

307. ETHICS AND 'SENSIBILITY'

If Prudence, though practically inseparable from Morality, is not to be confounded with the Moral Principle; still less may Sensibility, i.e. a constitutional quickness of Sympathy with Pain and Pleasure, and a keen sense of the gratifications that accompany social intercourse, mutual endearments, and reciprocal preferences, be mistaken, or deemed a Substitute for it. Sensibility is not sure pledge even of a GOOD HEART, though among the most common meanings of that many-meaning and too commonly misapplied expression.

393

So far from being either Morality, or one with the Moral Principle, it ought not even be placed in the same rank with Prudence. For Prudence is at least an offspring of the Understanding; but Sensibility (the Sensibility, I mean, here spoken of), is for the greater part a quality of the nerves, and a result of individual bodily temperament.

Prudence is an *active* Principle, and implies a sacrifice of Self, though only to the same Self *projected*, as it were, to a distance. But the very term Sensibility, marks its *passive* nature; and in its mere self, apart from Choice and Reflection, it proves little more than the coincidence or contagion of pleasurable or painful Sensations in different persons.

Alas! how many are there in this over-stimulated age, in which the occurrence of excessive and unhealthy sensitiveness is so frequent, as even to have reversed the current meaning of the word, *nervous*,—how many are there whose sensibility prompts them to remove those evils alone, which by hideous spectacle or clamorous outcry are present to their senses and disturb their selfish enjoyments. Provided the dunghill is not before their parlour window, they are well contented to know that it exists, and perhaps as the hotbed on which their own luxuries are reared. Sensibility is not necessarily Benevolence. Nay, by rendering us tremblingly alive to trifling misfortunes, it frequently prevents it, and induces an effeminate Selfishness instead,

—pampering the coward heart
With feelings all too delicate for use.

Sweet are the Tears, that from a Howard's eye
Drop on the cheek of one, he lifts from earth:
And He, who works me good with unmoved face,
Does it but half. He chills me, while he aids,
My Benefactor, not my Brother Man.
But even this, this *cold* beneficence,
Seems Worth, seems Manhood, when there rise before me

The sluggard Pity's vision-weaving Tribe,
Who sigh for Wretchedness yet shun the Wretched,
Nursing in some delicious Solitude
Their slothful Loves and dainty Sympathies.

> Sibylline Leaves, p. 180.

Lastly, where Virtue is, Sensibility is the ornament and becoming Attire of Virtue. On certain occasions it may almost be said to *become* Virtue. But Sensibility and all the amiable Qualities may likewise become, and too often *have* become, the pandars of Vice and the instruments of Seduction.

So must it needs be with all qualities that have their rise only in *parts* and *fragments* of our nature. A man of warm passions may sacrifice half his estate to rescue a friend from Prison: for he is naturally sympathetic, and the more social *part* of his nature happened to be uppermost. The same man shall afterwards exhibit the same disregard of money in an attempt to seduce that friend's Wife or Daughter.

All the evil achieved by Hobbes and the whole School of Materialists will appear inconsiderable if it be compared with the mischief effected and occasioned by the sentimental Philosophy of STERNE, and his numerous Imitators. The vilest appetites and the most remorseless inconstancy towards their objects, acquired the titles of *the Heart, the irresistible Feelings, the too tender Sensibility*: and if the Frosts of Prudence, the icy chains of Human Law thawed and vanished at the genial warmth of Human *Nature*, who *could help it*? It was an amiable Weakness!

> *Aids to Reflection.*

308. THE MAN MAKES THE MOTIVE

He need only reflect on his own experience to be convinced, that the Man makes the *motive*, and not the motive the Man. What is a strong motive to one man, is no motive at all to another. If, then, the man determines the motive, what determines the Man—to a good and worthy act, we will say, or a virtuous Course of Conduct? The intelligent Will, or the self-determining Power? True, *in part* it is; and therefore the Will is pre-eminently the *spiritual* Constituent in our Being. But will any reflecting man admit, that his own Will is the only and sufficient determinant of all he *is*, and all he does? Is nothing to be attributed to the harmony of the system to which he belongs, and to the pre-established Fitness of the Objects and Agents, known and unknown, that surround him, as acting *on* the will, though, doubtless, *with* it likewise? a process, which the co-instantaneous yet reciprocal action of the Air and the vital Energy of the Lungs in Breathing may help to render intelligible.

Aids to Reflection.

309. STOIC AND CHRISTIAN COMPARED

Of the sects of ancient philosophy the Stoic has been deemed the nearest to Christianity. Yet even to this Christianity is fundamentally opposite. For the Stoic attaches the highest honour (or rather, attaches honour *solely*) to the person that acts virtuously in spite of his feelings, or who has raised himself above the conflict by their extinction; while Christianity instructs us to place small reliance on a Virtue that does not *begin* by bringing the Feelings to a conformity with the Commands of the Conscience. Its especial aim, its characteristic operation, is to moralize the affections. The Feelings, that oppose a right act, must be wrong Feelings. The *act*, indeed, whatever the Agent's *feelings* might be, Christianity would command: and under certain circumstances would both command and commend it—commend it, as a healthful symptom in a sick Patient; and command it, as one of the ways and means of changing the Feelings, or displacing them by calling up the opposite.

Aids to Reflection.

310. THEOLOGY: MORALS

Too soon did the Doctors of the Church forget that the *Heart*, the *Moral* Nature, was the Beginning and the End; and that Truth, Knowledge, and Insight were comprehended in its expansion. This was the true and first apostasy—when in Council and Synod the divine Humanities of the Gospel gave way to speculative Systems, and Religion became a Science of Shadows under the name of Theology, or at best a bare Skeleton of Truth, without life or interest, alike inaccessible and unintelligible to the majority of Christians. For these therefore there remained only rites and ceremonies and spectacles, shows and semblances. Thus among the learned the substance of things hoped for (Heb. xi. 1.) passed off into *Notions*; and for the Unlearned the surfaces of Things became Substance. The Christian world was for centuries divided into the Many, that did not think at all, and the Few who did nothing but *think*—both alike *unreflecting*, the one from defect of the *Act*, the other from the absence of an *Object*.

Aids to Reflection.

311. IRRELIGIOUS FANATICISM

Young, beautiful was she; her parents' joy,
And the sole prop of their declining age.
And happy was she,—and perhaps had been
For ever happy,—but in evil hour,
Her lover took her to the theatre;—
Thence date her sorrow and her misery.
The Age: A Poem in Eight Books, Anon.

Coleridge comments: Not in the fictions of poetry but in the records of our criminal courts may we find similar results and consequences not less tragic from evening attendance on the Conventicle. Many a poor wretch has dated her fall, from the evil hour, Her lover took her to the Methodist Barn, or half-lit

397

Chapel.—But neither Theatre nor Conventicle can be wisely considered as the *cause* of the depravity, tho' both may be accessaries, and the latter more influentially, perhaps, than the former. For religious (more accurately, irreligious) Fanaticism is a species of Concupiscence—alike in its source, in its manifestations and in its products sensual.

MS.

312. FAITH AND BELIEF

'*Philosophy and Religion*' p. 5. Here we have strikingly exemplified the ill-effects of an ambiguous (i.e. double meaning) word even on highest minds. The whole Dispute between Schelling and Eschenmeyer arises out of this—that what Esch[enmeyer] asserts of *Faith* (the fëalty of the partial faculty even of Reason itself as merely speculative to the *focal* Energy—i.e. Reason+Will+Understanding=Spirit) Schelling understands of *Belief*, i.e. the substitution of the Will+Imagination+Sensibility for the Reason.

MS. note on Schelling.

313. DISINTERESTEDNESS ESSENTIAL

He, who begins by loving Christianity better than Truth, will proceed by loving his own Sect or Church better than Christianity, and end in loving himself better than all.

Aids to Reflection.

314. TOLERANCE?

We all know, that Lovers are apt to take offence and wrangle on occasions that perhaps are but trifles, and which assuredly would appear such to those who regard Love itself as Folly. These Quarrels may, indeed, be no proof of Wisdom; but still, in the imperfect state of our Nature the entire absence of the same, and this too on far more serious provocations, would excite a strong suspicion of a comparative indifference in the Parties who can love so coolly where they profess to love so well. I shall believe our present religious Tolerancy to proceed from the abundance of our charity and good sense, when I see proofs that we are equally cool and forbearing as Litigants and political Partizans.

Aids to Reflection.

315. BELIEF

Have you children, or have you lived among children, and do you not know, that in all things, in food, in medicine, in all their doings and abstainings they must believe in order to acquire a reason for their belief? But so it is with religious truths for all men. These we must all learn as children. The ground of the prevailing error on this point is the ignorance, that in spiritual concernments to believe and to understand are not diverse things, but the same thing in different periods of its growth. Belief is the seed, received into the will, of which the Understanding or Knowledge is the Flower, and the thing believed is the fruit. Unless ye believe (saith the Prophet) ye cannot understand: and unless ye be humble as children, ye not only *will* not, but ye *cannot* believe. Of such therefore is the Kingdom of Heaven. Yea, blessed is the calamity that makes us humble: though so repugnant thereto is our nature, in our present state, that after a while, it is to be feared, a second and sharper calamity would be wanted to cure us of our pride in having become so humble.

Aids to Reflection.

316. THE BIBLE

It is worthy of especial observation, that the Scriptures are distinguished from all other writings pretending to inspiration, by

the strong and frequent recommendations of knowledge, and
a spirit of inquiry. Without reflection, it is evident that neither
the one can be acquired not the other exercised.

Aids to Reflection.

317. 'THE RIGHT AND THE SUPERSTITIOUS USE OF THE SCRIPTURES DISTINGUISHED'

Curse ye Meroz, said the angel of the Lord; curse ye bitterly the
inhabitants thereof—sang Deborah. Was it that she called to mind
any personal wrongs—rapine or insult—that she or the house
of Lapidoth had received from Jabin or Sisera? No; she had
dwelt under her palm tree in the depth of the mountain. But
she was a *mother in Israel*; and with a mother's heart, and with
the vehemency of a mother's and a patriot's love, she had shot
the light of love from her eyes, and poured the blessings of love
from her lips, on the people that had *jeoparded their lives unto the*
death against the oppressors; and the bitterness, awakened and
borne aloft by the same love, she precipitated in curses on the
selfish and coward recreants who *came not to the help of the Lord,*
to the help of the Lord, against the mighty.

As long as I have the image of Deborah before my eyes, and
while I throw myself back into the age, country, circumstances,
of this Hebrew Bonduca in the not yet tamed chaos of the
spiritual creation;—as long as I contemplate the impassioned,
high-souled, heroic woman in all the prominence and individuality of will and character,—I feel as if I were among the first
ferments of the great affections—the pro-plastic waves of the
microcosmic chaos, swelling up against—and yet towards—
the outspread wings of the Dove that lies brooding on the
troubled waters. So long all is well,—all replete with instruction and example. In the fierce and inordinate I am made to
know and be grateful for the clearer and purer radiance which
shines on a Christian's paths, neither blunted by the preparatory

veil, nor crimsoned in its struggle through the all-enwrapping mist of the world's ignorance: whilst in the self-oblivion of these heroes of the Old Testament, their elevation above all low and individual interests,—above all, in the entire and vehement devotion of their total being to the service of their divine Master, I find a lesson of humility, a ground of humiliation, and a shaming, yet rousing, example of faith and fealty.

But let me once be persuaded that all these heart-awakening utterances of human hearts—of men of like faculties and passions with myself, mourning, rejoicing, suffering, triumphing—are but as a *Divina Commedia* of a superhuman—O bear with me, if I say—Ventriloquist;—that the royal Harper, to whom I have so often submitted myself as a *many-stringed instrument* for his fire-tipt fingers to traverse, while every several nerve of emotion, passion, thought, that thrids the flesh-and-blood of our common humanity, responded to the touch, that this *sweet Psalmist of Israel* was himself as mere an instrument as his harp, an *automaton* poet, mourner, and supplicant;—all is gone,—all sympathy, at least, and all example. I listen in awe and fear, but likewise in perplexity and confusion of spirit. . . .

Does not the universally admitted canon—that each part of Scripture must be interpreted by the spirit of the whole—lead to the same practical conclusion as that for which I am now contending;—namely, that it is the spirit of the Bible, and not the detached words and sentences, that is infallible and absolute? —Practical, I say, and spiritual too;—and what knowledge not practical or spiritual are we entitled to seek in our Bibles? Is the grace of God so confined,—are the evidences of the present and actuating Spirit so dim and doubtful,—that to be assured of the same we must first take for granted that all the life and co-agency of our humanity is miraculously suspended?

Whatever is spiritual, is *eo nomine* supernatural; but must it be always and of necessity miraculous? Miracles could open the eyes of the body; and he that was born blind beheld his

Redeemer. But miracles, even those of the Redeemer himself, could not open the eyes of the self-blinded, of the Sadducean sensualist or the self-righteous Pharisee;—while to have said, *I saw thee under the fig tree*, sufficed to make a Nathanael believe. . . .

. . . no man, I say, can recognize his own inward experiences in such Writings, and not find an objectiveness, a confirming and assuring outwardness, and all the main characters of reality, reflected therefrom on the spirit, working in himself and in his own thoughts, emotions, and aspirations—warring against sin, and the motions of sin. The unsubstantial, insulated Self passes away as a stream; but these are the shadows and reflections of the Rock of Ages, and of the Tree of Life that starts forth from its side.

On the other hand, as much of reality, as much of objective truth, as the Scriptures communicate to the subjective experiences of the Believer, so much of present life, of living and effective import, do these experiences give to the letter of these Scriptures. In the one *the Spirit itself beareth witness with our spirit*, that we have received the *spirit of adoption*; in the other our spirit bears witness to the power of the Word, that it is indeed the Spirit that proceedeth from God. If in the holy men thus actuated all imperfection of knowledge, all participation in the mistakes and limits of their several ages had been excluded, how could these Writings be or become the history and example, the echo and more lustrous image of the work and warfare of the sanctifying Principle in us?

Confessions of an Inquiring Spirit.

318. AN ALLEGORY

A beautiful Allegory of Persian Wisdom—its analogy to Prometheus—to Satan or Lucifer &c.

Anahid, the Egyptian Nëith, the Greek Athenè=Logos, Verstand. Harut and Murat, who obtained permission to descend from Heaven and become incarnate as Men, in order to try the sensual nature, and the possibility of its subordination to the Spiritual— [But they became sensually enamoured of *crossed out*] bringing with them the holy Word (Idea, Λόγος πρωτογένης) by which they descended and were enabled to re-ascend. But they became sensually enamoured of Anahid, who gave them hopes of yielding herself to their embraces, on condition of their communicating the Holy Word. Instead of trying they [were] *tempted*, and they gave the Word to Anahid—which instantly was lost to them, forgotten—and in the same instant, Anahid soared to the morning Star (Phosphor) and with her harp strung with sunbeams, plays to the Spheres, the Goddess of Love and Order. H[arut] and M[urat]=Reason and Will.

MS.

319. TASTE IN RELIGION

But when Count Zinzendorf and the founders of his Moravian Church had stript away the beautiful imaginative garment, they found it expedient to provide fig-leaves for naked nature;
Southey, *The Life of Wesley*, I. 143.

Coleridge comments: Metaphors are tricksy companions—Will o' the Wisps that often lead a man to say what he never meant; or call them fire-flies, that (on all momentous subjects) should be examined by the stronger light of the lamp of reflection, before they are let loose to ornament the twilight. Had the question been put, 'Is the exclusive love, which a man and woman of pure mind and inward dignity feel toward each other, and consecrate by a vow, only a gauze veil with which their imaginations clothe their lust to make it look charming?' who would return a more indignant No! than Robert Southey? who would turn away with more impatience from the person who had dared insult him by proposing the question?

P.S. These bewilderments of the first Moravians suggested to me, what I still hope to execute, an essay on the nature and importance of Taste (φιλοκαλία) in religion.—S. T. C.

320. TWO KINDS OF MYSTICS: BEHMEN AND FÉNELON

'*Antinous.*—What do you call Mysticism? and do you use the word in a good or in a bad sense?'

'*Nous.*—In the latter only: as far, at least, as we are now concerned with it. When a Man refers to *inward feelings* and *experiences*, of which Mankind at large are not conscious, as evidences of the truth of any opinion—such a Man I call a MYSTIC: and the grounding of any theory or belief on accidents and anomalies of individual sensations or fancies, and the use of peculiar terms invented or perverted from their ordinary significations, for the purpose of expressing these *idiosyncracies*, and pretended facts of interior consciousness, I name MYSTICISM. Where the error consists simply in the Mystic's attaching to these anomalies of his individual temperament the character of *Reality*, and in receiving them as permanent Truths, having a subsistence in the Divine Mind, though revealed to himself alone; but entertains this persuasion without demanding or expecting the same faith in his neighbours—I should regard it as a species of ENTHUSIASM, always indeed to be deprecated but yet capable of co-existing with many excellent qualities both of Head and Heart. But when the Mystic by ambition or still meaner passions, or (as sometimes is the case) by an uneasy and self-doubting state of mind that seeks confirmation in outward sympathy, is led to impose his faith, as a duty, on mankind generally: and when with such views he asserts, that the same experiences would be vouchsafed, the same truths revealed, to *every man* but for his secret wickedness and unholy will—such a Mystic is a FANATIC, and in certain states of the public mind a dangerous Member of Society. And most so in those ages and countries in which Fanatics of elder standing are allowed to persecute the fresh competitor. For under these predicaments, Mysticism, though originating in the singularities of an individual Nature, and therefore essentially anomalous, is nevertheless highly *contagious*. It is apt to collect a swarm and cluster *circum fana*, around the new *Fane*: and therefore merits the name of FANATICISM, or as the Germans say, Schwärmerey, i.e. *Swarm-making.*'

We will return to the harmless species—the enthusiastic Mystics: a species that may again be subdivided into two ranks. And it will not be other than germane to the subject, if I endeavour to describe them in a sort of allegory, or parable. Let us imagine a poor Pilgrim benighted in a wilderness or desart, and pursuing his way in the starless dark with a lanthorn in his hand. Chance or his happy genius leads him to an Oasis or natural Garden, such as in the creations of my youthful fancy I supposed Enos the Child of Cain to have found. And Here, hungry and thirsty, the way-wearied Man rests at a fountain; and the Taper of his Lanthorn throws its Light on an overshadowing Tree, a Boss of snow-white Blossoms, through which the green and growing Fruits peeped, and the ripe golden Fruitage glowed. Deep, vivid, and faithful are the impressions, which the lovely Imagery comprised within the scanty Circle of Light, makes and leaves on his Memory! But scarcely has he eaten of the fruits and drank of the fountain, ere scared by the roar and howl from the desart he hurries forward: and as he passes with hasty steps through grove and glade, shadows and imperfect beholdings and vivid fragments of things distinctly seen blend with the past and present shapings of his Brain. Fancy modifies Sight. His Dreams transfer their forms to real Objects; and these lend a substance and an *outness* to his Dreams. Apparitions greet him; and when at a distance from this enchanted land, and on a different track, the Dawn of Day discloses to him a Caravan, a troop of his fellow-men, his memory, which is itself half fancy, is interpolated afresh by every attempt to recall, connect, and *piece out* his recollections. His narration is received as a Madman's Tale. He shrinks from the rude Laugh and contemptuous Sneer, and retires into himself. Yet the craving for Sympathy, strong in proportion to the intensity of his Convictions, impels him to unbosom himself to abstract Auditors; and the poor Quietist becomes a Penman, and, all too poorly stocked for the Writer's trade, he borrows his phrases and figures from the only Writings to which he has had access, the sacred Books of his Religion. And thus I shadow out the enthusiastic Mystic of the first sort; at the head of which stands the illuminated Teutonic Thelosopher and Shoemaker, honest Jacob Behmen, born near Gorlitz, in Upper Lusatia, in the 17th of our Elizabeth's Reign, and who died in the 22d of her Successor's.

To delineate a Mystic of the second and higher order, we need only endow our Pilgrim with equal gifts of Nature, but these developed and displayed by all the aids and arts of Education and favorable Fortune. He is on his way to the Mecca of his ancestral and national Faith, with a well-guarded and numerous Procession of Merchants and Fellow-pilgrims, on the established Track. At the close of Day the Caravan has halted: the full moon rises on the Desart: and he strays forth alone, out of sight, but to no unsafe distance; and Chance leads *him* too to the same Oasis or Islet of Verdure on the Sea of Sand. He wanders at leisure in its maze of Beauty and Sweetness, and thrids his way through the odorous and flowering Thickets into open 'Spots of Greenery', and discovers statues and memorial characters, grottos, and refreshing Caves. But the Moonshine, the imaginative Poesy of Nature, spreads its soft shadowy charm over all, conceals distances, and magnifies heights, and modifies relations; and fills up vacuities with its own whiteness, counterfeiting substance; and where the dense shadows lie, makes solidity imitate Hollowness; and gives to all objects a tender visionary hue and softening. Interpret the

406

Moonlight and the Shadows as the peculiar genius and sensibility of the Individual's own Spirit: and here you have the other sort: a Mystic, an Enthusiast of a nobler Breed—a FÉNELON. But the residentiary, or the frequent visitor of the favored spot, who has scanned its beauties by steady Day-light, and mastered its true proportions and lineaments, he will discover that both Pilgrims have indeed been there! He will know, that the delightful Dream, which the latter tells, is a Dream of Truth; and that even in the bewildered Tale of the former there is Truth mingled with the Dream.

Aids to Reflection.

321. CONTROVERSY

And finally, and above all, let it be remembered by both parties, and indeed by controversialists on all subjects, that every speculative error which boasts a multitude of advocates, has its *golden* as well as its dark side; that there is always some truth connected with it, the exclusive attention to which has misled the understanding, some moral beauty which has given it charms for the heart. Let it be remembered that no assailant of an error can reasonably hope to be listened to by its advocates, who has not proved to them that he has seen the disputed subject in the same point of view, and is capable of contemplating it with the same feelings as themselves; (for why should we abandon a cause at the persuasions of one who is ignorant of the reasons which have attached us to it?) Let it be remembered, that to write, however ably, merely to convince those who are already convinced, displays but the courage of a boaster; and in any subject to rail against the evil before we have inquired for the good, and to exasperate the passions of those who think with us, by caricaturing the opinions and blackening the motives of our antagonists, is to make the understanding the pander of the passions; and even though we should have defended the right cause, to gain for ourselves ultimately from the good and the wise no other praise than the supreme Judge awarded to the friends of Job for their partial and uncharitable defence of his justice: 'My wrath is kindled against you, for ye have not spoken of me *rightfully*.'

Friend.

322. THE NEED OF TOLERATING INTOLERANCE

From this hint concerning Toleration, we may pass by an easy transition to the, perhaps, still more interesting subject of Tolerance. And here I fully coincide with Frederic H. Jacobi, that the only true spirit of Tolerance consists in our conscientious toleration of each other's intolerance. Whatever pretends to be more than this, is either the unthinking cant of fashion, or the soul-palsying narcotic of moral and religious indifference. All of us without exception, in the same mode though not in the same degree, are necessarily subjected to the risk of mistaking positive opinions for certainty and clear insight. From this yoke we cannot free ourselves, but by ceasing to be men; and this too not in order to transcend, but to sink below, our human nature. For if in one point of view it be the mulct of our fall, and of the corruption of our will; it is equally true, that contemplated from another point, it is the price and consequence of our progressiveness. To him who is compelled to pace to and fro within the high walls and in the narrow court-yard of a prison, all objects may appear clear and distinct. It is the traveller journeying onward, full of heart and hope, with an ever-varying horizon, on the boundless plain, that is liable to mistake clouds for mountains, and the mirage of drouth for an expanse of refreshing waters.

But notwithstanding this deep conviction of our general fallibility, and the most vivid recollection of my own, I dare avow with the German philosopher, that as far as opinions, and not motives, principles, and not men, are concerned; I neither am *tolerant*, nor wish to be regarded as such. According to my judgment, it is mere ostentation, or a poor trick that hypocrisy plays with the cards of nonsense, when a man makes protestation of being perfectly tolerant in respect of all principles, opinions, and persuasions, those alone excepted which render the holders intolerant. For he either means to say by this, that he is utterly indifferent towards all truth, and finds nothing so insufferable as the persuasion of there being any such mighty value or importance attached to the possession of the truth as should give a marked preference to any one conviction above any other; or else he means nothing, and amuses himself with articulating the pulses of the air instead of inhaling it in the more healthful and profitable exercise of yawning. That which doth not *withstand*, hath *itself* no standing place. To *fill* a station is to exclude or repel others,—and this is not less the definition of moral, than of material, *solidity*. We *live* by continued acts of defence, that involve a sort of offensive warfare. But a man's principles, on which he grounds his Hope and his Faith, are the life of his life. We live by Faith, says the philosophic Apostle; and faith without principles is but a flattering phrase for wilful positiveness, or fanatical bodily sensation. Well, and of good right therefore, do we maintain with more zeal, than we should defend body or estate, a deep and inward conviction, which is as the moon to us; and like the moon with all its massy shadows and deceptive gleams, it yet lights us on our way, poor travellers as we are, and benighted pilgrims. With all its spots and changes and temporary eclipses, with all its vain halos and bedimming vapours, it yet reflects the light that is to rise on us, which even now is *rising*, though intercepted from our immediate view by the mountains that enclose and frown over the vale of our mortal life.

This again is the mystery and the dignity of our human nature, that we cannot give up our reason, without giving up at the same time our individual personality. For that must appear to each man to be *his* reason which produces in him the highest sense of certainty; and yet it is *not* reason, except so far as it is of universal validity and obligatory on all mankind. There is a one heart for the whole mighty mass of Humanity, and every pulse in each particular vessel strives to beat in concert with it. He who asserts that truth is of no importance except in the signification of sincerity, confounds sense with madness, and the word of God with a dream. If the power of reasoning be the gift of the supreme Reason, that we be sedulous, yea, and *militant* in the endeavour to reason aright, is his implied command. But what is of permanent and essential interest to one man must needs be so to all, in proportion to the means and opportunities of each. Woe to him by whom these are neglected, and double woe to him by whom they are withholden; for he robs at once himself and his neighbour. That man's soul is not dear to himself, to whom the souls of his brethren are not dear. As far as they can be influenced by him, they are parts and properties of his own soul, their faith his faith, their errors his burthen, their righteousness and bliss his righteousness and his reward—and of their guilt and misery his own will be the echo. As much as I love my fellow-men, so much and no more will I be *intolerant* of their heresies and unbelief—and I will honor and hold forth the right hand of fellowship to every individual who is equally intolerant of that which he conceives such in me.—We will both exclaim—'I know not what antidotes among the complex views, impulses and circumstances, that form your moral being, God's gracious providence may have vouchsafed to you against the serpent fang of this error,—but it is a viper, and its poison deadly, although through higher influences some men may take the reptile to their bosom, and remain unstung'.

Friend.

410

323. A NATIONAL CHURCH

What are all these Mechanics Institutions, Societies for spreading Knowledge, &c. but so many confessions of the necessity and of the absence of a National Church?

MS.

324. MORAL LAW: FREEDOM AND OBEDIENCE

Who then shall dare prescribe a law of moral action for any rational being, which does not flow immediately from that Reason, which is the fountain of all morality? Or how without breach of conscience can we limit or coerce the powers of a free agent, except by coincidence with that law in his own mind, which is at once the cause, the condition, and the measure of his free agency? Man must be *free*; or to what purpose was he made a spirit of reason, and not a machine of instinct? Man must *obey;* or wherefore has he a conscience? The powers, which create this difficulty, contain its solution likewise: for *their* service is perfect freedom. And whatever law or system of law compels any other service, disennobles our nature, leagues itself with the animal against the godlike, kills in us the very principle of joyous well-doing, and fights against humanity.

Friend.

325. SELF-DECEPTION

The most common effect of this mock evangelical spirit, especially with young women, is self-inflation and busy-bodyism.

Table Talk.

326. THE PURE WILL THE END

As long as the spirit of philosophy reigns in the learned and highest class, and that of religion in all classes, a tendency to

411

blend and unite will be found in all objects of pursuit, and the whole discipline of mind and manners will be calculated in relation to the worth of the agents. With the prevalence of sophistry, when the pure will (if indeed the existence of a will be admitted in any other sense than as the temporary main current in the wide gust-eddying stream of our desires and aversions) is ranked among the *means* to an alien end, instead of being itself the one absolute end, in the participation of which all other things are worthy to be called good, commences the epoch of division and separation. Things are rapidly improved, persons as rapidly deteriorated; and for an indefinite period the powers of the aggregate increase, as the strength of the individual declines. Still, however, sciences may be estranged from philosophy, the practical from the speculative, and *one* of the two at least may remain. Music may be divided from poetry, and *both* may continue to exist, though with diminished influence. But religion and morals cannot be disjoined without the destruction of both: and that this does not take place to the full extent, we owe to the frequency with which both take shelter in the heart, and that men are always better or worse than the maxims which they adopt or concede.

Friend.

327. RELIGION MUST BE POSITIVE

The error of all sects, whether in religion or in philosophy, is commonly to be found, not in the positive of their characteristic tenets, but in the negative—*nil, nisi hoc*; not in the positions, but in the imposition. S. T. C.

MS.

REFERENCES

MANUSCRIPTS

Egerton and other manuscripts in the British Museum are referred to by folio number, the watermark being given where there is one.

Notebooks are referred to by numbers given them after Coleridge's death. Where an entry is dated I give the date; dating of other entries must await my edition of the notebooks now in preparation.

Marginalia, notebooks, and other manuscripts when not otherwise located, are in the possession of the Coleridge family.

I have not made any exhaustive search to see whether items I quote from manuscripts are printed elsewhere. A few of them may be; most of them are unpublished. And I have gone to the originals in each case. I have made minor changes in punctuation for the ease of the eye.

EDITIONS

Aids to Reflection, 1825.

Biographia Literaria, ed. Shawcross, 1907.

Essays on His Own Times, 1850.

Friend, 1818. With some additions from copies annotated by Coleridge, and some slight modifications in pointing and capitals.

Letters of S. T. Coleridge, ed. E. H. Coleridge, 1895.

The Philosophical Lectures of Samuel Taylor Coleridge, edited by Kathleen Coburn, 1949.

The Statesman's Manual, 1816.

Table Talk, 1835.

Unpublished Letters of S. T. Coleridge, ed. E. L. Griggs, 1932.

The Watchman, 1796.

NOTES

1. *Friend*, I. 191–2. The lines from Donne are from the 'Ecclogue 1613', *variatim*, the most important change being in the second line. Donne wrote, 'More of heaven's glory than a worldling can'. The lines do not appear in the 1809–10 edition of the *Friend*, and Coleridge's notes on Lamb's copy of Donne are dated 1811. See Coleridge's *Miscellaneous Criticism*, ed. T. M. Raysor, 131–45. See below, note 120.

   Warburton, William (1698–1779), Bp. of Gloucester, author of *The Divine Legation of Moses Demonstrated*, violent controversialist, friend and literary executor to Pope, and editor of a poor edition of Shakespeare.
2. Note on the front flyleaf of Tetens, J. N., *Philosophische Versuche über die menschliche Natur und ihre Entwickelung*, Leipzig, 1777. In the British Museum.
3. Notebook 44.
4. Notebook 17. *Cf. Anima Poetae*, 166–7, where the words between the two sets of asterisks are omitted.
5. Allsop, T., *Letters, Conversations and Recollections of S. T. Coleridge*, II. 85–6. Although I have not taken excerpts from either the two volumes of Coleridge's *Letters* edited by E. H. Coleridge, or the two volumes edited by Professor E. L. Griggs, which are recent enough to be available, I have made use of Allsop's collection, published in 1836 and now scarce. Allsop was a young man with domestic and financial problems who drew from Coleridge many interesting statements on social and other questions.
6. *Ibid.*, II. 134–7. The lines quoted are in the *Poetical Works* (1912), I. 77.
7. *Aids to Reflection*, 12–13.
8. *Ibid.*, 43–4.
9. *Philosophical Lectures*, 285; the subject under discussion was the abuse of child-labour in the cotton factories. *Cf.* items 282 and 286.

415

10. Notebook 14. *Cf. Unpublished Letters*, ed. E. L. Griggs, II. 108–9.

11. *Table Talk*, I. 109–10: May 1, 1830.

12. Notebook 17. *Cf. Anima Poetae*, 143. The memorandum begins in mid-sentence because part of a page of the notebook has been cut out.

13. MS. Egerton 2800, f. 7. Burchell, W. J., *Travels in the Interior of Southern Africa*, 2 vols. London, 1822–4, pp. 309–10.

14. *Table Talk*, I. 213–14: Sept. 28, 1830.

15. Notebook 15. The lines of verse are in the *Poetical Works* (1912), II. 1001. Coleridge was at this time waiting for a passage home, deeply discouraged because the voyage to Malta, taken to better his health of body and mind, had worsened it.

16. Note on Tetens, J. N., *op. cit.*, note 2 above.

17. *Table Talk*, II. 226: Aug. 10, 1833.

18. Notebook 50. He wrote in the same vein and phrase to Davy as early as 1804.

19. *Table Talk*, II. 2–3: Sept. 12, 1831.

20. Notebook 29.

21. Notebook 17.

22. *Table Talk*, II. 252: April 24, 1833.

23. *Ibid.*, I. 212.

24. *Friend*, I. 183–4. The lines quoted are from Milton, Sonnet 22, and Burns, 'Tam o' Shanter'.

25. Allsop, T., *Letters, Conversations and Recollections*, I. 202.

26. *Table Talk*, II. 96: Sept. 1, 1832.

27. *Ibid.*, I. 193–5: July 29, 1830. Spurzheim visited Coleridge at Highgate and after feeling the bumps of his skull opined that he lacked imagination. This gave rise to an amusing postscript in a letter to Green, MS. Egerton 2800, f. 188:

    P.S. The following is the etymological Note which (from the little less than idiocy of that same faculty of Locality, the size of which attracted the notice and excited the admiration of Professor *Spurz*heim, who consoled me therewith for the want, or evanescence, of the Organ of Ideality or Imagination) I looked and pothered after in vain when you were with me . . . (Watermark 1825).

28. *Ibid.*, I. 146: May 23, 1830.

29. *Aids to Reflection*, 72–3.

30. British Museum Add. MSS. 36, 532. See, as well as the next two, item 40. This note was taken at Coleridge's dictation, by another hand, and corrected by him.

Animal Magnetism, the nineteenth-century hypnotism, was associated chiefly with Mesmer and his disciples. It had a popular vogue discredited in many medical circles. In practice it appears to have had resemblances to modern psychiatric hypnotism; in theory it was inadequate and based on an erroneous physiology. For Coleridge on the subject, see *Philosophical Lectures*, especially pp. 104–5, 423–4.

Gymnotus electricus: the reference leads to a characteristically Coleridgian bypath. He might have read about the electric or Surinam eel (which gives off electric shocks) in many of the books of travel and natural history he read. It is interesting to note, however, that Alexander von Humboldt, whom he met in Rome in 1805 when the latter had just returned from a long South American expedition, was writing his *Versuche über die electrischen Fische* at that time. It is dated 'Rome in August, 1805', and in it von Humboldt gives a vivid description of the gymnoti and their victorious battles with wild horses. Coleridge, with the Ancient Mariner's phosphorescent water-snakes behind him, would be almost certain to discuss the subject, especially since phosphorescent fishes were to be seen off Civita Vecchia. From the casual reference here, I believe we stumble on a meeting between the Ancient Mariner and the German naturalist, between the blessed snakes and the gymnoti of Calabozo, and between all of them and a forerunner of modern psychiatry.

Gilbert. Perhaps Davies Gilbert, formerly Giddy, 1767–1839. He became President of the Royal Society in 1827 when Davy resigned on account of ill-health. His 'annals' possibly refers to the *Philosophical Transactions of the Royal Society*.

31. Note on Kluge, C. A., *Versuch einer Darstellung des Animalischen Magnetismus als Heilmittel*, Berlin, 1815.

32. *Ibid.*

33. Notebook 29.

34. *Poetical Works* (1912), I. 29.

Edwards, Bryan, *History, Civil and Commercial, of the British Colonies in the West Indies*, 2 vols., London, 1793.

Hearne, Samuel, *A Journey from Prince of Wales's Fort in Hudson's Bay, to the Northern Ocean*, London, 1795. *Cf.* Professor Lowes's use of this note in *The Road to Xanadu*, esp. pp. 127, 493.

35. *Friend*, I. 246–8. Wolff, C. F. von, *Annotations in Psychologia Rationalis*, § 24. Coleridge's annotated copy of the English edition is in the British Museum.

36. Allsop, T., *Letters, Conversations and Recollections*, I. 100.

37. Notebook 21. S. H. is Sara Hutchinson, sister of Mrs. Wordsworth, on whose account Coleridge suffered for many years the sorrows of unfulfilled love.

38. MS. Egerton 2801, f. 260. Watermark 1800.

39. Note on Webster, John, *The Displaying of Supposed Witchcraft*, London, 1677, p. 17. John Webster was a 'practitioner of physick' who in the happy temper of the time was able to denounce with vigour the unscientific credulity of men like Henry More in respect to witches, and to assert with confidence his own belief in astrology and the transmutation of metals. His *Displaying of Supposed Witchcraft* is full of medical and psychological explanations of witches and their alleged victims, a delightful book which Coleridge read with interest and respect. I believe he also knew Webster's *Metallographia*, 1661, which I can recommend to anyone who likes to see a lively mind at work. Coleridge in the *Philosophical Lectures* quotes a phrase about not being able to talk to the blind about colours and attributes it to John Penn. In my note to the passage (See *Philosophical Lectures*, p. 242 and p. 428) I say that I could not find it in Penn's *Works*. I have now found it, in John Webster, in the *Metallographia*, 1661, p. 31.

40. *Ibid.*, pp. 69–70.

41. Note on Southey, R., *Life of Wesley*, published in the edition by M. H. Fitzgerald, 1925, I. 215. Not having seen the original, I quote from this edition.

42. *Friend*, I. 177–8 fn.

43. *Ibid.*, I. 178.

44. Note on [Boyer, Jean de], Marquis d'Argens, *Kabbalistische Briefe*, Danzig, 1773. In the British Museum. *Cf.* another reference to the same difficulty: 'So the more anxiously and eagerly we strive to recollect a name, the less chance we have to remember it. The Nisus, or sensation of effort, stands between us and the thing sought for, consumes the attention, and, as long as it continues, eclipses its own object with its shadow.' Letter to Mr. Curtis, 22 Sept. 1816. *Lippincott's Magazine*. XIII. 702.

45. MS. note on his own *Watchman*, 1796. In the Ashley copy, in the British Museum. Vaccine inoculation (vaccination), was discovered by Jenner in 1798. The term began to appear immediately in medical journals, and public controversy raged for some years on the subject.

   Dr. Thomas Beddoes (1760–1808), one-time professor of chemistry at Oxford, and founder of the Pneumatic Institution, 1798, at Clifton, for the treatment of tuberculosis. He was a man of original mind, and his influence in his period, e.g. on Erasmus Darwin, the Wedgwoods, Coleridge, and in his profession, is more interesting and important than has been generally recognized. He is known chiefly as having sponsored the young Humphry Davy. But his literary and linguistic achievements were considerable, his concern for public health far ahead of his time, and his views on the need of educating the poor in principles of hygiene, on reforms in education generally and on the handling of children, on the need of increased employment for women, were as sound as they were daring. It was through his introduction that Coleridge first began to write for the London newspapers.

46. MS. Egerton 2801, f. 106. Watermark 1825.

47. Notebook 21. *Cf. Anima Poetae*, 84. *The Soother of Absence* was a projected work for which several fragments are extant.

48. MS. Egerton 2800, f. 86. *Asra* is Sara Hutchinson.

49. *Ibid.*, f. 158. Written about 1825 or later. Joseph Henry Green, a young surgeon, pupil and friend of Coleridge, became his literary executor.

50. Note on Weishaupt, Adam. *Apologie des Misvergnügens und Uebels*, 1790. On the front flyleaf.

51. Notebook 18. *Cf. Anima Poetae*, 254, which misses the portmanteau word.
52. MS. Egerton 2800, ff. 43–5. Watermark 1812.
53. Notebook 47.
54. *Table Talk*, 190–1: July 27, 1830.
55. *Friend*, III. 223–5.
56. *Table Talk*, I. 215: October 5, 1830.
57. *Essays on His Own Times*, I. 24: from the *Conciones ad Populum*, 1795.
58. Allsop, T., *Letters, Conversations and Recollections*, II. 123–6.
59. *The Statesman's Manual*, 1816, 50 fn.
60. *Friend*, III. 176–8.
61. Note on Weishaupt, Adam, 72. See note 50 above.
62. Notebook 54.
63. *Ibid.*
64. *Essays on His Own Times*, III. 702–3: from the *Courier*, November 2, 1814.
65. From the *Athenaeum*, March 13, 1909: also published in *Coleridge's* Shakespearean *Criticism*, edited by T. M. Raysor. 'The New System of Education' he refers to is the 'Madras System' of Dr. Bell. The principles are Dr. Bell's, the illustrations and expansions Coleridge's.
66. A note on a flyleaf of two works bound together: Maas, D. J. G. E., *Versuch über die Einbildungskraft*, Halle and Leipzig, 1797; and [Jacobi, F. H.], *Ueber die Lehre des Spinoza in Briefen an den Herrn Moses Mendelssohn*, Breslau, 1789. It is not clear to which work the note belongs.
67. Notebook 49.
68. *Essay on His Own Times*, I. 102–5: from the *Watchman*, 1796, No. 1.
69. MS. Egerton 2800, f. 157.
70. *Ibid.*, f. 71.
71. Note on L'Estrange, R. [translator], *The Travels of Monsieur de Thevenot in the Levant*, p. 31.
72. *Table Talk*, II. 63: July 8, 1832.
73. MS. Egerton 2801, f. 145. From what appears to be notes for a lecture to medical students.
74. MS. Egerton 2801, f. 74.

75. From the *Literary Remains*, II. 365–7. Note on a *Sermon on the Prevalence of Infidelity and Enthusiasm*, by Walter Birch. *Cf.* conclusion of item 113.

76. *The Statesman's Manual*, 1816, 36–7.

77. *Essays on His Own Times*, III. 920–2: from a letter to the *Courier*, September 21, 1811.

78. *Table Talk*, II. 96–7: September 1, 1832.

79. MS. Egerton 2801, f. 127. Watermark 1822. From a fragment on 'the polar logic', apparently part of a discussion with his son Hartley Coleridge. The manuscript clearly reads *Wheatley of Oriel*, but I believe Coleridge refers to Richard Whately (1787–1863), fellow of Oriel, 1811, and later Archbisop of Dublin. Whately was on the opposite side of many questions in which Coleridge was interested. He was contemptuous of Wordsworth, Plato and the Schoolmen, and by the date of Hartley Coleridge's brief fellowship at Oriel, was beginning to be known as a sharp controversialist on philosophical, theological, economic and social questions. 'His limitations were as conspicuous as his powers.' (D.N.B.)

    Francesco Sales. St. Francis of Sales, 1567–1622, was the subject of an essay by Leigh Hunt, 'The Gentleman Saint'.

80. MS. Egerton 2801, f. 57. Watermark 1827. Impetite is a word Coleridge invented to describe emotion as active rather than passive, and as a necessary word distinct from impulse or appetite. It does not appear in the N.E.D.

81. Notebook of 1808–10. Unnumbered. *Cf.* Simpson, Percy, *Shakespearian Punctuation*, Oxford, 1911.

82. *Friend*, I. 25–6.

83. *Table Talk*, II. 94–5: August 19, 1832.

84. *Table Talk*, II. 60–1: July 7, 1832.

85. Note on a back flyleaf of Swedenborg, E., *De Equo Albo de Quo In Apocalypsi*, Cap. XIX. *et dein De Verbo et Ejus Sensu Spirituali seu Interno, ex Arcanis Cœlestibus*, London, 1758. In the British Museum.

86. Note on Heinroth, J. C. A., *Lehrbuch der Anthropologie*, Leipzig, 1822, pp. 252–3. On J. H. Green's copy, in the British Museum. The annotations are generally condemnatory, e.g.,

'§ 45 I venture to denounce as *Trash*', 'An excellent Remark, an Oasis in this sandy Wilderness'.

87. Note on Grew, Nehemiah, *Cosmologica Sacra*, London, 1701. J. H. Green's copy, in the British Museum. Coleridge's marginalia display many of these facetious logical gambits.

88. *Table Talk*, I. 206–7: September 23, 1830.

89. *Ibid.*, I. 16: January 4, 1823.

90. *Ibid.*, I. 18: January 4, 1823.

91. *Ibid.*, I. 20: January 6, 1823.

92. Notebook 29.

93. *Table Talk*, I. 202–4: September 21, 1830.

94. Notes on Solger, K. W. F., *Philosophische Gespräche*, Berlin, 1817, pp. 129–32. Solger was a close friend of Ludwig Tieck; and J. H. Green studied with him in Berlin. Coleridge is in general disagreement with him as a Nihilist, and calls him, in another note, 'a biform Philosopher with the head of a Schelling and the Tail of a Fichte'.

95. Note on Southey, R., *The Doctor*, 1834, I. 209–10. In the British Museum. The notes are adversely critical, and possibly hark back to very early contentions between Southey and Coleridge. 'Interchapter II' is entitled *Aballiboozobanganorribo* and appears to refer to metaphysics equated with tabus, black magic, and other mysterious knowledge. In a letter to Caroline Bowles, Southey says he 'composed' the word *Aballiboozobanganorribo* 'seven– or eight and thirty years ago', i.e. about 1797–8. Coleridge's reference to 'common-place Sermons' is a dig at the fact that *The Doctor*, a curious farrago of a work, is made up from Southey's common-place books.

96. MS. Egerton 2801, f. 78.

97. *Table Talk*, I. 263–4: August 24, 1831.

98. Note on Schelling, F. W. J. von, *Philosophie und Religion*, Tübingen, 1804.

99. MS. Egerton 2801, f. 101. Occam, William of, d. 1349. Raymond of Sabunde's 'grand attempt' was his *Theologia naturalis sive liber creaturarum* which appeared with varying titles in various editions in the 1480's. *Cf. Philosophical Lectures*, notes, pp. 436–40, for further material on Occam, Raymond of Sabunde, and other scholastics.

100. Note on Ficinus, M., *Platonica Theologica*, Firenze, 1525. A note on the front flyleaf suggests that Coleridge bought the book in 'Messina, 9 Octr. 1805'.

101. MS. Egerton 2801, ff. 60–1. Watermark 1818. The reference to Dr. Kenn[e]y is probably to *Principles and Practices of Pretended Reformers in Church and State*, by A. H. Kenney, London, 1819. Kenney was a vigorous controversialist.

102. *Aids to Reflection*, 244–5 fn.

103. *Aids to Reflection*, 71, 73–4, corrected from a copy annotated by Coleridge, in the British Museum.

104. *Ibid.*, 77–8.

105. *Table Talk*, I. 88: July 23, 1827.

106. *Ibid.*, 104–5: April 30, 1830.

107. Note on Heinroth, J. C. See note 86 above.

108. *Friend*, I. 304 fn.

109. *Aids to Reflection*, 196–7.

110. *Friend* (1850) Appendix B, III. 294–6. From the first number of the 1809–10 edition.

111. *Friend*, III. 162–3.

112. MS. Egerton 2801, f. 260. Watermark 1800.

113. The notes on Kant, I., *Vermischte Schriften*, Halle, 1799, Bde I–II. These differ from the notes on another (J. H. Green's) copy of the same work, in the British Museum, published by H. Nidecker in the *Revue de Littérature Comparée*, 1927 (Vol. VII).

114. MS. Egerton 2801, f. 126. Watermark 1822. From a note on the 'polar logic'.

115. Notebook 44. The discovery of electricity belongs to the same year as the *Lyrical Ballads*, 1798, and Coleridge was well-read in the scientific papers on its development.

116. Note on Hartley, D., *Observations on Man*, London, 1791, I, 81

117. Notebook 47.

118. Note on Luther, M., *Colloquia Mensalia*, London, 1652, p. 362. Printed with small differences in *Literary Remains*, IV. 50.

119. MS. Egerton 2800, f. 46. Apparently notes for a lecture. The watermark is 1810.

120. MS. Egerton 2800, f. 53. The watermark is 1796, and the hand

early. The absence of Wordsworth's name among the modern poets (and the apparent acceptance of Ossian) also suggest an early date. There is nothing in the references to German literature that he might not have written before going to Germany in 1798. *The Latin Hexameter Romance on Attila* appears to refer to *Waltharius*, an epic of more than 1400 hexameter lines, written by Ekkehart I. *c.* A.D. 900–970. It is a story of the time of Attila, and the poem in style is said to look back to Virgil and forward to the mediaeval German epic, to be rough in metre, Teutonic in its Latin, and full of life and gusto. 'Of considerable importance in the history of literature.' Wright and Sinclair, *A History of Later Latin Literature*, London, 1931, p. 175.

The inclusion of Donne is interesting, especially if this note is as early as I think it is. Coleridge's enthusiasm for Donne was unusual in his time and to one visitor to Highgate, at least, 'unaccountable'. (See Lord Hatherley's *Memoirs*.) Hazlitt did not mention Donne in his lectures on the English Poets.

121. MS. Egerton 2800, f. 51.
122. Notebook 21. The words between the asterisks are omitted in *Anima Poetae*, 5. The omission of the qualifying clauses has given rise to confusion and argument about Coleridge's views.
123. MS. Egerton 2800, ff. 66, 54–5. (The fragments are arranged out of order in the manuscript volume.) The watermark 1820, and the analysis of the development of the romantic movement is intensely interesting coming (*a*) so early (*b*) from the intellectual fountain head.

As to the *Vittoria* of Beethoven, 'or *Wellington's Victory*', first performed in Vienna in 1813, and in England, Feb. 10, 1815, it was 'a work conceived on almost as vulgar a plan as the "Battle of Prague" and containing few traces of his genius' (Grove). The orchestra was apparently filled, by the musical mechanician who suggested and organized the production, with all sorts of gadgets and noisemakers, but the piece had in Vienna and in London 'a great run'. *Cf.* items 176–8.

Gruter, Jan (1560–1627), an immensely prolific editor and compiler, published in 1608, *Delitiae C. C. Italorum Poetarum*. . . ; in 1609, *Delitiae C. Poetarum Gallorum* . . .; in 1614, *Delitiae C. Poetarum Belgicorum*. . . . Bayle's Dictionary refers, in a long article on Gruter, to his *Deliciae Poetarum Italorum, Belgicorum, Gallorum*, in 9 volumes.

124. Note on de Boyer, IV. 134. See note 44 above.

125. *Table Talk*, II. 297–9: March 15, 1834.

126. *Ibid.*, I. 205: September 22, 1830.

127. *Ibid.*, II. 263–6: September 4, 1833.

128. Notebook 41.

129. Allsop, *Letters, Conversations and Recollections*, I. 101. Charles Matthews, the comedian, admired by Coleridge.

130. Notebook 17. *Anima Poetae*, 223, reads 'craned' for the last word.

131 *Table Talk*, II. 240–1: August 18, 1833.

132. *Ibid.*, I. 127–8: May 12, 1830.

133. *Ibid.*, I. 69: June 24, 1827.

134. *Ibid.*, I. 67–8: June 24, 1827.

135. *Friend*, III. 137–151.

136. Note on Coleridge, Hartley, *Lives of Northern Worthies*, edited by Derwent Coleridge with Coleridge's marginal notes, London, Moxon, 1852, I. 341.

137. *Table Talk*, II. 87: August 11, 1832.

138. *Ibid.*, I. 177–9: June 15, 1830.

139. *Ibid.*, I. 160: My 31, 1830.

140. MS. Egerton 2801, f. 249. Watermark 1823. The story of Elizabeth Melvill (Lady Colville) and her long prayer is given in Rev. James Kirkton's *The Secret and True History of the Church of Scotland, from the Restoration to the year 1678*, edited by C. K. Sharpe, Edinburgh, 1817, p. 16 n; the specimen of her verse is given there also, quoted from *Ane Godlie Dreame*, compylit in Scotish Meter, be M. M. Gentlewoman in Culross, at the Requeist of her Freindes, Edinburgh, 1603. (The poem was printed with an appendix of 'A Verie Comfortable Song', To the tune of 'Shall I let her goe?'). Coleridge's changes in the lines are as he describes them, with some other slight ones.

ll. 5–6 (of his extract) read, in the original,
'Thocht prick of iron do prick zou wonderous soir,
As noysum lusts that seek zour saull to slay:'
and l. 13 reads,
'Zour God is trew, zour blood is to him deir,'
and l. 15:
'Quhen clouds ar past, the weather will grow cleir.'

From reading the whole of this Pilgrimess's Progress, it is quite clear that Coleridge and the lady had in common: unhappy dreams, mental conflicts and guilt feelings, a vivid use of simple words and a strong sense of the pulse of a line. Their views of the operation of divine grace are, as might be expected, somewhat at variance, but Coleridge was always able to distinguish between theology and religion.

141. Note on Bishop Hacket, *A Century of Sermons*, 1675, p. 7.

142. Allsop, *Letters, Conversations and Recollections*, I. 194–6.

143. *Table Talk*, II. 399: July 5, 1834.

144. *Ibid.*, II. 230–3: August 15, 1833.

145. Note on Johnson, Samuel, *The Works of the Late Reverend Mr. Samuel Johnson, sometime Chaplain to the Right Honourable William, Lord Russell*, London, 1710.

146. *Table Talk*, I. 284–5: May 15, 1833.

147. *Ibid.*, II. 216–18: July 4, 1833.

148. *Ibid.*, II. 274–5: November 1, 1833.

149. Notebook 54. I include several comments on Dr. Johnson (see also 120) because I suspect Coleridge of comparing (and contrasting) himself with Dr. Johnson more than has been noticed. Were the personal resemblances and the critical differences almost equally irritating? For all about Aeolian harps, including how to play them, see Grigson, Geoffrey, *The Harp of Aeolus*, London, 1947, pp. 24–46. The essay, an illuminating study of the use by Coleridge and others of the Aeolian harp image, gives particular point to Coleridge's application of it to himself in this note. *See also* item 317.

150. Notebook 17. Distorted in *Anima Poetae* by the reading 'The Pope' (p. 223). I see no justification for the emendation. Coleridge meant the poet Pope. In the *Biographia Literaria*,

I. 145 (1907 edition), he refers to 'that good old man the present Pope'; the spurs obviously are not attached to him.

151. *Table Talk*, II. 296–7: March 5, 1834. *Tom Cringle's Log*, by [Michael Scott], in *Blackwood's Magazine*, 1829–33.

152. *Ibid.*, II. 108–18: February 16, 1833. Michael Scott, the scholar, who lived from about 1175–1234.

153. Notebook 47.

154. Notebook 43.

155. From a review of Lewis, M. G., *The Monk* in the *Critical Review* for February, 1797, 194–200. Reprinted in *A Wiltshire Parson and his Friends*, by Garland Greever.

156. Allsop, *Letters, Conversations and Recollections*, I. 105–7.

157. Notebook 16, the approximate date being October 20–November 20, 1805. *Cf. Anima Poetae*, 163.

158. *Friend* (1850) III. 325 (Appendix G.—from the 1809–10 edition of the *Friend*).

159. MS. Egerton 2800, f. 54. Watermark 1820.

160. Note on Steffens, H., *Caricaturen des Heiligsten*, 1819–21, II. 26. In the British Museum. The marginalia in Steffens are published by Nidecker in the *Revue de Littérature Comparée*, 1930.

161. Notes on Coleridge, Hartley, *Lives of Northern Worthies*, see note 136 above. Lamb used the phrase, 'Heywood, a prose Shakespeare', in a footnote to *Hieronimo, the Spanish Tragedy* in his *Specimens of the English Dramatic Poets*, 1808. The passage was quoted in a review of the *Specimens* in the *Annual Review* of 1808 of which Lamb wrote to Coleridge, asking if he had written it. If he had, surely he would have remembered that the iniquitous phrase was Lamb's before it was Hartley's.

162. Note on Southey, R., *Wesley*, I. 247. See note 41 above.

163. *Ibid*, I. 257, referring to Wesley's attacks on the Moravians.

164. MS. Egerton 2801, f. 194. Part of an outline and notes for *Aids to Reflection*. The word *chiro-cosmetics*, 'the art of adorning the hands', is attributed to Coleridge in the N.E.D.

165. Note on Hutton, James, *An Investigation of the Principles of Knowledge*, 3 vols., Edinburgh, 1794. On the title page.

Sarah Stoddart's brother was Sir John Stoddart, whom Coleridge knew in Malta, and who later became the editor of the *New Times*.

166. MS. Egerton 2800, f. 165. Watermark 18— [cut].
167. MS. Egerton 2801, f. 47. Watermark 1827. With the night-traveller who walks with his head over his shoulder, *cf.*

> ... one, that on a lonesome road
> Doth walk in fear and dread,
> And having once turned round walks on,
> And turns no more his head;
> Because he knows, a frightful fiend
> Doth close behind him tread.
>
> *The Rime of the Ancient Mariner*, ll. 446–51.

168. *Friend*, (1850), III. 323. Appendix G. From the 1809–10 edition.
169. Note on a copy of *The Statesman's Manual*, 1816, presented by Coleridge to James Gillman (Jr.). In the British Museum. There were fourteen lectures on the history of philosophy, but of only twelve of them were verbatim reports made. See *Philosophical Lectures, p.* 16.
170. MS. Egerton 2801, f. 57. Watermark 1827. He referred to his notebooks, from about 1827 onwards, as 'Flycatchers'.
171. MS. Egerton 2801, f. 126. Watermark 1822.
172. Note on Southey, R., *Wesley*, II. 57–9. See note 41.
173. MS. Egerton 2800, ff. 89–90. Watermark 1805.
174. MS. Egerton 2800, f, 87. Watermark 1811. A series of jottings which look as if they might have been put down as the thoughts occurred, preparatory to a reply to a review or an attack of some kind.
175. *Friend* (1850), III. 321–2. Appendix G. From the 1809–10 edition.
176. *Table Talk*, I. 214–15: October 5, 1830.
177. *Ibid.*, II. 220: July 6, 1833.
178. Notebook 52.
179. *Table Talk*, II. 218: July 6, 1833.
180. Notebook 15. Written in Italy, early in 1806. The painting referred to is *Diana and Her Nymphs in the Chase*, by Washington Allston, the American painter whom Coleridge met in Rome, and with whom he stayed for a time, at Olevano. Coleridge made detailed notes on the picture for use in the projected poem.

Allston's portrait of Coleridge is in the National Portrait

Gallery; another unfinished one is owned by Mr. H. W. L. Dana, in Boston.

181. MS. Egerton 2800, f. 69.

182. MS. Egerton 2800, f. 164.

183. Notebook 29.

184. MS. Egerton 2801, f. 58. Watermark 1827.

185. MS. Egerton 2800, f. 155. The 'fancy' in this should be set over against the practical sense of, say, item 201.

186. From a transcript by Sara Hutchinson copied from a journal or letters of Coleridge. It was reproduced in an article by G. H. B. Coleridge, in *Wordsworth and Coleridge*, Studies in honor of George McLean Harper, ed. E. L. Griggs, Princeton, 1939, pp. 135–65. I quote from the original transcript, and make some additions from another briefer account of this expedition, or rather the notes for this account, in Notebook 2. They are in very faded and rubbed pencil sometimes difficult to read.

187. Note on a copy of *Aids to Reflection* presented to Daniel Stuart. In the British Museum. The same note appears in a copy in the Harvard University Library. On it, and on Coleridge and the 'Glory', see Lowes, J. L., *Road to Xanadu*, 205, 470–1 (notes 138 and 139). And see Grigson, Geoffrey, *The Harp of Aeolus*, 1947, p. 40, where the connexion of the Glory with *Dejection* and *The Eolian Harp* is pointed out.

188. Notebook 29.

189. Notes on White, G., *The Works in Natural History of*, 2 vols., London, 1802. In Southey's copy, in the British Museum. The notes, not always exactly the same as my reading of them, were published in an edition of White's *Selborne*, by Grant Allen, 1902; I include one note that he omitted, the last one, and I omit his first one because it is not in Coleridge's hand.

    A learned German. Grellmann, H. M. G., *Historische Versuch über die Zigeuner*, 1783. Second edition. Göttingen, 1787.

190. Notebook 21. *Anima Poetae*, 222–3, omits the words between the asterisks.

    Bevereley, Robert, *The History and Present State of Virginia . . .* , London, 1705.

Lyonnet, Pierre, *F. C. Lesser's Théologie des Insectes avec des remarques de P. L. . . .* , Paris, 1742.

191. *Friend*, III. 169–175. The quoted lines are Milton's, *Paradise Lost*, X. 246–8.

192. Note on Oersted, H. C., *Ansicht der chemischen Naturgesetze*, Berlin, 1812, p. 42. In the British Museum. The marginalia are published by H. Nidecker in the *Revue de Littérature Comparée*, 1930.

193. *Ibid.*, pp. 87–9.·

194. Notes on Oken, L. von, *Erste Ideen zur Theorie des Lichts*, Jena, 1808, pp. 14 and 40. In the British Museum. For Coleridge on Goethe and Newton on light and colours, *cf. Philosophical Lectures*, pp. 405, 415.

195. Note on Schubert, G. H., *Allgemeine Naturgeschichte*, Erlangen, 1826. On a back flyleaf of J. H. Green's copy, in the British Museum.

The γυιλτ is, of course, opium.

Faraday's microphone: Faraday's published works, notebooks included, contain no reference to the microphone. I am indebted to the Librarian of the Royal Institution and to Mr. C. Martin, the editor of the Faraday notebooks, for a thorough search. But in the *Quarterly Journal of Science, Literature and Art*, July–December, 1827, there is an article on 'Experiments in Audition', by C. Wheatstone, which deals with what is called a microphone, i.e. a magnifier of sound. In the same number, a few pages farther on, is an article by Faraday on quite another subject. This fact; and perhaps the fact also that the publication came out under the auspices of the Royal Institution, where Faraday was director of the laboratory, may account for Coleridge's confusion of names. Wheatstone was later Sir Charles Wheatstone, the great inventor in the fields of telegraphy, acoustics, optics and electrical machinery.

196. Note on the *Kabbalistische Briefe*, IV. 114–15. See note 44.

197. MS. Egerton 2800, f. 167.

198. *Theory of Life*, ed. Seth B. Watson, 1848, pp. 28–32.

199. Notebook 29.

200. Note on Grew, Nehemiah, *Cosmologia Sacra*, p. 10. See note 87.

201. Notebook 38. (Flycatcher No. 6, 1829.)

202. *Friend*, III, 186–192. (I have omitted two long footnotes). Faraday's work on magnetism was just about to begin. No advance was made between the *De Magnete* (1600) of William Gilbert, whose chief discovery was the magnetic property of the earth, till Coulomb (1785) established the law of attraction and repulsion (varies inversely as the square of the distance.) Then came Oersted (1819) with his discovery of the electro-magnetic field, and the developments under Ampère, Faraday, Maxwell and others. Coleridge knew the work of Gilbert, Oersted and Faraday. He appears to be right about the dating of the compass in the 13th century. He may be thinking of Peter Peregrinus, to whom modern scholarship gives it; or he may have the old story from Gilbert that Marco Polo in 1260 introduced the compass from the East into Italy.

203. Notebook 45.

204. *Table Talk*, II. 51: May 3, 1832.

205. *Ibid.*, II. 147: April 8, 1833.

206. *Friend*, I. 325–9.

207. *Essays on His Own Times*, II. 320–9: from the *Morning Post*, March 19, 1800.

208. *Table Talk*, II. 13–14: December 17, 1831.

209. *Essays on His Own Times*, I. 8–10: from the *Conciones ad Populum*, 1795. Included later in the *Friend*, II. 244–6.

210. *Essays on His Own Times*, I. 230, II. 313–19, II. 406–8, II. 481 fn. These are all from contributions to the *Morning Post* of the dates cited. The last section is from the *Courier*, December 21, 1809 (*Essays on His Own Times*, II. 645–51).

211. *Friend*, III. 358–64.

212. *Table Talk*, I. 184–5: July 4, 1830.

213. *Ibid.*, I. 185: July 4, 1830.

214. *Ibid.*, I. 25–6: April 27, 1823.

215. MS. Egerton 2800, f. 107, (Watermark 1802) under the heading 'Notes on Brougham on the Colonial Policy of the European Powers'. The work, in two volumes, appeared in 1803. The British Museum copy belonged to Sir Joseph Banks, President of the Royal Society. I suspect that the pencil marks in it may

be Coleridge's. In 1802–3, Coleridge was seeing him occasionally and commented on his library (*Unpublished Letters*, I. 210), and the marked passages coincide with some that Coleridge commented on in the Egerton fragment. Perhaps there were limits, after all, to his readiness to 'enrich' the volumes of his friends.

216. *Table Talk*, I. 117–20: May 7, 1830.
217. *Ibid.*, I. 122–3: May 8, 1830.
218. *Ibid.*, I. 24: April 27, 1823.
219. *Ibid.*, I. 24–5: April 27. 1823.
220. Allsop, T., *Letters, Conversations and Recollections*, II. 191–3.
     Abel Drugger, in Ben Jonson's *The Alchemist*.
221. *Ibid.*, II. 228.
222. *Ibid.*, II. 112–14. For Coleridge's review of Clarkson's work on the Slave Trade, see item 286, from which are omitted, however, from limits of space, the mangled passages on Pitt.
223. *Ibid.*, II. 29. On Godwin and Burdett, see *ibid.*, II. 73–4.
224. *Table Talk*, II. 88: August 12, 1832.
225. Note on a copy of Irving, E., *For Missionaries after the Apostolical School*, London, 1825, presented to 'his dear friend and kind Instructor Samuel Taylor Coleridge' by the author. The work contains a long dedication to Coleridge as one who has been 'more profitable to my faith in orthodox doctrine, to my spiritual understanding of the Word of God, and to my right conception of the Christian Church, than any or all of the men with whom I have entertained friendship and conversation'. It also hints at deliberate contemporary misrepresentations of Coleridge's 'character and works'. The whole dedication is interesting, and touching.
226. MS. Egerton 2801, f. 207.
227. Note on the front flyleaf and title page of [Henry More]'s *Observations upon Anthroposophia Theomagica and Anima Magica Abscondita*, by Alagonomastix Philalethes, 1650. In the British Museum.
228. Allsop, T., *Letters, Conversations and Recollections*, II. 153–5.
229. *Essays on His Own Times*, I. 131–3: from the *Watchman*, No. III, March 17, 1796.

230. Allsop, T., *Letters, Conversations and Recollections*, I. 190–1.

231. *Ibid.*, II. 17.

232. Notebook 47.

233. Note on Southey, R., *The Doctor*, 1834, II. 61. In the British Museum. Frances Pattison was a favourite niece, sister of Sir John Taylor, Henry Nelson, and Rev. Edward Coleridge.

234. Allsop, T., *Letters, Conversations and Recollections*, II. 228–30.

235. MS. Egerton 2801, ff. 92–3. Watermark 1821.

236. MS. Egerton 2800, f. 171.

237. Allsop, T., *Letters, Conversations and Recollections*, II. 227.

238. *Essays on His Own Times*, III. 762–5: from the *Courier*, May 13, 1811.

239. MS. Egerton 2800, ff. 92–3. Watermark 1819.

240. Note on Hooker, R., *Ecclesiastical Polity*, 1682, Book I., p. 88. In Dr. Gillman's copy, from the Ashley collection in the British Museum.

241. Note on Mendelssohn, M., *Jerusalem, oder über religiöse Macht und Judenthum*. Frankfurt und Leipzig, 1791 (p. 87).

242. *Friend*, I. 294–5.

243. Note on Steffens, H., *Caricaturen des Heiligsten*, I. 216–17. See note 160 above.

244. Note on Tetens, J. N. See note 2 above.

245. *Table Talk*, I. 220: November 21, 1830.

246. *Essays on His Own Times*, I. 150–1: from the *Watchman*, No. IV, March 25, 1796. *Cf.* 307, thirty years later.

247. *Essays on His Own Times*, I. 16–17: From *Conciones ad Populum*, 1795.

248. Notebook 29, *c.* 1822.

249. MS. Egerton 2800, f. 170. Watermark 1820.

250. *Essays on His Own Times*, I. 89–91: from *Conciones ad Populum*, 1795.

251. Allsop, T., *Letters, Conversations and Recollections*, II. 112.

252. *Essays on His Own Times*, I. 187–9: from the *Morning Post*, December 31, 1799.

253. *Ibid.*, II. 633–6: from a letter to the *Courier*, December 20, 1799.

254. *Table Talk*, I. 226–8: June 25, 1831.

255. *Ibid.*, II. 25–6: March 3, 1832. The Reform Bill was passed in May, 1832.

256. MS. Egerton 2800, f. 136. *The Thoughts of an Honest Tory upon the present proceedings of that party in a letter to a friend in town*, 14 pp., 1710, was by Benjamin Hoadly. Coleridge might have read it in Somer's *Tracts*, reprinted in 1814.

    The Relation of Thuanus refers probably to the *History of His Own Time*, of J. A. de Thou, translated from the German edition of 1620 into English in 1729. It is a history of toleration. The *Argenis* of John Barclay (1621) is a romance, based on real persons and events, written for the purpose of denouncing political and religious feuds and conspiracies. Coleridge always praised 'this great work, for a great work it is' very highly. His annotated copy, or Southey's copy annotated by him, is in the British Museum.

257. MS. Egerton 2800, f. 123. Watermark 1799. This occurs in a paper of 'Observations on Egypt', written out of Coleridge's Mediterranean experiences in 1804–6, urging the British occupation and development of Egypt.

258. *Table Talk*, II. 21–2: January 28, 1832.

259. *Ibid.*, I. 174: June 6, 1830.

260. *Ibid.*, II. 17: December 18, 1831.

261. *Essays on His Own Times*, I. 273–4: February 1, 1800.

262. Note on L'Estrange, R. See note 71 above.

263. *Table Talk*, II. 312–13: May 3, 1834.

264. *Friend*, III. 322–5. The *worth-value* distinction Coleridge found in Kant (*Cf. Philosophical Lectures*, 364) in the *Metaphysic of Morals*. Kant, E., *Werke*, Berlin, 1912–21, Vol. IV. 293.

265. *Table Talk*, I. 196: August 20, 1830. Captain Basil Hall's *Travels in North America*, 1829, was not much liked in the U.S. on account of its Tory prejudices.

266. *Ibid.*, I. 150–1: May 28, 1830.

267. MS. Egerton 2800, f. 106. Watermark 1802. In notes on Brougham; see note 215 above.

268. *Table Talk*, II, 150–1: April 10, 1833.

269. *Ibid.*, II. 104–8: February 5, 1833.

270. *Ibid.*, I. 80–2: July 12, 1827.

271. MS. Egerton 2801, f. 157.

272. MS. Egerton 2800, f. 156. The watermark is a German one,

(n.d.) and the account appears to me part of the essays on Germany and German literature which were to have come out of his German travels in 1798-9.

273. *Friend*, III. 85–92. The insertions added to the 1818 edition are from a copy containing annotations by Coleridge (though copied by another hand).

274. Notebook 49.

275. *Table Talk*, II. 258: August 28, 1833.

276. *Essays on His Own Times*, II. 350–1: from the *Morning Post*, January 3, 1800.

277. *Ibid.*, II. 368–70: from the *Morning Post*, February 6, 1800.

278. *Ibid.*, II. 410–12: from the *Morning Post*, August 6, 1800.

279. *Ibid.*, I. 49–50: from *Conciones ad Populum*, 1795.

280. *Table Talk*, I. 27: April 27, 1823.

281. *Ibid.*, II. 317–18: May 19, 1834.

282. In March, 1818, the cotton spinners of Lancashire petitioned Parliament to shorten the factory hours for children, who were working from 5.30 a.m. to 8.30 p.m. Sir Robert Peel, the first baronet, father of the Prime Minister, took up their cause and drafted the bill for which he asked Coleridge's public support when his cause appeared threatened in both houses of Parliament.

283. Notebook 50.

284. *Essays on His Own Times*, III. 708 fn.: from the *Letters to Mr. Justice Fletcher* in the *Courier*, December, 3 1814. The letters, on the question of Irish relations to England, were signed 'An Irish Protestant'.

285. MS. Egerton 2800, f. 169. Watermark 1820.

286. *Edinburgh Review*, July 1808. The review runs to 25 pages in rather close print, and seems well worth the £20 Coleridge was paid for it. It has not, I think, been reprinted.

287. *Table Talk*, I. 49: May 8, 1824.

288. Manuscript note on a back flyleaf of *Sermons or Homilies of the United Church of England and Ireland* . . . , London, 1815. In the British Museum.

289. *Friend*, II. 221.

290. *Table Talk*, II. 34–6: April 4, 1832. In a notebook Coleridge refers to 'some of your sentimental Unitarians, *ex. gr.* Mrs.

Barbauld', and in another place he notices having difficulty
in making her understand why, though he refused to call
Unitarianism Christianity, he did not refuse to call Unitarians Christians. The conversation recorded here may have
been with her.

291. *Table Talk*, II. 188: May 18, 1833.
292. *Ibid.*, II. 292–3: February 22, 1834.
293. Note on Mendelssohn, M., *Morgenstunden, oder Vorlesungen
     über das Daseyn Gottes*. Frankfurt und Leipzig, 1790. In the
     British Museum. On a front flyleaf.
294. *Friend*, III. 104–8.
295. Note on Stillingfleet, E., *Origines Sacrae, or a Rational Account
     of the Grounds of Christian Faith, as to the Truth and Divine
     Authority of the Scriptures, &c.*, London, 1675, pp. 438–9. In
     the British Museum.
296. *Ibid.*, pp. 330–1. *Cf.* Wordsworth, *Prelude*, II. 203–32.
297. Notes on Jurieu's *The History of the Council of Trent*, in English
     translation, 1684. On pp. iv–ix, and pp. xxxii–xxxiii.
298. MS. Egerton 2801, f. 253. Watermark 1823. Eichhorn, J. G.
     (1752–1827), one of the early 'higher critics'; Coleridge knew
     him in Göttingen and left heavy annotations on his com-
     mentaries on the Old and New Testaments and on the
     Apocrypha. He by no means supported all of Eichhorn's
     views.
299. MS. Egerton 2801, f. 234. Watermark 1822. Coleridge was
     reading Scottish Church history. See note 140 above.
300. MS. Egerton 2801, ff. 252–3. Watermark 1823.
301. MS. Egerton 2801, f. 260. Watermark 1820. On the mountains
     of ice, ('and Ice mast-high came floating by') in *The Ancient
     Mariner*, see Lowes, J. L., *The Road to Xanadu*, esp. pp. 138,
     140–151. It is interesting to see Coleridge, as late as some date
     after 1820 (the Franklin expedition to the North Pole had
     perhaps revived old memories) using them as an image of
     'our mutual life'; these paragraphs strengthen the case of
     those who like to interpret the *Ancient Mariner* as allegorical
     of a longer voyage on a wider sea.
302. MS. Egerton 2801, f. 264. Mrs. W[ordsworth?].
303. Adam, Thomas, *Private Thoughts on Religion*, York, 1795. The

annotations are on Thomas Poole's copy, a gift from the Earl of Egmont, 15 June, 1804.

304. MS. Egerton 2800, f. 83. Every proposal made here by Coleridge has been carried out, though separately for the most part.

305. Note on Luther, M., *Colloquia Mensalia*, 1652, p. 121. In the British Museum.

306. MS. Egerton 2801, f. 131. In an article on 'the polar logic'.

307. *Aids to Reflection*, 51–6.

308. *Ibid.*, 67–8. In a note on a presentation copy to Daniel Stuart, now in the British Museum, Coleridge writes opposite this passage, 'This . . . is as it were the Vestibule to all the Reasoning in this volume, and to these pages therefore the Reader's attention is especially directed.'

309. *Ibid.*, 91–2. Coleridge rejected Kant's categorical imperative as a 'stoic principle'.

310. *Ibid.*, 184–5.

311. In the British Museum. Dated 1829.

312. Note on Schelling, F. W. J. von, *op. cit.* note 98 above.

313. *Aids to Reflection*, 101.

314. *Ibid.*, 103.

315. *Ibid.*, 187.

316. *Ibid.*, 9.

317. *Confessions of an Inquiring Spirit*, edited in 1840 by H. N. Coleridge, and with an introduction by J. H. Green in 1849, is an interesting small work, described as 'Seven Letters to a Friend concerning the bounds between the right, and the superstitious, use and estimation of the Sacred Canon; in which the Writer submissively discloses his own private judgment on the following Questions:

I. Is it necessary, or expedient, to insist on the belief of the divine origin and authority of all, and every part of, the Canonical Books as the condition, or first principle, of Christian Faith?—

II. Or, may not the due appreciation of the Scriptures collectively be more safely relied on as the result and consequence of the belief in Christ;—the gradual increase,—in respect of particular passages—of our spiritual discernment of their truth and authority supplying a test and measure of our own growth and progress as individual believers, without the servile fear that prevents or overclouds the free honor which cometh from love? 1 John iv. 18.'

The excerpts are from Letters III, VI, and VII.

318. Note on a flyleaf of Maas and Jacobi, *op. cit.*, note 66 above.

319. Note on Southey, R., *Wesley*, I. 143. See note 41 above.

320. *Aids to Reflection*, 381–6.

321. *Friend*, II. 45–6. Coleridge's copy of Behmen's *Works*, 4 vols., edited by William Law, London, 1764–81, is profusely annotated.

322. *Ibid.*, I. 158–63.

323. MS. Egerton 2801, f. 210.

324. *Friend*, I. 332–3.

325. *Table Talk*, II. 252: August 24, 1833.

326. *Friend*, III. 126–7.

327. Note on Southey, R., *Wesley*, I. 260–1. *Ed. cit.* note 41 above.

INDEX

(Note: The figures refer to the numbered sections of the text, but where p. followed by a number occurs it refers to the introductory and sub-introductory pages.)

439

INDEX

Auerbach's cellar, 152
Augustus Caesar, 210, 244
Austria, 210

Baader, F. X. von, 86
Bacon, Francis, 24, 81, 82, 93, 100,
    172; *Novum Organum*, 175, 198
Baillie, Dr., 27, 282
Baillie, Miss, 222
Banks, Sir Joseph, 215 (note)
Barabbas, 30
Barbauld, Mrs., 290 (note)
Barclay, John, *Argenis*, 256 and note
Batave, Lake, 115
Bayle, Pierre, *Dictionaire historique
    et critique*, 123 (note)
Beaumont, F. and Fletcher, J.,
    Pilgrim, Beggar's Bush, 161
Beaumont, Sir George, p. 211
Beck, C. D., 113
Beddoes, Dr. Thomas, p. 12, 45
    and note
Beethoven, Ludwig van, 123 and
    note, 176, 177, 178
Behmen, Jacob, p. 16, 40, 320, 321
    (note)
Bell, Andrew, p. 73, 65 and note
Berkeley, George, (Bp.), 105, 165
Berzylius, J. J., 30
Betham, Mathilda, p. 211
Beverley, Robert, *The History and
    Present State of Virginia*, 190
    and note
Birch, Walter, *Sermon on the Pre-
    valence of Infidelity and Euthusi-
    asm*, 75 and note
Black, Joseph, 198
Blackwood's Magazine, 151 and note
Blumenbach, J. F., 41, p. 221, 189,272
Böhme, Jacob, *see:* Behmen, Jacob
Bombyx Muscorum, 188

Bonaparte, 175, 210, 251, 252, 277
Bonduca, 317
Boswell, James, 145, 147
Bowder Stone, 186
Bowles, Caroline, 95 (note)
Boyer, Jean Baptiste de, Marquis
    d'Argens, *Kabbalistische Briefe*,
    44 and note, 124 and note, 196
    and note
Boyle, Robert, 190
Brande, W. T., 30
Brissot, J. P., 209
Bristol, 3, 65, p. 221, 166
British, Gems, 166; constitution,
    208, 282; sailors, 211; and
    Foreign, 274; Empire, 211, 267;
    Parliament, 282; Cabinet, 286
Britons, 65
Brocken, the, 152
Brougham, H. P., 215 and note, 267
    (note)
Browne, Sir Thomas, 30
Brücker, J., 52 fn.
Bruno, G., p. 16
Bull, George, (Bp), 95, 172
Bunyan, J., 139, 285
Buonaparte, *see:* Bonaparte
Burchell, W. J., *Travels in the
    Interior of Southern Africa*, 13
    and note
Burdett, Sir Francis, 223 (note)
Burke, Edmund, 146, 147, 205, 206,
    207
Burns, Robert, 24 and note, 120,
    149, 273
Butler, Bishop, 11, 104, 120
Buxtorf, Johann, 304
Byron, Lord, 123, 152

Cadiz, 211
Caesalpinus, André, 191

INDEX

Dryden, John, 120, 123, 258
Dunning, Mr., 216
Durham, Bishop of, 11

Edinburgh Magazine, 166
Edinburgh Review, 286 (note)
Edwards, Bryan, *History, Civil and Commercial, of the British Colonies in the West Indies*, 34 and note
Egmont, Earl of, 303 (note)
Egypt, Princess of, 117, 189, 210; Coleridge's Observations on, 257 (note)
Egyptian, *see:* Neith
Eichhorn, J. G., 272, 298 and note, 304
Ekkehart, I., *Waltharius*, 120 (note)
Elizabeth, Queen, 30, 81, 274, 280, 320
Ellis, John, 191
Elton, Oliver, p. 16
Emilia, *see:* Shakespeare, *Othello*
Empedocles, 157
England, Barbarism in, 140; cleanliness in, 262; and commerce, 261; Corn supply in, 263; history of, 250; marines of, 210; Jacobinism in, 276; rise of middle class in, 278; national characteristics, 273; view of Americans in, 266
England and America, 268
England and Ireland, 208, 269, 284 (note)
England, Church of, 269
England, King of, 272
English, the, 264, 265, 271, 273
English, Ballads, 120; classics, 81; Girls' Boarding Schools, 227; jury, 130; language, 75, 83, 152;

localities, 254; minister abroad, 275; nobility, 264; poetry, 120, 123; public, 97; romances, 120; style, 139; translators, 81; treatises on the Passions, 52; Unitarians, 304; and Ireland, 269; and Scotland, 26 (note),273
Englishman, 211, 268, 273, 276
Englishmen, 127, 268
Eolian Harp, *see:* Aeolian
Epictetus, 296
Epicurus, 294
Eschenmeyer, K. A., 41, 312
Esculapius, *see:* Aesculapius
Essequibo, 115
Euclid, 135
Europe, 52, 68, 100, 101, 121, 210, 261, 264, 272, 273, 277, 278, 286
European, adventurers, 286; tongues, 84; Powers, 215 (note)
Evangelicalism, 107
Evans, Mary, 5, 37

Falstaff, Sir John, *see:* Shakespeare, *Henry IV, Pt. I*
Fairfax, Thomas, Lord, 136
Faraday, Michael, 195 and note, 202 (note)
Fénelon, F. de S., 320
Fichte, J. G., 86, 94 and note
Ficinus, M., *Platonica Theologica*, 100 (note)
Fielding, Henry, 4; *Tom Jones*, 143
Fitzgerald, M. M., *see:* Southey, R., *Life of Wesley*
Fletcher, Mr. Justice, 284 (note)
Fox, C. J., 205, 207, 277
France, court of, 286; revolution in, *see also: French Revolution* in, 210, English in, 271; magnetic patients in, 41; Marat and, 101;

Green, J. H., p. 19, 27 (note), 49 and note, 86, 87 (note), 94 (note), 113 (note), p. 221, 195 (note), 274. *See also:* Coleridge, S. T., *Confessions of an Inquiring Spirit*

Greever, Garland, *A Wiltshire Parson and his Friends,* 155 (note)

Grellmann, H. M. G., 189 and note

Grew, Nehemiah, *Cosmologia Sacra,* 87, 200 and note

Griesbach, J. J., 304

Griggs, E. L., *see:* Coleridge, S. T., *Unpublished Letters,* and Coleridge, G. H. B., *Wordsworth and Coleridge*

Grigson, Geoffrey, *The Harp of Aeolus,* 149 (note), 187 (note)

Gruter, Jan, *Delitiae . . . Poetarum,* etc., 123 and note

Gymnotus Electricus, 30 and note

Haakedoorn, *see: Acadia detinens*

Hacket, Bishop, *A Century of Sermons,* 141 and note

Hall, Basil, 265 and note

Hall, Joseph, 120

Haller, Albrecht von, 77, 272

Hamlet, *see:* Shakespeare, *Hamlet*

Hanseatic, League, 272; Towns, 282

Harper, George McLean, *see:* Coleridge, G. H. B., *Wordsworth and Coleridge*

Harriott, Thomas, 198

Harris, John, the historian, 171

Hartley, D., *Observations on Man,* 116 (note), 165, 198

Harut, 318

Hatchett, Charles, 191

Hatherley, Lord, *Memoirs,* 120 (note)

Haydn, Joseph, 123

Hayward, Abraham, *Faust,* 152

Hazlitt, Mrs., *see:* Sarah Stoddart, 165

Hazlitt, William, 120 (note), 174, p. 211

Hearne, Samuel, *A Journey from Prince of Wales's Fort in Hudson's Bay, to the Northern Ocean,* 34 and note

Hebrew, scriptures, 127; Text, 304; *see also:* Bonduca

Hedwig, J., 191

Heinroth, J. C. A., *Lehrbuch der Anthropologie,* 86 and note, 107 and note

Helmont, J. B. von, 40

Henrietta Maria of France, wife of Charles I, 136

Henry VIII, 203

Heylyn, Peter, 164

Heyne, C. G., 272

Heywood, Thomas, 161 and note

Highgate, 27(note), 120(note), p. 221

Hindostan, 189

Hoadly, Benjamin, *The Thoughts of an Honest Tory,* 256 (note)

Hobbes, Thomas, 75, 307

Hogg, James, 273

Holland, 207, 282

Homer, 180, 287

Hone, William, 172

Hooker, Richard, 82, 222, p. 377, 240 (note)

Hookthorn, *see: Acacia detinens*

Horatio, *see:* Shakespeare, *Hamlet*

Hostess, *see:* Shakespeare, *Measure for Measure,* 135

Hottentots, 13

Howes, R. F., *see:* Armour and Howes

Hufeland, C. W., 41

Humboldt, Alexander von, *Versuche über die electrischen Fische,* 30(note)

INDEX